Insurance in the Baltic Countries

No. 7

OECD

ORGANISATION FOR ECONOMIC CO-OPERATION AND DEVELOPMENT

ORGANISATION FOR ECONOMIC CO-OPERATION AND DEVELOPMENT

Pursuant to Article 1 of the Convention signed in Paris on 14th December 1960, and which came into force on 30th September 1961, the Organisation for Economic Co-operation and Development (OECD) shall promote policies designed:

- to achieve the highest sustainable economic growth and employment and a rising standard of living in member countries, while maintaining financial stability, and thus to contribute to the development of the world economy;
- to contribute to sound economic expansion in member as well as non-member countries in the process of economic development; and
- to contribute to the expansion of world trade on a multilateral, non-discriminatory basis in accordance with international obligations.

The original member countries of the OECD are Austria, Belgium, Canada, Denmark, France, Germany, Greece, Iceland, Ireland, Italy, Luxembourg, the Netherlands, Norway, Portugal, Spain, Sweden, Switzerland, Turkey, the United Kingdom and the United States. The following countries became members subsequently through accession at the dates indicated hereafter: Japan (28th April 1964), Finland (28th January 1969), Australia (7th June 1971), New Zealand (29th May 1973), Mexico (18th May 1994), the Czech Republic (21st December 1995), Hungary (7th May 1996), Poland (22nd November 1996), Korea (12th December 1996) and the Slovak Republic (14h December 2000). The Commission of the European Communities takes part in the work of the OECD (Article 13 of the OECD Convention).

OECD CENTRE FOR CO-OPERATION WITH NON-MEMBERS

The OECD Centre for Co-operation with Non-Members (CCNM) promotes and co-ordinates OECD's policy dialogue and co-operation with economies outside the OECD area. The OECD currently maintains policy co-operation with approximately 70 non-member economies.

The essence of CCNM co-operative programmes with non-members is to make the rich and varied assets of the OECD available beyond its current membership to interested non-members. For example, the OECD's unique co-operative working methods that have been developed over many years; a stock of best practices across all areas of public policy experiences among members; on-going policy dialogue among senior representatives from capitals, reinforced by reciprocal peer pressure; and the capacity to address interdisciplinary issues. All of this is supported by a rich historical database and strong analytical capacity within the Secretariat. Likewise, member countries benefit from the exchange of experience with experts and officials from non-member economies.

The CCNM's programmes cover the major policy areas of OECD expertise that are of mutual interest to non-members. These include: economic monitoring, statistics, structural adjustment through sectoral policies, trade policy, international investment, financial sector reform, international taxation, environment, agriculture, labour market, education and social policy, as well as innovation and technological policy development.

FOREWORD

Worldwide, insurance and pension reform is high on the political agenda and it will certainly remain so in the years to come. This is no less the case in the Baltic countries. The Baltics have made important progress in these sectors, with inter alia, thorough reform of the public pay as you go (PAYG) pension scheme, including the establishment of a complementary privately funded pension regime and important improvements in the regulation and supervision of insurance activities with a view to integration to the EU. Accordingly, Baltic private pensions and insurance (and particularly life insurance) markets have great growth prospects for the years to come.

Over the past five years, the core objective of the OECD Insurance and Pension Reform Activity of the OECD's Baltic Regional Programme has been to analyse the issues and conduct dialogue among Baltic and OECD members, in order to provide recommendations which can assist policy reform in these fields. Given this aim, the present project which includes two connected publications in the insurance and private pensions fields, gathers high-quality analysis of the Baltic insurance and pension markets situation and regulation as well as experts' reports focusing on key policy issues and OECD insurance and pension guidelines. The issues were selected in accordance with the Baltic economies' needs and requests that emerged from among the topics raised in the Baltic Regional Programme meetings.

The private pensions publication released under the Private Pensions Series n°5 initially focuses on the description and study of the new Baltic pension schemes, their benefits, remaining weaknesses and future challenges. A comparative analysis introduces this part followed by three detailed studies prepared by Baltic experts dealing with pension reform and its progress in each country. A second section presents selected private pensions policy issues, inter alia, the expected consequences of investment regulation of pension funds in the Baltic States and the role of pension funds in private equity in these economies. This publication includes perspectives on these issues that were debated during the Pension Conference held on 23-25 April 2003 in Tallinn, and prepared in co-operation with the European Union.

The insurance publication released under Policy Issues in Insurance n°7 focuses on insurance markets situation in the Baltic countries and includes revised versions of papers highlighting major insurance policy issues discussed in Baltic workshops and that were deemed particularly relevant for Baltic policy makers and insurance market players in the future. Accordingly, the first section is organised around three reports dealing with, respectively, the life insurance, non-life insurance and reinsurance markets and their regulatory and supervisory framework, in the Baltic countries. The second section of this publication highlights selected policy issues including: compulsory insurance, taxation of life insurance products, liberalisation of insurance markets, environmental risks and insurance and financial integration.

The synergies stemming out of the combination of concrete and analytical reports, high-level Baltic and OECD experts' point of view on private pensions and insurance issues as well as policy recommendations and "best practices" will certainly make these publications unique reference tools for Baltic countries' policy makers and market players.

The views expressed here are the sole responsibility of the authors and do not necessarily reflect those of the Insurance Committee, the Working Party on Private Pensions, the Secretariat or the member or non- member countries. The two publications have been prepared by Flore-Anne Messy and Juan Yermo, both working for the Insurance and Private Pensions Unit of the Financial Affairs Division. These publications are published under the aegis of the activities of the Centre for Co-operation with Non-Members and on the responsibility of the Secretary-General of the OECD.

Eric Burgeat
Director
Centre for Co-operation with Non-Members

TABLE OF CONTENTS

5

PART 1

Baltic Insurance Market and Regulation

Analysis, Perspectives and Recommendations

THE DEVELOPMENT OF THE LIFE INSURANCE SECTOR IN THE BALTIC COUNTRIES

Janis Bokans

Abstract

This report provides an overview of the main figures of the life insurance markets in the Baltic States. After a short comparison with the life insurance markets in Central and Eastern European countries and OECD average, factors affecting the development of life insurance are discussed. The low income level (GDP per head) and the adverse demographic trends are the two main reasons limiting the growth of life insurance business in the Baltic States.

One of the prerequisites of a sound and well-functioning insurance market is the establishment of an adequate regulation and supervision. The survey therefore sketches out the regulatory and supervision framework of insurance activities in Estonia, Latvia and Lithuania. Key areas of regulations are highlighted such as market access, intermediaries and investment regulations. Taxation of insurance products, premiums and benefits are also analyzed.

The author concludes that the high GDP growth rate and the integration to the EU in 2004 should point to an optimistic forecast for the development of life insurance markets in the Baltic States. Finally, he provides some recommendations to promote Baltic life insurance markets.

TABLE OF CONTENTS

INTRODUCTION

This report was prepared at the request of the OECD as the culmination of the Baltic Regional Program launched in 1998 for the Financial Market Reform section. Beyond co-operation between OECD countries and Baltic States and OECD experts' missions to the Baltic countries, the Baltic Regional Program encompassed high-level insurance seminars and workshops held under OECD auspices. Workshops on insurance issues in the Baltic countries were held in Lithuania (1999), Latvia (2000) and Estonia (2002).

The Baltic life-insurance market survey was based on insurance market annual reports from the supervisory agencies of the respective Baltic States. The description of regulatory frameworks was developed from an analysis of laws, regulations and resolutions of the respective Baltic States, and on information from officials of their supervisory agencies.

The conclusions and recommendations reflected in the Perspectives of Life Insurance Market section are based on several sources: comparisons of observations in the best-practices documents and guidelines presented in OECD seminars and conferences; OECD guidelines on insurance regulation and supervision as summarized in OECD Insurance Guidelines for Economies in Transition, and the Insurance and Private Pensions Compendium for Emerging Economies; IAIS principles and standards; World Bank publications and working papers; and best-practices materials issued by the supervisory agencies and insurers associations of OECD countries.

CHAPTER 1

LIFE INSURANCE MARKETS IN THE BALTIC STATES

I. Historical background

After independence was restored in 1990, the Baltic States began to rebuild market economies. The separation of the financial system from that of the Soviet Union was one of the first tasks. Estonia, Latvia and Lithuania set up national insurance companies that took over the liabilities of Gosstrah (the Soviet state insurance monopoly) in their territories. Efforts to recover substantial financial resources related to insurance liabilities failed, however.

In 1992, Estonia reintroduced the kroon as its currency, and in 1993 Latvia reintroduced the lats, and Lithuania, the litas. Thus was hyperinflation cut, after reaching nearly 1,000% in 1992. But while market economy principles were restored, the legislation required to ensure their implementation was still being created. Private initiatives meantime developed rapidly. Commercial banks, insurance companies and other financial institutions were established. The first private insurance company appeared in the Baltic countries in 1990. Private insurance businesses developed quickly, though often without necessary expertise, which led to abuses.

Laws regulating insurance activities were passed by Lithuania in 1990, Estonia in 1992 and Latvia in 1993. At first, Ministries of Finance supervised the insurance business. A permanent insurance supervision authority was set up in Estonia in 1993, and in Latvia and Lithuania in 1995. From 1995 to 1997, all three states successfully completed the process of privatizing the state companies that had assumed the liabilities of Gosstrah. In the mid-1990s, the Baltic countries were granted considerable assistance through the EU's Phare project to improve insurance legislation and supervision. Lithuania passed new insurance laws in 1996; Latvia followed two years later. Life insurance was separated from non-life insurance by Estonia in 1992, by Latvia in 1994 and by Lithuania in 1996. The solvency control and insurance accounting principles as applied in the EU were introduced.

Starting practically from zero, private insurance markets in the Baltic States were established within a very short time. More than half of life insurance companies in the Baltic countries are owned by foreign insurers, demonstrating the stability and potential of the market.

It is important to note that despite the similarities, the Baltic States are very different, with diverse cultural, legislative and corporate environments. While the three states share common goals, above all to join the European Union, they must be approached as three markets, not one.

II. Life insurance markets: an update

A. *Structure of the life insurance markets*

At the end of 2002, there were nine life insurance companies in Lithuania, and six each in Latvia and Estonia, for a total of 21 in the Baltic States. The total has been quite stable, though the number in each country has varied. In Latvia, the number of life companies decreased from eight in 2000 to six in 2002 due to mergers, while in Lithuania three new licenses to provide life insurance were issued in 2001. There have been no serious bankruptcy cases in the Baltic life markets except in Estonia, where two companies were closed due to insolvency in 1999. In Lithuania, two non-life insurance companies are still liable for life insurance contracts concluded before 1997, when life and non-life businesses were legally separated. In 2002, these companies had 29% of total life premiums written and 57% of life technical reserves in Lithuania.

Life insurance providers in the Baltic States have an average density of 2.92 life insurance companies per million inhabitants. In Poland, by way of comparison, the figure is only 0.93. In all of the European Union, there were 805 life insurance companies at the end of 2000, translating to 2.14 insurance companies per million inhabitants. The average availability of life insurance services to Baltic States inhabitants is therefore higher than the EU average.

It is well known that isolated markets are less efficient than open markets. Since the earliest moves to restore market economies, the Baltic markets have tended to reduce restrictions on foreign capital inflow, particularly in the financial sector. In Latvia, the first insurance company with a foreign insurance group as a shareholder was established in early 1990. Currently in Lithuania, 84% of gross written life premiums belong to insurance companies in which a majority of shareholders (directly or indirectly – through mother companies or holdings) are foreign insurers or insurance groups. The comparable figure for Latvia is 74%, and for Estonia, 14%. The leading player in the Baltic markets is Codan Limited A/S, followed by Ergo Europa. Sampo PLC and Suomi Mutual are also present as shareholders of life insurance companies. The representative offices of world-known reinsurers such as SwissRe and General Cologne Re are also established in the Baltic countries.

It should be stressed that the banking sector and the insurance business have linkages. In Estonia, two life insurance companies are subsidiaries of banks; in Lithuania, three are. In Latvia, two life insurance companies are subsidiaries of financial groups in which banks are in leading positions.

As in other Eastern European countries, life insurance markets in the Baltic States are highly concentrated. In Lithuania, 56% of all written premiums belong to the Lietuvos Draudimas group. In Estonia, the market leader is Hansapanga Kindlustus, with a 47% market share. In Latvia, market concentration is not as high: the market leader, Ergo Latvija trivia, has only a 33% market share. As the number of market participants in each Baltic state is rather small, market concentration can reasonably be illustrated by the market share of the first two companies. In Estonia, this figure is 67%, in Latvia, 59%, and in Lithuania, 72%. Notably, market concentration indicators are decreasing yearly.

B. Life premiums

Gross written premium volume attributed to life insurance companies in the Baltic states totalled 83 million USD in 2002, divided as follows: in Latvia, 9 million USD; in Lithuania, 43.3 million USD, and in Estonia, 30.6 million USD. Over the last three years, average annual life insurance market growth in Estonia was 27%, and in Lithuania, 25%. These figures slightly exceed the Central and Eastern European average (24% for 1991-2000) and demonstrate that life insurance markets in Estonia and Lithuania consistently realize their potential. In Latvia, life insurance premiums fell dramatically in 2000, since tax incentives for life insurance were significantly diminished. In Latvia, over the last two years, life insurance premium volumes grew only by about 9%, and the total premium volume is half its 1999 level.

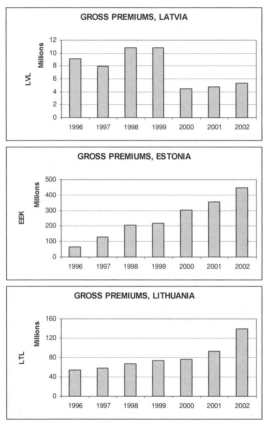

Source: Estonian, Latvian, and Lithuanian Financial Supervisory Authorities

In the first quarter of 2003, Baltic life markets witnessed accelerated growth. In Latvia, premium growth was 45% higher than in first-quarter 2002, and in Lithuania, it was even higher: 80%.

C. Premiums structure by insurance products

In the Baltic States, traditional life insurance products (term life, whole life, endowment, annuities) are available. In Latvia, 97% of all written life insurance premiums belong to the endowment insurance policy, 60% to individual contracts and the rest to group contracts. In Estonia, 72% of all written life insurance premiums belong to capital formative assurances, including 15% of unit-linked business; an additional 15% belong to annuities. Annuity (pension) contracts are the fastest-growing insurance business in Estonia – premiums written in this line rose 62% in 2001. In Lithuania, 94% of all written life insurance premiums belong to capital formative assurances, 65% to endowment type insurance and 9% to the unit-linked business. Marriage and birth insurance policies hold an important share – 26% of life assurance premiums in Lithuania -- whereas this class of insurance is negligible in Latvia and Estonia. In Estonia and Lithuania, unit-linked business rose from an insignificant volume in 1997-98 to important volumes today. In Latvia, this class of life insurance is practically not sold. Due to the peculiarities of new tax regulations, a universal life line has become very popular in Latvia since 2001.

Recently, catastrophic-illness coverage became available in the Baltic States, mostly as a rider to capital formation-type policies.

D. Distribution channels

Life insurance products in the Baltic markets are sold predominantly through branches or sales units of insurance companies. Tied agents are employed mainly by insurance groups including non-life and life companies, and they generally sell non-life products. The selling of life insurance is considered peripheral work. Brokers play a negligible part in the distribution of life insurance products, except in Lithuania, where about 20% of life premiums are collected through broker companies.

E. Life provisions, investments and investment income

At the end of 2001, life insurance companies in the Baltic States had accumulated life insurance funds (technical reserves) of 125 million USD, of which 8.5 million USD, or 6.7%, belonged to unit-linked business. The volume of technical provisions by country was: 67 million USD for Lithuania, 43 million USD for Estonia and 15 million USD for Latvia. In 2002, technical reserves rose by 20% and reached a volume of 150 million USD. In Lithuania, 88% of technical provisions investments are in government bonds. The next significant investment allocation is bank deposits, at 5%. Investments abroad account for about 5% of total investments of technical provisions. In Estonia, bonds constitute 43% of all investments, bank deposits, 31%, and shares, 18%. In Latvia, bonds constitute 35% of technical provisions investments, while bank deposits amount to 38%. Listed shares are practically absent from the investment portfolios of life insurance companies in Latvia. Investments abroad account for about 3% of total investments of technical provisions.

In Estonia, the average return on investments for life insurance companies was 6% in 2001. In Lithuania, return on investments of life insurance companies was 7.6% at the end of 2001. It should be noted that, until 2000, the profitability of Lithuanian government bonds was higher than interest rates on term deposits. This explains why life insurers in Lithuania prefer investing in government bonds. In Latvia, overall investment return of the insurance industry as of end-2001 was 7.2%.

It is important to note that scales of economy in the Baltic States are undersized, and the capital markets reflect this. Stock exchanges list small numbers of companies and companies seek listing more to raise their profiles than to acquire fresh capital to expand business. Recently, the HEX Group (Finland) acquired a majority of shares in the Tallinn Stock Exchange (now HEX Tallinn) and the Riga Stock Exchange (RSE). Therefore, insurers and other institutional investors will soon get direct access to the Nordic stock market.

F.   The significance of life insurance

Despite the remarkable growth of premiums, the life insurance market remains small in the Baltic States. In 2001, life insurance penetration (premiums to GDP) in Estonia represented 0.4%, in Lithuania, 0.2%, and in Latvia, 0.1%. These figures are far behind average life insurance penetration in OECD countries, which is 4.6%, and significantly lower than in Central and Eastern European countries (penetration rates in former Eastern bloc participants -- Poland, the Czech Republic, Hungary and Slovakia -- range from 1% to 1.4%). The following chart compares life insurance penetration in the Baltic States to the figures for selected CEE countries.

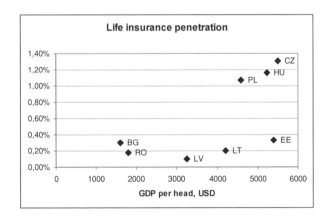

The same pattern is observed concerning life insurance density. Life insurance density in 2001 in Latvia represented 4 USD per capita, in Lithuania, 8 USD, and in Estonia, 17 USD. The average life insurance density in OECD countries accounts for about 1,150 USD. In the following chart life insurance density is compared to figures for selected CEE countries.

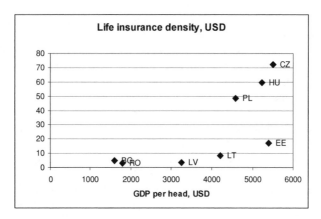

The share of life insurance in the overall insurance market in the Baltic States is significantly lower than in other markets. In Estonia and Lithuania, it is about 20%, while in Latvia the figure is only 5%, compared to an average of 62% in Europe and 35% to 43% in Poland, the Czech Republic, Hungary and Slovakia.

CHAPTER 2

FACTORS AFFECTING THE DEVELOPMENT
OF LIFE INSURANCE MARKETS

I. The economic environment

As described above, life insurance markets in the Baltic States are highly underdeveloped in comparison not only to EU and OECD averages but even to other CEE countries. Typically, a life insurance sector sees low insurance consumption when average income is low and accelerated demand after GDP per head exceeds a certain threshold.

The GDP per head in the Baltic States in 2000 was only about 15% to 17% of the EU15 average. In the Czech Republic, Hungary and Poland, this figure is in the 20% to 23% range. Income is the most important economic factor directly influencing insurance purchases. The average monthly wage in the Baltic States is 250 EUR, as compared to 350 EUR in Hungary and the Czech Republic, and 475 EUR in Poland and Slovakia. Monthly gross wages throughout the European Union average 1,900 EUR. Public surveys have found that about 60% of households in the Baltic States declare a disposable income per household member that is below the officially established cost of living, and this is most pronounced in rural areas. Household spending on housing, food and clothing together accounts for 60% to 70% of disposable income. The EU estimates that prices of foodstuffs in the Baltic States are 60% of the EU average, while wages are only 15% of the EU average. As life insurance products are not seen as being of prime necessity, the purchase of other products and services takes priority.

II. The demographic environment

Another factor influencing life insurance demand is family structure. The objective in acquiring insurance products is generally to protect dependents or family members -- most often children. The transition to a market economy in the mid-1990s caused a tremendous fall in birth rates in the Baltic States. The number of newborns at the end of the 1990s fell by about half from the level at the end of the 1980s. Moreover, there were more divorces or annulments than marriages. As a result, the proportion of singles and childless families rose significantly, reducing the demand for life insurance products.

III. Other competing financial products

There are well-developed commercial banks in the Baltic States, and the financial system is heavily bank-based. The leader in this field is Estonia; the number of banks in Latvia is also high. To illustrate the balance between the banking and life insurance sectors, consider the ratio of life insurance company assets to banking industry assets. In Latvia, the ratio is 0.8%. A considerable part of bank business includes providing for non-residents, but there is also strong competition to attract residents – physical persons.

One area of aggressive marketing policies today is long-term mortgage loans for the purchase of a house or an apartment. Interest rates for such loans are currently decreasing to unrealistic rates – in Latvia to 4.5%, in Estonia below 4%, thus attracting higher-income households. Interestingly, in Latvia, for example, the fixed interest rate of long-term (10-year) state treasury bonds is 5.125%. On the one hand, mortgage loans create insurable interest, thus fostering the demand for life insurance products; on the other, debt burden is often so high that it eliminates any other expenses, including life insurance products.

One way to attract clients with less income is consumer credit or leasing provided directly by banks or through subsidiaries – leasing companies. In Estonia, consumer credit rates decreased in one year to 14%, which is lower than typical Western European figures of 15% to 16%.

According to public surveys, about 40% of wage earners in Latvia still have no bank accounts. Banks fight for every new client, offering to open and maintain accounts for physical persons free of charge, as well as offering extremely low minimum requirements for initial deposits (as low as 17 USD) and high interest rates (up to 6% for five-year deposits). Banks thereby compete directly with life insurance savings products commonly designed for saving small amounts on a regular basis. To attract clients, banks realize large-scale aggressive advertising campaigns with slogans like "Loan sales" or "Deposits with special interest rates". Life insurance companies' marketing campaigns are fragmentary and less impressive compared to the banks' campaigns. As deposits and simple financial products are easier to understand than life insurance contracts, consumers usually prefer deposits.

CHAPTER 3

REGULATORY FRAMEWORK

The exclusive role of the state in encouraging the development of a life insurance market should be to ensure consumer protection and thereby strengthen their confidence in the long-term savings provided by life insurance companies. Commonly, this role is performed by specific regulations aimed at keeping the insurance market sound and well-functioning. This is achieved through appropriate restrictions on insurance operations to limit insurance market imperfections, and direct intervention when policyholders' interests are endangered directly. Nevertheless, overly restrictive regulations impede the development of the sort of competitive market most beneficial to policyholders. It is therefore essential to keep a fair balance between concrete market restrictions to protect policyholders' interests and the freedom to encourage competition and innovation.

After the restoration of independence in the 1990s, the Baltic States declared their will to become members of the European Union. EU membership requires that common principles and rules be observed in different areas, including the insurance sector. The process of adopting the *acquis communautaire* provided forceful incentives for the rapid and qualitative development of national legislation in the insurance field. In December 2002, the Baltic States successfully closed all 31 chapters of the *acquis communautaire*.

I.   The scope of regulation and supervision

All three Baltic States regulate insurance activities by special legislation that complements general legislation on business activities. The insurance regulations of all three states were reviewed by special EU expert missions, which found general compliance with EU insurance directives.

In Latvia, two laws regulate insurance activities:

- The Law on Insurance Companies and their Supervision, and

- The Law on Insurance Contracts.

The Law on Insurance Companies and their Supervision is a special law of the general Commercial Law, which regulates the establishment and governance of commercial enterprises. The Law on Insurance Contracts complements the Civil Code with special features concerning insurance contracts – the conclusion of the insurance contract, and the specific duties and rights of the insured, policyholder, beneficiary and insurer.

Regulations issued by the Financial and Capital Market Commission form the next layer in the regulatory hierarchy. This Commission issues binding rules, regulations and directives setting out requirements for the functioning of financial and capital market participants and the calculation and reporting of their performance indicators. In addition, the Commission has the right to issue recommendations on specific topics.

In Estonia, two special laws regulate insurance activities:

- The Insurance Law of the Republic of Estonia, and

- The Insurance Activities Act.

The latter was adopted in June 2000. The former was adopted in 1992 and amended six times. The adoption of the new Insurance Activities Law led to a considerable shortening of the former law, which now deals only with general provisions (terms), concepts and specialties of insurance contracts, and special kinds of pension insurance with income tax deduction. All other regulations are shifted to the new law.

The Insurance Activities Act is a special law of the Commercial Code of the Republic of Estonia that sets exclusions from the Commercial Code regarding insurance business activities.

Secondary regulations are issued by decree of the governor of the Bank of Estonia (Central Bank).

In Lithuania, there is the Law on Insurance of the Republic of Lithuania, which regulates insurance activities. This is a special part of the Law on Public Companies of the Republic of Lithuania. Other Lithuanian laws apply to insurance-connected relations to the extent they do not contradict the Law on Insurance of the Republic of Lithuania. There is no dedicated law on insurance contractual relationships. Regulations on insurance contracts, terms of indemnity payment, the calculation of cash surrender value and other regulations concerning insurance relations are incorporated in the Law on Insurance of the Republic of Lithuania. Separate legislation including an Insurance Activities Law and an Insurance Contract Law is to be drafted soon.

The State Insurance Supervisory Authority has the right to issue legal acts in accordance with the powers established by the Law on Insurance. For example, the law establishes powers regarding general insurance policy terms by which an insurance company must guide its activities when establishing specific policy conditions; a list of financially credible reinsurance companies in other countries; methods of building up insurance technical provisions; calculation methods, limits of solvency margins, etc.

II. Supervisory authorities

The insurance supervisory authorities in the Baltic States have different degrees of independence within their state executive structures. The common features are that supervisory authorities have legally defined objectives, tasks and rights and that they are financed from fees of financial and capital market participants.

In Latvia, the insurance sector is supervised by a special institution – the Financial and Capital Market Commission, which was established by, and operates according to, the Law on the Financial and Capital Market Commission. The Commission began its activities on 1 July 2002 when it assumed the functions of the Insurance Supervision Inspectorate and the Securities Market Commission, as well as Bank of Latvia functions regarding supervision of commercial banks and credit unions.

The Commission is an independent and autonomous public institution. It is governed by a Council, whose chairperson and deputy are appointed by Parliament for six-year terms. The other three members of the Council are also directors of functional departments. The Commission is financed by the fees of financial and capital market participants.

The Commission's main functions are to regulate and monitor the management of the financial and capital market and its participants. Regarding insurance companies, the Commission has exclusive rights to issue or revoke licenses. The Commission also has the authority to issue regulations and directives governing the activities of insurers and insurance intermediaries, to request and receive information necessary for performing supervision functions, and to set forth restrictions on insurers' activities.

In Estonia, insurance supervision is carried out by the Financial Supervision Authority (Finantsinspektsioon), which supervises all financial and capital market participants. The Financial Supervision Authority operates from the Bank of Estonia (Estonia Central Bank) with autonomous competence and a separate budget financed by fees paid by the subjects of financial supervision. Day-to-day activities of the Supervisory Authority are managed and organized by a Management Board, which is an executive body. A Supervisory Board, the decision-making body, plans the activities of the Supervisory Authority and monitors Management Board operations. The Chairman of the Supervisory Board is the Minister of Finance. The Minister of Finance and the President of the Bank of Estonia are Supervisory Board members by virtue of office. Four additional members (two each) are appointed by the Government and the Board of the Central Bank.

In Lithuania, the State Insurance Supervisory Authority at the Ministry of Finance conducts the supervision of the insurance business. The Director of the Supervisory Authority is appointed, and can be dismissed, by the Minister of Finance.

The decision-making body of the Authority is the Board. Licenses to engage in the insurance business and permits to engage in insurance intermediation activities are issued by decision of the Board. The Board of the Supervisory Authority is appointed and dismissed by proposal of the Director of the Supervisory Authority, with approval from the Minister of Finance. The Director of the Supervisory Authority heads its Board. Regulations issued by the Supervisory Authority require Government approval.

The Supervisory Authority of insurance companies is supported by levies from the insurance premiums.

The State Insurance Supervisory Authority cooperates with other financial sector supervisory bodies and there are plans to form a Commission for the Co-ordination of

Regulation and Supervision of Financial Institutions and Insurance Companies in Lithuania.

The Supervisory institutions of all three Baltic States are members of the International Association of Insurance Supervisors.

III. Market openness (market access)

The openness of the market is a key issue for emerging markets, as it provides the necessary know-how concerning life insurance products, new marketing and distribution approaches and methods of management and organization of the insurance business. Market openness to foreign insurers enables fair competition and reasonable insurance prices.

Baltic insurance markets were open to foreign insurers from the origin of the private markets in 1990. The sole requirement was to operate through a daughter company -- foreign insurers must establish a joint stock insurance company and obtain a license from the insurance supervision institution. The participation of foreign investors is not limited.

Recent legal developments extend the possibilities for foreign insurers to provide insurance in the Baltic States.

Upon authorization of the Supervisory Authority of Lithuania, insurance companies from World Trade Organization (WTO) countries may establish branches in Lithuania. Branches must maintain property equivalent to half of required authorized capital of a joint stock insurance company.

Upon the accession of the Republic of Lithuania to the European Union, insurers from EU countries will have the right to provide insurance services on a single license basis through establishing branch as well as directly (freedom to provide services). In a few non-life insurance classes, insurance companies from WTO countries can now provide insurance services directly, whereas in life insurance this is still not allowed.

As in Lithuania, legislation in Latvia stipulates that upon the accession of the Republic of Latvia to the European Union, insurers from EU countries will have the right to provide insurance services on single license basis by establishing branches as well as directly (freedom to provide services).

There are no restrictions regarding insurers from specific countries or groups of countries establishing branches in Estonia, although authorization from the Financial Supervision Authority is, of course, required. If an insurer registered in a European Union member state wishes to open a branch in Estonia, the insurer need only inform the Financial Supervision Authority and submit the information and documents specified in the common regulations (Insurance Directives) of the EU.

IV. Licensing requirements

Any activity defined in national legislation as belonging to the insurance sector is subject to licensing. An exception applies to insurance provided by the state on a mandatory basis (state social insurance), which is covered by special legislation. Reinsurance activities are regulated differently. In Estonia, reinsurance activities are subject to licensing, while in Latvia there is no direct requirement for licensing if an undertaking provides reinsurance only. Licensed direct insurers can provide reinsurance, too. A foreign reinsurer may provide reinsurance in Latvia without restrictions. In Lithuania only direct insurance activities are subject to licensing.

Insurance legislations in all the Baltic States clearly state that an insurer may engage in insurance business only once licensed by the Supervisory Authority. There are some common prerequisites for starting an insurance business. To restrict business risks and ensure transparency, legislation in all the Baltic States presupposes that insurance companies can deal only with insurance business and that no business entity may provide insurance service without appropriate authorization, that is, licensing. Life and non-life business must be separated, although this restriction does not apply to accident insurance and health insurance provided by an insurer licensed to provide life insurance. Licences are issued for specific classes of insurance, and commonly non-life activities of life insurance companies (accident and health insurance) must be licensed separately.

License applications must include specified documentation. First, general information on the insurance business entity is required: articles of association, notice of payment of share capital, list of shareholders, list of management board and supervisory board members, and information on the insurer's auditor and actuary. Second, specific insurance business information is required: a scheme of operations, general terms of insurance contracts, the organizational structure of the insurance company, internal accounting rules and information relating to the information-technology (IT) systems to be used. In all three Baltic States, legal requirements on operating schemes are basically similar. A scheme of operations must contain the principles of, and bases for, the calculation of tariffs and technical provisions, principles of reinsurance cover and revenue forecast, and a balance sheet showing the basic categories of assets and liabilities for the first three years of activity. Estimates of business launching expenses and information on sources for covering them (the organizational fund) must be provided, too. In addition, Latvia requires a description of the rules for information system protection and procedures for identifying unusual and suspicious financial transactions.

In Latvia, the Supervisory Authority can refuse to issue a license if planned insurance activities are not economically sustainable; the applicant's close links to third parties may endanger its stability and prevent the Financial and Capital Market Commission from adequately performing its supervisory functions; or the business reputation and financial stability of company shareholders are doubtful. A license can also be refused if the chairperson, members of the executive board, the executive director, the chief accountant, the chairperson or members of the audit committee do not meet the "fit and proper" requirements set by law. The Financial and Capital Market Commission must examine an application for the issue of a license to provide insurance and make a decision within three months of the receipt of all necessary documents. A decision of the Financial and Capital Market Commission to refuse to issue a license must be argued and it may be appealed before a court within one month of the receipt of the refusal.

In Estonia, grounds for refusal are defined more broadly. An activity license must be issued if the information and documents submitted make it possible to verify that facilities exist to carry on insurance activities and that the interests of policyholders and insured persons are sufficiently protected. The interests of policyholders and insured persons are considered sufficiently protected if the activities of an insurer comply with the requirements set by insurance legislation and the insurer is able, at all times, to perform its obligations.

A decision to issue or refuse an initial license should be issued by the Minister of Finance within three months of receipt of the application and all required information and documentation from the applicant.

In Lithuania, the Board of the Supervisory Authority shall make a decision concerning the issue of a license to engage in insurance business within four months of the submission of an application and will inform the applicant thereof in writing. The Board of the Supervisory Authority, when notifying the applicant of a decision to refuse issuance of a license to engage in insurance business, should submit a written list of the reasons for refusal, informing the Companies' Registrar at the same time. Any decision to refuse to grant a license to engage in insurance business may be appealed in court.

V. Corporate governance

Given the long-term nature of contractual relationships between insured persons and an insurance company in the life assurance business, corporate governance principles are critical, especially concerning with-profit policies, unit-linked business and annuities. Corporate governance in this case does not mean only fit and proper management, but also special procedures for the disclosure of relevant information to the insured persons.

The OECD Principles of Corporate Governance makes the board's responsibility clear in ensuring the strategic guidance of the company and the effective monitoring of management by the board. In the Baltic States, these principles are broadly included in the legislation concerning general-purpose corporations. The recently adopted Commercial Law in Latvia follows modern practices of corporate governance. A similar situation prevails in Estonia, with its Commercial Code. The situation in Lithuania (the Law on Public Companies) is, however, a bit less favourable. Special insurance legislation presents more direct instructions. Insurance legislation in the Baltic states outlines the responsibilities of the board and management to ensure appropriate accounting and financial reporting systems, independent auditing of financial statements and internal monitoring of risks. There are legal requirements in insurance legislation to establish comprehensive internal control systems based on a clear organizational structure and well-defined responsibilities and competences. Several internal regulations are prescribed by straightforward legislation. These are internal regulations on investment policies and procedures, on calculation of technical reserves, on ceding liabilities to reinsurers, etc. To ensure compliance with internal regulations, an internal audit service must be in place as well. In Lithuania, legislation stipulates that any outsourcing of investment management, claims administration, bookkeeping or other functions must be disclosed.

VI. Accounting requirements

It is commonly recognized that insurance accounting differs from general business accounting due to its inverted production cycle. The Baltic States are no exception and have special regulations concerning annual financial statements of insurance companies. Generally, financial statements should be drawn up in accordance with commonly accepted accounting principles. Content and layouts of financial statements generally should comply with requirements set in the European Community Insurance Accounting Directive 91/674/EEC. Latvia and Estonia harmonized their insurance accounting regulations with the aforementioned directive at the end of the 1990s, whereas Lithuania issued relevant regulations in 2000. Latvia and Estonia impose requirements to prepare consolidated financial statements for insurance undertakings in an insurance group, so as to be in line with the European Community Directive on supplementary supervision of insurance undertakings in an insurance group (98/78/EC). In Lithuania, a chart of accounts is prescribed by regulations from the cabinet of ministers, while Latvia makes the chart of accounts facultative, and insurance companies have the option to draw up their own chart of accounts. The chart must be approved by the Management Board of the insurance company.

Valuation rules for regulatory and shareholders' purposes are the same, following the on-going concern principle.

VII.   Solvency requirements

Minimum capital resources on top of insurance liabilities are required for insurers in all Baltic States. In general, excess capital consists of two parts: constant minimum capital required initially at the establishment of the insurer and continually adjusted overhead. The calculation of minimum capital resources for life insurance businesses follows the procedure established by European Community Directive 2002/83/EC. In general, minimum capital (solvency margin) is equal to 4% of mathematical (life) technical provisions of the insurance company, plus 0.3% of the capital at risk, which is equal to maximum payouts under life policies in force minus mathematical provisions. At the same time, requested capital resources at any time must be higher than constant minimum capital. Constant minimum capital in Latvia is required at a level of 3 million EUR for life insurance companies; in Lithuania, of 1.16 million EUR (LTL 4 million) for companies engaged in life insurance; and in Estonia, of 0.77 million EUR (EEK 12 million).

VIII.   Regulation of technical provisions and investments

All three Baltic states require a setting aside of technical provisions in an amount sufficient to cover financial liabilities arising from insurance contracts. An insurer must calculate technical reserves for each insurance contract or contract group separately. The executive board of an insurer must formulate and approve the procedures for technical reserve formation and is liable for compliance with such procedures. An insurer must submit the procedures for technical reserve formation to the supervisor.

Technical provision must be calculated on a prudent basis, using appropriate mortality, morbidity and disability statistics. In Lithuania, the application of particular statistical tables or parameters is subject to the authorization of the Supervisory Authority. In Estonia, a responsible actuary of the insurance company is entrusted to draw up mortality tables for life insurance and assess the accuracy of the mortality tables used. In Latvia, the statistical tables used for the calculation of technical provisions are subject to approval from the management board of the insurer.

Regulations concerning calculations of life insurance technical reserves (or mathematical reserves) prescribe the use of the prospective calculation method as a basic approach, although the retrospective method may be applied if the prospective method cannot be applied to a particular type of insurance contract. Mathematical technical provisions should not be less than the guaranteed surrender value, if it is established in the insurance contract. Companies are allowed to reduce life insurance technical reserves by applying Zilmer's method, that is, reserves reduced by acquisition costs. In Lithuania, the total amount by which the life insurance technical provision is reduced at the moment an insurance contract is concluded should not exceed 4% of the sum assured.

The technical interest rate used in calculating the mathematical (loss cover) reserves must not be higher than the interest rate established under a careful evaluation of income expected from life assurance equity investment; and this is subject to a ceiling established by the supervisor. In Lithuania, the technical interest rate does not exceed 60% of the weighted average of the annual interest rate on Government bonds issued in national currency. The technical interest rate must be calculated regularly, according to Government bond emissions of the last 12 complete calendar months, but not to exceed 3.5%. As of 1 January 2003, the maximum technical interest rate in Lithuania was set at 3.25%. In Latvia, the management board of the insurer approves the technical interest rate, which is not to exceed the average of the last three years' return on committed assets.

Committed assets covering technical provisions are subject to quantitative regulation to ensure that investment portfolios are sufficiently diversified and spread. Four main categories of investments are permitted to cover technical provisions: bonds and other fixed-interest instruments, shares and other equity securities, deposits with credit institutions and real estate. Loans are not included as admissible assets unless secured by mortgage. Maximum levels of investment by category are established; there are no minimum levels of investment in particular categories. Investment in a given asset is limited as a proportion of all committed assets covering technical provisions. In Estonia, quantitative restrictions are established in respect to gross technical reserves, while in Lithuania and Latvia they are set in respect to technical reserves net of reinsurance. The following table summarizes the main quantitative restrictions.

	Latvia	Estonia	Lithuania
Real estate	No more than 10% in one piece and no more than 25% in buildings and parcels of land taken together	No more than 10% in one piece and no more than 15% in buildings and parcels of land taken together	No more than 10% in one piece and no more than 20% in buildings and parcels of land taken together
Shares and other equity securities	No more than 5% issued by one issuer, listed only	No more than 5% issued by one issuer, no more than 10% if the proportion of securities does not exceed 40%, listed only	No more than 20% in listed shares no more than 5% in non-listed shares
Bonds and other debt securities	No more than 5% issued by one issuer; listed only. This restriction must not apply to debt securities issued by central and local governments. No more than 10% in mortgage bonds issued by one issuer, no more than 25% in mortgage bonds taken together	No quantitative restrictions	No more than 10% in municipal securities; no more than 20% in listed debentures; no more than 5% in non-listed debentures
Bank term deposits	No more than 25% with one credit institution	No quantitative restrictions	No more than 10% with one credit institution and no more than 30% in bank term deposits taken together
Loans	No more than 10% to one mortgage loan and no more than 25% to mortgage loans taken together	No more than 5% in debenture loans in total; other loans, no quantitative restrictions	No more than 5% to one mortgage loan and no more than 15% to mortgage loans taken together

In Estonia, insurers may conclude transactions involving securities, which are characterized by the right or obligation of purchase or sale (derivative instruments), but only for the purpose of managing risk arising from fluctuation of the value of the insurer's assets.

Restrictions on investments abroad (representing technical provisions) are fairly liberal. Regulations in Lithuania permit investment in member states of the European Economic Area (EEA) and the Organization for Economic Co-operation and Development (OECD). Latvia permits investment in Lithuania, Estonia or an OECD member state. Regulations in Estonia allow investment in states of Zone A of the

OECD. Investments abroad are limited indirectly by a requirement for currency matching of assets to liabilities. Insurance technical provision funds shall be invested in assets expressed in terms of the currency in which the insurer's commitments are expressed. In general, the mismatch of assets to liabilities comprises not more than 20% in the particular currency and not more than 7% of total assets in other currencies.

In all three Baltic States, supervisors have the right to intervene in investment operations of the insurer. In Estonia, the Insurance Supervisory Authority has the right to prohibit an insurer from concluding a transaction that may result in the committed assets of the insurer not complying with regulatory provisions. In Lithuania, the Board of the Supervisory Authority has the right to restrict investments that may adversely affect the financial stability of the insurance company, as well as when such an investment might have a negative effect upon the business of the insurance company. In Latvia, the Financial and Capital Market Commission has the right to request a change in the composition and structure of assets accepted as cover for technical reserves. This can be done if the existing composition and structure of assets prejudices, or may prejudice, the financial stability of the insurer and the interests of insurance policyholders, and also if the Commission detects excessive reliance on any asset category or a high predominance of illiquid assets.

The assets covering other liabilities including the solvency margin are not subject to quantitative regulations.

IX. Reinsurance (cession to reinsurers)

In the Baltic States there is no requirement to reinsure accepted risks with a specific reinsurer. While an insurer can freely choose a reinsurer, the insurer has an obligation to compile and analyze information concerning the capability of the reinsurer to meet its liabilities. In general, the regulation and supervision of risk transfer to reinsurers follow OECD recommendations[1]. In all Baltic States, reinsurance programs must be presented as a part of the business plan when the company is licensed. The reinsurance program comprises a description of the risks to be reinsured, the planned reinsurers and the type of reinsurance treaty.

In Lithuania, the Board of the Supervisory Authority has issued extensive regulations concerning the criteria for choosing a reinsurer. A new version of the Criteria for Choosing a Reinsurer took effect on 1 January 2003. Reinsurers are classified into three categories, with the first category requiring suitable ratings from Standard & Poor's, Fitch IBCA or Moody's. Cession volumes are limited depending on the category of reinsurer. However, the Supervisory Authority Board may, in view of the insurer's needs and the reinsurer's reliability, agree upon the insurer's intention to exceed the restrictions of ceded insurance. To receive this type of agreement, the insurer is obliged to submit a special reinsurance program on the whole portfolio of insurance

---

[1] OECD Recommendation of the Council on the Assessment of Reinsurance Companies, OECD Council 1998.

risks. The Supervisory Authority has the right to examine reinsurance cover of direct insurers on an ongoing basis.

In Latvia, the executive board of an insurer shall formulate and approve a reinsurance program and is liable for compliance with this program. Without reinsurance, an insurer may not conclude an insurance contract with a single policyholder if the liabilities assumed by the insurer in accordance with this contract exceed 20% of its own funds.

An insurer must notify the Financial and Capital Market Commission when a reinsurance contract is concluded. When verifying an insurer's annual report, the Financial and Capital Market Commission assesses the placement of reinsurance and its volume. Based on its assessment, the Financial and Capital Market Commission has the right to require an insurer to set up technical reserves in the full amount or to change the placement of reinsurance.

In Estonia, the Insurance Supervisory Authority has the right to issue a precept to an insurer concerning a reinsurance contract concluded by the insurer if the contract may damage the interests of policyholders or insured persons, or harm the financial situation of the insurer.

The amount of all possible commitments of an insurer engaged in life insurance arising from one insurance contract or with regard to one object of insurance may exceed 10% of the funds owned by the insurer only if fulfilment of the insurer's commitment with regard to the part exceeding 10% is ensured by a reinsurance contract.

X. Actuaries

The function of the actuary as an expert in the evaluation and management of financial risks is quite new in the Baltics; this is still not a well-known profession. Before World War II, a few mathematicians in Estonia and Lithuania specialized in actuarial issues, but the tradition was lost during 50 years under Soviet rule.

Requirements for actuaries in life insurance companies were introduced in the legislation in the mid 1990s. By the rationale of the legislation rationale, the actuary's role is more that of an official than a professional; the actuary is listed along with company officials, including executive officers and the chief accountant. Moreover, the actuary is often a member of the Executive Board, although in Estonia the management board of an insurer engaged in life insurance must include a responsible actuary.

As stated explicitly in the legislation, an actuary's main responsibility is to assess the financial stability of insurers. (The regulations include more detailed explanations.)

In Latvia, according to the Financial and Capital Market Commission regulation, the actuary must prepare an actuarial report meant to supplement the annual financial statement. This report must include solvency margin calculations, the calculations on technical reserves and an evaluation of the adequacy of assets covering technical reserves (a "liquidation test"), a comparison of the actual and projected rates of return on assets, and a sensitivity test.

In Lithuania, the amounts and changes of insurance technical provisions reflected in the financial statements must be approved by the actuary.

In Estonia, the actuary must assess the accuracy and sufficiency of tariffs, calculate the amount of technical provisions based on actuarial methods, verify the accuracy and compliance of the technical provisions with legal requirements and the compliance of own funds with the minimum limit of owner's equity (the solvency margin). In addition, a responsible actuary should draw up mortality tables for life insurance and assess the accuracy of the mortality tables used, calculate the surrender values of insurance contracts and conduct an actuarial profit analysis of individual contracts and contracts of the same class. A responsible actuary must assess the influence of reinsurance contracts entered into or to be entered into on technical provisions, indemnities to be paid, surrender values and actuarial profit in the context of individual contracts and contracts of the same class.

National actuarial associations in all three Baltic States are members of the International Actuarial Association. The Estonian actuarial association is an associate member, but the Latvian and Lithuanian actuarial associations are observer members of the *Groupe Consultatif Actuariel Européen.*

XI. Intermediaries

Insurance intermediaries play a significant role in the overall life insurance industry. Insurance agents and brokers remain customers' major interlocutors and are usually the only information source for potential customers. It is therefore essential that intermediaries maintain high professional standards as regards both the particularities of life assurance products and the fair treatment of customers.

In the Baltic States, insurance intermediaries are subject to regulations and supervision. Under the insurance legislation, only adequately certified persons are permitted to provide insurance intermediation.

In Estonia, insurance legislation intermediation is defined simply as an insurance activity divided into insurance agents' and insurance brokers' activities. The intermediaries' main duties are defined in legislation as well. Insurance agents shall inform the client of possible variations of the insurance contract, of the terms and conditions of the contract, and particularly on insurance premiums, restrictions and exclusions related to the contract. The insurance broker moreover shall determine the insurance interests of the client and recommend to the client the best insurance contract.

Only natural persons who have received training in the insurance field may operate as insurance agents or brokers. Before beginning agent's or broker's activities, a person must obtain a certificate to be listed as an insurance intermediary by the Insurance Supervisory Authority. The official list is publicly available at the Internet home page of the Insurance Supervisory Authority. Insurance brokerage activities may be performed only on behalf of an insurance brokerage company, and only companies whose share of capital is at least EEK 1 million may operate as insurance brokers. An insurance intermediary must keep in his possession separate records of the assets of policyholders and insurers.

In Latvia, the legal framework for brokers and agents is slightly different. Latvian legislation defines insurance intermediation not as an insurance activity but as a special service activity that can be used by insurers, reinsurers and potential policyholders. An insurance agent is defined as a natural person representing the interests of an insurer, while an insurance broker is an independent insurance intermediary, and his or her professional activities must include the representation of interests of the persons planning to conclude insurance (or reinsurance) contracts. An insurance brokerage service can be provided only on behalf of a brokerage company with minimum capital of LVL 30,000. In Latvia, insurance agents may register themselves only with the Financial and Capital Market Commission, while insurance brokers must obtain certificates issued by the Financial and Capital Market Commission. In addition, an insurance brokerage firm must obtain a license from the Financial and Capital Market Commission before starting operations, and shall insure its third-party liability in case its actions cause losses to policyholders, insurers or other interested persons.

In Lithuania, an insurance agent is defined as a legal entity operating on behalf of, and using funds of, one or two separate insurance companies that are engaged in different branches of insurance, and an insurance broker as a legal entity (a public or a private company) carrying out insurance broker functions by authorization of an insurance company. Companies may engage in insurance brokerage only after receiving a permit issued by the Lithuania Insurance Supervisory Authority Board.

XII.   Treatment of failing insurers

Appropriate measures to prevent bankruptcies of insurers are essential to the stability of an insurance market. Regulations must therefore contain special rights for supervisors to permit proportional interventions. The supervisor should at the same time regularly and properly review and analyze the solvency position and operating conditions of the insurer to detect potential irregularities as early as possible.

In all three Baltic States insurers must submit monthly, quarterly and yearly reports to the supervising authority. These reports are analyzed to compare the solvency ratio, sufficiency of technical reserves, asset diversification and quality and reinsurance cover with requirements set out in regulations.

In Latvia, if indications of irregularity are discovered, the supervisor has the power to convene a meeting with the executive board or call a shareholders meeting of an insurer to discuss the situation. The supervisor is further entitled to request, on the basis of statements submitted and an analysis of examinations, a plan to improve the insurer's financial position and establish a time limit for its implementation. If the irregularity concerns investments, the Financial and Capital Market Commission may require changes in the structure of investments. If the irregularity concerns reinsurance cover, the supervisor has the right to require an insurer to set up technical reserves in the full amount, or change the placement of reinsurance. Regarding the sufficiency of technical reserves, the supervisor may instruct the insurer on the necessary amount of technical reserves if the insurer has not followed instructions from the Financial and Capital Market Commission on the formation and calculation methods of technical reserves. If matters worsen, the supervisor has the right to suspend the insurer's license. When a license is suspended, the insurer cannot conclude new contracts but must fulfil liabilities relative to valid insurance contracts. As an ultimate measure to avoid and insurer's insolvency and protect its policyholders, the Financial and Capital Market Commission may require the insurer to transfer all concluded insurance contracts, or parts thereof, to another insurer who has agreed to accept such contracts.

In Lithuania, the Supervisory Authority Board must examine the financial position of insurance companies and exercise control over their establishment of insurance technical provisions. The Supervisory Authority Board has the right to receive information needed in carrying out its supervisory functions and to inspect insurance companies and examine their financial activities, reinsurance contracts, rates of insurance contributions and adherence to rules on insurance types. It has the right to apply legal sanctions when companies have taken risks that may affect the interests of policyholders, the insured, third parties or beneficiaries.

When irregularities emerge, the Director of the Supervisory Authority has the right to issue warnings to the insurer. Ultimately, the supervisor has the right to suspend the insurance companies' licenses to engage in insurance business.

In Lithuania, the supervisor has the right to take over an insurance company. The Supervisory Authority Board has the right to appoint a temporary administrator for the period when the insurance company's supervisory board has its powers suspended, or the board or chief administrator is dismissed. Once a temporary administrator is appointed, the temporary administrator shall take over all powers of the supervisory board, the board and the chief administrator of the company; whereupon their decisions shall become unlawful and unenforceable. The main task of the temporary administrator is to institute a detailed audit of the insurance company within three months of his appointment and to prepare a written opinion on the state of the company's assets and liabilities. If it is established in the course of the audit that the insurance company is insolvent and will be unable to avoid bankruptcy, the temporary administrator must inform the Supervisory Authority Board of the initiation of bankruptcy proceedings.

The Board of the Supervisory Authority, in seeking to save an insurer from insolvency, and/or seeking to protect policyholders' interests, has the right to oblige the insurer to transfer the rights and obligations of insurance contracts to another insurer willing to take over those rights and obligations.

The insurance technical provision funds of an insurance company in liquidation should be used only to settle creditors' claims of policyholders, the insured, beneficiaries and third persons arising from insurance contracts. Insurance technical provision funds and assets in which insurance technical provision funds are invested cannot be drawn on to settle the claims of other insurance obligations.

In Estonia, an activity license may be revoked if the share capital, own funds or technical provisions of the insurer do not meet regulatory requirements or the insurer is unable to perform its assumed obligations, and the interests of policyholders are insufficiently protected. If owned funds decrease below the minimum limit set by the regulation, the insurer must submit a plan for the restoration of the financial situation to the Insurance Supervisory Authority.

As in Lithuania, the supervisor in Estonia has the right to take over insurer management in what is known as a "special regime". A special regime may be established when circumstances enable an activity license to be declared invalid or when there is reasonable suspicion that such circumstances may arise. The objective of a special regime is to ascertain the possibility of bringing the insurer's activities into compliance with the law and of acting to protect policyholders' interests. A special regime must be established by a decision of the supervisor, who appoints the special regime trustee. A special regime trustee is required to act first in the interests of policyholders and has the rights of the management board, supervisory board and general meeting of the insurer during the special regime. The authority of the management board, supervisory board, general meeting, procurator and other representatives of the insurer is suspended during a special regime unless otherwise prescribed by the decision to establish the special regime. The special regime trustee has the right to suspend compliance with resolutions of the management board, supervisory board or general meeting of the insurer. During a special regime, the insurer is prohibited from concluding new insurance contracts and extending existing contracts, increasing sums insured and paying indemnities, unless otherwise provided for in the decision to establish the special regime. A special regime trustee may transfer the insurance portfolio of an insurer or a part thereof to another insurer.

XIII. Protection of policyholders

Protection of insurance consumers is a threefold problem. First, consumers must be duly informed about contract particularities; this helps avoid unfair selling of insurance products that fail to meet the real needs of clients or are not fully transparent to them. Second, policyholders must have some protection against losing insurance cover due to an insurer's inability to fulfil its obligations. Last, there must be an adequate legal framework and institutional arrangements for settling disputes between insurers, policyholders and concerned third persons.

In all three Baltic States, the insurance contract is the subject of specific regulations. These regulations impose obligatory content for insurance contracts. They require an explicit presentation of the amount of insurance premiums, the sum that is insured separately for each insured risk and benefit, and the procedure for determining benefits in each insured event, as well as the surrender amount and the conditions for receiving it. For participating life contracts, the various types of bonuses and the procedures use in calculating and granting them must be stated. Unit-linked life insurance contracts must indicate relevant assets and the procedure for calculating the sum insured. Latvian insurance legislation explicitly requires insurance contracts to be clear and understandable. Insurers are obliged to inform customers of the terms of an insurance contract before concluding it.

A policyholder has the right to reconsider the purchase of an individual life insurance contract within a fixed period from the conclusion of the contract. In Latvia, this period is 15 days, and in Lithuania, 30 days.

For a personal insurance contract that lasts more than one year, the insurer informs the policyholder in writing at least once a year of taxes that apply to insurance premiums and benefits, of changes in such conditions, and of bonuses granted.

In bankruptcy cases, regulations commonly prescribe using life insurance technical provision funds only to settle the claims of policyholders and beneficiaries. Payment of other obligations of an insurance company in bankruptcy cannot come from insurance technical provision funds or property in which insurance technical provision funds are invested.

Latvia created a Fund for Protection of the Insured to safeguard the interests of the insured in the event of a bankruptcy. If the assets of the bankrupt company are insufficient to cover insurance claims, the fund covers the remainder up to 100% of insurance indemnity, but not more than LVL 2,000 to one policyholder (natural person). To establish the Fund for Protection of the Insured, insurance joint stock companies contributed 1% of total gross insurance premiums received from natural persons.

XIV.   Tax incentives

Considering the social and economic role of life insurance, the establishment of tax incentives is an important part of overall insurance regulations in a particular country.

Regulations concerning the taxation of life insurance have several common features in the Baltic States. Tax relief up to a certain ceiling is commonly granted to long-term endowment-type life insurance contracts oriented toward capital formation.

In Estonia, premiums paid under the pension insurance policy are deductible from taxable income in respect to personal income tax, with a ceiling of 15% of annual income. A contract is qualified for tax relief if it involves payments of the insurance pension after 55 years of age. No personal income tax is applied to pension benefits paid under a pension policy, while lump sum benefits are taxed at the rate of 10% instead of the regular 26%.

In Latvia, premiums for endowment insurance are not subject to personal income tax if the contract term is five years or longer, with a ceiling of 10% of annual income. The payout under such a policy is also tax-free. It is important to note that the ceilings are a composite of contributions under a life insurance policy and contributions to the voluntary pension fund.

In Lithuania, personal income tax does not apply to premiums paid by individuals for life insurance contracts that exceed 10 years. This incentive is subject to a ceiling of four times the amount of the minimum monthly wage (set by the Government) per annum. This is a composite incentive for life, accident and sickness insurance premiums. Indemnities received are not subject to tax.

Latvia and Lithuania provide corporate income tax relief to employers who take out endowment policies for the benefit of employees. The ceilings for tax relief are the same as for policies taken out by persons themselves. In Latvia, insurance payouts for policies taken out by an employer are subject to the personal income tax at the regular rate, while in Lithuania, received insurance benefits are not subject to tax.

Estonia provides no tax incentives for premiums paid by employers for life insurance policies on behalf of their employees.

It should be noted that the taxation regime in Latvia was changed dramatically in recent years. Up to 1999, insurance premiums paid by employers to benefit their employees were tax-free with no ceiling. In 2000, this advantage was eliminated, causing an enormous fall in the life insurance market. In 2001, tax incentives were restored with the above-mentioned ceilings.

XV. Regulations summary

In general, insurance regulations in the Baltic States are in line with concepts of deregulation meant to facilitate a competitive and efficient insurance market.

The essence of insurance supervision in the Baltic States is now more financial than technical. There are no requirements for prior approval of rates, tariffs or policy conditions. Instead, regulations concerning market entrance (licensing) and ongoing operations require the maintenance of a sound financial position and solvency margins adequate to insurance commitments; and they establish "fit and proper" requirements for managers, and minimum requirements for systems of internal risk management and control.

Baltic insurance markets are open to foreign insurers; in general, the participation of foreign investors is not limited. Recent legislative developments extend the possibilities for EU insurers to provide insurance in Baltic States by establishing branches or directly (freedom to provide services).

As Baltic States will soon become EU member states, regulations on insurance accounting, solvency and investments of technical provisions should conform to EU directives.

EU and World Bank expert missions in 2001-2002 found that insurance-sector regulation and the financial reporting framework in the Baltic States generally comply with such requirements.

Notwithstanding, several shortcomings of regulation and supervision should be noted.

"Fit and proper" conditions for top management are still too general, and there is little practical supervision to enforce requirements on an ad hoc basis. The enforcement of good corporate governance practices is thus handicapped for now.

Some weaknesses in policyholders' protection should also be mentioned. The general mode for settling disputes between insurers and policyholders stated in the regulatory framework is to apply to a court. Supervision institutions commonly adjudicate policyholders' complaints, but they have no judgment rights. There are no alternative ways of dispute resolution, such as an ombudsman, at present.

Although the Baltic States all regulate and supervise intermediaries, considerable gaps remain when compared to the regulation of intermediation in Western countries. Furthermore, there is a complete lack of self-regulation in the form of professional standards and code of conduct, an essential shortcoming.

CHAPTER 4

PERSPECTIVES OF THE LIFE INSURANCE MARKET

I. Overall economic development and life insurance markets

The experience of emerging markets shows a correlation between the level of wealth and life insurance consumption. At a certain threshold of GDP per capita, life insurance consumption tends to grow quickly before reaching a mature equilibrium. In the Baltic States, GDP per head averages three times less than that of the EU-15, when expressed in the Purchasing Power Standard (PPS), EU data show. Households surveys find that food, housing and clothing account for 60% to 70% of expenditures. A majority of households lack the resources to make contractual savings with insurance companies. Fortunately, there are positive signs. Baltic States' GDP has shown steady growth, amid overall stability, in recent years, reaching 5%-6% annually. Integration into the EU in 2004 should point to an optimistic outlook in coming years, with positive signs for the life insurance market, too. As mentioned, the life insurance market has developed at a rate of more than 20% for each of the last three years, and preliminary figures for 2003 are even more significant, including 70% growth for life insurance premiums in Lithuania.

II. Reforms of pensions systems in the Baltic States

Looking at the role of life insurance in the UK and Ireland as a provider of old age pensions savings, and considering as well the experience of pension reforms in South America, it becomes clear that pension reforms are important in developing personal responsibility and as a powerful incentive for the development of a life market.

In the mid-1990s, when pension reform concepts were developed in all three Baltic states, the general purpose or reform strategy was defined as that of creating a financially stable, risk-diversified pension system based on social security contributions, which would involve both PAYG and capital-accumulation components. According to the reform concepts, the new pension systems were to be established with three tiers, or pillars:

Pillar I – compulsory state pension insurance, based on PAYG principle;

Pillar II – compulsory funded pension scheme;

Pillar III – private voluntary pension savings.

The second-pillar pension scheme in Latvia, which redirected part of social insurance contributions for old-age pensions to the investment fund, began operating on 1 July 2001. In Estonia, a mandatory second (funded) pension scheme was introduced on 1 July 2002. In Lithuania, the introduction of a mandatory funded second pillar is still pending, but is scheduled for 1 January 2004. In general, the second pillar is organized as a pool of assets managed by an asset management company.

The third (voluntary) pillar was introduced in Latvia and Estonia in 1998 and in Lithuania in 2000 by special legislative acts. The role of life insurance companies in the third (voluntary) pillar differs in the Baltic States. In Latvia, voluntary pension savings are legally assigned to the special financial institutions. However, tax allowances are similar for contributions to pension funds and for long-term endowment life insurance. In Estonia, participation in the voluntary third pillar can take two forms: units-of-pension funds managed by private fund managers or pension insurance policies offered by insurance companies. A special license is required to provide pension insurance. In Lithuania, voluntary accumulation for old age can be arranged by pension funds or insurance companies.

Life insurance markets will benefit from the introduction of a second pillar no sooner than 20 years, when accrued pension capital will be converted to annuities. In the voluntary third-pillar pension scheme, Baltic life insurance companies could play an active role, as tax treatments are similar to those applied to pension funds.

CHAPTER 5

RECOMMENDATIONS FOR PROMOTING LIFE INSURANCE

It is widely recognized that life insurance, in a system where relatively small amounts of money (premiums) paid by policyholders are accumulated and invested, is an important part of developing a sound national economy. This system allows individuals with relatively low incomes to save and invest over the long run. Such mobilized capital is also a considerable resource to invest in local capital markets, thus leading to capital market growth. It is therefore essential to recognize the importance of life insurance and to promote it through a proper state strategy built on legislation and supervision. As life insurance products are usually more complex than term deposit with banks, it is necessary for life insurance market participants to make efforts and provide resources to incite potential customers to purchase life insurance products.

I. Regulation and supervision

To eliminate regulatory shortcomings concerning good corporate governance it is reasonable to extend regulations in keeping with the recommendations of the International Association of Insurance Supervisors (IAIS). Fitness and propriety testing should be carried out continuously to allow effective intervention by a Supervisory Agency when necessary. The Supervisory Agency, moreover, should have appropriate and effective sanctions procedures to dismiss key persons who do not meet "fit and proper" requirements. Measures should also be taken to enforce the effective internal control of insurance enterprises and to raise the independence of a life insurance company's chief actuary.

To improve confidence in insurance services, the establishment of an ombudsman should be given priority.

The introduction of comprehensive professional standards for insurance intermediaries and independent financial advisers should be hastened.

II. Pension reforms

The reformed pension systems in the Baltic States include funded components, both compulsory and voluntary. Unfortunately, laws on compulsory funded pension schemes do not allow life insurance companies to participate in the capital accumulation phase. Therefore, consumers have no option to arrange with the same financial institution additional long-term protection, such as long-term care insurance or catastrophic-illness insurance. As life insurance companies have experience in asset management, in might make sense to include life insurance companies in the compulsory funded pension scheme as eligible asset managers.

Pension reforms are complex, difficult and onerous for governments. It is not surprising that they targeted public relations campaigns to the introduction of mandatory funded schemes. However, the rising wealth of future pensioners greatly depends on deliberate, voluntary savings. It would seem advisable for governments to finance public-information campaigns to explain the necessity of voluntary savings for retirement and the role of long-term life insurance as a part of old-age care. Governments, after all, started pension reforms with the aim of shifting from full reliance on state aid to greater personal responsibility. Governments must consequently promote voluntary savings. However, officials often consider such activities as unethical lobbying for a particular private business sector.

III. Distribution of life insurance products

The purchase of a life insurance policy generally constitutes an informed choice to endow dependents with necessary funds and to provide income for retirement. The potential consumer must, therefore, have some sense of his own financial planning, based on appropriate advice. Present distribution models, based on agents selling standard endowment contracts, do not reflect either the awareness of potential consumers or the variety of consumer needs in different life cycles. To increase sales volume, insurance and broker companies must train sales forces to bring their competence toward financial-adviser standards. Insurance products must be more flexible, expressed in clear language, and set out benefits and costs explicitly. As governments encourage long-term insurance through tax incentives, it is essential for agents and brokers to be able to provide advice on income declarations. Not all residents are required to declare income, and some lack knowledge of how to do so properly, but having a tax incentive on a life policy makes this necessary.

Regulators must, therefore, increase legal requirements on the competence of intermediaries and call on them to observe a code of conduct.

IV. Education

According to public survey results in Latvia, about 50% of respondents know little to nothing about capital formation in life insurance. This means that half the potential insurance market cannot be reached. "Insurance literacy" campaigns could considerably raise the life insurance market volume. It is in the interest of all life insurance companies to pool their resources and launch educational campaigns to disseminate information on life insurance. All the Baltic States have national Associations of Insurers and Associations of Brokers which could join in such activities. Given the potential social and economical role of life insurance, governments should support these campaigns. A good example of what can be done is the guide, "What You Should Know About Buying Life Insurance" issued by the American Council of Life Insurance. The idea of the booklet is expressed in the subheading: "What questions to ask when you're buying life insurance".

V. Technology

Modern communications technology is an important accelerator of insurance sales volume. About 39% of Estonians have Internet access, and 29% of the adult population owns a home computer. In Latvia, 17% of inhabitants use the Internet, and in Lithuania, 14% do. The main use of the Internet in the financial area is Internet banking. Statistics show that Estonia has more than 400,000 people who use Internet banking, Latvia has 150,000 and Lithuania has 130,000, and the numbers are constantly growing. Combined with an educational campaign, the Internet could help reach many more potential customers. Undoubtedly, the purchase of life insurance requires personal contact with an agent, broker or representative of insurance company. Many people have little idea of how much life cover costs and what the investment return is. Internet sites with calculators for needed life cover and retirement information, illustrations and examples could stimulate potential customers to make contact with insurers or intermediaries.

Conclusions

Although life insurance markets in the Baltic States are highly underdeveloped in terms of insurance premium penetration and density, the necessary prerequisites are in place for rapid growth. Insurance regulation and supervision frameworks largely correspond to EU regulations and IAIS principles. As the Baltic States demonstrate high rates of GDP growth, the widespread expectation is that wealth and consequently the consumption of life insurance will increase considerably in the near future. Governments could promote the development of the life insurance sector by improving regulations and by putting more emphasis on personal responsibility in the reformed pension system. The life insurance industry itself could promote the market by modernizing distribution channels and methods and by developing targeted educational activities.

BIBLIOGRAPHY

P.Sneijers. Insurance Services Statistics. EU Statistics in Focus. Industry, trade and services. Theme 4 – 43/2002.

S.Stapel. The GDP of the Candidate Countries. EU Statistics in Focus. Theme2-28/2001.

B.Galgoczi. Wage trends in Central and Eastern Europe. ILO, Labour Education 2002/3, N 128, pp. 39-44.

Capital Markets and Financial Intermediation in the Baltic States, IMF Country report Nr. 03/115, 2003.

OECD Recommendation of the Council on the Assessment of Reinsurance Companies. OECD Council, 1998.

G. Dickinson. Encouraging a Dynamic Life Insurance Industry: Economic Benefits and Policy Issues. OECD workshop on Insurance in the Baltic States, Riga, 2000.

EU Statistics in Focus, 28/2001

Guidance Paper for Fit and Proper Principles and their Application. IAIS, 2000.

Developing Life Insurance in the Economies in Transition. OECD Workshop on Insurance in the Baltic States. Riga, 2000.

OECD Principles on Corporate Governance. OECD, 1999.

Latvia Insurance Market Statistics. Finance and Capital market Commission:

http://www.fktk.lv/en/

Lithuania Insurance Market Statistics. State Insurance Supervisory Authority:

http://www.vdpt.lt/en/

Estonia Insurance Market Statistics. Financial Supervision Authority:

http://www.fi.ee/eng/

INSURANCE IN THE BALTIC STATES:
A COMPARATIVE STUDY OF THE NON-LIFE SECTOR

Robert B. K. Pye

Abstract

This report is devoted to a comparative analysis on the development of the non-life insurance sector in the Baltic Countries. In this perspective a first part of the paper presents an overview of the evolution of the non-life insurance market in the three Baltic States as compared to other transition economies and OECD countries.

The second part of the paper is dedicated to the current and past development of this market, its strengths and difficulties. The legal and regulatory framework of the non-life insurance sector in the Baltic's is also sketches out. The various distribution channels of the non-life insurance sector and in particular the development of e-insurance in the Baltic States is lastly presented.

The study ends by a series of recommendations addressed to Baltic policy makers and insurance managers in order to further develop the non-life segment of the insurance sector and to facilitate their future integration in the European Union.

TABLE OF CONTENTS

ACKNOWLEDGEMENTS

The author is grateful for the invaluable cooperation of the official host country supervisory authorities and local insurers associations of the three Baltic States for providing statistical data and background materials used in this paper. Their comments and suggestions on draft versions of this paper were of tremendous assistance. Finally, my sincere thanks to Sofia Despotidou, whose help on this paper was invaluable. Any remaining errors are the sole responsibility of the author.

INTRODUCTION

Since achieving independence from the Soviet Union in 1991, Estonia, Latvia and Lithuania – collectively known as the Baltic States – have each forged their own path down the long road of transition, attempting to move from a Communist command-style economy to a democratic free-market orientation. Yet, the process continues to be an arduous one, especially in light of the legacy of the Communist system that so dominated these countries and their inhabitants over the past century. Consequently, each of the Baltic States, as results show, has achieved a different level of progress in the transformation process.

An integral part of the transition process in each of the three states has involved the development of a viable domestic financial-services sector, whose three main pillars – banking, capital markets and insurance – are essential elements in the functioning of a dynamic market economy. While often overlooked by its more glamorous colleagues, the insurance sector plays a pivotal role in the functioning of an efficient and effective financial-services sector, both as a provider of risk coverage and as an institutional investor in the local and global economy (Pye, 2003; OECD, 1997; Skipper, 1997; EBRD, 1996). Yet, despite its importance, very little research has been conducted on the development of the insurance sector in transition economies.

Given this situation, the purpose of this paper is to examine the development of the insurance sector in the context of Estonia, Latvia and Lithuania, and specifically to provide a comparative study of the development of the non-life segment from the onset of the transition. In doing so, attention is given to the implications for the insurance sector stemming from the Baltic States' planned accession to the European Union (EU), along with five other transition economies (the Czech Republic, Hungary, Poland, Slovakia and Slovenia). Together, these eight transition economies are hereafter referred to as the EU Accession Countries Eight (EU-AC8).

This paper is presented in four main sections. In Chapter 1, the author examines the evolution of the insurance market in the transition economies of Central and Eastern Europe (CEE) and the Newly Independent States (NIS) between 1990-2001, with special attention given to the progress of the three Baltic States. This is facilitated by a comparative analysis of premium income data for the non-life insurance sector using a common denominator; insurance density rates; and insurance penetration rates. Chapter 2 forms the main body of the paper, identifying the development of the insurance sector in each of the Baltic States with regard to the historical and cultural context; the legal and regulatory environment; the development of the non-life market, with specific reference to major non-life classes; and an overview of distribution channels used. In Chapter 3, the author draws conclusions based on the analysis and provides some recommendations, which, while primarily directed at policymakers, have clear implications for insurance providers and consumers.

CHAPTER 1

THE EVOLUTION OF THE INSURANCE MARKET
IN CEE AND THE NIS

In examining the evolution of the insurance sector in the Baltic States it is appropriate to highlight their progress in relation to other transition economies. Subsequently, the performance of the insurance sectors in the three Baltic countries is compared and contrasted with other transition countries in CEE and the NIS, using a number of forms of analysis, including a comparative analysis of premium income data using a common denominator; insurance density rates; and insurance penetration rates. References are also made to the relative position of each Baltic state to the EU-AC8 grouping and the EU in general.

Yet, before beginning the actual analysis, it is prudent to address one key issue pertaining to data comparability. To be specific, during the early phases of the transition process (1990-95) the host countries of CEE and the NIS experienced a high degree of economic volatility. A simple review of inflation rates based on average annual consumer prices for this period reveals a number of the host countries affected by high rates of inflation, and in some cases hyperinflation. In terms of specific average inflation rates, CEE achieved a rate of 325%; the Baltic States, 253%; and the remaining NIS, 1,285%. The EU-AC8 grouping did somewhat better, with an average for the period of 139%.

The high degree of economic volatility during the early phases of the transition process also had a profound impact on exchange rates. This, in turn, has made a transposition of nominal growth rates in local currencies using a common denominator, such as US dollars, highly problematic.

However, the situation in most host countries has improved since 1995, with inflation rates generally stabilizing at more acceptable levels. Rates of inflation during the more recent 1996-2001 period averaged, by groupings, 33% for CEE, 7.5% for the Baltic States, 31% for the NIS, and 8.9% for the EU-AC8. Moreover, most of this volatility in CEE and the NIS can be attributed to a few host countries within the groupings. To be specific, for CEE, Bulgaria's inflation rate hit its highest peak to date at 1,082% in 1997, while Romania had an average annual inflation rate of 63%, and Serbia and Montenegro of 56%, between 1996-2001. In the NIS, while Russia, Ukraine and Uzbekistan have each experienced double-digit inflation rates, the situation in Belarus remains problematic, with an average annual inflation rate of 116% for the period.

Given the severity of economic volatility in CEE and the NIS between 1990-95, it is appropriate to devote more attention to the data from the 1996-2001 period. This latter period is also more reflective of the actual development of the insurance sector since the onset of the transition process.

46

In regard to the Baltic States, Exhibit 1 provides a profile of the economic conditions in each of the three countries between 1993-2002, which corresponds to the available insurance data presented in the main part of this paper.

I.   A comparative review of premium income

To provide a general feel for the data and for the overall magnitude of the sector, it is appropriate to translate the premium income data from local currencies into a common denominator. Accordingly, Exhibit 2 provides a basis for comparison of premium income in CEE and the NIS between 1990-2001, using US dollars as the common denominator. While this measure is subject to a degree of exchange rate volatility across the region, this has not been the case with regard to the Baltic States, where rates have generally been stable during 1996-2001 (See Exhibit 1).

In reviewing the data, a number of important points are worth note. First, there is the clear dominance of non-life over life insurance. Data for the 1996-2001 period show that in 1996, non-life insurance accounted for an average of around 77% of total activity for CEE and the NIS. Over the years this has very slowly decreased, but the non-life sector has continued to dominate, accounting for some 65% of total insurance business in 2001.

Exhibit 1, Basic Economic Indicators for the Baltic States, 1992-2002

Indicator / Host Country	1992	1993	1994	1995	1996	1997	1998	1999	2000	2001	2002
Population (annual average, in millions)											
Estonia	1.562	1.527	1.507	1.492	1.476	1.462	1.454	1.446	1.437	1.429	1.421
Latvia	2.657	2.606	2.556	2.530	2.502	2.480	2.458	2.439	2.42	2.401	2.382
Lithuania	3.747	3.737	3.724	3.718	3.712	3.707	3.704	3.701	3.700	3.700	3.699
GDP (in millions of local currency)											
Estonia (Kroons)	13,054	21,610	29,867	40,897	52,423	64,045	73,538	76,327	87,236	96,571	106,496
Latvia (Lats)	1,005	1,467	2,043	2,329	2,807	3,269	3,592	3,890	4,348	4,813	5,195
Lithuania (Litai)	3,406	11,590	16,904	24,781	31,529	38,520	43,555	42,608	44,698	47,498	50,679
GDP (in millions of US dollars)											
Estonia	$1,078.8	$1,637.1	$2,297.5	$3,556.3	$4,368.6	$4,607.6	$5,215.5	$5,192.3	$5,131.5	$5,487.0	$6,415.4
Latvia	na	$2,189.6	$3,648.2	$4,394.3	$5,103.6	$5,636.2	$6,088.1	$6,593.2	$7,127.9	$7,639.7	$8,379.0
Lithuania	na	$2,695.3	$4,226.0	$6,195.3	$7,882.3	$9,630.0	$10,888.8	$10,652.0	$11,174.5	$11,874.5	$13,697.0
GDP per Capita (in US dollars)											
Estonia	$690.7	$1,072.1	$1,524.5	$2,383.6	$2,959.7	$3,151.5	$3,587.0	$3,590.8	$3,571.0	$3,839.7	$4,514.7
Latvia	na	$840.2	$1,427.3	$1,736.9	$2,039.8	$2,272.7	$2,476.9	$2,703.2	$2,945.4	$3,181.9	$3,517.6
Lithuania	na	$721.3	$1,134.8	$1,666.3	$2,123.5	$2,597.8	$2,939.7	$2,878.1	$3,020.1	$3,209.3	$3,702.9
Growth in Real GDP[1]											
Estonia	-14.2%	-8.8%	-2.0%	4.3%	3.9%	9.8%	4.6%	-0.6%	7.1%	5.0%	5.8%
Latvia	-34.9%	-14.9%	2.2%	-0.9%	3.7%	8.4%	4.8%	2.8%	6.8%	7.9%	6.1%
Lithuania	-21.3%	-16.2%	-9.8%	3.3%	4.7%	7.0%	7.3%	-1.8%	4.0%	6.5%	6.7%
Inflation Rate (annual average)[2]											
Estonia	1076.0%	89.8%	47.7%	29.0%	23.1%	11.2%	8.1%	3.3%	4.0%	5.8%	3.6%
Latvia	951.2%	109.2%	35.9%	25.0%	17.6%	8.4%	4.7%	2.4%	2.6%	2.5%	1.9%
Lithuania	1020.5%	410.4%	72.1%	39.6%	24.6%	8.9%	5.1%	0.8%	1.0%	1.3%	0.3%
Exchange Rate (annual average)											
Estonia (Kroons per US dollar)	12.1	13.2	13.0	11.5	12.0	13.9	14.1	14.7	17.0	17.6	16.6
Latvia (Lats per US dollar)	na	0.67	0.56	0.53	0.55	0.58	0.59	0.59	0.61	0.63	0.62
Lithuania (Litai per US dollar)	na	4.3	4.0	4.0	4.0	4.0	4.0	4.0	4.0	4.0	3.7
Foreign Direct Investment (FDI) (in millions of US dollars)[3]											
Estonia	$80	$156	$212	$199	$111	$130	$574	$222	$324	$343	$300
Latvia	na	$50	$279	$245	$379	$515	$303	$331	$400	$170	$250
Lithuania	na	$30	$31	$72	$152	$328	$921	$478	$375	$439	$395

Sources: EBRD (2000-03), Euromonitor (2002), and the Author's own calculations.

Notes: 1) Estimates for Real GDP represent weighted averages formulated by the EBRD; **2)** Inflation Rates are based on annual changes in Consumer Prices; **3)** FDI figures are based on Balance-of-Payments (BoP) data.

Exhibit 2, Premium Income (in US Dollars) by Insurance Type in CEE and the NIS, 1990-2001

Host Country (in millions of US Dollars)	1990 Total	1990 Life	1990 Non-Life	1991 Total	1991 Life	1991 Non-Life	1992 Total	1992 Life	1992 Non-Life	1993 Total	1993 Life	1993 Non-Life	1994 Total	1994 Life	1994 Non-Life	1995 Total	1995 Life	1995 Non-Life
Albania							3.32	0.00	3.32	11.40	0.00	11.40	11.77	0.00	11.77	14.48	0.00	14.48
Armenia																		
Azerbaijan													0.60			3.91	-	-
Belarus										26.36	1.71	24.66	23.88	1.88	21.99	39.73	1.87	37.86
Bosnia-Herzegovina																34.22	0.00	34.22
Bulgaria							0.10	0.00	0.09	0.20	0.05	0.15	225.55	67.35	158.20	274.70	93.38	181.32
Croatia										459.44	15.68	443.77	451.89	15.60	436.29	539.20	30.28	508.92
Czech Republic	894.67	342.44	552.22	488.24	157.01	331.23	594.36	184.53	409.83	801.25	202.24	599.00	1,010.00	257.57	752.43	1,272.89	348.10	924.79
Estonia	na	na	na	na	na	na	5.98	1.28	4.70	14.46	2.41	12.05	26.50	2.56	23.95	47.67	3.72	43.96
FYR Macedonia							102.50	3.20	99.30	102.50	3.20	99.30	104.31	5.63	98.68	143.07	10.00	133.07
Georgia																		
Hungary	629.70	68.92	560.78	831.72	171.31	660.41	746.20	97.28	648.92	798.67	184.11	614.56	894.43	229.45	664.99	946.81	282.01	664.80
Kazakhstan													4.35	-	-	11.17	-	-
Latvia										22.33	7.03	15.29	32.32	9.59	22.73	60.45	17.06	43.40
Lithuania										13.02	6.05	6.98	26.75	13.25	13.50	30.96	13.21	17.75
Moldova							4.97	-	-	5.27	-	-	6.71	3.74	2.97	14.57	5.99	8.58
Poland	737.86	54.26	683.60	1,402.11	196.73	1,205.39	1,527.21	397.60	1,129.62	1,708.39	489.57	1,218.82	1,802.91	558.43	1,244.48	2,326.38	771.63	1,554.75
Romania	344.46	131.38	213.08	144.09	23.43	120.66	65.57	10.20	55.37	60.39	5.78	54.60	99.06	9.75	89.30	142.56	15.48	127.08
Russian Federation				203.50	124.59	78.91	466.04	106.36	359.68	1,188.38	522.93	665.45	3,419.05	1,949.21	1,469.84	6,118.54	1,078.87	5,039.67
Serbia & Montenegro													313.37	-	-	503.56	4.39	499.17
Slovakia	399.16	94.43	304.74	191.38	59.01	132.37	221.38	64.73	156.64	243.22	59.37	183.85	280.72	66.20	214.52	360.46	86.00	274.47
Slovenia				417.36	28.26	389.09	404.75	30.23	374.52	418.71	44.29	374.43	488.84	70.12	418.72	863.92	127.86	736.07
Ukraine										187.50	83.32	104.18	436.91	185.75	251.16	166.23	41.49	124.74
Uzbekistan																		

Continued...

Exhibit 2, Premium Income (in US Dollars) by Insurance Type in CEE and the NIS, 1990-2001 (Cont'd.)

Host Country (in millions of US Dollars)	1996 Total	1996 Life	1996 Non-Life	1997 Total	1997 Life	1997 Non-Life	1998 Total	1998 Life	1998 Non-Life	1999 Total	1999 Life	1999 Non-Life	2000 Total	2000 Life	2000 Non-Life	2001 Total	2001 Life	2001 Non-Life
Albania	14.52	0.00	14.52	8.09	0.01	8.08	10.17	0.02	10.15	13.37	0.03	13.34	14.03	0.06	13.97	20.63	1.22	19.42
Armenia				0.87	0.00	0.87	1.67	0.00	1.67	2.07	0.00	2.07	2.37	0.00	2.37	3.72	0.00	3.72
Azerbaijan	8.59	0.14	8.45	13.64	0.22	13.41	14.89	0.41	14.48	14.86	0.30	14.57	13.65	0.28	13.37	na	na	na
Belarus	57.42	2.48	54.94	47.69	2.12	45.57	53.09	1.51	51.57	61.20	0.53	60.67	81.08	0.79	80.29	85.79	na	na
Bosnia-Herzegovina	43.42	0.29	43.13	71.51	2.02	69.48	73.57	2.42	71.15	119.88	7.75	112.13	119.52	9.54	109.98	110.01	8.04	101.97
Bulgaria	208.53	47.38	161.15	116.76	10.80	105.96	132.28	16.08	116.20	168.73	17.24	151.50	182.25	20.78	161.47	218.36	39.86	178.49
Croatia	573.37	47.66	525.71	567.14	63.93	503.21	636.19	92.22	543.97	610.75	96.45	514.30	545.86	91.47	454.39	614.30	111.47	502.83
Czech Republic	1,484.98	405.49	1,079.48	1,513.76	400.32	1,113.44	1,696.51	463.32	1,233.19	1,804.68	575.65	1,229.03	1,794.94	589.90	1,205.04	2,124.86	744.26	1,380.60
Estonia	66.43	5.37	61.06	75.84	9.22	66.62	87.71	14.64	73.07	91.34	14.73	76.62	93.77	17.90	75.86	101.31	20.22	81.09
FYR Macedonia	134.18	0.44	133.74	105.12	0.92	104.20	103.06	1.17	101.89	105.03	1.37	103.66	88.56	1.34	87.22	86.73	1.35	85.38
Georgia				4.33	0.12	4.21	6.49	0.06	6.42	7.11	0.11	7.00	9.04	0.06	8.98	na	na	na
Hungary	1,000.92	316.17	684.76	1,042.04	341.29	700.75	1,144.72	418.46	726.27	1,254.77	505.76	749.01	1,360.57	629.24	731.34	1,464.12	610.96	853.16
Kazakhstan	14.75	-	-	44.20	1.16	43.04	52.66	0.39	52.26	48.81	0.31	48.50	57.31	0.01	57.30	90.69	0.65	90.04
Latvia	73.99	17.20	62.46	115.55	14.71	92.88	149.35	17.36	130.04	160.29	19.05	141.15	156.72	7.89	146.46	152.13	7.07	145.06
Lithuania	46.13	13.57	32.55	63.30	14.56	48.74	99.12	16.63	95.20	101.41	18.51	91.32	109.27	19.07	90.20	119.49	23.21	96.28
Moldova	21.09	10.95	10.15	29.80	14.57	15.23	18.58	5.93	12.65	8.81	0.71	8.10	9.44	0.52	8.92	na	na	na
Poland	3,040.74	1,033.41	2,007.33	3,734.24	1,234.09	2,500.14	4,453.89	1,536.67	2,917.21	4,626.30	1,739.34	2,886.96	4,785.12	1,627.21	3,157.91	5,402.20	1,878.78	3,523.41
Romania	178.41	17.38	161.03	181.93	11.27	170.66	272.09	22.47	249.62	278.74	32.98	245.76	310.65	49.17	261.48	344.53	72.77	271.76
Russian Federation	7,228.71	1,521.22	5,707.49	7,662.60	1,392.34	6,270.26	4,269.22	1,241.57	3,027.65	3,928.43	1,444.04	2,484.39	6,063.79	2,829.45	3,234.35	9,472.60	4,784.25	4,688.36
Serbia & Montenegro	397.86	2.18	395.68	486.60	3.77	482.82	264.99	2.30	262.69	451.39	2.31	449.08	266.00	1.42	264.58	279.43	2.33	277.10
Slovakia	449.05	115.46	333.59	505.01	140.58	364.43	604.59	184.28	420.31	571.47	205.54	365.93	591.38	245.61	345.76	658.23	286.73	371.50
Slovenia	899.66	148.65	751.01	811.45	143.26	668.20	927.43	158.35	769.08	942.69	170.00	772.69	866.03	167.76	698.27	947.79	202.50	745.29
Ukraine	173.67	18.28	155.39	219.57	9.98	209.59	322.11	5.25	316.85	281.86	1.84	280.02	392.65	1.84	390.81	564.38	2.93	561.45
Uzbekistan										19.16			17.27			21.10		-

Sources: Wherever possible the researcher has utilized data obtained directly from host country sources (local insurers' association and/or the respective supervisory authority).

Notes: 1) Wherever possible the researcher has utilized data obtained directly from host country sources (local insurers' association and/or the respective supervisory authority); **2)** Gross Premium Income (GPI) figures given in US dollars are based upon the appropriate average annual exchange rates as reported by the EBRD.

A second point that comes to light is that not only is the life insurance sector yet to take off in any great way in CEE and NIS countries, but it has yet to take firm root in many of them. Actually, this should not be so surprising given that under the former Communist system life insurance was often viewed by domestic consumers as a non-essential product, given the dynamic role of the state. With the onset of the transition period this situation has been compounded by the high economic volatility experienced in most host countries in the region, which has played havoc with consumers and providers alike. For consumers, this has not only had an adverse effect on their ability to buy life insurance, but on the economic utility of such policies given high rates of inflation. The latter issue has also been a fundamental problem for providers, especially in light of the limited range of investment opportunities available to them in the respective host countries.

Third, the distribution of life and non-life insurance differs between the countries of CEE, the NIS and the EU. For example, in the EU during 2001 life insurance activity accounted for 63% of overall activity, with non-life responsible for just 37%. In contrast, even in the more economically advanced EU-AC8 grouping the distribution favored non-life over life by a 3-to-1 margin. In the Baltic States, the spread was even more pronounced in 2001, with activity in the non-life sector highest in Latvia, at 95%, followed by Lithuania, with 81% and Estonia with 80%. This imbalance represents a significant gap between East and West that will certainly need to be addressed by each of the Baltic States and the EU.

Fourth, in terms of the non-life sector, it should be noted that motor insurance, both motor third party liability (MTPL) and motor own damage (Casco), has been a key source of insurance business within CEE and the NIS. To be specific, in 2001 motor insurance policies constituted 66.9% of all non-life premiums in Estonia, 47.1% in Latvia, and 44.6% in Lithuania. In Lithuania, where legislation making MTPL compulsory took effect in 2002, spending on motor insurance has increased significantly to account for 59.7% of all non-life premiums.

Most insurers operating in these transition economies view motor insurance cover, especially compulsory MTPL, as a means of introducing local consumers, notably private individuals, to their more extensive lines of life and non-life insurance products. Yet, it remains to be seen whether this will prove to be an effective means of educating consumers on the merits of a Western-style insurance system. For many insurers in these transition economies it is also proving to be a costly education process, since for reasons already cited MTPL is financially often a marginal line of business, and in some cases unprofitable. This education process is essential, however, to redressing the very low level of "insurance culture" in CEE and the NIS, which is a direct product of the insurance system that operated under the former Communist economic model (Pye, 2003, 2000; Faulkner, 2002; Aubrey-Jones, 1996a, 1996b). It should be noted that the term "insurance culture" refers to level of customer knowledge and usage of various insurance instruments within a given host country. This is also a topic that will be addressed later in the paper in an overview of the Baltic insurance markets.

Finally, to put this all into perspective, it is prudent to discuss the relative size of the three Baltic markets. In 2001, Latvia had the highest values in relative dollar terms for both total and non-life insurance activity, followed by Lithuania and Estonia. However, the amount of premium income generated by these countries shows them to be very small markets. Even together, their insurance markets had a total value of just $364 million in 2001, of which the non-life segment accounted for $322 million (86.5%).

In terms of the EU-AC8, this positioned the three Baltic States at the very bottom of the grouping for both life and non-life segments during the same year. In examining the data, the gap between the Baltic States and the rest of the EU-AC8 grouping becomes evident. For instance, Slovakia, the next country up from the Baltic states in the grouping, generated more than four times the total insurance premiums of Latvia, the Baltic leader, and more than two and a half times that of its non-life segment.

In comparison to the EU, the very small size of the three Baltic markets becomes even more apparent. In 2001, according to Swiss Re data, the EU as a group generated $697.3 billion in total premium income, of which the non-life segment accounted for nearly $266 billion (38%) and life insurance the balance of $431.3 billion (62%). In respect of non-life insurance, Germany spent the most, with $68 billion. At the other end of the spectrum, Luxembourg had the smallest non-life insurance market in the EU, valued at $770 million. Thus, the Baltic States clearly have considerable ground to cover if they hope ever to reach comparable EU levels. For a more complete picture of the progress of the Baltic States, it is appropriate to examine the data based on both insurance density and penetration rates.

II. Insurance density rates

Insurance density rates measure premium volume in relation to a host country's population, that is, how much money per capita is spent annually on insurance-related products. This measure is a useful indicator, as host-country populations generally remain constant over short periods, although in CEE and the NIS, population levels have generally been flat or in some cases gradually decreased over time. In the case of the Baltic States, the latter applies (See Exhibit 1).

By comparison, premiums in US dollars have been utilized. As noted, this measure is subject to possible deviations stemming from fluctuations in exchange rates. Exhibit 3 provides a profile of density rates for non-life insurance in the host countries of CEE and the NIS between 1990 and 2001.

Data analysis has been conducted for three time periods, namely a six-year (1996-2001), eight-year (1994-2001), and 12-year (1990-2001) spread. Individual averages were calculated for the non-life insurance segment based on these three periods, which in turn were plotted against one another using a multiple line chart to identify the trends and respective groupings of host countries. For the purposes of grouping and to minimize the impact of economic volatility associated with the early years of transition, the more recent six-year (1996-2001) period was used as a base line while ensuring that data from the other two periods also fell within the bands identified.

An analysis of the data in Exhibit 3 reveals six host-country groupings for the non-life insurance segment, as follows:

Group One (Less than $5.00 per capita): Armenia ($0.69), Georgia ($1.23), Azerbaijan ($1.61), Moldova ($2.50), Kazakhstan ($3.89), and Albania ($3.93).

Group Two ($5.00-19.99 per capita): Belarus ($5.74), Ukraine ($6.41), Romania ($10.08), and Bulgaria ($17.67).

Group Three ($20.00-$34.99 per capita): Lithuania ($20.45), Bosnia-Herzegovina ($22.49), the Russian Federation ($28.91), and Serbia and Montenegro ($33.47).

Group Four ($35.00-$54.99 per capita): Latvia ($49.18), Estonia ($49.95), and the FYR Macedonia ($51.28).

Group Five ($55.00-$99.99 per capita): Slovakia ($68.08), Hungary ($73.21), and Poland ($73.26).

Group Six (More than $99.99 per capita): Croatia ($111.83), the Czech Republic ($117.24), and Slovenia ($370.86).

As is evident, the Baltic States are in the middle of the six host-country groupings, whereby a higher amount of per capita spending correlates to greater development in the insurance market in a given country. Thus, of the 23 host countries examined, Lithuania ($20.45) is in the bottom half with a ranking of 11th, while Latvia ($49.18) and Estonia ($49.95) are ranked in the top half, respectively holding the 15th and 16th positions. In addition, results from Latvia and Estonia show more than twice the level of per capita spending on non-life products as their southern neighbor, Lithuania. By comparison, the density rates achieved by Latvia and Estonia are less than half the threshold level found in the most advanced transition economies in Group Six, at $99.99, and well below that of the market leader, Slovenia, with average per capita spending of $370.86.

In terms of the host-country groupings, during 1996-2001 the CEE countries achieved an annual average density rate of $79.45, while the Baltic States together were at $39.86, and the remaining NIS at $6.37. Overall, the EU-AC8 had the highest density rate for the period, with $102.78 per capita spending on non-life cover.

On the basis of year-end data for 2001 only the Group Six countries – Slovenia, the Czech Republic and Croatia – have achieved density ratings in line with existing EU member countries. It should be noted that for the Czech Republic and Croatia, this was at the tail end of the grouping, respectively above and below the rather low density rates set by Greece, with $114 per capita spending. Only Slovenia, with a density rate of $379.28, managed to position itself above Greece and Portugal, both of which have population more than five times greater. Average density for the EU in 2001 was $620, a level only Slovenia has come close to achieving.

In terms of overall performance, the three Baltic states are not only at the bottom of the EU-AC8 grouping for density rates in the non-life segment, but they are even surpassed by a number of other transition economies. This represents a difficult situation for both Estonia and Latvia, but Lithuania lags even further behind. Thus, there is a real question whether the three Baltic States will achieve insurance density rates comparable to EU levels prior to their formal accession. Based on current evidence, the outlook would appear doubtful, although both Latvia and Estonia could reduce the gap. However, Lithuania's low levels of per capita spending on non-life insurance, and even more so with regard to life insurance, are a very serious concern. These will surely have major implications in the development and viability of any indigenous insurance market. Nevertheless, it is promising that in 2002 the Lithuanian non-life insurance market increased dramatically by 65% to $171.4 million, which equated to per capita spending rising to a level of $46.35. Even this dramatic increase, fueled mostly by compulsory MTPL, is below the density rates achieved by Estonia and Latvia, well below those in the other EU-AC8, and far off EU average levels. Thus, the outlook for Lithuania's domestic insurance market continues to warrant attention.

As noted, insurance density rates are subject to exchange rate volatility, which could partially explain some host country differences. Moreover, purchasing power generally varies between host countries, as do the costs associated with various insurance products, producing further differences. It is therefore necessary to evaluate premium income levels in relation to another host country measure, GDP, which is used to calculate insurance penetration rates.

III. Insurance penetration rates

Insurance penetration rates measure insurance activity in terms of premium volume as a share of GDP. As such, they measure the insurance industry's significance in relation to a country's total domestic economic activity, or GDP. This is a useful measure because it is not affected by currency fluctuations; the calculation uses only the national currency with respect to both premium income and GDP. Exhibit 4 provides insurance penetration rates for countries within CEE and the NIS between 1990-2001 for the non-life segment.

As was the case in examining insurance density rates, three specific time periods have been relied upon to analyze the data on penetration rates, namely a six-year (1996-2001), eight-year (1994-2001), and 12-year (1990-2001) spread. On this basis, individual host country averages were calculated for the non-life element; they were then plotted using a multiple line chart for each category. This process identified the main trends and respective host country groupings. Due to aforementioned concerns about economic volatility, the most recent six-year (1996-2001) period was used as a base line for the grouping process, while ensuring that the data from the other two periods also fell within the bands identified.

Exhibit 3, Non-Life Insurance Density Rates in CEE and the NIS, 1990-2001

Host Country (in US dollars, as shown)	Year											
	1990	1991	1992	1993	1994	1995	1996	1997	1998	1999	2000	2001
Albania			1.04	3.60	3.70	4.49	4.44	2.43	3.03	3.94	4.08	5.63
Armenia								0.28	0.54	0.67	0.76	1.20
Azerbaijan					na	na	1.08	1.70	1.81	1.82	1.65	na
Belarus				2.37	2.13	3.68	5.35	4.45	5.05	5.96	7.90	na
Bosnia-Herzegovina							12.62	20.02	19.78	29.85	27.90	24.78
Bulgaria			0.01	0.02	18.70	21.52	19.22	12.70	14.03	18.41	19.74	21.94
Croatia				97.40	93.93	109.23	114.76	111.01	119.90	113.88	100.28	111.15
Czech Republic	86.34		39.74	58.01	72.81	89.50	104.59	108.01	119.74	119.44	117.22	134.43
Estonia	na	na	3.01	7.89	15.89	29.46	41.37	45.57	50.26	52.99	52.79	56.75
FYR Macedonia				48.25	50.95	68.00	67.72	52.34	50.89	51.50	43.14	42.08
Georgia								0.78	1.19	1.29	1.65	na
Hungary	60.69	63.78	62.78	59.61	64.71	64.88	67.05	68.88	71.66	74.22	72.60	84.85
Kazakhstan					na	na	na	2.78	3.44	3.26	3.87	6.08
Latvia				5.87	8.98	17.35	25.19	37.79	53.32	57.87	60.52	60.42
Lithuania				1.87	3.63	4.78	8.77	13.15	25.70	24.67	24.38	26.02
Moldova			na	na	0.68	1.97	2.29	3.42	2.84	1.85	2.07	na
Poland	19.40	31.57	29.49	31.73	32.32	40.30	51.99	64.71	75.46	74.66	81.67	91.07
Romania	14.84	5.20	2.43	2.40	3.93	5.60	7.11	7.56	11.08	10.93	11.66	12.16
Russian Federation		0.53	2.42	4.49	9.93	34.07	38.67	42.62	20.63	16.98	22.22	32.35
Serbia & Montenegro					na	47.38	37.44	45.58	24.75	42.25	24.83	25.97
Slovakia	75.48	25.11	29.58	34.60	40.20	51.25	62.14	67.75	78.01	67.85	64.03	68.72
Slovenia		194.55	187.36	187.78	210.52	370.07	377.39	336.28	387.45	390.64	354.09	379.28
Ukraine				2.00	4.84	2.42	3.04	4.12	6.31	5.62	7.92	11.45
Uzbekistan										na	na	na

Source: Wherever possible the researcher has utilized data obtained directly from host country sources (local insurers' association and/or the respective supervisory authority).

Notes: 1) Insurance Density Rates (premium income in US Dollars / population); **2)** Premium income figures given in US Dollars are based upon the appropriate average annual exchange rates reported by the EBRD; **3)** Population figures are based upon Euromonitor International data, with the exception of Armenia, Azerbaijan, Kazakhstan, and Uzbekistan, which rely on EBRD data.

Exhibit 4, Non-Life Insurance Penetration Rates in CEE and the NIS, 1990-2001

Host Country (in % of GDP terms)	Year											
	1990	1991	1992	1993	1994	1995	1996	1997	1998	1999	2000	2001
Albania			0.51%	0.96%	0.61%	0.59%	0.54%	0.35%	0.33%	0.36%	0.37%	0.47%
Armenia							0.27%	0.05%	0.09%	0.11%	0.12%	0.18%
Azerbaijan			na	na	na	na	0.38%	0.34%	0.33%	0.32%	na	na
Belarus				0.67%	0.46%	0.36%	0.38%	0.33%	0.34%	0.51%	0.63%	na
Bosnia-Herzegovina						1.99%	1.50%	1.75%	1.74%	2.16%	2.21%	2.12%
Bulgaria			1.07%	1.40%	1.62%	1.38%	1.63%	1.02%	0.91%	1.17%	1.28%	1.32%
Croatia				4.10%	2.99%	2.69%	2.63%	2.52%	2.53%	2.58%	2.47%	2.56%
Czech Republic	1.72%	1.30%	1.37%	1.75%	1.83%	1.77%	1.87%	2.10%	2.17%	2.24%	2.34%	2.43%
Estonia	na	na	0.44%	0.74%	1.04%	1.24%	1.40%	1.45%	1.40%	1.48%	1.48%	1.48%
FYR Macedonia				3.96%	2.91%	2.98%	3.03%	2.79%	2.85%	2.82%	2.43%	2.44%
Georgia								0.12%	0.16%	0.25%	0.30%	na
Hungary	1.70%	1.98%	1.74%	1.59%	1.60%	1.49%	1.52%	1.53%	1.54%	1.56%	1.53%	1.60%
Kazakhstan					na	na	na	0.19%	0.24%	0.29%	0.31%	0.40%
Latvia				0.70%	0.62%	0.99%	1.22%	1.65%	2.14%	2.14%	2.05%	1.90%
Lithuania				0.26%	0.32%	0.29%	0.41%	0.51%	0.87%	0.86%	0.81%	0.81%
Moldova			na	na	0.26%	0.51%	0.53%	0.69%	0.66%	0.69%	0.57%	na
Poland	1.10%	1.54%	1.34%	1.42%	1.36%	1.29%	1.49%	1.85%	1.86%	1.89%	1.97%	1.96%
Romania	0.56%	0.42%	0.28%	0.21%	0.30%	0.36%	0.46%	0.48%	0.60%	0.70%	0.71%	0.70%
Russian Federation		0.38%	0.42%	0.36%	0.53%	1.51%	1.36%	1.47%	1.12%	1.28%	1.25%	1.51%
Serbia & Montenegro					na	na	2.35%	2.45%	1.67%	2.58%	2.44%	2.56%
Slovakia	2.12%	1.22%	1.33%	1.56%	1.47%	1.49%	1.69%	1.78%	1.97%	1.86%	1.80%	1.86%
Slovenia		3.08%	2.99%	2.95%	2.91%	3.93%	3.98%	3.67%	3.93%	3.85%	3.85%	3.96%
Ukraine			0.00%	0.35%	0.69%	0.34%	0.35%	0.42%	0.76%	0.89%	1.25%	1.49%
Uzbekistan										na	na	na

Sources: Wherever possible the researcher has utilized data obtained directly from host country sources (local insurers' association and/or the respective supervisory authority).

Notes: 1) Insurance Penetration Rates (premium income / GDP); **2)** Premium income figures utilized are obtained directly from host country sources (local insurers' association and/or the respective supervisory authority); **3)** GDP figures are those reported by the EBRD.

An analysis of non-life insurance penetration rates in Exhibit 4 reveals four main host country groupings, as follows:

Group One (Less than 1%): Armenia (0.11%), Georgia (0.21%), Kazakhstan (0.29%), Azerbaijan (0.31%), Albania (0.41%), Belarus (0.44%), Romania (0.61%), Moldova (0.63%), **Lithuania (0.71%)**, and Ukraine (0.86%).

Group Two (1.0%–1.59%): Bulgaria (1.22%), the Russian Federation (1.33%), **Estonia (1.45%)**, and Hungary (1.55%).

Group Three (1.6%–1.99%): Slovakia (1.83%), Poland (1.84%), **Latvia (1.85%)**, and Bosnia-Herzegovina (1.91%).

Group Four (More than 1.99%): the Czech Republic (2.19%), Serbia and Montenegro (2.34%), Croatia (2.55%), the FYR Macedonia (2.73%), and Slovenia (3.87%).

Based on these four host country groupings, we can see some further delineation within the three Baltic States. Lithuania (0.71%) is again in the bottom half of the grouping, ranking just ninth out of 23 host countries, while Estonia (1.45%) is just above the middle, ranked 13th, and Latvia (1.85%) is in the top half, ranked 17th. The relatively low average annual penetration rate in Lithuania only provides further evidence of the lack of development in the insurance sector there. More interestingly is that relative to GDP, the Estonian insurance sector is less prominent than the Latvian sector, a reversal from the findings based on insurance density rates.

A review of the annual data for the period would seem at first to offer a rather mixed picture for each of the Baltic States. For Lithuania, the situation continues to look bleak, with a decline in the penetration rate evident from the peak of 0.87% in 1998. With increased spending on non-life insurance in 2002, the penetration rate has improved to 1.25%, but this still contrasts sharply with levels found in the EU-AC8 grouping and among current EU member states.

In Estonia, the insurance penetration rate was extremely flat at 1.48% between 1999 and 2001. The 2002 data show an increase to 1.61%, a positive sign but also one that points to the less developed nature of the local insurance market. Interestingly, there does not appear to be any direct correlation between movements in density rates and GDP rates of growth. Moreover, the effects of inflation have been relatively minimal, so this cannot account for the situation.

As regards Latvia, the data show a clear wave effect, with a rising, a peak and then a trough. Starting in 1994, the insurance penetration rate rose steadily to a peak of 2.14% in 1998; it leveled off there for a year, coinciding with a period of relatively stable GDP real growth. However, since 1999 the penetration rate has fallen as GDP has grown in real terms. The 2002 data show a continuation of this trend, with a penetration rate of 1.88% for non-life insurance. Thus, the Latvian insurance market would seem to be losing ground relative to GDP growth, when in relation to the EU-AC8 and EU, it clearly needs to be gaining ground.

Overall, a review of the host country data shows that while insurance penetration rates have predominately increased during the period, there have been fluctuations in a number of host countries, some of which could be viewed as slight hiccups in the growth process.

As noted, most of the premiums generated in the non-life segment stem from motor insurance policies. This was the case in most of those host countries achieving the market leader position that comprise the latter two bands of average annual penetration activity between 1996-2001. Interesting exceptions could be found in Serbia and Montenegro, Croatia and the FYR Macedonia, where property insurance was the primary contributor to premiums in the non-life branch.

Given the general over-reliance on motor insurance in the non-life segment, the key question is whether this type of activity will propel the market forward, exposing customers to other insurance products, or prove a costly detour, with low premium rates adversely affecting the profitability of insurers and further hampering market development. The answer is important, given the obvious impact it will have on the future of insurance in CEE and the NIS.

In terms of specific host-country groupings, the average annual penetration rate during 1996-2001 was 1.92% for the CEE, 0.93% for the three Baltic States, and 0.52% for the rest of the NIS. The rate for the EU-AC8 was 1.91%, just slightly below that of the CEE grouping. Yet, as of 2001, CEE and the EU-AC8 had reached near parity, at an average penetration rate of 2%.

In comparison, the EU rate for 2001 stood at 2.68%, ranging from just 1% in Greece to 4.12% in the Netherlands. Regardless, the EU-AC8 and CEE average penetration rate of 2% for 2001 placed them above the levels of three other EU member states: Greece, Finland and Sweden. This, as is evident, does not apply equally to all EU-AC8 members, since several countries are below the 2% threshold. In ascending order, they are: Lithuania (.81%), Estonia (1.48%), Slovakia (1.86%), Latvia (1.90%), and Poland (1.96%). Despite positive movement by Estonia, and to a lesser degree by Lithuania, the situation does not bode well for EU accession. Even Latvia, with the highest non-life insurance penetration rate of the Baltic States, looks likely to have serious problems after a further decline in the rate in 2002.

IV. Conclusion

The data show clearly the dominance of non-life insurance over life cover. It is also apparent that the life sector is vastly underdeveloped in the CEE and NIS countries. The region does, however, show signs of limited growth, especially in those countries that have achieved a necessary level of economic stability. This is particularly applicable to the EU-AC8, although there are a number of host country deviations.

Overall, an analysis of the data shows that the development of the individual insurance markets in the three Baltic States has not reached the levels found in EU member states. While the development level in Estonia, and to a lesser degree in Latvia, is somewhat more promising, Lithuania continues to lag behind the other two countries. However, in terms of overall market size, Lithuania clearly offers the greatest potential of the three countries.

Nevertheless, the Baltic States, even combined, currently represent a very small market for insurance products. This situation may make local operations economically unviable for insurers, with forthcoming integration within the EU. This in turn might result in Estonia, Latvia and Lithuania being served by foreign branch operations rather than having their own indigenous insurance sector. Prior to making such presumptions, however, it is appropriate to examine in greater detail how the insurance sector, and particularly the non-life segment, has developed within each of the Baltic States.

CHAPTER 2

THE DEVELOPMENT OF THE INSURANCE SECTOR
IN THE BALTIC STATES

In the first part of this chapter, the author will examine the development of the insurance sector in each of the Baltic States with regard to the historical and cultural context as well as the legal and regulatory environment. In the second part, the discussion will focus on the development of the non-life market, with specific reference to major non-life classes; and on an overview of distribution channels. A review of the data will provide a more accurate picture of the non-life insurance sector in each of the Baltic states, in the past, at present, and as we look to the future.

I.   The Baltic market: myth or reality?

It has been well over a decade since Estonia, Latvia and Lithuania reasserted their formal independence as sovereign nations. While referred to collectively as the Baltic States because of their position along the shores of the Baltic Sea, it would be a mistake to consider these three countries as a single homogeneous market. Each host country has developed a unique national identity and character, and each traditionally has been fiercely independent (Leonard, 2000). Nevertheless, in regard to their past trials and tribulations, and their likely future direction, they do have much in common.

In early 1918, Estonia, Latvia and Lithuania each declared independence from the crumbling Russian Empire. This independence was short-lived, however, as foreign forces soon occupied the region -- first the invading Germans and then the forces of the newly formed Soviet Union, seeking to reclaim territory they considered their own. In 1919, after joining forces and with a degree of foreign intervention, the Baltic States each realized the dream of full statehood. That dream lasted until 1940, when Soviet forces again occupied the region. In 1941, the advancing Germans ousted the retreating Soviets, and that occupation was reversed only in 1944, when the Soviets recaptured the region.

Under Soviet rule, all forms of nationalism in the Baltic States were ruthlessly suppressed and the Communist ideology was adopted as the sole political model. Under the process of "Stalinization," the state assumed near-complete control of all aspects of the economy. The people of the Baltic States yearned for their independence.

It was not until the Gorbachev era, more than 40 years later, that the Estonians, Latvians and Lithuanians dared openly to raise the issue of independence again. In the spring of 1990 each of the three states openly sought independence; this was not formally recognized by the Soviets until the early autumn of 1991. By the end of that year the Soviet Union had officially ceased to exist, dissolving into its constituent republics. While the former republics quickly re-formed as the Commonwealth of Independent States (CIS), the three Baltic States rejected calls to join the grouping, looking instead to the rest of Europe, and the West.

Besides sharing a common past, the Baltic states have expressed a common future direction with their individual desire for further integration with the rest of Europe, and in particular the EU. In that regard, Lithuania was the first to open accession talks with the EU, in 1995, followed by Estonia in 1997, and finally Latvia in 2000. On 17 April 2003, their common goal was realized when the EU formally invited each of the three states, along with seven others, to join their ranks in the expansion program planned to culminate in mid-2004 with an EU expansion from its current 15 member countries to a total of 25.

However, while the Baltic States view joining the EU as an important step in the transition process, it will surely not solve all of their problems. On the contrary, it may underscore the fact that there are cultural, economic and political gaps that continue to divide the East and the West. The question, therefore, remains whether the Baltic States, along with the rest of the EU-AC8 grouping, will be able to bridge these gaps. This is extremely relevant to the development of the insurance sector within the Baltic States, and to the financial services sector in general. It is therefore appropriate to provide an overview of the development of the insurance sector.

II. The insurance sector in the Baltic States: a historical perspective

A. Insurance tradition

Of the three Baltic states, Estonia was first to establish an insurance business, with the creation in 1832 of the Livonian Society for Mutual Insurance of Crops against Hail. However, Lithuania, the eldest member of the Baltic States, also claims the longest-running insurance organization in the region, with the establishment of the State Insurance Institution of Lithuania *(Lietuvos Draudimas)* in 1921. Latvia also had an established tradition of insurance activities dating to the 1920s, mainly via a number of mutual insurers. However, the insurance tradition in each of the three states was to change dramatically when Soviet forces occupied the region in 1940 and reoccupied it in 1944.

B. Insurance, Communist-style

Between 1945 and 1946 the Soviet leadership nationalized all remaining domestic insurers operating in the Baltic States, along with all other aspects of the local economy. The Soviet regime ceded all insurance activities to its own *Gosstrakh* (State Insurance), which acted under the Soviet Ministry of Finance. In 1948, this model was adjusted slightly to accommodate a two-tier system, whereby *Ingosstrakh* (International State Insurance) took full responsibility for all forms of insurance requiring foreign (hard) currency, due to the international nature of the coverage, while Gosstrakh retained control of all domestic insurance business. In 1958, the state further refined the role of Gosstrakh by dividing it into separate operating units for each of the 15 republics, although Gosstrakh retained central control of these via the Ministry of Finance in Moscow. Thus, in the case of the Baltic States, while each had its own separate operating unit, they effectively had no real autonomy.

Under the Soviet insurance system, the state provider established premiums at almost arbitrary levels for each of the few products it offered and for which the state was the sole underwriter. Premiums charged bore little correlation to the actual risks involved, given the nature of the cover. Premium payments were used to offset both losses incurred via claims during the year and the operating expenses of the provider. Subsequently, surpluses from operations were absorbed by the state and deficits guaranteed by it. With respect to non-life products there was little or no attempt to estimate or provide for future liabilities that had not materialized during the course of the year.

One key element of the system that has had a dramatic impact on the insurance culture was the nature of the agency issue. Under the Soviet insurance system, the obligation to sell an insurance policy and obtain the respective premium was the responsibility of the state's insurer agent, and the failure to collect it did not relieve the state from its responsibility to cover any losses that might arise. In the event of such a claim, the state would merely deduct the prescribed premium payment from the amount of the claim settlement.

In terms of the range of offerings, while both life and non-life insurance policies were widely available to the general public, they were often very simple in nature, which reflected the state's dominant role within society. Life insurance products were generally seen as non-essential luxuries that offered little economic value to customers. As for non-life insurance, these focused mostly on motor, household and numerous compulsory types of cover. The compulsory classes were widely resented by locals as merely another form of taxation on their already meager incomes, even though these classes, and especially agricultural insurance, often generated heavy losses for the state insurer. Most other types of insurance coverage were seen as non-essential under the Communist system since the state guaranteed the citizen's basic needs, from health care, education and employment to pensions.

As regards commercial insurance, since the state owned all aspects of the economy there was little need to use insurance instruments to hedge against possible risks (fire, financial loss, etc). The concept of liability insurance was virtually unknown under the Communist insurance system. In addition, in 1956 the Soviets effectively abolished property insurance for all state-owned enterprises (SOEs), covering any outstanding claims from the state budget.

Given these conditions, it was common across the SOE sector either to not utilize insurance products or to accept only very basic insurance cover, which was often well below the actual value of what was being insured. The sole exception to this was activities related to international operations (marine, goods-in-transit [cargo] for export orders, and aviation liability for overseas flights), which were insured by the respective state provider and international reinsurance markets utilized to offset the associated risks.

This combination of factors has had an adverse impact on the development of the insurance sector in the Baltic states, as it did across the countries of CEE and the various republics of the then Soviet Union. This is especially true of the low level of "insurance culture" exhibited by both individual and business customers. Aubrey-Jones (1996b) accurately summed up the legacy of the Soviet insurance system and its impact on "insurance culture" by stating that:

> "This inverse method of handling the business has left its influence on the way in which much insurance is bought and sold today. Many assureds, corporate as well as private, simply have not learnt their responsibility to go out and seek insurance protection. On the other side, among some of the insurers, the idea of formulating products their customers really want, and then learning to sell them is, in itself, still relatively novel."

C. The insurance market in transition

During the late 1980s, Mikhail Gorbachev, the Soviet leader, enacted his program of *perestroika*, which involved a series of economic reforms aimed at revitalizing the failing Soviet economic model from within. One aspect of this process was the Law on Cooperatives, which effectively ended the state monopoly over the insurance sector by permitting the establishment of other local insurers. However, as is well known, Gorbachev's reforms proved a case of too little too late.

The independence of the Baltic States in the autumn of 1991 and the demise of the Soviet Union at the end of the same year effectively ended the Soviet insurance system. Consequently, it also ended the vast branch network of both Gosstrakh and Ingosstrakh. While Ingosstrakh suffered far less upheaval, each of the Baltic States was quick to nationalize its local Gosstrakh branch. In Estonia, the new state insurer was known as *Eesti Kindlustus*, originally created in 1940; in Latvia, the local branch was transformed into *Latva*; and in Lithuania, the new state provider returned as *Lietuvos Draudimas*, which traced its roots to 1921.

However, the collapse of the Soviet insurance system also created a vacuum in the market, which newly created insurers soon filled. This situation was complicated by inadequate insurance legislation, especially as regards the establishment of acceptable levels of share capital. This led to a glut of insurers, all fighting over the same limited pool of potential customers. To make matters worse, many of the would-be insurers lacked the necessary know-how and/or resources to effectively run a Western-style insurance business. Not surprisingly, a number of these insurers eventually went out of business, further eroding the already low level of "insurance culture" among the customer base.

Exhibit 5 provides comparative data on the number of insurers active in each of the Baltic States between 1994 and 2002. Accordingly, it is appropriate to examine the situation in each of the Baltic States in greater detail, focusing on non-life insurers.

Exhibit 5, Number of Insurers in the Baltic States, 1994-2002

Host Country	Year								
Type of Insurer	1994	1995	1996	1997	1998	1999	2000	2001	2002
Estonia									
Life	4	5	7	8	9	6	6	6	5
Non-Life	14	17	17	15	13	11	8	8	8
Composite	1	-	-	-	-	-	-	-	-
Total	19	22	24	23	22	17	14	14	13
Latvia									
Life	11	10	9	8	8	8	8	6	6
Non-Life	31	27	21	20	19	19	17	15	14
Composite	-	-	-	-	-	-	-	-	-
Total	42	37	30	28	27	27	25	21	20
Lithuania									
Life	2	2	2	4	4	5	6	9	9
Non-Life	0	0	25	28	28	27	22	22	22
Composite	34	25	9	-	-	-	-	-	-
Total	36	27	36	32	32	32	28	31	31

Sources: **Estonia**: Finantsinspekstsioon / Estonian Financial Supervision Authority (EFSA)(2001-03) and Eesti Vabariigi Kindlustusinspektsioon / Estonian Insurance Supervisory Authority (EISA)(1997-01); **Latvia**: Finanšu un kapitala tirgus komisija (FKTK) / Financial and Capital Market Commission (FCMC)(2001-03) and Valsts Apdrošinašanas Uzraudzibas Inspekcija (VAUI) / Latvian State Insurance Supervision Inspectorate (SISI)(1997-03); **Lithuania**: Valstybine Draudimo Priežiuros Tarnyba (VDPT) / State Insurance Supervisory Authority (SISA)(formerly Draudimo Reikalu Taryba / State Insurance Council)(1996-03).

In Estonia, during 1994 there were four active life insurers, 14 non-life insurers, and the state-owned *Eesti Kindlustus,* which acted as a composite insurer handling both life and non-life coverage. Throughout the 1990s, foreign insurers moved into the Estonian market alongside domestic start-ups, which inevitably increased the level of competition. As a result, between 1996 and 2000 there was a general consolidation in the number of non-life insurers active in the Estonian market. This occurred through a combination of factors: pro-active supervision, leading to the revocation of the licenses of troubled insurers, and the creation of a few insurance groups through mergers. Nonetheless, in 1999 three non-life insurers with a combined market share of 10% were declared insolvent and forced into bankruptcy by the state regulator, a significant event for the market. The repercussions of these failures further damaged customer perceptions of the insurance sector. By the end of 2002, there were just eight non-life insurers active in Estonia, seemingly a near-optimum level for the market.

As for the state provider, in 1995 *Eesti Kindlustus's* composite status ended, with its activities being separated into a life and non-life operating company, although the Estonian authorities retained sole ownership over both. In 1996, the Estonian government formally privatized *Eesti Kindlustus*, selling its stake to the local bank *Hoiupank.* This was significant, as Estonia became the first of the Baltic States to shed its holdings in the former state insurer. Since then, *Eesti Kindlustus* has changed hands and its name several times. It is now known as *If Eesti*, and is owned by the Swedish/Finnish insurance group If Property & Casualty.

The situation with regard to the development of the Latvian insurance market has been somewhat different. In 1994, there were 42 active insurers operating in the country, with 11 offering life insurance and 31 providing non-life coverage. However, by 2002 there were only 20 insurers still active, of which 14 were non-life insurers. It should be noted that almost all of the attrition was due to intervention by the state regulator, withdrawing licenses from insurers deemed to be in distress. The volume of insolvencies did little to bolster the already low insurance culture evident in the country, which also suffered from other problems affecting the broader financial sector. Thus, while the number of life and non-life insurers has effectively fallen by half between 1994-2002, further rationalization seems both likely and necessary in light of the limited potential offered by the Latvian insurance market.

As for the state-owned insurer Latva, the firm was divided in 1992 into two operating units, with Latva retaining the life insurance business and its non-life activities being ceded to Balta, a joint venture between itself and the Danish insurer Baltica. In 1997, the Latvian government finally privatized Latva, selling its holdings in the former monopoly to the renamed Balta Group, thereby transferring the dominant domestic insurer to foreign interests.

Compared to the progress exhibited by Estonia, and to a lesser degree Latvia, the development of the Lithuanian insurance market continues to lag. In general, the problem stems from far too many insurers chasing a very limited number of customers in a country that, like the other Baltic States, has a very low level of insurance culture.

In 1994, there were a total of 36 active insurers, most of them acting as composite insurers transacting both life and non-life insurance business. During 1997, the division between the two types of activity was formalized, although life and non-life insurers were still allowed to transact both forms of business with customers. By 2002, there were a total of 31 insurers operating in the Lithuania market, 22 of them active in non-life insurance. While this would seem a modest decrease, it must be remembered that the state regulators have had their hands full during the period issuing new licenses and revoking others due to a high number of insolvencies. Moreover, given the underdeveloped nature of the Lithuanian insurance market, it is clear that the large number of insurers will have to be reduced further, especially in the non-life segment. This will be necessary if Lithuania is to reach the same level of progress as the other Baltic States.

As for the Lithuanian state's role in the insurance sector, while Lietuvos Draudimas was privatized by public share subscription in 1994, it was not until 1999 that the remaining 70% stakeholding was finally sold off to the Danish insurer Codan, itself controlled by the Royal & SunAlliance Insurance Group based in the United Kingdom.

III. The legal and regulatory environment

Given the upheaval brought by the process of transformation, each of the CEE and NIS countries has had the opportunity to dramatically reshape its legal environment. Faced with this challenge, some host countries have sought to adopt a Westernized system, some to rehabilitate the Communist-era system, and others to attempt a hybrid of the two. Nevertheless, the creation of an effective and efficient legal environment has proven difficult, especially as regards the establishment of laws governing private commercial activities, where there has been a general shortage of practical experience. Moreover, the absence of commercial codes, especially in the NIS, or their outdated nature, as in the CEE and the Baltic states, has tended to aggravate the situation. The path to legal reform has been an arduous one.

The development of an efficient and effective legal environment for the operation of a Western-style insurance sector has also proven difficult. While responsibility for insurance activities has generally remained under the auspices of the host country's Ministry of Finance, in most situations the state's role has changed dramatically. Undoubtedly, the key change has been the realignment of the insurance industry away from state control to that of an open market, with a variety of insurers offering products in a competitive environment. A fundamental element of this shift has led to the adoption of the Western principle of insurance whereby premium rates are correlated directly to the nature of the coverage and the associated risks. Moreover, many host countries have already sought to reduce, partly or in full, their controlling interests in former state insurers via privatization. Changing the "insurance culture" of the local population has proven to be the most difficult of tasks.

In the legal and regulatory environment of the Baltic States, each country resorted after independence in 1991 to the commercial codes that were in use during the 1920s and 1930s. The problems associated with using such an outdated system, however, soon became evident. Accordingly, given the Baltic States' desire to establish strong ties with Western Europe, they soon began adopting the commercial codes used within the EU. The Baltic States, along with other EU-AC8 members, also moved to adopt the various EU directives on insurance activities. As a result, the legal context for insurance and its supervision in the Baltic States has increasingly been harmonized with EU directives, of which three generations have been established. These directives form part of a concerted effort by the EU to create a single market for all financial services. This is not to say that EU insurance directives represent the ideal vehicle for transformation, rather that they are a better guide to development than what these countries had relied upon.

While adopting EU standards would seem to be relatively easy, actually implementing the directives has proven more difficult. In that regard, progress to date in each Baltic state on establishing the necessary legal and regulatory environment for insurance activities very much reflects the level of development in the respective host country market. A comparative overview of the host country specifics follows.

A. *Insurance legislation*

Estonia

The Insurance Activities Act (1 August 2000) superseded both the Insurance Law of the Republic of Estonia (5 November 1992) and the Amendment Act of the Insurance Law (1 June 1999). The more recent Insurance Activities Act now brings Estonia into line with existing EU directives.

MTPL was first made obligatory by the Law on Traffic Insurance (1 October 1993), which was superseded first in 1995 and more recently by the Motor Third-Party Liability Act (1 June 2001). The new MTPL Act removed statutory tariffs on MPTL insurance, allowing insurers free range to compete for this line of business, provided they submit rating schedules to the authorities for verification of the methodology used for calculations.

Latvia

The Law on Insurance Companies and their Supervision (1 September 1998) and the Law on Insurance Contracts (1 September 1998) supersede the Law on Insurance (1993) and the Law on the State Insurance Supervision Inspectorate (1995).

MTPL was first made obligatory by the Law on Motor Third-Party Liability Compulsory Insurance (September 1997).

Lithuania

The Law on Insurance of the Republic of Lithuania (10 July 1996) superseded insurance legislation of 1990. Also of note is the Law on Investment Amounts of the Authorized Capital and Technical Provisions for Insurance Companies (24 July 1998).

Lithuania was the last of the Baltic States to make MTPL obligatory, through the Law on Compulsory Motor Third-Party Liability Insurance of Vehicle Owners and Possessors' (1 April 2002).

B. Licensing / supervision

Estonia

Since June 2001, the *Finantsinspekstsioon* (Estonian Financial Supervision Authority, or EFSA) has effectively had full responsibility for licensing and supervision of all insurance activities, along with all other financial services activities, in Estonia. In regard to insurance activities, this new combined agency supersedes the *Eesti Vabariigi Kindlustusinspektsioon* (Estonian Insurance Supervisory Authority, or EISA).

Latvia

Since July 2001, the *Finanšu un kapitāla tirgus comitia,* or FKTK (Financial and Capital Market Commission, FCMC) has had full responsibility for licensing and supervision of all insurance activities, along with all other financial services activities, in Latvia. In regard to insurance activities, this new combined agency supersedes the *Valsts Apdrošināšanas Uzraudzības Inspekcija,* or VAUI (Latvian State Insurance Supervision Inspectorate, or SISI).

Lithuania

Since 1996, the *Valstybinė Draudimo Priežiūros Tarnyba,* or VDPT (State Insurance Supervisory Authority, SISA) has had sole responsibility for licensing and supervision of all insurance activities in Lithuania. This organization supersedes the *Draudimo Reikalų Taryba* (State Insurance Council).

C. Activity

Estonia

Licensed insurers may conduct either life or non-life insurance business but not both. Any insurer licensed to conduct reinsurance business may do so provided it retains sufficient capital. Foreign insurers' branch operations are permitted.

Latvia

Licensed insurers may conduct either life or non-life insurance business but not both. At present, reinsurance business is not subject to licensing. Foreign insurers' branch operations have been permitted since April 2003.

Lithuania

Licensed insurers may conduct life, non-life or credit insurance business but not a combination thereof. While both accident and health insurance are non-life insurance classes, life insurers are allowed to transact these lines of business. Any insurer licensed to conduct reinsurance business may do so provided it retains sufficient capital. Foreign insurers' branch operations are allowed for insurers originating from World Trade Organization (WTO) member countries.

D. Minimum capital requirements

Estonia

From 1 January 1997 (based on average annual exchange rates for 2002) the minimum capital requirements were set at:

Non-Life Insurers = EEK 5 million (USD 0.3 million)

Non-Life Insurers with liability and/or credit = EEK 10 million (USD 0.6 million)

Non-Life Insurers with reinsurance activities = EEK 20 million (USD 1.2 million)

Life Insurers = EEK 12 million (USD 0.7 million)

For insurers involved in two or more of the above non-life lines of business, the minimum capital requirement is the higher amount.

Latvia

From 15 April 2003 (based on average annual exchange rates for 2002) the minimum capital requirements were set at:

Non-Life Insurers = EUR 2 million (USD 2.3 million)

Non-Life Insurers with liability = EUR 3 million (USD 3.4 million)

Life Insurers = EUR 3 million (USD 3.4 million)

Mutual Non-Life Insurers = EUR 1.5 million (USD 1.7 million)

Mutual Non-Life Insurers with liability = EUR 2.3 million (USD 2.6 million)

Mutual Life Insurers = EUR 2.3 million (USD 2.6 million)

Lithuania

From 10 July 1996 (based on average annual exchange rates for 2002) the minimum capital requirements were set at:

Non-Life Insurers = LTL 2 million (USD 0.5 million)

Life Insurers = LTL 4 million (USD 1 million)

Credit Insurers = LTL 7 million (USD 1.9 million)

Insurance Brokers = LTL 10,000 (USD 2,700)

E. Compulsory insurance

Estonia

In Estonia, there are four main compulsory classes of insurance: 1) MTPL; 2) aviation liability; 3) professional indemnity for lawyers, notaries, auditors, bailiffs, insurance brokers; 4) liability for emergency services (fire and rescue).

Workmen's compensation insurance is to become compulsory during 2003.

Latvia

In Latvia, there are three main compulsory classes of insurance: 1) MTPL; 2) professional indemnity for doctors and dentists (related solely to their medical work), insurance brokers, notaries, auditors, certain bankruptcy administrators and owners of sources of radiation; 3) liability insurance for contractors before tendering for construction work.

While tariffs for MTPL remain in place, insurers actually heavily discount these due to intense competition.

Lithuania

In Lithuania, there are four main compulsory classes of insurance: 1) MTPL; 2) professional indemnity for real estate assessors, lawyers, notaries, auditors, surveyors, ship owners, pharmaceutical/drug testers, insurance brokers and customs brokers; 3) liability insurance for contractors before tendering for construction work; and 4) aircraft operators.

The Lithuanian government sets tariff rates only for MTPL, which, for political reasons, are kept very low.

F. Customer rights

Estonia

There is no insurance ombudsman in Estonia, and the EFSA is not equipped to handle customer complaints.

Latvia

There is no insurance ombudsman in Latvia, and the FKTK / FCMC is not equipped to handle customer complaints.

Lithuania

While there is no official insurance ombudsman in Lithuania, the VDPT / SISA does handle customer complaints.

IV. The non-life insurance market

As noted, while the three Baltic insurance sectors have all been moving toward greater integration with the EU, the level of development achieved has varied in Estonia, Latvia and Lithuania. Thus, it is appropriate both to examine the situation with respect to individual host country markets and to undertake a comparative analysis of the three markets. The former will be examined via a review of gross premium income and claims paid data in local currencies between 1997 and 2002. For the latter, the same data will be used, but for the sake of comparison it will be translated into US dollars and presented graphically to aid the reader. In addition, a discussion of the data will address the size and leading trends, as well as the strengths and weaknesses of each market.

A. Individual host country markets

Exhibit 6a provides data on the development of the insurance market in Estonia between 1997 and 2002. The amounts shown are in millions of Estonian kroons (EEK).

In regard to the composition of gross premium income, the data clearly show that motor insurance (voluntary MTPL, compulsory MTPL and Casco) has consistently been the dominant driver in the non-life sector during the period. On average, motor insurance business accounted for 68.3% of all non-life premiums during the six years analyzed, with compulsory MTPL at 36.4%, motor hull (Casco) at 30%, and voluntary MTPL at just 1.9%. Interestingly, while compulsory MTPL was the leading form of non-life insurance between 1997 and 2000, during 2001 the volume of motor hull (Casco) insurance edged slightly ahead of it, and expanded its lead thereafter. In comparing figures for 1997 and 2002, the amounts spent on motor insurance have increased by more than 60% for motor hull (Casco) while compulsory MTPL has shown only a 25% increase in overall volume. Voluntary MTPL remains a minor source of premium income.

The only other major source of gross premium income during the period originated from property insurance, accounting on average for 21.3% of the total non-life sector. It should be noted that spending on property insurance has risen consistently each year since 1997, above Estonia's average annual inflation rate of 6% for the period.

Other growing sources of premiums include a number of personal lines, such as accident and travel, and general liability insurance. In fact, while the first two non-life lines have posted fairly steady growth during the period, the outlook for general liability insurance looks more favorable to insurers. Of course, once Estonians become more legally aware and assertive of their rights, this situation is likely to change.

The data on claims paid generally mirror the situation noted above, with motor insurance again dominating. In this respect, compulsory MTPL was the primary source of claims, accounting for on average 41.8% of all claims paid, followed by motor hull (Casco) with 34.6%, and then voluntary MTPL with a mere 1%. Again, the combination of compulsory and voluntary MTPL was the main source of claims paid until 2001, when it surrendered that position to motor hull (Casco). On the basis of volume of claims paid, a comparison of the data from 1997 and 2002 reveals that motor insurance has grown 43% for compulsory MTPL, and 75% for motor hull (Casco), while voluntary MTPL has been relatively flat.

Exhibit 6a, Gross Premium Income vs. Claims Paid in the Estonian Insurance Market, 1997-2002

Type of Insurance (in millions of EEK)	1997 Gross Premium Income	1997 Claims Paid	1997 Claims %	1998 Gross Premium Income	1998 Claims Paid	1998 Claims %	1999 Gross Premium Income	1999 Claims Paid	1999 Claims %	2000 Gross Premium Income	2000 Claims Paid	2000 Claims %	2001 Gross Premium Income	2001 Claims Paid	2001 Claims %	2002 Gross Premium Income	2002 Claims Paid	2002 Claims %
Total Life:	128.152	25.312	19.8%	206.467	41.027	19.9%	216.483	68.604	31.7%	304.325	58.415	19.2%	356.900	54.483	15.3%	446.1908	61.1945	13.7%
Total Non-Life:	926.024	380.417	41.1%	1,030.320	546.67	53.1%	1,126.263	580.662	51.6%	1,288.686	616.950	47.9%	1,427.197	712.842	49.9%	1,718.270	912.436	53.1%
Accident	20.688	4.699	22.7%	28.906	8.640	29.9%	30.796	12.252	39.8%	34.480	14.236	41.3%	35.675	15.961	44.7%	37.003	16.942	45.8%
Health	0.134	0.086	64.2%	0.696	0.032	4.6%	0.421	0.274	65.1%									
Travel	22.121	4.177	18.9%	30.337	6.573	21.7%	32.346	6.930	21.4%	40.375	9.214	22.8%	43.187	11.037	25.6%	47.413	11.386	24.0%
Motor Hull (CASCO)	236.524	92.509	39.1%	278.063	190.706	68.6%	327.367	203.196	62.1%	385.773	209.635	54.3%	476.606	276.972	58.1%	600.155	370.496	61.7%
Railway Rolling Stock (CASCO)										0.823	0.0	0.0%	2.852	0.0	0.0%	3.766	1.035	27.5%
Aircraft Hull (CASCO)	0.180	0.008	4.4%	0.113	1.431	1266.4%	0.258	0.0	0.0%	0.086	0.0	0.0%	0.161	0.382	237.3%	0.026	0.0	0.0%
Marine (CASCO)	7.271	2.324	32.0%	7.682	9.416	122.6%	2.439	1.678	68.8%	3.018	2.011	66.6%	4.429	2.856	64.5%	4.836	2.270	46.9%
Goods-in-Transit (Cargo)	14.052	2.177	15.5%	13.436	7.041	52.4%	11.73	4.774	40.7%	14.211	2.409	17.0%	21.069	3.454	16.4%	20.257	7.081	35.0%
Property	185.568	71.601	38.6%	211.389	75.145	35.5%	232.917	94.025	40.4%	275.620	103.433	37.5%	317.322	119.749	37.7%	395.990	141.974	35.9%
Motor Third Party Liability (MTPL)	386.967	195.904	50.6%	399.944	233.514	58.4%	434.460	242.774	55.9%	475.978	244.963	51.5%	456.616	263.975	57.8%	516.565	344.953	66.8%
Motor Vehicle Liability (Voluntary)	26.311	4.273	16.2%	22.837	5.974	26.2%	20.19	8.225	40.7%	19.832	5.229	26.4%	21.933	5.596	25.5%	24.223	4.286	17.7%
Liability for Aircraft Ownership	0.278	0.0	0.0%	0.184	0.0	0.0%	6.144	0.0	0.0%	0.122	0.0	0.0%	0.262	0.0	0.0%	0.456	0.0	0.0%
Liability for Ship Ownership							0.143	0.0	0.0%	0.038	0.0	0.0%	0.063	0.0	0.0%	0.193	0.0	0.0%
General Liability	8.933	0.447	5.0%	14.476	1.796	12.4%	13.43	1.979	14.7%	18.646	8.393	45.0%	24.76	4.547	18.4%	42.290	3.211	7.6%
Liability Insurance for Notaries	1.174	0.052	4.4%	1.088	0.081	7.4%	1.058	0.046	4.3%	1.366	0.121	8.9%	2.317	0.304	13.1%	1.490	1.473	98.9%
Credit				0.217	0.0	0.0%	1.125	0.0	0.0%	0.375	1.196	318.9%	0.375	0.747	199.2%			
Suretyship	13.718	2.160	15.7%	18.182	4.882	26.9%	14.930	4.383	29.4%	14.403	13.906	96.5%	11.264	6.975	61.9%	10.542	4.980	47.2%
Miscellaneous Financial Loss	2.105	0.000	0.0%	2.770	1.447	52.2%	2.497	0.126	5.0%	3.540	2.204	62.3%	8.306	0.287	3.5%	13.065	2.350	18.0%
Total Life & Non-Life	1,054.176	405.729	38.49%	1,236.777	587.705	47.52%	1,342.746	649.266	48.35%	1,593.011	675.365	42.40%	1,783.097	767.325	43.03%	2,164.461	973.631	44.98%

Sources: Finantsinspektsioon / Estonian Financial Supervision Authority (EFSA)(2001-03); Eesti Vabariigi Kindlustusinspektsioon / Estonian Insurance Supervisory Authority (EISA)(1997-01), and the Author's own calculations.

72

Exhibit 6b, Gross Premium Income & Claims Paid in the Latvian Insurance Market, 1997-2002

Type of Insurance (in millions of LVL)	1997 Gross Premium Income	1997 Claims Paid	1997 Claims %	1998 Gross Premium Income	1998 Claims Paid	1998 Claims %	1999 Gross Premium Income	1999 Claims Paid	1999 Claims %	2000 Gross Premium Income	2000 Claims Paid	2000 Claims %	2001 Gross Premium Income	2001 Claims Paid	2001 Claims %	2002 Gross Premium Income	2002 Claims Paid	2002 Claims %
Total Life:	**6.654**	**3.572**	**53.7%**	**7.838**	**2.557**	**32.6%**	**6.734**	**2.617**	**38.9%**	**4.488**	**2.018**	**45.0%**	**4.283**	**2.134**	**49.8%**	**5.379**	**1.946**	**36.2%**
Total Non-Life:	**56.698**	**9.872**	**17.4%**	**77.231**	**19.481**	**25.2%**	**83.722**	**29.612**	**35.4%**	**88.497**	**30.023**	**33.9%**	**88.617**	**34.343**	**38.8%**	**93.862**	**36.920**	**39.3%**
Accident	1.710	0.163	9.6%	2.402	0.433	18.0%	3.229	0.426	13.2%	2.473	0.568	23.0%	2.592	0.853	32.9%	2.335	0.803	34.4%
Health	3.879	2.019	52.0%	5.409	2.685	49.6%	8.044	4.422	55.0%	8.730	6.423	73.6%	10.429	7.968	76.4%	11.835	9.033	76.3%
Travel	0.577	0.127	22.0%	0.677	0.174	25.7%	0.839	0.236	28.1%	0.970	0.188	19.4%	1.268	0.321	25.3%	1.522	0.399	26.2%
Motor Hull (CASCO)	6.389	3.082	48.2%	10.056	6.131	61.0%	12.334	10.863	88.1%	14.327	11.542	80.6%	16.885	12.838	76.0%	20.528	12.792	62.3%
Railway Rolling Stock (CASCO)	0.013	0.0	0.0%	0.108	0.0	0.0%	0.0006	0.0	0.0%	0.260	0.0	0.0%	0.157	0.0	0.0%	0.159	0.0045	2.8%
Aircraft Hull (CASCO)	0.127	0.0	0.0%	0.208	0.133	64.1%	0.438	0.021	4.7%	0.465	0.166	35.8%	0.131	0.0001	0.1%	0.119	0.0	0.0%
Marine (CASCO)	0.492	0.018	3.6%	0.624	0.159	25.5%	0.517	0.221	42.8%	0.414	0.089	21.4%	0.647	0.228	35.2%	0.876	0.167	19.0%
Goods-in-Transit (Cargo)	2.709	0.193	7.1%	2.915	0.230	7.9%	4.376	0.682	15.6%	3.642	0.246	6.7%	3.719	0.394	10.6%	2.907	0.220	7.6%
Property	14.028	1.748	12.5%	18.600	1.948	10.5%	16.488	3.917	23.8%	17.501	3.409	19.5%	16.911	3.377	20.0%	16.356	4.281	26.2%
Motor Third Party Liability (MTPL)	13.968	0.856	6.1%	19.905	5.022	25.2%	21.861	7.064	32.3%	23.467	6.453	27.5%	24.629	7.755	31.5%	25.342	8.271	32.6%
Motor Vehicle Liability (Voluntary)	1.947	0.455	23.4%	2.536	1.216	47.9%	1.492	0.986	66.0%	0.175	0.0022	1.3%	0.153	0.0007	0.5%	0.182	0.0027	1.5%
Liability for Aircraft Ownership	0.223	0.0	0.0%	0.241	0.0001	0.0%	0.287	0.00002	0.0%	0.294	0.003	1.0%	0.097	0.0	0.0%	0.242	0.0	0.0%
Liability for Ship Ownership	0.006	0.0	0.0%	0.060	0.015	24.7%	0.172	0.008	4.8%	0.034	0.041	123.0%	0.130	0.021	16.2%	0.202	0.002	0.9%
General Liability	8.605	0.204	2.4%	8.841	0.488	5.5%	9.008	0.229	2.5%	11.295	0.420	3.7%	8.532	0.388	4.5%	8.524	0.420	4.9%
Credit	0.117	0.002	1.8%	0.113	0.638	564.2%	0.307	0.002	0.5%	0.598	0.034	5.7%	0.454	0.016	3.4%	0.281	0.082	29.0%
Suretyship	0.001	0.0	0.0%	0.086	0.0	0.0%	0.674	0.028	4.2%	0.922	0.059	6.4%	0.812	0.027	3.3%	1.070	0.396	37.0%
Miscellaneous Financial Loss	1.906	1.004	52.7%	4.450	0.209	4.7%	3.655	0.506	13.8%	2.933	0.380	13.0%	1.073	0.156	14.6%	1.380	0.048	3.5%
Total	**120.049**	**23.316**	**19.4%**	**162.300**	**41.520**	**26.6%**	**174.178**	**61.840**	**35.5%**	**181.482**	**62.064**	**34.2%**	**181.516**	**70.821**	**39.0%**	**193.104**	**76.786**	**39.2%**

Sources: Finanšu un kapitāla tirgus komisija (FKTK) / Financial and Capital Market Commission (FCMC)(2001-03), Valsts Apdrošināšanas Uzraudzības Inspekcija (VAUI) / Latvian State Insurance Supervision Inspectorate (SISI)(1997-01), Latvijas Apdrošinātāju Asociācija (LAA) / Latvian Insurers Association (LIA)(1998-03), and the Author's own calculations.

73

Property insurance was the only other major source of claims paid in the non-life segment, with an annual average of 16.3% for the six-year period. The volume of claims paid for this insurance line has also been rising steadily, almost doubling in 2002 compared to 1997. Over the six years, the accident, travel and general liability insurance classes have also been a significant source of claims paid. In regard to the first two classes, the claims paid data indicate a trend whereby the amounts are increasing at a slightly higher growth rate than premiums. As for general liability insurance, the level of claims paid has been decreasing since its peak in 2000.

In examining the claims ratio (claims as a percentage of premiums), we find that there has been a steady increase in almost all non-life insurance classes, while others have experienced volatility, with peaks and troughs. The latter category applies to several Casco lines of insurance (aircraft, railway rolling stock and marine), voluntary MTPL, goods-in-transit (cargo), general liability, liability for notaries, credit, suretyship, and miscellaneous financial loss. It should be noted that with the exceptions of voluntary MTPL, goods-in-transit (cargo) and suretyship, these lines of business have had relatively small volumes of premiums and claims. The high volatility in the claims ratio for travel insurance, and especially in credit insurance, eventually resulted in both lines being withdrawn. While far from beneficial to the development of the sector, such action might have to be taken by insurers for other problematic lines of business if they are unable to reduce the claims ratio to a more manageable, and profitable, level. As for those insurance classes experiencing a steady and/or escalating claims ratio, this includes the major classes of motor insurance (compulsory MTPL and Casco) and property, as well as some smaller and developing lines, including travel and accident.

One of the more worrisome findings from the data is that the growth rate of premium income does not appear to be keeping pace with claims paid, as expressed via the growing claims ratio. If this trend continues, it will have serious implications for the range of non-life insurance offerings, as well as the future development of the Estonian non-life insurance sector. Based on the 2002 data, this would seem especially relevant to motor insurance (compulsory MTPL and Casco), which remains the main driver in the non-life segment. Moreover, growing problems in other non-life classes, including accident, property, travel, suretyship and miscellaneous financial loss, should not be overlooked, as these represent the future sources of growth in the non-life segment.

Exhibit 6b presents data for the development of the insurance sector in Latvia between 1997-2002, expressed in the local currency, Latvian lats (LVL).

In terms of composition, while motor insurance (voluntary MTPL, compulsory MTPL and Casco) was the dominant force in the Latvian insurance market, it accounted on average for only 43.8% of all non-life activity during the 1997-2002 period covered. Of this, compulsory MTPL business accounted for an average of 26.3%; motor hull (Casco), 16%; and voluntary MTPL just 1.5%. Other key sources of premium income in the non-life segment included property insurance, with an annual average of 20.1%, general liability at 11.5%, and health insurance with 9.6%.

On the surface this would suggest that the Latvian non-life insurance market is slightly more balanced overall than, for example, the situation in Estonia. It should be noted, however, that MTPL insurance is sold at a very low premium level by insurers in Latvia. While the Latvian authorities nominally set premium rates for compulsory MTPL, there is intense competition among insurers for this line of business, leading them to offer customers as much as a 40% discount off official rates. In the past, the low claims ratio has made this palatable for insurers, yet it remains questionable how much longer insurers can effectively subsidize their MTPL business. Claim levels have been rising, and in 2002 accounted for 32.6% of gross premiums for this line of coverage.

In terms of claims paid, in addition to rises in compulsory MTPL, there has been a steady and significant increase in most other non-life classes in Latvia. In fact, the growth rates of claims paid for both health and motor hull (Casco) insurance have greatly exceeded the rate of growth for their respective premiums. While the situation with motor hull (Casco) has improved from its peak in 1999, it continues to be problematic for insurers. Regarding health insurance, the level of claims paid between 1997 and 2002 has certainly not been healthy for insurers and has been increasing steadily in volume. As for property insurance, the amount of claims paid has fluctuated somewhat but remains low, though it continues to increase at a faster rate than the level of premium income.

As for the claims ratio, a review of averages for 1997-2002 indicates growing problems with a number of non-life insurance classes, mainly with health and motor hull (Casco) insurance, with an average of 64% for health and 69% for motor hull (Casco). Yet, a review of the more recent 2002 data shows a much more disturbing picture, similar to the situation in Estonia, with a number of non-life classes posting increasingly higher claims ratios. If this situation continues, then it could be problematic for development of the Latvian non-life sector, which remains less developed than its northern neighbor, Estonia.

Data presented in Exhibit 6c show development of the insurance market in Lithuania during the 1997-2002 period, with amounts expressed in millions of Lithuanian litai (LTL).

A review of the averages for premium income during the period indicates that motor insurance (Casco and MTPL) is again the dominant non-life insurance class in Lithuania. Yet, in a reversal of the scenario noted for Estonia and Latvia, averages for the period show that motor hull (Casco) is the main source of premiums, with 24.7%, while MTPL accounted for 19.8%. Interestingly, property insurance had a 22.7% average over the six-year period, higher than that of MTPL.

However, 2002 data paint a different picture. As noted, MTPL moved at the start of April 2002 from being a voluntary insurance class to a compulsory one. An examination of the 2002 data thus shows a dramatic jump in premiums for compulsory MTPL, accounting for 40% of all activity in the year. Moreover, the 2002 figures represent only eight full months of activity with MTPL being a compulsory class. Thus, the level of activity should increase further for 2003, reflecting a full year's worth of premium activity.

Exhibit 6c, Gross Premium Income & Claims Paid in the Lithuanian Insurance Market, 1997-2002

	Year																
	1997			1998			1999			2000			2001			2002		
Type of Insurance (in millions of LTL)	Gross Premium Income	Claims Paid	Claims %	Gross Premium Income	Claims Paid	Claims %	Gross Premium Income	Claims Paid	Claims %	Gross Premium Income	Claims Paid	Claims %	Gross Premium Income	Claims Paid	Claims %	Gross Premium Income	Claims Paid	Claims %
Total Life:	68.239	34.682	59.6%	66.634	22.300	33.6%	74.043	39.387	63.2%	76.286	27.669	36.3%	92.845	34.365	37.0%	139.634	43.117	30.9%
Total Non-Life:	194.963	68.260	29.9%	380.781	131.489	34.5%	365.285	156.060	42.7%	360.782	149.277	41.4%	385.118	147.055	38.2%	634.310	242.673	38.2%
Accident	13.211	5.824	44.1%	17.049	3.993	23.4%	17.708	3.863	21.8%	16.161	3.839	23.8%	18.128	5.630	31.1%	20.523	7.009	34.2%
Health	10.175	2.158	21.2%	23.374	3.495	15.0%	14.310	2.425	16.9%	14.942	2.870	19.2%	18.118	3.418	18.9%	19.454	4.354	22.4%
Travel	.	.		0.002	0.0	0.0%	0.012	0.006	47.3%	0.020	0.008	40.7%	0.058	0.010	17.0%	0.070	0.024	33.8%
Motor Hull (CASCO)	41.999	20.421	48.6%	93.997	55.241	58.8%	97.000	65.003	67.0%	98.585	49.644	50.4%	109.092	66.331	60.8%	125.269	90.017	71.9%
Railway Rolling Stock (CASCO)	0.911	0.904	99.2%	0.396	0.833	210.1%	0.387	0.205	53.1%	0.080	0.0	0.0%	0.043	0.0	0.0%	0.028	0.0	0.0%
Aircraft Hull (CASCO)	0.030	0.109	361.1%	9.666	0.056	0.6%	5.583	-0.003	0.0%	5.128	0.028	0.6%	-0.040	0.130	-326.0%	9.400	0.145	1.5%
Marine (CASCO)	0.602	0.077	12.8%	12.716	2.616	20.6%	9.939	0.362	3.6%	6.889	17.980	261.0%	2.854	3.452	120.9%	2.111	11.591	549.1%
Goods-in-Transit (Cargo)	11.949	1.052	8.8%	6.385	0.468	7.3%	4.300	0.978	22.7%	5.555	1.046	18.8%	6.165	7.182	116.5%	6.022	2.213	36.8%
Property	62.448	15.028	24.1%	84.050	13.499	16.1%	85.300	30.431	35.7%	78.395	27.275	34.8%	80.796	19.178	23.7%	100.294	40.834	40.7%
Motor Third Party Liability (MTPL)	19.112	5.784	30.3%	71.072	33.402	47.0%	64.998	32.971	50.7%	58.036	25.349	43.7%	62.847	22.111	35.2%	253.782	54.926	21.6%
Liability for Aircraft Ownership	0.0004	0.0	0.0%	0.0	0.0	0.0%	0.110	0.0	0.0%	0.065	0.0001	0.2%	0.315	0.0	0.0%	0.574	0.001	0.2%
Liability for Ship Ownership	.	.		0.0	0.0	0.0%	1.028	0.0	0.0%	6.166	0.0	0.0%	5.855	0.0	0.0%	2.674	0.0	0.0%
General Liability	6.807	0.028	0.4%	32.890	3.384	10.3%	27.359	3.371	12.3%	28.406	4.220	14.9%	20.308	4.644	22.9%	23.699	7.651	32.3%
Credit	1.600	0.592	37.0%	4.394	0.869	19.8%	12.706	2.181	17.2%	12.322	6.610	53.6%	13.734	5.130	37.4%	17.156	8.308	48.4%
Suretyship	25.165	6.274	24.9%	22.843	13.625	59.6%	23.080	14.196	61.5%	27.887	10.371	37.2%	40.768	9.743	23.9%	44.707	15.423	34.5%
Miscellaneous Financial Loss	0.944	0.000	0.0%	1.948	0.007	0.4%	1.467	0.061	4.2%	2.147	0.036	1.7%	6.076	0.097	1.6%	8.486	0.077	0.9%
Legal Expenses	.	.		0.0	0.0	0.0%	0.0	0.0	0.0%	0.0	0.0	0.0%	0.001	0.0	0.0%	0.062	0.0	0.0%
Total	263.192	92.932	36.7%	447.315	153.789	34.4%	439.328	195.437	44.5%	437.068	176.936	40.5%	477.963	181.420	38.0%	773.843	285.690	36.9%

Sources: Valstybine Draudimo Priežiuros Tarnyba (VDPT) / State Insurance Supervisory Authority (SISA)(formerly Draudimo Reikalu Taryba / State Insurance Council)(1997-03), Lietuvos Drauiku Asociacija (LDA)/ Lithuanian Insurance Association (LIA)(1998-03), and the Author's own calculations.

The only other significant source of premium income in the non-life segment comes from suretyship insurance, which has generally been increasing in volume over the 1997-2002 period. Approximately 95% of this suretyship business stems from customs bonds that are purchased by customers involved in import-export activities. Yet, these types of customs bonds have suffered from a degree of fraud and misuse, as well as problems originating with the Lithuanian customs authorities. So while the suretyship class is growing, its high-risk nature makes it a potential time bomb for insurers.

In terms of other non-life insurance classes, there are signs of growth in the accident, health, credit and general liability lines of coverage, although the amounts have been quite low overall. On the other hand, the situation with regard to marine (Casco) insurance has been rather problematic. In fact, since reaching a peak in 1998 generated ever-decreasing levels of premium income. Moreover, between 2000 and 2002, the level of premiums generated was greatly outstripped by very high claims, especially in 2000 and 2002.

In that respect, the averages for the claims paid data between 1997 and 2002 reveal that in a number of non-life insurance classes, claims are rising at a faster rate than the respective premium income levels. Given that the Lithuanian insurance market is less developed than those in Estonia or Latvia, this is reason for concern. In volume terms, the rise in claims paid in the motor (Casco) class averaged 39% over the six-year period, while MTPL was at 19% and property insurance at 17%. As regards MTPL, the fact that this class was introduced as a compulsory line only in April 2002 would suggest that the full effects of claims paid have yet to be realized.

In regard to the claims ratio data, a review of the averages for 1997-2002 indicates growing problems with a number of non-life insurance classes. This is evident in three of the four main Casco classes, namely marine, railway rolling stock and motor. While the level of activity in Casco for railway rolling stock is minimal, the claims ratio results for marine and motor during the period are reason for serious concern. Since 2000, Casco for marine activities has generated heavy losses for insurers in comparison to a very small amount of premium income. As for motor hull (Casco), in 1997 the claims ratio for this class was around 49%, yet by 2002 it had grown to almost 72% and looks likely to continue to increase. If MTPL follows a similar trend, as seems likely, then it could be quite detrimental to the development of the non-life segment in Lithuania.

Other lines posting high average claims ratios include credit, suretyship, goods-in-transit (cargo) and property insurance. While the volume of business in goods-in-transit (cargo) insurance has been relatively low, the same cannot be said of the other three lines. While credit insurance has been a growing line of business, its claims ratio was rather volatile in 1997-2002, which does not bode well for insurers. As for suretyship, while the claims ratio has been improving since the very rough 1998-99 period, it remains a problematic class for reasons previously cited. As for property insurance, this was the second biggest stream of premium income between 1998-2001, before the surge in MTPL pushed it down to the third spot. Unfortunately, the claims ratio, rather volatile during the six-year period, has been increasing in magnitude.

While a review of the individual host country markets provides insight into the development of the various non-life components shaping the market, it is also important to gauge the situation via a comparative analysis of the data.

B.   Comparative data

Exhibit 7 provides a graphical representation of the development of the non-life insurance sector with respect to both gross premium income and claims paid in each of the Baltic States for 1997-2002, using US dollars as a common denominator to facilitate comparison.

In general, the Baltic States appear to be following similar paths of development, though with different rates of progress. To reiterate, the non-life market in Estonia is the most developed of the three, followed by Latvia, and with Lithuania much further behind.

A review of average annual growth rates demonstrates that while premium income and claims paid are both growing fairly steadily in all three countries, claims paid are growing at a faster rate. This is the case even adjusted for varying host country rates of inflation. Using 1997 as a base year, we see that the real average annual growth rate for premium income was 4.7% for Estonia, 7% for Latvia, and 33.3% for Lithuania. In terms of claims paid, the real average annual growth rates were 11.6% in Estonia, 30% in Latvia, and 41.7% in Lithuania. If this trend continues, as appears likely, then insurers in the region will be faced with difficulties, quite possibly impeding the further development not just of the non-life sector but of the general insurance market. A review of the evidence shows the problem to be most acute in Latvia, where between 1998-1999 claims paid exploded to a very high level, then continued fairly steadily growth. The non-life insurance markets in Estonia and Lithuania have also suffered from rising levels of claims paid, which spiked during 1997-98, and have continued to grow at rates more closely correlated with growth in premiums. The exception to this occurred in Lithuania during 2002, when compulsory MTPL significantly boosted in the volume of premium income.

Having identified the overall situation in the non-life segment it is appropriate and prudent to examine the development of the major individual components in each of the Baltic States between 1997 and 2002, which is covered by Exhibits 8-13.

In terms of development of personal insurance classes, Exhibit 8a provides an overview of the accident insurance class, while Exhibit 8b does the same for health, and Exhibit 8c for travel insurance.

The data in Exhibit 8a shows that accident insurance remains underdeveloped as an insurance class. In Estonia, activity in this line of insurance seems to have leveled off, as it has in Latvia, but with a higher dollar value of premiums generated, and in Lithuania at even higher dollar amounts but with fairly steady growth. Yet, in both Estonia and Latvia, the level of claims paid has continued to grow during the period, despite the minimal growth in premiums generated. In Lithuania, claims paid were almost at the same level in 2002 as in 1997, with a slight trough evident in the interim years.

Based on a review of Exhibit 8b we can see that health insurance has been a non-starter in Estonia, while in Lithuania it remains a marginal line of business. Only in Latvia has health insurance made an impact. Yet, while the level of premium income has grown from $6.7 million in 1997 to $19.1 million in 2002, claims paid have increased at a slightly greater rate, growing from $3.5 million in 1997 to $14.6 million in 2002. The situation in Lithuania is similar to that of Latvia, but on a much smaller scale and with a much more favorable claims ratio.

Overall, as can be seen from Exhibit 8c, travel insurance remains a very small component of the personal lines. In Lithuania, the business is almost non-existent. In both Estonia and Latvia, travel insurance has been growing very modestly; in Estonia, the claims ratio remains quite low, while this is not the case in Latvia.

In regard to motor insurance, which remains the dominant driver in the non-life sector, Exhibit 9a reviews the development of motor hull (Casco) insurance, and Exhibit 9b covers the combination of voluntary and compulsory MTPL.

Before examining the motor insurance branch in detail, it is appropriate to provide some relevant background. According to various sources, in 2002 there were approximately 2.685 million vehicles in the region, with Estonia accounting for 675,000, Latvia 810,000, and Lithuania 1.2 million. Based on these figures, vehicle ownership as a percentage of overall population would be 48% in Estonia, 34% in Latvia and 32% in Lithuania. However, many of the vehicles in the region, notably passenger cars, are in excess of 10 years old and not necessarily in use. Moreover, many of the passenger cars are low-value Lada types, dating from the Soviet era.

Exhibit 7, Total Non-Life Insurance in the Baltic States, 1997-2002

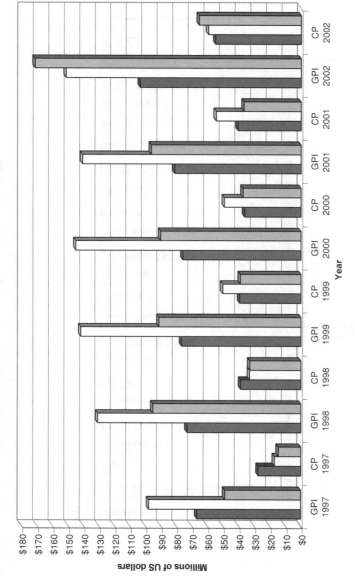

Sources: Estonia: Finantsinspekstsioon / Estonian Financial Supervision Authority (EFSA)(2001-03) and the Eesti Vabariigi Kindlustusinspektsioon / Estonian Insurance Supervisory Authority (EISA)(1997-01); **Latvia:** Finanšu un kapitāla tirgus komisija (FKTK) / Financial and Capital Market Commission (FCMC)(2001-03) and the Valsts Apdrošināšanas Uzraudzības Inspekcija (VAUI) / Latvian State Insurance Supervision Inspectorate (SISI)(1997-03); **Lithuania:** Valstybinė Draudimo Priežiūros Tarnyba (VDPT) / State Insurance Supervisory Authority (SISA)(formerly Draudimo Reikalu Taryba / State Insurance Council)(1997-03).

Exhibit 8a, Accident Insurance in the Baltic States, 1997-2002

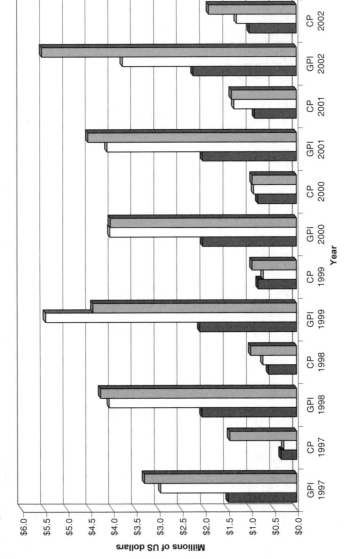

Sources: Estonia: Finantsinspekstsioon / Estonian Financial Supervision Authority (EFSA)(2001-03) and the Eesti Vabariigi Kindlustusinspektsioon / Estonian Insurance Supervisory Authority (EISA)(1997-01); **Latvia:** Finanšu un kapitāla tirgus komisija (FKTK) / Financial and Capital Market Commission (FCMC)(2001-03) and the Valsts Apdrošināšanas Uzraudzības Inspekcija (VAUI) / Latvian State Insurance Supervision Inspectorate (SISI)(1997-03); **Lithuania:** Valstybinė Draudimo Priežiūros Tarnyba (VDPT) / State Insurance Supervisory Authority (SISA)(formerly Draudimo Reikalų Taryba / State Insurance Council)(1997-03).

Exhibit 8b, Health Insurance in the Baltic States, 1997-2002

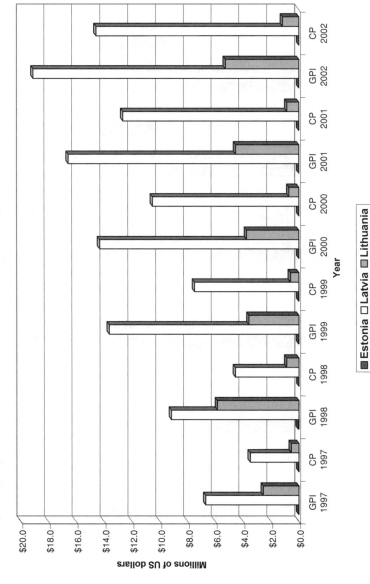

Millions of US dollars

Year

■ Estonia □ Latvia ■ Lithuania

Sources: Estonia: Finantsinspektsioon / Estonian Financial Supervision Authority (EFSA)(2001-03) and the Eesti Vabariigi Kindlustusinspektsioon / Estonian Insurance Supervisory Authority (EISA)(1997-01); **Latvia:** Finanšu un kapitāla tirgus komisija (FKTK) / Financial and Capital Market Commission (FCMC)(2001-03) and the Valsts Apdrošināšanas Uzraudzības Inspekcija (VAUI) / Latvian State Insurance Supervision Inspectorate (SISI)(1997-03); **Lithuania:** Valstybine Draudimo Priežiuros Tarnyba (VDPT) / State Insurance Supervisory Authority (SISA)(formerly Draudimo Reikalu Taryba / State Insurance Council)(1997-03).

81

Exhibit 8c, Travel Insurance in the Baltic States, 1997-2002

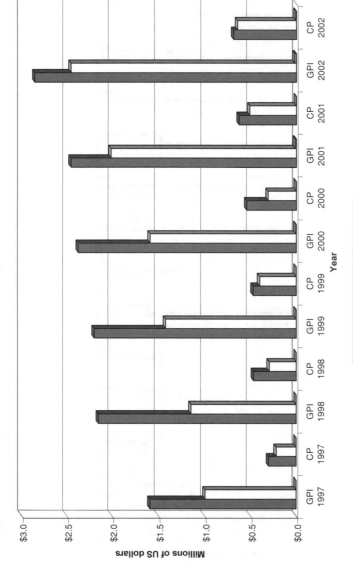

Legend: ■ Estonia □ Latvia ■ Lithuania

Y-axis: Millions of US dollars ($0.0, $0.5, $1.0, $1.5, $2.0, $2.5, $3.0)

X-axis (Year): GPI 1997, CP 1997, GPI 1998, CP 1998, GPI 1999, CP 1999, GPI 2000, CP 2000, GPI 2001, CP 2001, GPI 2002, CP 2002

Sources: Estonia: Finantsinspektsioon / Estonian Financial Supervision Authority (EFSA)(2001-03) and the Eesti Vabariigi Kindlustusinspektsioon / Estonian Insurance Supervisory Authority (EISA)(1997-01); **Latvia:** Finanšu un kapitāla tirgus komisija (FKTK) / Financial and Capital Market Commission (FCMC)(2001-03) and the Valsts Apdrošināšanas Uzraudzības Inspekcija (VAUI) / Latvian State Insurance Supervision Inspectorate (SISI)(1997-03); **Lithuania:** Valstybine Draudimo Priežiuros Tarnyba (VDPT) / State Insurance Supervisory Authority (SISA)(formerly Draudimo Reikalu Taryba / State Insurance Council)(1997-03).

82

Exhibit 9a, Motor Hull (CASCO) Insurance in the Baltic States, 1997-2002

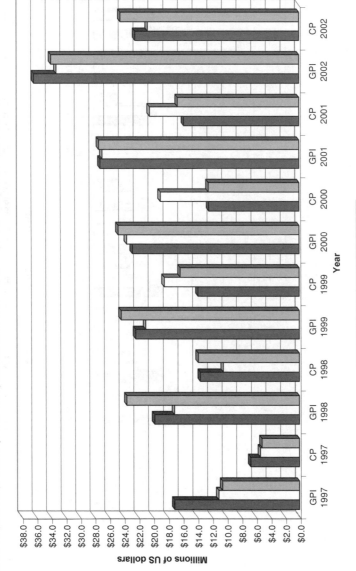

Sources: Estonia: Finantsinspekstsioon / Estonian Financial Supervision Authority (EFSA)(2001-03) and the Eesti Vabariigi Kindlustusinspektsioon / Estonian Insurance Supervisory Authority (EISA)(1997-01); **Latvia:** Finanšu un kapitāla tirgus komisija (FKTK) / Financial and Capital Market Commission (FCMC)(2001-03) and the Valsts Apdrošināšanas Uzraudzības Inspekcija (VAUI) / Latvian State Insurance Supervision Inspectorate (SISI)(1997-03); **Lithuania:** Valstybine Draudimo Priežiuros Tarnyba (VDPT) / State Insurance Supervisory Authority (SISA)(formerly Draudimo Reikalu Taryba / State Insurance Council)(1997-03).

83

Exhibit 9b, MTPL (Total) Insurance in the Baltic States, 1997-2002

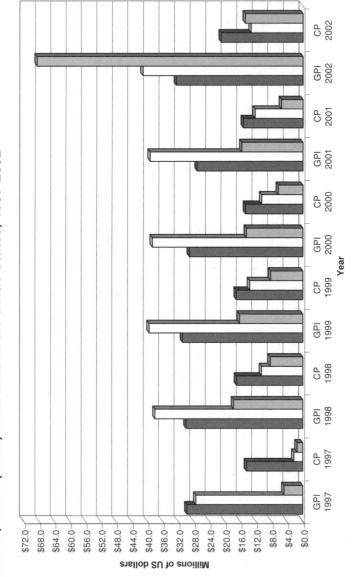

Millions of US dollars

Year

■ Estonia □ Latvia ■ Lithuania

Sources: Estonia: Finantsiinspekstsiooon / Estonian Financial Supervision Authority (EFSA)(2001-03) and the Eesti Vabariigi Kindlustusinspektsioon / Estonian Insurance Supervisory Authority (EISA)(1997-01); **Latvia:** Finanšu un kapitala tirgus komisija (FKTK) / Financial and Capital Market Commission (FCMC)(2001-03) and the Valsts Apdrošinašanas Uzraudzibas Inspekcija (VAUI) / Latvian State Insurance Supervision Inspectorate (SISI)(1997-03); **Lithuania:** Valstybine Draudimo Priežiuros Tarnyba (VDPT) / State Insurance Supervisory Authority (SISA)(formerly Draudimo Reikalu Taryba / State Insurance Council)(1997-03).

Exhibit 10, Goods-in-Transit (Cargo) Insurance in the Baltic States, 1997-2002

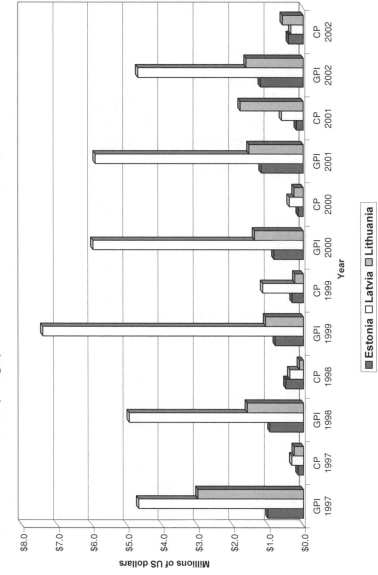

Sources: **Estonia:** Finantsinspektsioon / Estonian Financial Supervision Authority (EFSA)(2001-03) and the Eesti Vabariigi Kindlustusinspektsioon / Estonian Insurance Supervisory Authority (EISA)(1997-01); **Latvia:** Finanšu un kapitāla tirgus komisija (FKTK) / Financial and Capital Market Commission (FCMC)(2001-03) and the Valsts Apdrošināšanas Uzraudzības Inspekcija (VAUI) / Latvian State Insurance Supervision Inspectorate (SISI)(1997-03); **Lithuania:** Valstybine Draudimo Priežiuros Tarnyba (VDPT) / State Insurance Supervisory Authority (SISA)(formerly Draudimo Reikalu Taryba / State Insurance Council)(1997-03).

Exhibit 11, Property Insurance in the Baltic States, 1997-2002

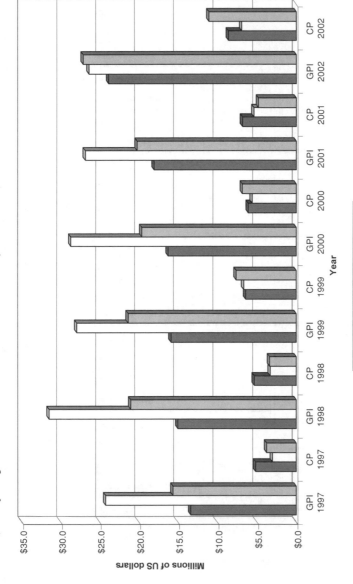

Millions of US dollars

Year

■ Estonia □ Latvia ■ Lithuania

Sources: Estonia: Finantsinspektsioon / Estonian Financial Supervision Authority (EFSA)(2001-03) and the Eesti Vabariigi Kindlustusinspektsioon / Estonian Insurance Supervisory Authority (EISA)(1997-01); **Latvia:** Finanšu un kapitāla tirgus komisija (FKTK) / Financial and Capital Market Commission (FCMC)(2001-03) and the Valsts Apdrošināšanas Uzraudzības Inspekcija (VAUI) / Latvian State Insurance Supervision Inspectorate (SISI)(1997-03); **Lithuania:** Valstybine Draudimo Priežiuros Tarnyba (VDPT) / State Insurance Supervisory Authority (SISA)(formerly Draudimo Reikalu Taryba / State Insurance Council)(1997-03).

Exhibit 12, General Liability Insurance in the Baltic States, 1997-2002

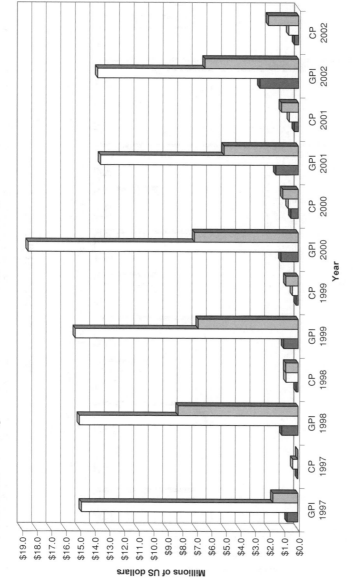

Sources: Estonia: Finantsinspektsioon / Estonian Financial Supervision Authority (EFSA)(2001-03) and the Eesti Vabariigi Kindlustusinspektsioon / Estonian Insurance Supervisory Authority (EISA)(1997-01); **Latvia:** Finanšu un kapitala tirgus komisija (FKTK) / Financial and Capital Market Commission (FCMC)(2001-03) and the Valsts Apdrošinašanas Uzraudzibas Inspekcija (VAUI) / Latvian State Insurance Supervision Inspectorate (SISI)(1997-03); **Lithuania:** Valstybine Draudimo Priežiuros Tarnyba (VDPT) / State Insurance Supervisory Authority (SISA)(formerly Draudimo Reikalu Taryba / State Insurance Council)(1997-03).

87

Exhibit 13, Pecuniary Loss Insurance in the Baltic States, 1997-2002

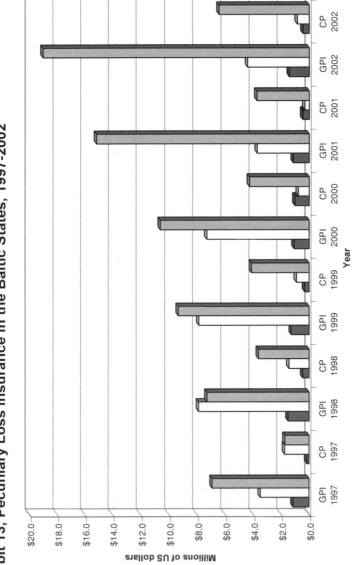

Sources: Estonia: Finantsinspektsioon / Estonian Financial Supervision Authority (EFSA)(2001-03) and the Eesti Vabariigi Kindlustusinspektsioon / Estonian Insurance Supervisory Authority (EISA)(1997-01); **Latvia:** Finanšu un kapitāla tirgus komisija (FKTK) / Financial and Capital Market Commission (FCMC)(2001-03) and the Valsts Apdrošinašanas Uzraudzibas Inspekcija (VAUI) / Latvian State Insurance Supervision Inspectorate (SISI)(1997-03); **Lithuania:** Valstybine Draudimo Priežiuros Tarnyba (VDPT) / State Insurance Supervisory Authority (SISA)(formerly Draudimo Reikalu Taryba / State Insurance Council)(1997-03).

In terms of the road network, Estonia has about 16,430 km (10,268 miles) of roads, mostly in good condition; Latvia has 20,820 km (12,800 miles), generally in somewhat poorer shape; and Lithuania has a network of 73,650 km (46,031 miles), largely unpaved and, given economic realities, unlikely to be upgraded soon. To compound matters, the Baltic States' northern location subjects the region to cold weather for much of the year. Snow and ice not only damage paved roads but make driving difficult. That said, the level of driving skills in the region is generally said to be good.

A review of the data in Exhibit 9a provides clear evidence of the growth of motor hull (Casco) insurance during the 1997-2002 period; the level of premium income generated by this line of insurance had grown significantly in each of the Baltic States. At the end of 2002, the level of premiums was $36.2 million in Estonia, $33.9 million in Lithuania, and $33.1 million in Latvia. This represents a growth factor of 2.1 for Estonia, 3 for Lithuania and 3.2 for Latvia from the 1997 figures. However, the level of claims paid also grew steadily in each country, and at a much faster rate than was the case with premium income. Using the same basis for comparison, claims paid in 2002 amounted to $24.3 million in Lithuania, $22.3 million in Estonia, and $22.3 million in Latvia. Thus, the multiplier for claims paid for 1997-2002 was 3.4 for Estonia, 3.9 for Latvia, and a very high 4.8 for Lithuania. If this trend continues, it could be detrimental for insurers offering motor hull (Casco) insurance, especially given heavy competition for the business, which keeps premium rates low and coupled with limited consumer purchasing power. In this regard, Lithuania is currently the most exposed of the Baltic States.

The situation in the voluntary and compulsory MTPL insurance class, as shown by Exhibit 9b, presents a similar scenario to that discussed above, but with some host country deviations. In general, the commodity nature of the MTPL offering, combined with intense competition by insurers for this line of business, has kept rates to customer quite low. Nevertheless, the level of claims paid has continued to rise and looks likely to continue doing so. To put this into perspective, a comparison of 1997 and 2002 data shows a growth factor for premium income at just 1.1 for Estonia, 1.5 for Latvia, and a very high 14.4 for Lithuania. As noted, in Lithuania the MTPL class received a significant boost in premiums when it was made into a compulsory line in April 2002. Therefore, in the comparative data for 1997-2001 in Lithuania, the premium income for MTPL shows a growth factor of 3.3. An examination of claims paid data for 1997 and 2002 reveal a growth factor of 1.5 in Estonia, 5.9 in Latvia, and 10.3 in Lithuania. Again, looking at the situation in Lithuania prior to MTPL being compulsory, we find that the multiplier for claims paid in 1997-2001 was only 3.9.

The situation in Latvia would seem quite volatile, given the low income streams for MTPL, coupled with rising costs. This could lead to financial difficulties among insurers and in turn have an adverse affect on policyholders and the non-life market in general. For the same reasons, the situation for MTPL in Lithuania could prove even more dangerous for all concerned. Furthermore, the fact that various Lithuanian governments have been slow, for political reasons, to enact compulsory MTPL could make this a political "hot potato" if customer confidence in the insurance sector continues to decrease.

The level of activity in goods-in-transit (cargo) insurance is shown in Exhibit 10. As is evident, the volume of activity within this class of insurance is negligible in both Estonia and Lithuania. In Lithuania, the amount of claims paid for 2001 exceeded not only the premiums for that year, but even surpassed the sum of claims paid in all other years. Only in Latvia, with its long tradition of serving as an East-West transit gateway, has goods-in-transit insurance shown any prominence. Latvia's developed port and rail facilities handle the vast bulk of cargo within the region. This should present further growth opportunities for insurers operating in Latvia licensed to offer such coverage.

Exhibit 11 illustrates the development of the property insurance class. In 1997, property insurance was the primary source of premium income in both Latvia and Lithuania. Yet, by 2002 it had been forced down to third position, behind the motor branch (MTPL and Casco). In Estonia, property insurance was also a significant non-life class during the early 1990s, but developments in motor insurance laws propelled these forward shortly thereafter. Hence, property insurance was consistently the third main source of premium income in Estonia through the 1997-2002 period. Given the prominence of the property class in the three Baltic States, it is worth greater attention.

Property insurance can be divided into two customer groups: individual physical persons (personal) and legal individuals (commercial). While such data is available for Estonia and Latvia, it is not readily available for Lithuania. In Estonia, between 1997 and 2002 an average of 55% of total premiums was related to commercial customers, while the other 45% went to cover personal property. Interestingly, commercial and personal customers accounted for on average 69% of all claims paid for the period, and personal customers for 31%. In Latvia, commercial customers generated 77% of total premiums for the same period, while the remaining 23% went to cover personal property. The claims paid for the period were 69% for commercial customers and 31% for personal property.

In general, property insurance remains greatly underdeveloped within the Baltic States. Again, the very low level of "insurance culture" stemming from the nature of the former insurance system has continued to play a role in the region, as have host country economic conditions, which in general are poor but improving. Much work needs to be done by insurers to educate the commercial customer base to the benefits of insurance products.

In the case of commercial customers, the low insurance culture stems primarily from the fact that the Soviet regime effectively abolished the need for property insurance for state-owned enterprises (SOEs) in the late 1950s. Nevertheless, insurance awareness within the commercial sector has increased since independence, greatly facilitated by increasing levels of foreign direct investment (FDI) in the local economies. Local firms with foreign capital participation have not only been a source of customers for local insurance products, but their use of these products to hedge against potential risks has had a demonstration and contagion effect on other commercial businesses. They have had a similar impact on their own employees, potential personal customers. Still, many domestically owned firms remain underinsured as a result of basic economic considerations, especially among the cash-strapped firms still under state control.

As to the personal customer segment, a combination of factors has hampered the development of the property insurance class, including low disposable incomes and a high proportion of individuals in rented accommodations. That said, awareness of property insurance products is reportedly high in the Baltic States, and as economic conditions improve and home ownership becomes more widespread, this situation should change. The problem is what to do in the meantime, not only for insurers looking for business but for personal customers looking to protect their limited assets.

A review of the comparative data on property insurance for 1997-2002 shows that premium income has been rising in both Estonia and Lithuania, although with fluctuations in the latter. In Latvia, the level of premium income seems to have peaked in 1998, at $31.5 million, and then fluctuated around the $27 million level. As for claims paid, while they have generally been rising in each of the Baltic States, the claims ratio has remained low, in sharp contrast to the general trend for most other non-life insurance classes. Nevertheless, the level of activity within the property insurance class remains low, and until local conditions improve it would seem likely that this will remain the situation.

While general liability insurance is often a substantial class within a developed market economy, as shown in Exhibit 12, it has yet to take hold in the Baltic States, despite its being a compulsory line of coverage for a number of professionals and general contractors. In Estonia, the level of activity has been very low, while in Lithuania, business has generally been higher but still limited. As regards Latvia, general liability insurance has shown some progress, with premiums fluctuating between $13 million and $18 million and with claims paid remaining minimal. In all three countries this line remains greatly underdeveloped, which surely will need to change with forthcoming integration into the more developed EU.

The data covered in Exhibit 13 show pecuniary loss, which is a combination of credit, suretyship and miscellaneous financial loss insurance lines. As with general liability, these non-life insurance lines remain an untapped source of potential development. Of course, there are problems with regard to "black business" activities within these types of insurance. As discussed, in Lithuania the problem stems from suretyship activities (customs bonds), which will need to be addressed. As for Latvia, most of the premiums generated here stem from miscellaneous financial loss, which in fact was used for legal but dubious purposes as a tax optimization scheme. In 2002, the primary insurer of this line of business was placed into bankruptcy, so it is hoped that this type of activity will now cease.

In closing, having identified the overall market structure in each of the Baltic States as well as the various individual elements within the non-life insurance segment, it is appropriate to now focus the discussion on the various distribution channels used.

V. Distribution channels

The nature of insurance products, like other offerings in the financial service sector, is often unique and based on personal relationships. Moreover, given the low level of insurance culture in the Baltic States, it has been essential for insurers to establish a strong connection with their customers. It is therefore prudent to examine the primary distribution channels available, as well as their usage for sales of non-life insurance products within the context of the Baltic States, including direct sales via insurers' own branch networks and tied agents; agencies; brokers; and the role of e-commerce within the non-life sector.

It should be noted that direct marketing of insurance products (via call centers) has not yet been used in Estonia and Lithuania, and in Latvia it has been rather unsuccessful due to the low insurance culture of both operators and customers. In the case of bancassurance, while insurers and banks have generally been cooperating in this regard, the level of activity generated remains small. However, this could represent an untapped means of distribution in the future.

A. Direct sales via insurers (branch networks and tied agents)

Across the Baltic States, the company insurance agent as well as agents tied to a specific insurer continues to be the most common mode of distribution for non-life insurance products, as for life policies. Accordingly, major insurers have each sought to develop their own domestic branch networks and/or to expand the number of tied agents working on their behalf. Fortunately for the former state insurance providers (Eesti Kindlustus, now If Eesti in Estonia; Latva, now Balta, part of the Balta Group of insurers in Latvia; and Lietuvos Draudimas in Lithuania) this was a relatively easy process, since these providers inherited an extensive branch and agent network from Gosstrakh when the Soviet system collapsed. In addition, the former state insurers have had a head start establishing strong brand recognition within their respective host country markets.

In all three Baltic States, insurance agents are classed as "insurance intermediaries" and must satisfy certain requirements as well as have a license to operate from the respective regulatory authority.

B. Agencies

In general, insurance agencies have not been a specific feature in the Estonian and Lithuanian non-life markets. However, in Latvia insurance agents have grouped together for such purposes, although they have usually attached themselves to a single insurance provider. Agents working as part of an agency are treated as "insurance intermediaries" and governed under the same criteria noted.

As for other forms of agencies, a number of simple non-life classes are sold via a variety of outlets, including automotive dealerships, leasing companies, lawyers, banks, post offices, travel agents and petrol stations. Some of these agencies are class-specific, for example travel agents acting as a conduit for travel insurance and car dealerships for motor insurance (MTPL and Casco). Within the motor hull (Casco) class, insurers have insisted upon physically inspecting vehicles prior to issuing the policy as a means of minimizing potential fraud. Other agencies have taken the form of strategic alliances. For instance, in Latvia the insurer Balta has formed an alliance to sell simple MTPL coverage through the Norwegian firm Staoil and its countrywide network of petrol stations.

C. Brokers

Over the years, insurance brokers have been gaining an increasingly prominent role within the sector. In fact, brokers in each of the Baltic States have formed associations that lobby for their interests.

Relations between insurers and brokers have generally been good, though at times difficult. Insurers, already faced with difficult operating conditions and fierce competition for business, sometimes see brokers as unwanted middlemen who cut into their profitability and distance them from their customers. However, given the low level of insurance culture in the Baltic States, as in most CEE and NIS states, brokers are in a good position to help develop personal relationships with customers. Brokers can offer independent advice to customers on the range of insurance offerings as well as the quality of insurance providers, since they are not necessarily tied to a specific insurer, as agents are. Yet, as noted, that very relationship can sometimes cause friction between the insurer and the broker. For example, in some competitive segments, like MTPL, which is sold as a commodity offering, brokers sometimes show very little loyalty to specific insurers, which can lead to difficulties. Likewise, some insurers have attempted to lure customers away from brokers.

The rules and regulations governing the activities of insurance brokers are generally similar across the Baltic States, in that the brokers are required to have certification by local regulatory authorities, meet certain capital requirements, and carry adequate professional indemnity insurance.

As for the number of brokerage firms operating, in 2002 there were 13 in Estonia, 29 in Latvia, and 92 in Lithuania. In addition, there were a number of individual brokers operating, although they generally transact a small volume of business. Most of the brokerage firms focus on small-to-medium enterprises as well as offering services to individual customers.

D. The role of e-commerce within the non-life insurance sector

A number of studies and articles highlight the tremendous opportunities available to those willing and able to design and implement e-commerce strategies that are both effective and efficient. E-commerce can also be used to improve operational effectiveness within a given organization. That said, within the more conservative insurance sector, the adoption rate of such strategies and tactics has thus far been mixed.

In the Baltic States, the necessary enabling environment for e-commerce activities remains rather low, despite a fairly e-friendly attitude of the population. According to the market research firm Taylor Nelson Sofres, Estonia had the highest percentage of population using the Internet in 2002, at 39%, followed by Lithuania, with 18%, and Latvia, at 17%. In all three countries, the primary means of connection to the Internet was at the workplace, followed by the university and home. Yet, Estonians, Latvians and Lithuanians were not found to make significant use of the Internet for online shopping, but more for informational and communication purposes.

As economic conditions improve in each of the Baltic States, this situation might change. Thus far, Estonia, with its 39% usage rate, appears best positioned of the three countries to adopt the Internet for such activities, perhaps promoted by the growing Finnish influence in the country.

In regard to insurance activities, a number of local insurers and brokers have established their own web sites. However, thus far this channel apparently is being used mostly to provide information on products and quotations to customers, as opposed to making sales. Moreover, the very nature of some insurance offerings, like motor hull (Casco), require a visual inspection of the vehicle prior to the quotation and offer of coverage. Hence, the Internet is not an appropriate medium for all types of non-life offerings.

Internally, e-commerce offers insurers an opportunity to improve their operational effectiveness. This can be done with electronic data systems that allow a more effective and efficient processing of claims, and which provide useful statistics and help identify fraudulent claims. Yet, the key to success, as found in a vast array of other business activities, is the ability of the firm to manage such knowledge effectively rather than fall into the trap that many firms have, by collecting the knowledge but failing to use it to benefit business activities.

CHAPTER 3

CONCLUSIONS AND RECOMMENDATIONS

The stated aim of this paper was to examine the development of the insurance sector within the Baltic States and specifically to provide a comparative study of the non-life insurance segment. Based on the findings of this study a number of important themes arise, from which conclusions are drawn and appropriate recommendations offered.

In general, the path of development of the insurance sectors in each of the Baltic States closely mirrors the level of country-specific economic, political and social transition achieved to date. While forthcoming accession to the EU hopefully will benefit the countries in many respects, many of the gaps that have divided East and West still exist and will continue to present problems with regard to integration. Accordingly, the ability of the Baltic States to bridge these gaps effectively will be vital to their success within the framework of the EU, and within the world economy in general.

Conclusions regarding the non-life insurance sector in the Baltic States have been drawn on the basis of a number of factors, including the size of the individual markets, their positioning relative to other countries, their sources of current and future activity, the level of host country development, and a comparative assessment of the three countries. Each of these factors is addressed, along with the conclusions reached.

The volume of activity in dollar terms for non-life insurance products in Estonia, Latvia and Lithuania has been rather small; individually and even collectively. Based on 2002 data, the Baltic States together generated premium income of $426.3 million, of which Lithuania accounted for $171.4 million (40%); Latvia, $151.4 million (36%); and Estonia, $103.5 million (24%). For the group, this represented a doubling of premium income from 1997. Of even greater concern is the fact that claims paid actually tripled during the period, and the trend of rising claims ratios looks likely to continue. With EU accession planned for mid-2004, this might make it economically unviable for some insurers to continue with purely domestic operations, increasing the likelihood that these countries will be served by branch operations. This situation undoubtedly will affect the development of the financial services sector in the three countries.

As regards the positioning of the non-life insurance markets in the Baltics relative to other transition economies, the evidence shows that they are generally more advanced than others in the NIS grouping. In relation to the CEE countries, the development level in the Baltic States positions them in the upper half of the grouping. However, in regard to the EU-AC8, the Baltic States find themselves at the bottom of the grouping, with a significant gap between them and the market leader Slovenia, whose non-life insurance sector is comparable to those in the EU.

In relation to the EU, evidence from the insurance density and penetration rates is mixed. Analysis of density rates demonstrates that the Baltic States are not only well below the EU average but, based on 2001 data, well below levels in Greece, which had the lowest density rates of any EU member state. While Latvia and Estonia could effectively reduce this gap before formal accession or shortly thereafter, the situation in Lithuania looks less favorable, given its very low per capita spending on insurance products. In terms of penetration rates, the picture is somewhat brighter for some but still difficult for others. Comparative data for 2001 show that the EU average penetration rate was almost 2.7%, which only Latvia, at 1.9%, came close to realizing, followed by Estonia, at 1.5%, and Lithuania, with just 0.81%. Overall, host country economics and a low level of insurance culture continue to play major roles in the development of the region's insurance market. This places each of the Baltic States in a difficult situation given their planned accession to the EU.

In terms of areas of activity, the main source of premium income in the non-life segment for insurers operating in the Baltic States continues to be motor insurance policies (MTPL and Casco). As for motor hull (Casco), the growth in premium income is being surpassed by claims paid, a fact that is further exacerbated by rising repair costs and in some cases fraudulent claims. A similar situation is being experienced with the MTPL class, but with somewhat different ingredients. In MTPL, the commodity nature of the offering has given rise to increasing competitive pressures that keep premium rates low. Coupled with an increasing claims ratio, this equals lower profit margins for insurers. This makes motor insurance (MTPL and Casco) a poor engine for driving growth in the non-life segment. Nevertheless, many foreign and local insurers active in the region seem to be relying heavily on motor insurance to provide not only growth but, more importantly, to introduce consumers to their other product offerings, and hopefully in the process to enhance the low "insurance culture" in the Baltic states. While this education process is essential, it is sure to be resource-intensive, and in the end may not actually yield the necessary critical mass of customers required to support operations.

As for other non-life insurance classes, considerable scope remains for further development, such as general liability coverage, and personal lines such as health, accident and travel. This is true even in the property insurance class, which is a significant source of premiums that, if properly nourished, could offer even more opportunities for insurers while providing protection and security to customers.

However, there is reason for concern that some types of business, such as pecuniary loss, are not being regulated as closely as they should be, given the risks to stakeholders. In the past, there has been evidence that certain aspects of the insurance mechanism have been perverted for what can be termed "black business" activities, involving capital transfer, tax evasion and insurance fraud. Given the Baltic states' geographic proximity to Belarus and the Russian Federation, more must be done not only to combat these "black business" activities but to work with host country governments and their regulatory authorities to prevent an economic "iron curtain" from separating the expanding EU from the rest of Europe. This is especially important given the traditional Baltic role as a bridge between East and West.

Each of the Baltic states has taken important steps over the past decade to transform its insurance systems along international lines, including liberalizing markets, adopting international standards of risk management, permitting foreign entrants into the sector, and relinquishing control of the former state insurers via privatization. A key element of this process has been the creation of an effective and efficient legal environment in which insurance operations can function. This has meant adopting several EU directives, many of which still need to be harmonized. The state role in the insurance sector is now concentrated primarily in a supervisory capacity.

Supervision of the insurance sector in each of the Baltic States has generally been quite good. Local authorities have not shied away from dealing with situations by revoking licenses of insurers deemed to be in distress, or from forcing some of them into insolvency via bankruptcy proceedings. Yet, these acts, while beneficial to the market, do not necessarily instill confidence in the minds of consumers, who are troubled by such developments and already suffer from a low "insurance culture". In fact, the supervision process has been hampered by a number of resource issues (knowledge, expertise, funds, etc.), which, despite the best intentions of supervisory staff, make proactive supervision difficult. This is especially the case in Latvia and Lithuania, where there remain a high number of market participants (insurers and brokers). Moreover, as the three pillars of financial services – banking, capital markets and insurance – continue to converge, the need will rise for a more united approach to supervision. In Estonia and Latvia, this issue has been addressed by merging the respective regulatory authorities, but in Lithuania they remain separate.

Estonia appears to have the more developed of the Baltic insurance markets, followed by Latvia and then Lithuania. However, with a much larger population base, Lithuania would seem to have the greatest potential of the three countries, provided economic conditions continue to improve. All three countries continue, however, to suffer from a low insurance culture that is a byproduct of the former Soviet insurance system. While a general awareness of insurance products and their uses has developed within the main urban centers, this is not necessarily the situation in rural areas. Thus, while the insurance culture is showing signs of improvement, much work remains to be done. Economic conditions continue to be difficult and are not yet to the level where most people have sufficient disposable income to consider voluntarily purchasing insurance products, which would seem to be viewed as a luxury that many can ill afford.

In conclusion, a review of the data would appear to paint a picture of the non-life insurance markets in the Baltic States as underdeveloped and offering limited potential, especially in comparison to the rest of the EU-AC8 grouping, not to mention EU member states. This would also seem to describe the life insurance market in the Baltic States, which is even less developed. However, to simply dismiss the Baltic States would negate their tremendous potential and deny the dynamic nature of Estonians, Latvians and Lithuanians. It would also negate the importance of developing an efficient and effective insurance sector in each of these countries that should not be understated, given its vital role as one of three key pillars of financial services, alongside banking and capital markets.

Given these considerations, the author offers the following three recommendations, which while aimed primarily at policymakers, both internal and external to the Baltic States, also have implications for other stakeholders, including supervisory authorities, insurers, intermediaries and customers (existing and potential). The recommendations offered generally aim to facilitate further market development.

I. Fostering and developing a positive insurance culture

It is vital to the future development of the non-life segment, and the insurance industry as a whole, to educate the local population on the relative benefits and costs of using insurance products. Accordingly, the host country government and its supervisory authorities could work not only with insurers but with intermediaries to facilitate this aim. The process must be centered around educating consumers on how the insurance system functions and how insurance instruments (life and non-life) can be best used for their benefit.

In marketing terminology, the education process should focus on the "AIDA" concept of creating awareness (A), interest (I), desire (D) and action (A). As noted, there is a general awareness of insurance offerings and a degree of interest, but more must be done to promote desire to use such products and for consumers, completing the cycle, to safeguard their own interests by securing such coverage. This process must not be limited to urban centers but also be promoted in rural areas. This education process should be targeted at work environments as well as schools and universities. Since brokers and agents undoubtedly will play a vital frontline role in this education process, they should receive adequate training to do so. In this regard, the local insurance association and brokers association should work together with the assistance of the host country government.

As for incentives, host country governments should be careful about providing tax relief for non-life insurance activities, as these are often more appropriate to life coverage. However, certain types of tax incentives for health, general liability and property insurance classes should be considered as a means of further developing a positive insurance culture.

II. Strengthening customer confidence and security within the financial services sector

The first main aspect of this recommendation focuses on the state's role as primary supervisor, and the second on its responsibility to safeguard consumers' rights.

As regards supervision, given the movement in the financial services sector toward providing one-stop shopping for customers, it is essential that supervisory authorities merge their activities under one unified supervisory authority. Both Estonia and Latvia have already done this; Lithuania has not. This is, however, about more than just moving three separate supervisory functions into one building under a joint heading. The unification of banking, capital markets and insurance supervision needs to be about creating a culture whereby knowledge, expertise and best practices are leveraged through coordination of activities. This culture will take time to develop, and it must be given every possible positive encouragement.

Once unified supervision is established, cooperative links with other supervisory authorities in the region should be forged and/or strengthened. While this obviously will include the other Baltic States as well as the EU, it should also encompass neighboring countries such as Sweden, Finland, the Russian Federation, Belarus, Poland and Ukraine. The OECD and other international bodies should play vital supporting and facilitating roles in this. By working together, best practices can be shared and experience and knowledge leveraged to benefit all.

Supervision of insurance activities could be expanded to cover more fully brokers (insurance intermediaries), who are vital, given their growing importance and connection to customers. In addition, resources should be set aside for the purposes of conducting more onsite inspections and for training staff.

The second main recommendation involves safeguarding consumers' rights. This could be facilitated by the establishment of an ombudsman's office. At present, none of the Baltic States has an official ombudsman for insurance activities. Yet, an ombudsman should not be confined to insurance activities but encompass the full financial services sector, combining banking and capital markets. Moreover, serious consideration should be given to connecting the financial services ombudsman to the respective supervisory authority, which will facilitate the information flow between the two bodies and in turn help foster a more secure sector.

III. Developing the non-life market

The non-life insurance market in the Baltic States remains fairly underdeveloped, with some classes problematic and others in need of encouragement. As regards the problematic classes, there are as noted growing problems in the motor insurance class, primarily with respect to MTPL coverage. The host country government and the respective supervisory authorities should therefore direct additional resources toward proactively monitoring the MTPL class, ensuring that rates charged reflect the technical nature of the coverage. In addition, they should take steps to prevent dumping of rates, especially by insurers that have access to additional sources of capital, whether through a foreign parent or a domestic partner.

A MTPL fund could be established in each host country, as it has been in Estonia with the Estonian Traffic Insurance Fund and in Latvia via the Latvian Traffic Bureau. This fund should be able to monitor the MTPL class, with access given to insurers and supervisory authorities to safeguard all parties concerned.

Appropriate measures need to be taken to combat the growing problem with fraud in the motor branch. This applies to other non-life insurance classes, as well.

As for the issue of encouraging further development in the non-life classes, this could include general liability, property and personal lines such as health, accident and travel.

In sum, the Baltic States – Estonia, Latvia and Lithuania – have each made tremendous progress over the last decade in transforming their insurance sectors. However, much remains to be done, especially with their forthcoming accession to the EU. It is the author's sincere hope that the three recommendations offered in this paper will, if implemented, help each of the Baltic States to further develop its non-life insurance markets for the benefit of all those concerned: policymakers, supervisory authorities, insurers, insurance intermediaries and customers.

BIBLIOGRAPHY

Aubrey-Jones, S. (1996a) Developments in Eastern Europe – Part II. *European Insurance Market*, No. 122, 6 December, pp. 407-409.

Aubrey-Jones, S. (1996b) Developments in Eastern Europe – Part I. *European Insurance Market*, No. 121, 22 November, pp. 397-399.

AXCO (2003) *Insurance Market Report on Latvia: Non-Life*. AXCO Insurance Information Services Ltd., London, United Kingdom, February.

AXCO (2002) *Insurance Market Report on Estonia: Non-Life*. AXCO Insurance Information Services Ltd., London, United Kingdom, June.

AXCO (2001) *Insurance Market Report on Lithuania: Non-Life*. AXCO Insurance Information Services Ltd., London, United Kingdom, September.

Baur, P. (2002) The impacts of EU enlargement on the insurance markets of the Eastern European candidate countries. *Insights*, Swiss Re, Zürich, Switzerland, December.

Birkmaier, U. and Codoni, C. (2002) World insurance in 2001: Turbulent financial markets and high claims burden impact premium growth. *Sigma*, No 6, Swiss Re, Zürich, Switzerland.

Birkmaier, U. and Helfenstein, R. (editors) (2000) Europe in focus: Non-life markets undergoing structural change. *Sigma*, No 3, Swiss Re, Zürich, Switzerland.

EBRD (2003) *Transition Report Update*. European Bank for Reconstruction and Development (EBRD), London, United Kingdom, May.

EBRD (2002) *Transition Report 2002: Agriculture and Rural Transition*. European Bank for Reconstruction and Development (EBRD), London, United Kingdom, November.

EBRD (1996) *Transition Report 1996: Infrastructure and Savings*. European Bank for Reconstruction and Development (EBRD), London, United Kingdom, November.

Euromonitor International (2002) *European Marketing Data and Statistics 2003, 38th edition*. Euromonitor International, London, United Kingdom.

Faulkner, J. (2002) Culture and Corruption – The Development of Insurance in Post-Communist Countries. Conference Proceedings of the *"UK Insurance Economists Conference,"* Nottingham, Nottinghamshire, United Kingdom, 10-11 April.

Finantsinspektsioon (2003) www.fi.ee/

Finantsinspektsioon (2003) *Yearbook 2002.* Finantsinspektsioon / Estonian Financial Supervision Authority (EFSA), Tallinn, Estonia.

Finantsinspektsioon (2002) *Insurance Yearbook 2001.* Finantsinspektsioon / Estonian Financial Supervision Authority, Tallinn, Estonia.

FKTK (2003) www.fktk.lv

FKTK (2003) *Latvian Insurance Market in Figures, 1997-2001.* Finanšu un kapitāla tirgus komisija (FKTK) / Financial and Capital Market Commission (FCMC), Riga, Latvia.

Leonard, A. (2000) *Insurance in the Baltic States.* Insurance Research & Publishing Ltd. (IRP), Loughton, Essex, United Kingdom.

OECD (1997) *Insurance Regulation and Supervision in Economies in Transition.* Center for Co-operation with Economies in Transition (CCET), Organization for Economic Co-operation and Development (OECD), Paris, France.

Ollerma, Siiri (1997) *Insurance Market and Insurance Regulation in Estonia 1992-1996.* Eesti Vabariigi Kindlustusinspektsioon / Estonian Insurance Supervisory Authority (EISA), Tallinn, Estonia.

Pye, R. B. K. (2003) The Evolution of the Insurance Sector in Central and Eastern Europe (CEE) and the Newly Independent States (NIS) of the former Soviet Union. In Conference Proceedings of the *"IX Dubrovnik Economic Conference (9DEC): Banking and the Financial Sector in Transition and Emerging Market Economies,"* Croatian National Bank, Dubrovnik, Croatia, 26-28 June.

Pye, R. B. K. (2000) The Lion Roars Back into Budapest: The Generali Group in Hungary, a Series of Cases. In Conference Proceedings of *"Insurance in Central and Eastern Europe,"* IBC Global Conferences, London, United Kingdom, 15-16 May.

Rantama, J. (2001) Financial supervision in the Baltic countries. *Baltic Economies – The Quarter in Review*, No 4, Bank of Finland Institute for Economies in Transition (BOFIT), pp. 4.

Rüstmann, M. (2001) Insurance industry in Central and Eastern Europe – current trends and progress of preparations for EU membership. *Sigma*, No 1, Swiss Re, Zürich, Switzerland.

Skipper, H.D. (1997) *Foreign Insurers in Emerging Markets: Issues and Concerns.* Occasional Paper 97-2. Center for Risk Management and Insurance, Georgia State University, Atlanta, GA, USA.

Taylor Nelson Sofres (2003) *Global eCommerce Report 2002.* www.tnsofres.com/ger2002/.

VDPT (2003) www.vdpt.lt

VDPT (2002) *Insurance in Lithuania, Annual Overview 2001.* Valstybinė Draudimo Priežiūros Tarnyba (VDPT) / State Insurance Supervisory Authority (SISA), Vilnius, Lithuania.

VDPT (2001) *Insurance in Lithuania, Annual Overview 2000.* Valstybinė Draudimo Priežiūros Tarnyba (VDPT) / State Insurance Supervisory Authority (SISA), Vilnius, Lithuania.

Yuko, K. (1999) *Technology Spillovers Through Foreign Direct Investment.* William Davidson Institute Working Papers Series, University of Michigan, Ann Arbor, Michigan, USA, No 221, January.

REINSURANCE ISSUES IN THE BALTIC COUNTRIES

Adrian Leonard

Abstract

The following study deals with reinsurance markets' issues in the Baltic States and in particular the availability and soundness of the reinsurance coverage in these markets. To this extent, it first overviews consolidation and foreign ownership developments in the insurance markets of Baltic States, since both trends are major drivers of the shrinking demand for open market reinsurance in these markets. It then sketches out the pros and cons of the development of local reinsurance activities by Baltic insurers. The report describes the evolution of the local reinsurance markets, that have first grown rapidly and are in turn today in a contraction phase. The author argues that the explanation for this evolution is that reinsurance activities were at first often developed for tax avoidance purposes. This phenomenon is today increasingly overseen by the financial supervisory authorities and limited by the regulatory framework of each Baltic States.

The next part of the paper is devoted to the development of the regulatory framework related to reinsurers at the international and EU level and at Baltic level. Actually, as in a majority of countries, reinsurance activities in the Baltic States are slightly regulated: to operate as a reinsurer in the Baltic States, companies only need to apply for a license to underwrite this business. However, In Lithuania specific requirements are imposed on insurers when selecting a reinsurer. The report ends with a series of recommendations addressed to the Baltic States and also provides examples of different alternatives that have been experienced in various countries to reinsure specific kind of activities and risks.

TABLE OF CONTENTS

INTRODUCTION

As development continues in the insurance markets of the countries of the former Soviet Baltic – Latvia, Lithuania and Estonia – both their need for reinsurance and its supply from the international market are changing dramatically. The changes are happening from country to country, and from company to company. As well as being directly affected by trends in international reinsurance markets such as concentration and limitation of supply, cyclical pricing and a general move toward more technical underwriting, significant local factors in the development of the three markets are also driving change. These include consolidation among insurers, foreign ownership, the maturing of compulsory motor insurance markets, market liberalization, and the ongoing but sluggish modernization of local underwriting technique.

These local influences are occurring at different paces in Latvia, Estonia and Lithuania. In addition, the external influences have a varying impact depending on the stage of development of local influences. As a result, cession rates in the Baltic markets are in flux, and valid generalizations about reinsurance in the region are few. Cession rates vary from market to market, based on each local insurance economy's current development, and from company to company, based on its individual circumstances. Thus in recent years, cession rates have not followed predictable overall trends (despite coincidental similarity in 2001, the most recent year for which complete statistics are available).

Baltic insurance market
Cession rates by country, 1998-2001

	1998	1999	2000	2001
Estonia	24.2%	31.4%	30.1%	33.4%
Latvia	47.9%	44.3%	43.3%	35.4%
Lithuania	39.7%	34.6%	29.2%	33.2%

Source: Compiled by the author from published sources (selected Bibliography)

Although many smaller companies in the region are still reliant on reinsurance, the combination of effects has tended to reduce the region's overall demand for *open-market* reinsurance capacity, both local and foreign. Yet, despite consolidation, smaller companies continue to remain important, especially in Latvia and Lithuania, at least for now. Smaller companies tend to buy significant amounts of proportional reinsurance capacity and, for those that can afford to do so, excess of loss protection for their retained risk. The number of small companies buying proportional reinsurance is one of two major reasons that the Baltic region's level of insurance premium retention is lower than that in most other regions of Central and Eastern Europe and the Commonwealth of Independent States (CIS). The other is foreign ownership leading to cessions to parent companies, which is discussed in detail in Chapter 2.

Unfortunately, for insurers reliant on proportional reinsurance capacity, many foreign reinsurers see the Baltic markets as unattractive. The markets and even the largest companies are small relative to those in other Central European countries, such as Hungary and Poland. Because of their low premium volume, it is not uncommon for a single foreign reinsurer to accept 100% of a treaty for a small Baltic insurer, an extremely rare practice in Western Europe. In addition, European reinsurers are working aggressively to eliminate catastrophe coverage from proportional reinsurance treaties. Such moves require insurers that rely on proportional reinsurance to purchase additional catastrophe excess of loss reinsurance protection. For some this may be an unaffordable necessity. Improved data collection can, however, bring catastrophe excess of loss reinsurance costs down.

David Wansbrough-Jones, formerly CEE and CIS reinsurance underwriter for Tryg-Baltica International, estimates that the entire CEE and CIS region generated non-life earned premium income of USD 15.411 billion in 2002, just 1.2% of the world market. The Baltic States contributed USD 405 million of this – about 0.0031% of the world's non-life premium. Mr Wansbrough-Jones further estimated that the CEE and CIS regions generated 1.35% of the world's total reinsurance premium. For the Baltic States, he estimated that USD 81 million was ceded to reinsurers in 2002.

CEE and CIS market overview, USD millions, 2002

Region	Non-life premium income	Share re-insured
Central Europe*	$8,215	16%
Russia and neighbours	$5,531	7%
South Central Europe	$1,055	15%
Baltic states	*$405*	*20%*
Central Asia	$139	12%
Caucasus^	$66	47%
Total	**$15,411**	**12%**

* including Slovenia ^ primarily fronting
Source: David Wansbrough-Jones, Tryg-Baltica International

Adding to reinsurers' challenge, little is known about the risks ceded through this small volume of cessions. Data collection is limited in the Baltic States – insurers collect too little information about the risks they insure – leading to actions such as

Swiss Re's withdrawal from motor reinsurance treaty underwriting in the region. Even in Estonia, where compulsory motor third party liability insurance has more than eight years' history, data is insufficient for proper actuarial analysis.

Competition between insurers exacerbates this problem, especially in the case of proportional treaties, where reinsurers' returns are based solely on the pricing approach of the cedant. When competition for market share and the need for cash flow drive pricing below economic levels (a phenomenon certainly not limited to the Baltic countries), proportional reinsurers are directly affected. Further, insurers' poor risk assessment and incorrect calculation of probable maximum loss figures have led to the setting of insufficient premium rates. Mr Wansbrough-Jones summed up the factors discouraging reinsurers from participating in the CEE and CIS region as follows:

1. Poor results overall for motor and catastrophe reinsurance.
2. Complexity of the region and its "unknown factors".
3. Small markets.
4. Small margins (5% profit on treaty at best, but overall probably a loss of 5% to 20%).
5. Small shares of treaties are not cost effective.
6. Bigger shares are needed but they require more research resources, but...
7. Reinsurers face constant shareholder pressure to reduce costs.

Meanwhile, some efforts are being made to increase and enhance the reinsurance business transacted within the region between local risk carriers, notably in Latvia. In June 1999, shareholders of privately owned Baltikums Insurance Group launched Riga Re, the Baltic States' first locally owned reinsurer. It began primarily as a retention vehicle for the direct operations of the Baltikums Group, but soon branched out to accept ceded premiums from other Baltic insurers, and later from other post-Soviet countries, including Russia, Ukraine and Kazakhstan.

Also in Latvia, the insurance association is working to increase risk-sharing between local insurers, a project which Latvian-owned companies and others are pursuing. Parex Insurance, part of a privately owned banking and insurance group, states: "As a member of the Latvian Insurers Association, the company is actively involved in implementing a program of mutual risk reinsurance and co-insurance in Latvia. The main Latvian partners of the company are Balta and BTA."

Such risk-sharing programs do mean that premium stays local, but they carry an inherent challenge. In other Central European countries, the widespread use of co-insurance was intended to divide among insurers' risks that were otherwise unacceptable under the obligatory treaties provided by reinsurers. As a result, many reinsurance treaties with foreign companies now specifically exclude co-insurance and assumed reinsurance risks. As reinsurance underwriting discipline increases among major reinsurers, such exclusions are becoming more common, requiring insurers either to retain co-insurance risk, or obtain specific "facultative" reinsurance for individual risks assumed from a professional reinsurer. International reinsurers are increasingly unhappy about accepting co-insurance and retrocessional risks through treaties, since underwriting control is removed by another generation. Munich Re, the world's largest reinsurer, is understood to have widely introduced in Central Europe a restrictive clause to limit its co-insurance exposures under conventional fire insurance treaties. The clause limits the reinsured share of an accepted co-insurance risk to the same proportion as that of the original risk assumed.

Recommendations

Improved data collection and underwriting skill will improve the attractiveness of Baltic insurance companies to international reinsurers, potentially increasing reinsurance supply and the choice of reinsurers willing to assume the region's excess insurance risk. Initiatives promoting risk analysis and valuation, as well as training for insurance professionals (in co-operation with local insurance associations, reinsurers and organisations such as the Chartered Insurance Institute) will improve the attractiveness of the Baltic insurance market, despite its size. Continued Professional Development (CPD) schemes and other programs encourage ongoing training. The collection of risk data by individual insurers and through central bodies such as motor bureaus allows both insurers and reinsurers to analyze claims trends and insurance pricing over time. The introduction of standardized data formats for the recording of risk information (such as those developed through CRESTA) would add further transparency to risk. Recommendations regarding risk sharing and other retention tools are made in Chapter 3,VI.

CHAPTER 1

CONSOLIDATION AND FOREIGN OWNERSHIP

Consolidation and foreign ownership are major drivers of the shrinking demand for open market reinsurance in the Baltic markets. As an entrepreneurial fervour swept post-Soviet Europe, the tiny Baltic States were quickly overpopulated with small, undercapitalized insurers (as were most CIS and CEE countries). As they grew, most of these insurers relied heavily on foreign reinsurers to supply both the treaty reinsurance needed to support the risk which they assumed, and for the technical expertise they usually lacked for functions such as product design. A round of collapses and consolidation followed through the 1990s, beginning in Estonia, where the process is essentially complete and moving southward to Latvia and Lithuania, where it continues.

In many cases, the key to consolidation has been foreign investment, which gathered speed in the late 1990s as established insurers, primarily from Scandinavia and Germany, rushed to acquire the best of the local companies. The investments they made immediately reduced demand for reinsurance among local companies. The foreign owners have tended to be large, well-capitalized insurance companies that do not require as much of the proxy capital that open-market reinsurance provides.

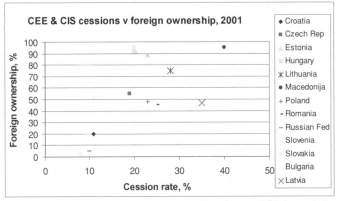

Source: Compiled by the author from published sources (See Selected Bibliography)

In addition, foreign owners tend to boost the capital of their Baltic subsidiaries upon acquisition, allowing the companies to retain more risk on their own balance sheets. Thus, even those that have not seen their reinsurance buying centralized, or drawn into a group retention program, may have less need for proportional reinsurance. For many exposures, better-financed insurers have moved toward greater use of excess of loss protections. For example, Lietuvos Draudimas, the former Lithuanian monopoly, now retains all of its motor risk, protecting the book only through excess of loss cover for catastrophe exposures.

However, foreign owners often cede a significant share of subsidiaries' premium income to parent companies or group holding companies, leaving little risk on the books of local subsidiaries or branches. Ceding premium to a central group company can have several advantages for the group and the subsidiary, including the ability to implement a cost-effective and co-coordinated group investment program, to develop a group-wide outward reinsurance strategy comprising a balanced and co-ordinated retention scheme and a group reinsurance program, and the ability to circumvent potentially unattractive investment restrictions that may be required of subsidiaries in some countries.

In some cases, reinsurance through the parent has approached 100%, as was the case with the insurers of the Zurich Financial Services Group that operated in the Baltic states until they entered run-off in 2003. In 1995, Macedonia, with 0% foreign ownership, ceded 10% of its premium, but by 2001, after international insurer QBE had purchased the former local monopoly, cessions increased to 40% but were channelled to the parent. Such private cessions distort market-wide retention and reinsurance figures, as the reports of regulators and associations tend not to distinguish between open-market and internal cessions.

In all three Baltic countries the former state-owned monopolies have remained dominant for personal lines and small commercial business, though they have been subdivided into life and non-life companies. All have now been sold to "strategic" insurance-company investors. By the end of March 2000, the market share of foreign-owned insurers (defined as companies in which foreign owners hold 50% or more of the company's capital) exceeded 80% in Lithuania and Estonia. That placed those two countries second only to Hungary among the EU candidate countries in terms of the penetration of foreign ownership. Latvia, in contrast, at the time had the lowest foreign ownership of eight candidates considered, at less than 10%, but that was shortly to change with the sale of Balta, the non-life arm of the former Latvian monopoly.

I.   Consolidation and foreign ownership – Latvia

Concentration has reduced the number of Latvian non-life insurers by one-third since 1998, to 14. Meanwhile, Latvian ownership of the equity in Latvian insurers fell below half in 2001, and was 47.4% at the end of 2002. Scandinavian companies had 21%, and other European investors had 27%. Six insurers operated as subsidiaries of foreign insurers, two were owned outright by foreign insurers, and more than 10% of the share capital of two others was foreign-owned. According to Ministry of Finance figures, cessions for all non-life insurers in Latvia fell from 37% of premiums written in 2001 to 28% of premiums written in 2002.

After its privatization through stock-market quotation, Balta, the non-life arm of the former Latvian monopoly, was finally sold to a strategic investor late in 2001. Codan Forsikrings A/S of Denmark, part of the Royal & SunAlliance Group, bought the company following a bidding battle with Sampo of Finland, whose Baltic acquisitions are now part of the Swedish If P/C Insurance Group.

Balta, like fellow Codan subsidiary Lietuvos Draudimas (the former Lithuanian monopoly), continues to purchase reinsurance on the open market. This is in contrast to, for example, If Eesti Kindlustus, the former monopoly in Latvia now owned by Sweden's If Group, and the related, smaller If companies in Latvia and Lithuania. They purchase reinsurance through their parent company, reducing total regional cessions significantly and the amount of open-market reinsurance premium available even more. However, it is understood that discussions are under way to rationalize reinsurance buying practices at the Codan subsidiaries, which would reduce open-market cessions further.

Largest Latvian non-life insurers ownership, country of ownership

Company	Owner	Country of owner
Balta Group	Codan Forsikrings A/S; Royal & SunAlliance Group	Denmark; UK
ERGO, apdrošinātāju grupa	Ergo International AG	Germany
BTA	Latvian companies	Latvia
Parekss Apdrošināšanas	Individuals (Valery Kargin, Viktor Krasovitsky)	Latvia
Balva	SOVAG, Ingosstrakh	Russia
Rīgas Slimokase	N/A	Latvia
Baltikums	Individuals (Aleksandrs Peškovs, Sergejs Peškovs, Andrejs Kočetkovs, Oļegs Čepuļskis)	Latvia
If Latvia	IF P&C Insurance Co Ltd.	Sweden
Seesam	Pohjola Group plc, American International Group Inc.	Finland, USA

Source: Compiled by the author from published sources (See selected Bibliography)

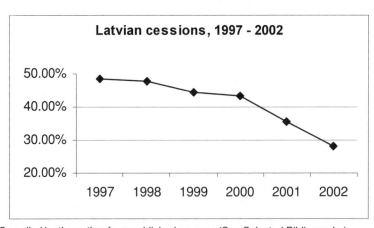

Source: Compiled by the author from published sources (See Selected Bibliography)

More detailed figures from Latvia show the ascent of cessions in that country: reinsurers' share of gross written premiums, excluding deductions for compulsory motor liability insurance, were 48.5% in 1997, 47.9% in 1998, 44.3% in 1999, 43.3% in 2000, and 35.4% in 2001.

While many insurers' cessions are falling, independent Latvian insurers continue to rely on reinsurance from leading international reinsurers. Parex, for example, is locally owned and operates insurance companies as part of a financial services group. It has reported that it has both treaty and facultative reinsurance contracts in place to cover a variety of risk classes, and that up to 75% of assumed risk is transferred to reinsurers under treaties established to cover many lines of business.

Parex has reported that its main reinsurer is Gerling Global Re, although this reinsurer, once the seventh-largest in the world, ceased operations in 2002, and is now in run-off. However, Parex states that it has concluded reinsurance contracts with other leading international reinsurers including Lloyd's of London, Swiss Re, General Cologne Re, ERC Frankona Re, The Copenhagen Re (also now in run-off), Colonia (part of the Axa group), and Converium (formerly Zurich Re).

II. Consolidation and foreign ownership – Estonia

Nowhere has the Baltic insurance markets' consolidation been more complete than in Estonia, the smallest of the Baltic trio with fewer than 1.5 million inhabitants. From a peak of 17 non-life insurers in 1996, only six remain (seven if one includes the mutual Estonian Traffic Insurance Foundation, the motor guarantee fund) after the withdrawal of Zurich Financial Services, the smallest player in the market, as part of its overall withdrawal from Central Europe.

Estonian non-life insurers: ownership, and parent's country

Company	Owner	Country of owner
AS If Eesti Kindlustus	IF P&C Insurance Co Ltd.	Sweden
Ergo Kindlustus AS	Ergo International AG	Germany
Seesam Rahvusvaheline Kindlustus AS	Pohjola Group plc (50.5%, AIG Inc (49.5%)	Finland, USA
Salva Kindlustus AS	UB Aprodišinâšana, individuals	Latvia, Estonia
Nordea Kindlustuse Eesti AS	Tryg i Danmark	Denmark
AS Inges Kindlustus	Ingosstrakh	Russia
Zurich Kindlustus Eesti AS (in run-off)	Zurich Financial Services	Switzerland

Source: Finantsinspektsioon data

Five of the six remaining Estonian insurers are completely foreign-owned following the sale of privately owned Nordika Kindlustus AS to Tryg Baltica in October 2001. Only Salva is partially owned by Estonian citizens, although Latvians own a considerable share in a rare example of successful cross-border insurance company ownership within the Baltics. Increased foreign ownership has seen premium flow outside of the country through parent-company group reinsurance buying programs. However, it has also seen retentions increase, as local companies' capitalization is strengthened. Both have the effect of reducing open-market cessions.

If Eesti provides an example of both. If is the successor of the former monopoly Eesti Kindlustus, and through a merger in 2000 of Sampo Estonia and Sampo's own local acquisition, Polaris. The combined entity retained 91.5% of the companies' combined premium in 2002, compared to 81.9% in 1998, on a *pro forma* basis. However, in 1998 the dominant direct predecessor, Eesti Kindlustus group, retained 90.8%. Eesti's cession level, acquisitions notwithstanding, has changed little, but that of Sampo and Polaris has increased, as the former entities are now part of a well-capitalized group with a greater local risk appetite.

Eesti's retention may have changed only a little, but the direction of its cessions has changed completely. It reveals that in 2002 it had reinsurance contracts with sister companies in the If Skadeförsäkring Holding AB Group – If Eesti's parent company – under which, that year, it had accrued or paid premiums of EEK 44.6 million and to which it had payable premiums of an additional EEK 26,538. The accrued, paid and payable cessions obviously reflect more than 2002's outward business alone, since for the year If Eesti reported total cessions of EEK 51.7 million. The figures indicate that companies in the If Group are the If Eesti's subsidiary's dominant or sole reinsurer.

Estonian non-life insurance cessions, 1997 – 2001, EEK 000

	Gross premiums	Cession	Net premiums	Cession rate
1997	926,024	241,496	684,528	26.08%
1998	1,030,320	245,025	785,295	23.78%
1999	1,126,263	353,800	772,463	31.41%
2000	1,289,686	387,741	901,945	30.06%
2001	1,427,197	472,904	954,293	33.14%

Source: Compiled by the author from published sources (See selected Bibliography)

The increase in cessions driven by the rise in foreign ownership is visible over time across the Estonian insurance market. Total retention of the seven active Estonian non-life companies in 2002 was 64.9%, compared to 76.2% in 1998. Part of the explanation for the overall increase in cessions lies in the maturation of the market, causing the smaller companies to grow, fed in part by proportional treaty capacity from continental reinsurers and parent companies. While the larger groups' retentions have remained relatively high and stable, and their reinsurance strategies have not changed dramatically, the smaller players have decreased their risk appetite as their premium income has grown. However, all but one of the seven companies active in Estonia in 2000 and 2001 increased its cessions in 2001.

Numerous changes in ownership in the intervening years make direct comparisons difficult, but some of the drivers of changing retentions can be identified. Ergo was formed from former local insurers BICO and Leks, which together retained 68.3% of their premium income in 1998, compared to 69.3% for Ergo in 2002. Those with falling retentions, however, had a greater impact, and Seesam had the largest. It retained 70.3% in 1998, but since has grown dramatically through several portfolio acquisitions. In 2002, it retained only 29.18%, providing the largest aggregate block of open-market cessions in the Estonian market. As the company retains its independence and thus limits its cessions to majority owner Pohjola, in 2003 it concluded reinsurance agreements with Pohjola, Swiss Re, GeneralCologne Re and Munich Re.

Estonian insurers' premiums cession rates, 2001– 02

Company	2000	2001	change
If Eesti	18%	10%	-44%
Ergo	29%	30%	+3%
Seesam	63%	67%	+6%
Salva	59%	61%	+3%
Nordea	12%	15%	+25%
Inges	48%	59%	+23%
Zurich *	73%	89%	+22%
Total	**31%**	**34%**	**+10%**

* now in run-off
Source: Compiled by the author from published sources (See selected Bibliography)

Estonian insurers' premiums and cessions, 2002, EEK 000

Company	Gross premium	Ceded premium	Retention
If Eesti	610,820	51,684	91.54%
Ergo	433,884	133,140	69.31%
Seesam	280,932	198,967	29.18%
Salva	161,175	110,288	31.57%
Nordea	87,192	7,789	91.07%
Inges	74,216	45,649	38.49%
Zurich *	48,738	47,631	2.27%
Total	**1,696,957**	**595,148**	**64.93%**

* now in run-off
Source: Compiled by the author from published sources (See selected Bibliography)

Salva's retention rate was 40.4% in 1998, but fell to 31.6% in 2002, providing the second largest portion of Estonian ceded premiums to the open market. Zurich, now in run-off following the strategic withdrawal of its parent company from non-life operations in Central and Eastern Europe, saw its retention fall from 20.1% in 1998 to 2.27% in 2002, its final full year of operations, as it ceded even more premium to its cash-hungry parent.

III. Consolidation and foreign ownership – Lithuania

The Lithuanian market remains the most fragmented and underdeveloped of the three Baltic countries, although the introduction of motor third-party liability insurance in 2002 has spurred growth, as well as influencing reinsurance practice. Meanwhile, consolidation has changed the structure of the market, as weaker players have fallen away. Some 20 companies were actively writing non-life insurance in July 2003, with eight bankrupts in liquidation. This compares to 30 active non-life companies during 1998.

According to data from the State Insurance Supervisory Authority, Lithuania's non-life reinsurers ceded LTL 127.8 million of premiums in 2001, or 33.2% of written premium. In 2000, insurers ceded LTL 105.3 million, or 29.2% of premium, but cession rates were nearly 40% in 1998. However, approximately 50% of motor business was ceded in 2001. The increase in the overall cession rate marked the reversal of a steady decline in cessions. It was brought on in part by the pending introduction of compulsory third-party liability insurance for motor vehicles, which was made mandatory from April 2002. Sales began in January that year. However, generalizations about the level of cessions in Lithuania are fraught. Between 2002 and 2001, nine insurers significantly increased their retention (by more than 5% of premium income), while eight increased their cessions by 5% of premium income or more.

Lithuanian non-life cession rates

Year	Total written premium, LTL m	Cession rate
2001	385.1	33.2%
2000	360.8	29.2%
1999	365.3	34.6%
1998	380.8	39.7%

Source: Compiled by the author from published sources (See selected Bibliography)

Reinsurers' share of all claims paid in Lithuania in 2001 was LTL 44.7 million, or 30.4% of paid claims (but 98.3% of marine liability insurance claims). Of total cessions in 2001, German reinsurers accepted 37.9%; UK reinsurers, 24.4%; and Swiss reinsurers, 15.0%. According to the insurance supervisor, in 2001 the principle reinsurers of Lithuanian companies were Munich Re, Swiss Re, GeneralCologne Re, Lloyd's of London, and Gerling Global Re (which ceased underwriting in 2002).

Largest Lithuanian non-life insurers' ownership, country of ownership

Company	Owner	Country of owner
Lietuvos draudimas AB	Royal & SunAlliance Group, EBRD/IFCEE	UK
Ergo Lietuva UAB	Ergo International AG	Germany
Lindra UAB	Powszechny Zaklad Ubezpieczen SA	Poland
If draudimas UAB	If P&C Insurance Co Ltd.	Sweden
Baltijos garantas UAB / Baltik garant	Privately held ... Ingosstrakh	Russia
Baltikums Draudimas UAB	Baltikums Apdrošinašanas Grupa	Latvia
Nord L/B draudimas UAB	Norddeutsche Landesbank Girozentrale (Nord LB)	Germany

Source: Compiled by the author from published sources (See selected Bibliography)

Seven companies that wrote 85% of Lithuanian non-life insurance premium in 2002, or LTL 511 million, are controlled or owned outright by foreign insurers. Impacts on cessions similar to those experienced in the markets to the north can be expected to result from foreign involvement in Lithuania: as local ownership falls, cessions to foreign parents will increase, decreasing the need for open-market reinsurance.

Scandinavian and German insurers dominate ownership of the Lithuanian insurance market, primarily the same players as in Estonia and Latvia, and thus the same mix of outward reinsurance strategies are common. The largest company, Lietuvos Draudimas (the former Gosstrakh), is owned by Codan A/S of Denmark, itself a subsidiary of Royal & SunAlliance Group of the UK.

As with its sister company in Latvia, Lietuvos Draudimas has not yet rationalized its reinsurance purchasing through the parent group. For 2002, Lietuvos Draudimas concluded reinsurance contracts with Swiss Re, GeneralCologne Re, ERC Frankona Re, Hannover Re, PartnerRe, SCOR, Sorema, Royal & SunAlliance, Gerling Global Re and Cigna Re Europe, using the broking services of Marsh, Aon and Willis. According to its annual reports, less than 10% of its total cessions are ceded to Royal & SunAlliance and Hermes Kreditversicherungs, its joint-venture partner in credit insurance subsidiary Lietuvos Draudimo Kreditų Draudimas. A rationalization of reinsurance buying by Lietuvos Draudimas is anticipated.

Lietuvos Draudimas: cessions to group companies, LTL 000

	2000	2001	2002
Total cessions	4,928	42,147	29,769
Cessions to Codan companies	314	439	432
Cessions to Hermes	0	2,210	1,877
Share of cessions to affiliates	6.37%	6.29%	7.76%

Source: Lietuvos Draudimas

The impact of foreign ownership is clear even with smaller companies, although the effect may be different. In late 1999, Latvia's Baltikums Apdrošinašanas Grupa (40% owned by privately held Riga Re) acquired the Latvian insurer Eurogarantas, which was then ranked 12th in the local market. Its cession rate nearly tripled in 2000, from about 11% to more than 33%, and by 2002 had risen to 55.5%.

Baltikums Draudimas premiums and cession, LTL 000

	1996	1997	1998	1999	2000	2001	2002
Written premiums	1,807	3,475	6,362	7,277	9,152	7,768	27,279
Cessions	0	180	937	827	3,075	2,252	15,127
Cession rate	0.00%	5.18%	14.73%	11.36%	33.60%	28.99%	55.45%

Source: Baltikums

IV. Recommendations

The total population and insurance premium spending of each of the Baltic States, and of the entire region, is relatively small compared to the large losses that could result from a major industrial fire, aviation loss, natural catastrophe or other large loss event. Thus, it is essential that Baltic insurers spread the risk they assume beyond the borders of their home countries and the region. Cessions to the international market allow the increased spread of risk, either through group risk-sharing programs, which share risk within a pan-European or international insurance group, or through open-market reinsurance cessions to international reinsurers with a diverse risk base and the ability to withstand larger losses. The cost of such cessions is the outflow of insurance premium, but the benefit is greater security for the ultimate policyholders and increased insurance market stability.

Although for international insurance groups, the advantages of centralized investment and group reinsurance buying hold strong appeal, some policy actions could encourage the retention of premiums by insurers. One is to ensure that the investment restrictions placed on local insurers are manageable and afford access to a wide range of possible investment strategies (while ensuring, of course, that policyholders' funds are not unnecessarily imperilled). A reporting regime that requires the disclosure of cessions to related companies would assist insurance supervisors in developing a true picture of internal and external cessions, without creating an onerous additional reporting requirement. Finally, where open-market cessions represent a significant portion of an insurer's outward reinsurance strategy, ensuring a diversified program that employs multiple reinsurers of reorganized minimum financial strength will help to ensure that insurers do not face an overwhelming counter-party credit risk, which can arise from the failure of an individual reinsurer, as the Parex example in chapter 2 illustrates.

CHAPTER 2

LOCAL INWARD REINSURANCE

Most insurance markets at some point in their development include a local reinsurance component, just as most governments at some point consider ways to prevent premium from leaving local markets through reinsurance arrangements with foreign reinsurers. Reinsurance premium often appears to insurers to be an excellent source of income, with relatively little in the way of associated expenses. For example, a negotiable and clear-cut ceding commission under a proportional motor treaty can be paid to an insurer instead of the potentially volatile cost of maintaining an agent network, conducting advertising campaigns, and absorbing the other costs associated with acquisition of personal-line insurance policies. Likewise, with facultative acceptances or co-insurance, fellow insurers or intermediaries usually take on much of the client-facing role.

However, many insurers around the world have come to realize the single great disadvantage of dabbling in reinsurance: underwriting decision-making is delegated to a third party which may or may not deploy reinsurers' capital as the reinsurer would see fit. In addition, the payment of reinsurance claims usually lags significantly behind the payment of direct claims, distorting the true picture of the reinsurers' liabilities. The cost of sufficient technical analysis of policies may make assuming many risks uneconomic in view of the premium available, and claims can be very, very large.

Nonetheless, the Baltic countries have seen the rapid development of local reinsurance markets, followed by their equally rapid contraction. Part of the explanation for this cycle is that in many cases local reinsurance acceptance has been related to money laundering activities (particularly the avoidance of payroll taxes), to questionable solvency enhancement schemes designed to artificially reduce liabilities, and to outright fraud.

For example, Latvia's longstanding connections to Russia mean that many Latvian insurers had accepted reinsurance premiums from the east. In 1998, non-domestic reinsurance contributed 3% of total Latvian premium and 7% of claims. However, in many of these transactions no underlying risk existed. In other cases, companies have used affiliated offshore companies to reinsure property that presents no real risk, sometimes paying premiums equal to the value of the insured property. Fortunately, both practices are on the decrease, as Baltic financial services supervisors become more experienced, and as foreign investors reduce local companies' participation in such schemes.

Speaking at the Annual Marcus Evans Conference on Insurance in the CEE and Russia in 2002, Gvido Romeiko, head of licensing at the Latvian Financial and Capital Markets Commission, said the signals that reveal the existence of such transactions are excessively high tariffs, unjustified levels of sums insured, the insurance of non-typical risks (such as the notorious insurance of a local reservoir against fire risk), the involvement of unknown brokers, and "mystical or unclear reinsurance operations", which often involve reinsurance in countries where "supervision is conducted oddly, not at all, or only internally".

Supervisors in the Baltic countries are combating the practice through various measures involving greater scrutiny of regulated companies' reinsurance arrangements and counter-parties. "It is not likely that non-classical insurance can be eliminated, but states can combat it," Mr Romeiko said, adding that "irreversible changes [in tax laws, for example] have decreased demand for non-classical insurance." Certainly, any reduction in these practices should be welcomed by mainstream foreign reinsurers, who may not wish to participate in such transactions.

I. Local inward reinsurance – Lithuania

In its review of 2001, the Lithuanian Insurance Supervisory Authority states: "A small amount of reinsurance was transacted in Lithuania amounting to LTL 2.6 million. The rest was carried forward to other countries." The retained reinsurance premium represents less than 1% of total non-life market premium in 2001. However, Lithuanian insurers accepted a significant volume of inward reinsurance premium, and retroceded all but this fraction. Local reinsurance acceptances were LTL 35.2 million in 2001, or 9.14% of total non-life market premium, but 92% of the premium was retroceded.

Lithuanian insurers' accepted reinsurance premium, LTL

Year	direct insurance	accepted reinsurance	total	reinsurance share of total
2001	349 896 814	35 221 151	385 117 965	9.15%
2000	335 850 950	24 930 920	360 781 870	6.91%
1999	331 588 697	33 698 727	365 287 424	9.23%
1998	329 963 448	50 844 432	380 807 880	13.35%

Source: Lithuanian Insurance Supervisory Authority

However, local cessions appear to be tailing off. For example, Lietuvos Draudimas cut its accepted reinsurance premium volume by almost 75% in 2002, to just LTL 229,000. In many cases, foreign investors have discouraged insurers from accepting reinsurance premiums, preferring them instead to focus on primary underwriting, marketing and distribution.

Motor was the line which saw the highest local cession rate. The supervisor reported in 2000: "The [motor third-party liability] insurance class had the greatest amount of written premiums for accepted reinsurance – LTL 9.2 million (15.9% of all [gross written] motor vehicle liability premiums)." Overall, reinsurers accepted 19.7% of total motor risk, the supervisor reported, which illustrates the high level of local cession of motor liability risk. This local reinsurance boom in motor reversed the shrinkage of the local market and reflects the growing primary market for motor third-party liability (MTPL) cover. It remains the greatest current impact on cession rates for the 11 Lithuania insurers licensed to write compulsory MTPL.

Lietuvos Draudimas: some reinsurance data, LTL 000

	2000	2001	2002
Inward reinsurance premiums	508	901	229
Inward reinsurance claims	137	250	481
Co-insurance premiums	0	14	0
Outward proportional premiums	4,640	38,557	23,419
Outward non-proportional premiums	288	3,590	6,350

Source: Lietuvos Draudimas

Lithuania's introduction of compulsory motor on 1 April 2001 was the last such action in the Baltic region (Kaliningrad notwithstanding), and served to boost total Lithuanian premium spending dramatically. That, in turn, drove increased demand for reinsurance – unfortunately at a time when international reinsurance markets were suffering a demand squeeze. This made small, immature markets such as Lithuania unattractive to many international reinsurers, who could choose to deploy their capital elsewhere, where certainty is greater and superior data collection affords better risk transparency.

Many insurers chose initially not to reinsure the additional exposure to MTPL, due in part to the perceived low risk. Limits were set at LTL 60,000, and premiums ranged from LTL 110 to LTL 1,700 based on a variety of factors, although the base premium was set at LTL 220. Uninsured drivers were to face fines of LTL 300 to LTL 500, although on 28 March 2002 this was reduced by Parliament to just LTL 100. Eleven companies were initially granted permits to offer the new product: Lindra, Lietuvos Draudimas, Ergo Lietuva, Baltic Polis, Lietuvos Zemes Ukio Draudimas, Industrijos Garantas, Baltikums Draudimas, If Draudimas, Baltik Garant, Snoro Garantas, and LTB Draudimas. In the first six months of 2002, MTPL accounted for just over half of all Lithuanian non-life premiums.

On 18 January 2001, Edvinas Vasilis-Vasiliauskas, director of the State Insurance Supervisory Authority, told the news service Insurance in Central & Eastern Europe that "as reinsurance rates rise, Lithuanian cedants were increasingly turning to less well-known and less expensive reinsurers, rather than the big-name companies that previously dominated." However, part of the shift appears to have been intended to reduce insurers' retained liabilities. Co-operative reinsurers in some cases accepted a large share of individual insurers' risk under proportional MTPL treaties, and in return paid large ceding commissions. With low MTPL limits and the long tail of motor injury claims, and considering the pervasiveness of cash-flow underwriting, the practice was an understandable strategy for gaining a foothold in the nascent, competitive MTPL market.

Predictably, claims began to escalate rapidly. By 30 September 2002, premium of LTL 215.3 million had been written in the line. As premium growth began to tail off, claims paid increased rapidly, growing, for example, by 32.5% in September and 26.7% in October, when total claims reached LTL 26.2 million, or 11.58% after less than a year. Claims grew by 21.4% in November, to 13.57% of premium. In December, claims escalated an additional 16.1%, ending the year at more than 15% of premium, before any long-tail claims were paid. In January 2003, the 11 MTPL insurers wrote premium of LIT 14.3 million, compared to claims of LIT 5.7 million, or 39.86%, and the reality of the economics of MTPL began to sink in.

In June 2002, the Supervisor's office introduced new regulations which tightened up Lithuanian insurer's ability to cede premiums to reinsurers, local or foreign, which have not been granted a financial security rating by Standard & Poor's, Moody's or Fitch, or which have a rating below triple-B. The new rules should prevent insurers from ceding business to local or foreign reinsurers for reasons relating primarily to presentational or solvency-compliance issues (although it must be recognized that the legitimate purpose of reinsurance is to enhance solvency through risk transfer).

II. Local inward reinsurance – Estonia

Locally accepted reinsurance premium peaked in Estonia in 1999. That year, insurers underwrote reinsurance premium totalling EEK 74.2 million, equal to 5.22% of total gross Estonian premium. By 2002, the total had fallen by about two-thirds, to EEK 24.3 million, or just 1.10% of total premium income. The rise and fall were sudden, following a rapid escalation in the mid-1990s. The growth in appetite for reinsurance is illustrated by licensing: in 1997, the Licensing Commission of the Ministry of Finance granted seven licenses to existing insurers allowing them to write specific reinsurance products. However, the acceptance of large shares of reinsurance and co-insurance risk by inexperienced underwriters is one of a litany of reasons behind the failure of several Estonian insurers in the late 1990s.

Development of Estonian accepted gross non-life reinsurance premium, 1994 - 2002 (kroons m)

Year	1994	1995	1996	1997	1998	1999	2000	2001	2002
Accepted reinsurance	1	1.666	27.035	31.052	35.079	74.241	64.789	49.145	24.278
Total gross premium	345	550	823	1,085	1,272	1,417	1,659	1,832	2,189
Reinsurance share	0.29%	0.36%	3.28%	2.86%	2.75%	5.22%	3.92%	2.67%	1.10%

Source: Compiled by the author from Finantsinspektsioon data

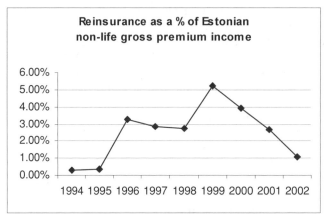

Source: Compiled by the author from Finantsinspektsioon data

The 2001 accounts of Ergo Kindlustus illustrate its rapid retreat from local reinsurance business, following the acquisition by the German insurer of the post-merger Ergo Kindlustus predecessor BICO-Leks Insurance from Alte Leipziger in 2000. BICO-Leks wrote reinsurance premium in 2000 of EEK 143,441, of which it retroceded EEK 7,418. In 2001, as an Ergo subsidiary, the company accepted reinsurance premiums of just EEK 1,679, and retained the entire amount, while releasing EEK 256,477 from its provisions for unearned reinsurance premiums. The 2000 account shows how reinsurance claims were passed on to retrocessionnaires: of EEK 206,315 in claims that year, reinsures met some EEK 153,682.

The experience has been mirrored in other companies. As local ownership among Estonia's insurers continues to decrease, the rate of local reinsurance acceptance is likely to continue its slide. Almost all insurers active in the market today have sufficient backing from their parent companies, should they require it, to allow them to accept almost any risk likely to be presented to them without support from co-insurers or reinsurers.

III. Local inward reinsurance – Latvia

Latvia's reinsurance market was the one most involved in reinsurance arrangements intended to avoid taxes or insure simply to profit the reinsured, and as such the country appeared to have a relatively buoyant local insurance market until recent years. However, such practices are being phased out, due in part to the efforts of the legislature and supervisor. In 1999, more than 10% of Latvian cessions went to other insurance companies in Latvia, but by 2001 the total had fallen to about 6%. Over the same period, cessions to Russian insurers fell from 28.8% of total Latvian cessions to 6.3%.

Destination of Latvian cessions, 1999-2001

Home country of reinsurer	1999	2000	2001
Germany	16.7	16.5	21.5
Great Britain	14.8	27.6	14.5
Ireland	10.5	11.8	13.6
USA	1.1	10.3	10.1
Lithuania	5.3	5.4	10.1
Sweden	1.7	4.0	8.9
Latvia	10.2	5.4	6.3
Russia	28.8	3.9	6.2
Finland	2.2	2.1	3.9
Austria	5.7	5.5	2.2
Switzerland	1.2	1.3	2.2
Others	1.9	6.0	0.6

Source: Latvian Financial and Capital Markets Commission

In the late 1990s, reinsurers began assuming more of the risk from Latvian insurers' accepted reinsurance portfolios. From 0.0% in 1998, the local market retroceded 71.2% of its inward non-life reinsurance risk in 2001. Non-life reinsurance acceptances increased dramatically that year, from LAT 2.6 million in 2000 (2.86% of total non-life premium income), to LAT 4.2 million, or 4.51% of gross premiums in 2001. Acceptances tailed off in 2002, however, falling to LAT 3.7 million, or 3.82% of the non-life market.

Local cession in Latvia is notable because of the presence of Riga Re, self-described as "the first national reinsurance company in the history of the Baltic states." It remains the only locally owned reinsurer in the region, with four years in operation as of June 2003. The business is tiny by international standards, with share capital of USD 4.4 million, supported by guarantees from the Baltikums group, its trans-Baltic parent. However, Riga Re also fronts for international reinsurers or acts as a straight intermediary when the limits required demand it.

Riga Re premium and cessions

	2002	2001	2000	1999 *
Gross written premiums	3,844,453	3,463,452	1,919,661	321,357
Ceded premiums	2,703,324	2,638,364	1,408,554	17,762
Cession rate	70.32%	76.18%	73.38%	5.53%

* seven months. Source: Riga Re

Riga Re's business was initially focused on cessions from related companies in the Baltikums Insurance Group, and in 1999 some 99% of its premium income came from

Latvian cedants, of which 76% was from Group companies. However, Riga Re quickly expanded eastward, opening offices in Kiev and St Petersburg in 2000, and in Moscow in 2001. In that year, only 32% of its accepted reinsurance premium came from Latvia, followed by Russia (21%), Kazakhstan (20%), and Ukraine (19%). The bulk of its business – about two-thirds – is property and cargo.

Riga Re declares that "among our partners and clients are companies whose offers are not substantial enough to be attractive for larger international reinsurance organizations, or [have been] declined because of limitations in respect of origin of business." Riga Re is, of course, a buyer of foreign retrocession, and historically has retained only 25% to 30% of its premium. It now offers property capacity of up to USD 5 million per risk, and in 2002 posted profit of LVL 338,000 on gross premium of LVL 3.84 million. It reported paid and outstanding claims of LVL 476,000 during the year.

IV. Local inward reinsurance – outlook

Global market trends are running contrary to these considerations. According to *Reinsurance: A retreating or resurgent market?,* a report by global reinsurance broker Aon in February 2003:

> *"The most significant trend across all classes of business has been the quest by [reinsurance] buyers for financial security, the so-called 'flight to quality'. This received extra focus [in 2002] with increased movement of security ratings by the various agencies resulting in a number of 'AAA' companies being downgraded, including Munich Re, Swiss Re, GE Frankona, Employers Re and Top Layer Re. Gerling also became a well-known casualty of the market conditions, with a dramatic fall in security rating from 'AA' to 'BBB' over less than a 12-month period."*

The so-called flight to quality has been under way for several years, and has had several impacts. The most marked is the increasing dominance of large reinsurers, and the concurrent withdrawal and exit of many smaller participants in the reinsurance market, notably the reinsurance arms of insurance companies.

The top four global reinsurance groups accounted for 47% of total international non-life reinsurance premium in 2001, according to *Reinsurance Magazine.* The top 20 groups accepted non-life reinsurance premium of $74 billion, probably more than 80% of the total reinsurance premium ceded in the world. Today, insurance companies in developed markets increasingly seek extremely well-capitalized, experienced reinsurance companies that can demonstrate financial strength as well as reinsurance expertise.

Meanwhile, fewer and fewer insurers are also writing reinsurance. Some of the largest recent exits include St Paul and Zurich Financial Services, which spun off their reinsurance subsidiaries into exchange-listed, stand-alone companies (respectively, Platinum Re and Converium). Generali, Aviva (formerly CGNU), Gerling, Winterthur, The Hartford, ARIG and Folksam have completely or almost completely exited the reinsurance market. Axa has closed its reinsurance offices in the United States and

London, Sirius closed Scandinavian Re, and ALM Brand let Copenhagen Re fail. These decisions by insurers to withdraw from reinsurance were largely the product of poor results, and have not only driven reinsurance market concentration even further, but have caused cedants to think carefully about the staying power of their current and potential reinsurance partners.

Legislation around the world is also driving the concentration of cessions into the hands of fewer, larger players. Insurance supervisors' scrutiny of reinsurance transactions has become increasingly comprehensive. For example, in 2000, Finanstilsynet, the Danish financial services supervisor, introduced regulations requiring insurers to register reinsurance programs electronically. Each program is reviewed annually. The strength of reinsurers is assessed against five key criteria: reserving provisions as a percentage of net premium income; gearing ratios; combined ratios; return on equity; and return on investment. The supervisor has the authority to insist that insurers rectify perceived weaknesses in their reinsurance cover. Such practice is becoming widespread, and in 2002 Lithuania's supervisor published a set of criteria for choosing a reinsurer (see Chapter 4, IV).

V. Conditions in the global reinsurance market

Concurrently, reinsurance practice is changing. Following a long cyclical downturn in reinsurance pricing, the global marketplace is experiencing a "hard market" characterized by rising reinsurance prices and narrowed terms and conditions. For many of the young insurance companies in the Baltic States, the current hard market is the first cyclical upturn that they have experienced. Reinsurers are cutting ceding commissions and insisting on greater risk transparency. Some have withdrawn altogether from certain countries and lines of business, after soft-market efforts to build a presence can no longer be justified, and particularly for proportional business, which relies on insurers' original pricing. For example, GeneralCologne Re has exited the Polish market, and Swiss Re has ceased underwriting motor treaties in the Baltic States.

Thomas Holzheu, senior economist for Swiss Re, said in late June that the hard market is likely to persist for the foreseeable future, and can be maintained as long as capacity is constrained and underwriting discipline is maintained. One factor in the sustainability of current market conditions is the collapse in investment return potential: insurers and their reinsurers are no longer able to make up for serious underwriting losses through returns on invested premiums and reserves. Instead, underwriting must yield a profit without relying on investment income.

This, too, has had an effect on Baltic insurers. One aspect of the move by the major reinsurers toward technical underwriting is the increasingly common exclusion of accepted co-insurance and reinsurance risk under Central European insurers' property and casualty insurance treaties. Foreign reinsurance partners are attempting to introduce new disciplines in Baltic markets involving the levels of sums insured in relation to premium and probable maximum losses, and the division of co-insurance shares among local insurers. This introduction of discipline will translate, in many cases, into a refusal to accept certain risks under established treaties.

Complicating the situation for local insurers wishing to underwrite large risks is the increasing unwillingness of many foreign reinsurers to underwrite facultative reinsurance in areas where the number of treaties and the amount of premium is small. As reinsurers move into a period of increased technical discipline, such facultative undertakings often prove financially unacceptable, as the costs of both administration and claims can outweigh the premium. Some foreign reinsurers will continue to underwrite facultative risks as part of the service package they provide to major treaty reinsurance clients, though others have explicitly halted the practice, insisting that facultative business, too, must stand on its own as potentially profitable based on the premium and expected loss.

If foreign reinsurers increasingly exclude accepted co-insurance and reinsurance risks, and if they are unwilling to write local facultative risk, where will the risk go? One answer is into local facultative reinsurance markets. It is here where the greatest potential lies for developing reinsurance acceptances in the Baltic countries, although discipline and the support of well-capitalized parent companies or shareholders, or the co-operation of a strong and interested foreign reinsurer or group of reinsures, will be essential.

VI. Recommendations

Risk-sharing between local insurers can reduce premium outflow and boost insurers' profitability when losses do not occur, but as reinsurers retreat from co-insurance risk the danger increases of crippling retained losses assumed through co-insurance. Measured risk-taking through pooled capacity is a relatively safe and efficient way of retaining local premium, but when underwriting controls are weak, and in the absence of robust reinsurance support, such risk-sharing can occasionally lead to catastrophic losses. It is essential that the foundation of such risk-sharing is skilled underwriting, and that insurers are confident that assumed co-insurance risk is either protected by reinsurance, or sufficiently limited so as not to imperil solvency. Since probable maximum loss figures related to specific large risks are often badly underestimated, the underwriting and the limits of risk assumption are linked. The development of forma risk-sharing pools is one solution. Two examples of such pools are outlined in Chapter 5. As described in Chapter 1, I, numerous education-based programs can help with the challenge.

An equally important strategy is to ensure that insurers implement effective, resilient actuarial analysis of liabilities arising from co-insurance and reinsurance contracts, including incurred but not reported liabilities, and that they reserve for these liabilities appropriately (as indeed should be the case for insurance liabilities). However, this is easier said than done: the recent collapse of Independent Insurance, a leading UK liability insurer, was largely due to its under-reserving strategies. UK regulators and insurer-appointed actuaries failed to spot consistent under-reserving.

A number of strategies can be adopted to deal with the problem of illegitimate reinsurance, often described as "non-traditional" or "non-classical" reinsurance. Critically, the approach should be to control demand, rather than supply. Restrictions on cessions such as those introduced by Lithuania (see Chapter 4, IV) in response to increasing non-classical reinsurance purchasing are an effective strategy. Likewise, programs of outward reinsurance assessment such as that introduced by Finanstilsynet, the Danish financial services supervisor (see Chapter 3, IV above) allow the effective monitoring of reinsurance purchasing practices. Central to the analysis of reinsurance buying should be the assessment of risk transfer: reinsurance purchases that do not transfer significant amounts of risk from the balance sheet of the insurer to that of the reinsurer must have some other purpose. When no risk transfer is evident, the search for the true purpose of a reinsurance contract must begin.

CHAPTER 3

LEGISLATIVE DEVELOPMENTS

Regulation of reinsurers varies dramatically around the world. In most countries, however, reinsurers are not required to meet any regulatory requirements that differ from those of insurance companies, based on the assumption that reinsurance is a business transacted between informed, sophisticated professionals, and thus reinsurance buyers do not need the regulatory protection provided to consumers. In most cases, such countries require only the licensing of entities that wish to transact reinsurance business. Such is the case in the Baltic countries: to operate as a reinsurer, companies need only apply for a license to underwrite reinsurance, in the same way that they might apply to underwrite motor damage or life insurance. When reinsurance is regulated, more often the regulation is imposed on insurers, limiting the types or sources of reinsurance they are permitted to count toward their solvency calculations, as is the case, for example, in Lithuania (see Chapter 4 IV).

"It is worth noticing," states the European Commission Fast-track Reinsurance Supervision *Project's* 18 June 2003 paper *Overview and issues for consideration by the Insurance Committee,* "that all major jurisdictions which supervise reinsurance do so on the basis of the rules for direct insurance." In some other countries, regulations set specific guidelines for the operation and solvency of reinsurance entities. However, in the case of European Union member countries, the question of supervision of reinsurance entities is soon to be narrowed through the introduction of a reinsurance directive.

I.   International Accounting Standards

Policy decisions covering the accounting techniques employed by insurers in the European Union are soon to be overtaken by the implementation of International Accounting Standards, which the European Union requires member states to implement. Standards for insurance companies are under development, and are the subject of severe controversy and conflicts between insurers and the London-based International Accounting Standards Board (IASB). They are due to be introduced and mandatory for insurers in EU member states on or after 1 January 2005. They will have very serious implications for the reporting of insurance companies' liabilities, including a requirement for the reporting of gross liabilities without consideration of reinsurance recoveries.

The current draft of the IASB's accounting standards for insurers includes provisions that would apply to all insurance contracts, including reinsurance contracts, issued and held, and would eliminate catastrophe and equalization provisions, require a loss recognition test, and require an insurer to keep insurance liabilities in its balance sheet until they are discharged, cancelled or expired. *In addition, insurers would be required to present insurance liabilities without offsetting them against related reinsurance assets.*

Under the new regime, an insurer could not adopt a new accounting policy that involves any of the following, although it may continue using existing accounting policies that involve them:

1. Measuring insurance liabilities on an undiscounted basis.

2. Measuring insurance liabilities with excessive prudence.

3. Reflecting future investment margins in the measurement of insurance liabilities.

4. Using measurements that implicitly measure contractual rights to future investment management fees at an amount that exceeds their fair value as implied by a comparison with current fees charged by other market participants for similar services.

5. Using non-uniform accounting policies for the insurance liabilities (and related deferred acquisition costs, if any) of subsidiaries.

The proposals would also:

1. Exempt an insurer from accounting for an embedded derivative separately at fair value if the embedded derivative meets the definition of an insurance contract.

2. Require an insurer to un-bundle (that is, account separately for) deposit components of some insurance contracts, to avoid the omission of assets and liabilities from its balance sheet.

3. Limit reporting anomalies when an insurer buys reinsurance.

4. Permit an expanded presentation for insurance contracts acquired in a business combination or portfolio transfer.

5. Address limited aspects of discretionary participation features contained in insurance contracts or financial instruments.

The proposals would require disclosure of:

1. The amounts in the insurer's financial statements that arise from insurance contracts.

2. The estimated amount, timing and uncertainty of future cash flows from insurance contracts.

3. The fair value of the insurer's insurance liabilities and insurance assets.

II. The EU reinsurance directive

The existing European Reinsurance and Retrocession Directive dates to 1964, and goes no further than to establish the right of reinsurance companies from one EU member state to establish them in another. However, the Reinsurance Directive is widely misunderstood. While it allows reinsurers within the EU the freedom of establishment and freedom to provide services, it does so in the 1960s' sense: it abolishes restrictions on freedom of establishment *based on nationality*, with "companies and firms to be treated in the same way as natural persons who are nationals of Member States ... whereas no company or firm may be required ... to fulfil any additional condition [or] be required to obtain any special authorization not required of a domestic company or firm." Today, freedom of establishment means much more, including the right to operate in other member states under home-state supervision and local control, without licensing in the host state, and with freedom to establish branches on the basis of the "Single Passport" for insurance entities.

The cumulative effect of the Reinsurance Directive, European Single Market law, and the Third Life and Non-life Insurance Directives has been that it is now possible for reinsurers to trade across EU frontiers without needing to apply for a license outside their home state. However, reinsurance is not directly affected by the Third Directives because, while reinsurance companies in the UK and some other countries such as Sweden are licensed under the same rules as insurers, they are not licensed at all in some European countries, and are only indirectly regulated through their cedants. Nor are they covered by the EU's First, Second and Third Insurance Framework Directives. Thus, at present no harmonized framework for reinsurance supervision exists in the European Union.

In 2000, member states and the European Commission agreed to start a project to assess the possibility of establishing a harmonized framework for reinsurance supervision in the EU. Active work is under way, on a fast-track basis, to develop a new European reinsurance directive that would address the current lack of uniform supervision of reinsurers. The project had aimed at presenting a European Commission proposal on a reinsurance directive by late in 2003, following an Insurance Committee Reinsurance Subcommittee meeting on 9 September 2003, although Parliamentary elections have delayed the presentation. However, speaking at a Comité Européen des Assurances event in Brussels in late November 2003, Alexander Schaub, Director General of the European Commission's Internal Market Directorate, indicated that progress on the directive is a high on the agenda. "We aim to propose a directive for supervision of reinsurance early next year... [It] will involve a delicate balance between sufficient solvency to ensure a secure and robust system, without overburdening [reinsurers] with excessive capital requirements," he said.

European parliamentarians should soon be considering the full, formal draft proposal of Europe's reinsurance directives, which would harmonize the supervision and regulation of reinsurers in all EU member states. The proposed regulations would introduce to all member states a supervisory regime similar to the one that exists in the UK, based on the national supervision of primary insurance companies. (This is the approach adopted by the Reinsurance Subcommittee of the International Association of

Insurance Supervisors, which is also developing a schedule of minimum requirements for the supervision of reinsures.) The directive would disallow the offsetting of reinsurance liabilities with pledged assets. At the time of writing, various member states were discussing the level of the solvency margin that reinsurers should be required to maintain. Current proposals by the Commission call for higher solvency margins for reinsurers than those required of primary insurers, but insurers and reinsurers (including the Comité Européen des Assurances and the International Underwriting Association of London) have argued that the margin should be set at the same level as for direct insurance companies. In either case, the directive should ensure that capitalization of all reinsurers reaches a specified minimum.

As the European Commission addresses reinsurance supervision, it continues its work on so-called Solvency 2 proposals to update statutory insurance company solvency margins. Thus, it is intended that the initial solvency provisions of a reinsurance directive would be updated following the introduction of new solvency rules for insurers, since reinsurance company regulation will be based on insurance company regulation. The European Commission Fast-track Reinsurance Supervision project's 18 June 2003 paper *Overview and issues for consideration by the Insurance Committee* sets out the basics of the current proposals as follows:

Element of a fast-track regime -- Commission Services' proposals

License or passport solution	License
Scope of authorization	It shall permit a reinsurance undertaking to carry out life, non-life or both kinds of reinsurance. Licensing should not be based on further specified insurance classes.
Scope of regime	Pure reinsurers and reinsurance captives. The application also to direct insurers accepting inwards reinsurance is to be considered.
Treatment of technical provisions	Current rules in the direct insurance directives should be used.
Equalization provisions/reserves	Equalization provisions/reserves would be required for credit reinsurance, but there would be an option for member states to require them also in other reinsurance lines. The issue whether such provisions/reserves amounts could be counted against the solvency margin is to be considered.
Use of actuarial methods	Encouraged, but no formal legal requirement.
Solvency margin, minimum guarantee fund	Is to be considered.
Investment rules	A "prudent person" approach should be used.
Asset cover rules	The technical provisions – not the full solvency margin – should be covered by quality assets.
Accounting, financial reporting and statistics	The current requirements in the direct directives should apply also to reinsurance undertakings.
Reinsurance/retrocession reduction factor	Is to be considered.
Powers of intervention for supervisors	In principle the same as for direct insurance undertakings, including the Solvency I amendments.
Withdrawal of license	To the extent possible the same procedural arrangements as for revoking a direct insurance license should be used.
Use of internal models	Should not be allowed in a fast-track reinsurance regime.

Source: EC Fast Track Reinsurance Supervision Project MARKT/2513/03

The European Commission's Insurance Committee is to consider certain detailed points of the proposals. In June 2003, Commission Services presented alternatives for discussion.

III. Recommendations

Clearly, European Union regulation governing the supervision of reinsurers is relatively close, as are new requirements for insurance accounting. The former will allow the simple introduction of qualitative standards for acceptable reinsurance partners: supervisors will be able to limit cessions to countries that meet EU or equivalent solvency and supervision standards. Quick passage through the European Parliament could see a reinsurance directive in force before the end of 2004, although European Parliament elections could slow the process. Policymakers in Estonia, Latvia and Lithuania should follow the development of the directive and set their regulatory agenda accordingly. New accounting standards for insurance are also on the near horizon. They will require all insurers in the European Union to increase significantly their fiscal transparency, and will allow supervisors to make like-for-like comparisons between insurers and reinsurers throughout the European Union. Early adoption of the IASB's insurance accounting standards is encouraged by the board. However, at present it is far from certain that the current proposals will be adopted without significant amendments.

IV. Lithuania

On 20 March 2002 the Lithuanian government published additional amendments and supplements to Chapter 2 of the *Insurance Law 1996*. The chapter was amended substantially, and renamed *Insurance Contract, Reinsurance and Co-insurance* from simply *Insurance Contract*. Significant changes were introduced, primarily to allow the establishment of foreign insurers from WTO member countries, following the accession of Lithuania to the WTO.

Under the 1996 law, all licensed insurers were permitted to accept reinsurance in their licensed classes, and all were broadly permitted to cede an undefined portion of their assumed risk to foreign insurers or reinsurers considered and listed as "financially credible" by the Insurance Supervisory Authority. Such credibility was outlined by a 26 May 1998 resolution of the Supervisory Authority titled *On Financially Credible Foreign Insurance and Reinsurance Companies*, which stated that credibility would be determined by the ratings assigned by international agencies.

The 2002 amendments continued to grant insurers the right to act as reinsurers, but introduced several changes regarding outward reinsurance cessions. Explicit permission was granted for Lithuanian branches of foreign companies to cede risk to their foreign parents, provided the parent company is located in a WTO member country, and is a locally licensed reinsurer. Lithuanian insurers were further permitted by the amendments to reinsure an unspecified portion of accepted risks to local or foreign insurance or reinsurance companies. The supervisor's list of financially credible re/insurers was abandoned by the amendment; in its place the Board of the Insurance

Supervisor was granted broad authority to set criteria for insurers to follow when selecting reinsurance partners.

The Board acted quickly to set such rules, and published on 18 June 2002 its Resolution No. 113, *Criteria for Choosing a Reinsurer*, which took effect on 1 January 2003. The criteria are set out in full in Appendix 1. In summary, they introduced requirements intended to ensure that all insurers entrust their outward reinsurance to a diverse panel of reinsurance providers. The criteria do so by limiting strictly the proportion of gross premium individual insurers are permitted to cede to individual reinsurers.

Under the criteria, any reinsurer rated at least BBB by Standard & Poor's or Baa2 by Moody's is permitted to accept cessions of up to 30% of an insurers' gross premium income. Reinsurers based in countries with a sovereign debt rating that is at least as good as that of Lithuania, and that are supervised by that country's regulator, are permitted to accept cessions of up to 20% of an insurer's gross premium income, and 40% of an insurance group's total premiums. No more than half of this second-category limit may be allocated to a single reinsurer. Reinsurers which fail to meet the standards of either category will be permitted to accept cessions of up to 5% of an insurer's gross premium income (10% for insurance groups), with no single third-category reinsurer exceeding a limit of 3% (5% for a group).

The March 2002 amendments to the Insurance Law 1996 also introduced legislation surrounding the previously unregulated but commonplace practice of co-insurance, whereby insurers share large local risks proportionally. However, the law does not refer specifically to the cession of risk assumed through co-insurance.

CHAPTER 4

MODELS FOR RETENTION

Many countries and insurance economies have adopted programs intended to increase insurance premium retentions and maximize the efficiency of insurance buying. These range from mandatory cession programs in countries including China and India, where a specified share of gross premiums has been payable under statute to a monopoly state-owned reinsurer, to systems under which insurance market bodies have developed mutual, insurer-owned reinsurers to provide reinsurance to owner companies. Such models can have many benefits, provided they are well-considered, although many have failed. Formal risk pools are more common, and provide an alternative to informal co-insurance and risk sharing. They also offer advantages, and can be formed by insurers with or without the assistance or backing of the state. Two recent examples follow.

I.   Czech Aviation Pool

In June 2003 a group of Czech insurers, including *Ceská pojistovna as, Kooperativa as, CSOB pojistovna as,* and *Pojistovna Ceske sporitelny as,* which together hold a commanding share of the Czech insurance market, formed a pool to insure aviation risks. The companies will each retain a share of the aviation risks the pool underwrites, and collectively purchase reinsurance on the open market at a more attractive price than would be available if each company were to buy an aviation reinsurance program for its own, obviously much smaller aviation portfolio. Such pools have several advantages. They allow local insurers between them to retain a greater portion of premium and risk. A single large loss is unlikely to deal a crippling blow to a single insurer. Because the number of risks is limited and the exposure is very specific, the insurers should be able to purchase reinsurance which ensures that exposures are capped at a level affordable for the insurers involved, retaining the maximum amount of premium and risk in the Czech Republic. Many such pools have been extremely successful.

As appealing as aviation and other underwriting pools appear, they can be fraught with pitfalls. One of the major reinsurance failures in recent years involved the collapse of Fortress Reinsurance, an aviation reinsurance pool financed by blue-chip Japanese insurance companies. The key shortcoming in the case of Fortress (and in many other failed pools such as Unicover Workers' Compensation Pool) was poor underwriting control. If pool managers – using the risk capital provided by others – fail to assess risk adequately and price insurance policies accordingly, the result can be catastrophic losses for the insurers involved. In the case of Fortress Re, its insolvency forced Taisei Fire & Marine Insurance Company Ltd., a major Japanese insurer, to cease operations. However, provided sufficient controls are in place and pool retentions are not too onerous for individual members, pools can attract expert underwriting talent and the attention of reinsurers, which bring further underwriting and risk assessment expertise. Both can lead to a robust, successful and potentially profitable insurance vehicle that maximizes local retention without jeopardizing participating insurers' solvency.

II. Mutual Taiwanese fire and catastrophe protections

Following the catastrophic Chi Chi earthquake in the autumn of 1999, Taiwan and its insurers recognized the extent to which the rapidly industrializing island republic and its insurers were exposed to catastrophic loss. More recently, that awareness has led to the formation of a mutual insurance pool to cover industrial fire risks, and the development and placement of a catastrophe bond to cover earthquake exposures, supporting a state-backed earthquake insurance pool.

The intention of the new fire pool is to reduce reinsurance costs and prevent competitive pricing, which can lead to underpricing of risks and thus damaging loss ratios if a major property loss event occurs. The plan is led by the former state-controlled Central Re Corporation, Taiwan's recently privatized local reinsurer (itself an example of the successful transition of a state-owned reinsurance entity into a viable open-market reinsurer), and is supported by local insurers through an industry association. The scheme remains in the planning stage, but has the potential to improve local retention and distribute risk within (rather than outside of) the Taiwanese market. However, the same risks apply as those mentioned above. It is essential that such retention projects receive explicit reinsurance protection, and that each participating insurer is sufficiently reinsured for the specific exposures assumed through the pool to prevent insolvency in the case of catastrophic loss. Underwriting authority must be granted judiciously to capable and qualified underwriters and centralized rather than simply extended to all relevant underwriters in participating companies. Widespread distribution of underwriting authority inevitably leads to the degradation of pool risks, and ultimately to unacceptable losses.

III. Recommendations

When assessing co-insurance, pooling and other premium retention projects, and the associated exposures that insurers carry through them, it is critical to remember that large losses do occur. For example, on 22 November 2002, a large fire took place at the Spolchemie chemical plant in Usti nad Labem, Bohemia, Czech Republic. The claim cost about USD 75 million, thought to be the largest Czech fire loss in history. It was insured through the local co-insurance market by the insurers Ceska Pojistovna, Kooperativa and IPB. However, as much as 90% of the loss is expected to fall to international reinsurers. The loss came as reinsurers began vociferous calls for the elimination of co-insurance risk in reinsurance treaties. As stated in the introduction, Munich Re, the world's largest reinsurer, is leading the charge for reduction of co-insurance exposures under conventional fire insurance treaties, and is said to have introduced a clause widely across Central Europe that limits cover for accepted co-insurance: if a reinsured accepts, say, 25% of a risk on a co-insured basis, the reinsurance protects only 25% of the accepted risk. In other words, local insurers are being required to retain a lot more of the risk they swap among themselves. The policy is certain to reduce local co-insurance and facultative reinsurance, and demands that participants in any such co-insurance or pooling arrangements ensure that sufficient valid reinsurance coverage is in place to cover potential catastrophic losses.

SELECTED BIBLIOGRAPHY

Leonard, Adrian: *Insurance in the Baltic States*. Insurance Research & Publishing, London, November 2000.

The Central and Eastern European insurance markets on their way to the EU, Munich Reinsurance Company, Munich, December 2000

Estonian Insurance Yearbook 2001, Estonian Financial Supervision Authority, Tallinn, December 2002

If Eesti Kindlustus Annual Report 2002.

Ingosstrakh Insurance Company Consolidated Financial Statements, 31 December 2001.

Insurance in Lithuania Annual Overview 2001, State Insurance Supervisory Authority Under the Ministry of Finance, Vilnius, October 2002.

Insurance in Lithuania Annual Overview 2000, State Insurance Supervisory Authority Under the Ministry of Finance, Vilnius, October 2001.

Insurers in Estonia, Estonian Financial Supervision Authority, Tallinn, April 2003.

Latvian Insurance Market In Figures 1997-2001, Financial and Capital Market Commission, Riga 2002.

Lietuvos Draudimas Annual Report 2002, Vilnius, March 2003.

Lietuvos Draudimas Annual Report 2001, Vilnius, April 2002.

Norddeutsche Landesbank Annual Report 2002, Hannover, June 2003.

Parex Bank Annual Report 2002, Riga, April 2003.

Salva Kindlustus Financial Report 2002, Tallinn, June 2003.

APPENDIX 1: LITHUANIA'S "CRITERIA FOR CHOOSING A REINSURER"

STATE INSURANCE SUPERVISORY AUTHORITY
UNDER THE MINISTRY OF FINANCE
LITHUANIA

BOARD RESOLUTION NO. 113
ON CRITERIA FOR CHOOSING A REINSURER

18 June 2002

APPROVED by
the Board of the State
Insurance
Supervisory Authority
under
the Ministry of Finance,
Resolution No.113,
18 June 2002

CRITERIA FOR CHOOSING A REINSURER

1. The following criteria for choosing a reinsurer shall be due to each insurance company and branch established in the Republic of Lithuania by an insurance undertaking from the foreign state enjoying the World Trade Organisation's (WTO) membership rights and registered in the Republic of Lithuania (hereinafter – insurer).

2. Insurer may reinsurer an accepted risk or part of that risk in another insurance or reinsurance company, branch established in the Republic of Lithuania by an insurance undertaking from the foreign state that is enjoying the World Trade Organisation's (WTO) membership rights, or (re)insurance company of a foreign state (hereinafter – reinsurer).

3. The accepted risk transfer to reinsurance may be aimed at reduction of insurance risk or solvency margin, more effective use of the capital owned or increasing of possibilities to accept other insurance risks.

4. Insurer is obliged to have the matching cover for his accepted risks at any time.

5. Insurer shall choose a reinsurer according to his reinsurance strategy approved internally not less than once a year (life insurers – once in three years) which would involve all risks assumed. The reinsurance strategy shall involve:

5.1 type and scope of reinsurance programs, amounts of insurance risk remaining within the company;

5.2 criteria for choosing a reinsurer and(or) approved list of reinsurers;

5.3 principals for internal control of the reinsurance program.

6. In choosing a reinsurer, insurer is obliged to respect the security principal and be aware of the reinsurer including the following information:

6.1 exact reinsurer's name, address of his headquarters, also (if) ratings provided by rating agencies through last three years, otherwise, adequate permissions for reinsurance business with regard to the legislation established by the state it belongs as a person;

6.2 reinsurance business scope, including insurance and reinsurance written premiums;

6.3 financial data of reinsurance business of last three years, including Balance sheet and Profit and loss account;

7. Insurer shall choose reinsurer who would meet the following requirements:

7.1 reinsurer shall have the right to carry out reinsurance upon a risk accepted from insurer approved by certain permits as far as it is set out by the legislation established by the state it belongs as a person.

7.2 reinsurer's own capital shall be not less than the minimum authorised capital compulsory to insurance companies registered in Lithuania who engage in certain insurance branch risk insurance;

8. In choosing a reinsurer and transferring insurance risk amounts onto him, insurer is obliged to respect the reinsurer's liability. Conditionally, reinsurers shall be classified:

8.1 reinsurer shall adhere to the first category if he has been granted a financial strength rating not lower than the following:

8.1.1 BBB by Standard & Poor's;

8.1.2 BBB by Fitch IBCA;

8.1.3 Baa by Moody's.

8.2 reinsurer who does not adhere to the first category, shall adhere to the second, if he belongs as a person to the state which, according to a rating of a long-term investment in a foreign currency by any of the agencies identified in paragraph 8.1 is not lower than the Republic of Lithuania, and the reinsurer is directly supervised by insurance or similar supervisory institution of that state;

8.3 reinsurer who does not comply with the provisions of the two categories, shall belong to the third category.

9. In setting reinsurer's compliance with the provisions set out in paragraph 8, only new ratings (provided not earlier than through last three years) shall be regarded.

10. In choosing a reinsurer and amounts of insurance risks transferred to him, insurer is obliged to regard the following criteria (reinsurer's share in insurance premiums shall mean the amount of insurance and reinsurance premiums written by insurer through a financial year which belongs to reinsurer):

10.1 the premiums share of one reinsurer of the first category shall comprise not more than: 30%;

10.2 the premiums share of reinsurers of the second category shall comprise not more than:

10.2.1 20% per insurance class per reinsurer;

10.2.2 40% per insurance class of all reinsurers;

10.2.3 10% of total premiums per reinsurer;

10.2.4 20% of total premiums of all reinsurers;

10.3 the premiums share of reinsurers of the third category shall comprise not more than:

10.3.1 5% per insurance class per reinsurer;

10.3.2 10% per insurance class of all reinsurers;

10.3.3 3% of total premiums per reinsurer;

10.3.4 5% of total premiums of all reinsurers.

11. In case when risks of compulsory insurances in the Republic of Lithuania are reinsured, insurer is obliged to regard the following criteria in choosing a reinsurer:

11.1 the premiums share of reinsurers of the second category shall comprise not more than:

11.1.1 10% per compulsory insurance class per reinsurer;

11.1.2 20% per compulsory insurance class of all reinsurers.

11.2 the premiums share of reinsurers of the third category shall comprise not more than:

11.2.1 3% per compulsory insurance class per reinsurer;

11.2.2 5% per compulsory insurance class of all reinsurers.

12. The Supervisory Authority Board, in respect with insurer's needs and reinsurer's reliability, may agree upon the insurer's intentions to exceed the restrictions specified in paragraphs 10 and 11 for ceded reinsurance. To receive this type of agreement the insurer is obliged to submit the following information:

12.1 reinsurance program on the whole portfolio of insurance risks;

12.2 reinsurance program in detail concerning the insurance classes which are intended for excess of restrictions of paragraphs 10 and 11, including types, scopes and contract drafts of reinsurance programs;

12.3 reasoned grounds for the need to exceed the restrictions specified in paragraphs 10 and 11;

12.4 reasoned grounds for the choice of reinsurers concerned for transfer of a risk share in excess of restrictions specified in paragraphs 10 and 11;

12.5 information specified in paragraph 6 concerning every reinsurer who is entitled for transfer of a risk share in excess of restrictions specified in paragraphs 10 and 11;

12.6 information to prove fulfillment of requirements indicated in paragraph 7;

12.7 information on connections to the insurer of every reinsurer concerned for transfer of a risk share in excess of restrictions specified in paragraphs 10 and 11;

12.8 if reinsurer is a person of a foreign state and his reinsurance business is directly supervised insurance or similar supervisory institution of that state, the supervisor's conclusion about the reinsurer's compliance with the requirements on solvency margin, calculation and investment of technical provisions set out in the state.

13. The agreement defined in paragraph 12 shall be provided for one year if not decided otherwise.

PART 2

Policy Issues in Insurance in the Baltic States

OECD Experiences and Recommendations to Baltic Countries

COMPULSORY INSURANCE IN OECD COUNTRIES

INFORMATION AND RECOMMENDATIONS FOR THE BALTIC STATES

Marcel Fontaine and Hélène de Rode

Abstract

This report deals with a subject of paramount importance in OECD countries and in emerging economies: the case for mandatory insurance. Drawing from an analytical listing and study of the experiences of selected OECD countries in this respect, the authors are considering the rationale of the development of compulsory insurance and its pros and cons. On this ground, they establish criteria to assess the desirability of making insurance compulsory, and provide a critical view of the principal forms of compulsory insurance reviewed in the paper.

The two last sections of the report focus on the experiences of countries in transition as regards to compulsory insurance – and particularly the Baltic Countries. After sketching out the situation of these countries, the authors provide a series of recommendations especially on the desirability and technical aspects of the introduction of compulsory insurance addressed to Baltic policymakers and insurance market players.

TABLE OF CONTENTS

INTRODUCTION

In a previous paper one of the authors took a comparative look at insurance contract law in OECD countries in an effort to extract guidelines on legislative policy that might be of help to countries in Central and Eastern Europe anxious to provide a sound legal framework for their developing insurance markets[1].

The present paper is similar in intent. However, it focuses on a single aspect, one nevertheless of no little importance: compulsory insurance. Some OECD countries have seen a remarkable growth in compulsory insurance, while in others it remains uncommon. In Central and Eastern Europe, compulsory insurance is at times regarded as a leftover of the former economic system and its place and provisions looked at askance in a market economy.

The first edition of this study, published in 1997[2], made recommendations to the benefit of Central and Eastern European countries in general. This new, updated, edition is more particularly aimed at the three Baltic States.

Preceded by a review of compulsory insurance in OECD countries (Chapter 1), the practice will be subjected to critical analysis (Chapter 2) and information derived that could be useful to countries in Central and Eastern European, more specifically to the Baltic countries (Chapter 3).

---

[1] FONTAINE, M., (1993) "Le droit du contrat d'assurance dans les pays de l'OCDE: étude comparative, orientations de *lege ferenda*", In *Aspects fondamentaux des assurances*, OECD, Paris, pp. 259-301.

[2] FONTAINE M. and DE RODE H., Mandatory insurance in OECD countries, in OECD Proceedings, *Insurance Regulation and Supervision in Economies in Transition*, Paris, 1997, pp. 73-138.

CHAPTER 1

COMPULSORY INSURANCE IN VARIOUS OECD COUNTRIES

I. Method

This paper covers most of the OECD countries, twenty countries in Europe and five elsewhere. A selection had to be made because of the need to complete work within a reasonable period of time. It was guided by the availability of sources of information (despite reservations which will be indicated later); greater consideration also had to be given to countries with a wide range of compulsory insurance.

This new edition includes three countries belonging to Central Europe (the Czech Republic, Slovakia and Poland) which have in the meantime already developed some experience in compulsory insurance in a market economy. The same could be said of the three Baltic States, but they have been considered separately in Chapter 3, since this study is mostly aimed at stating recommendations for their benefit.

The data used in preparing Chapter 1 came from a variety of sources. The starting point was an earlier study by the authors relating to compulsory insurance in Belgian law and in comparative law[1].

Various publications dealing with compulsory insurance were subsequently consulted, such as the substantial body of work on this topic issued by the French journal *Risques* in 1993 [2] and the proceedings of a colloquium held in Belgium in 1998[3] [4]. Most updating information came from OECD delegations, some from members of the *Comité Européen des Assurances* [5].

The information gathered on compulsory insurance varied from country to country; in some cases there was an abundance of documentation and in others very little. Lists of compulsory types of insurance obtained from different sources often contradicted each other. Furthermore, the dates on which given types of insurance

---

[1] FONTAINE, M. and PAULUS-DE RODE H., (1979) *Les assurances obligatoires. Droit belge, droit comparé, de lege ferenda*, Centre de Droit des Obligations, Université Catholique de Louvain, Louvain-la-Neuve, 2 volumes of 287 and 123 pp.

[2] *Risques*, n° 12/1993.

[3] The proceedings have been published in the *Bulletin des Assurances* (Brussels), 2001, Dossier n° 7, L'obligation d'assurance - Analyse économique et juridique, 201 pp.

[4] Other interesting studies have also been published by I. CISSE, Assurances obligatoires en Afrique, *Risques*, 1998, pp. 101-110 and E. PAVELEK, Seguros obligatorios y obligacion de asegurarse, *Rev. esp. de seguros*, 2001, pp. 235-275.

[5] A number of colleagues from the *International Insurance Law Association* (AIDA) had provided valuable information for the first edition.

became compulsory, often varied widely from list to list. This could perhaps be explained by the fact that such regulations are often subject to frequent amendment. As a rule, the earliest date available was taken. For some countries, lack of sufficient information on the dates when the different types of compulsory insurance were introduced led us to omit any references to such dates.

Since compilation of an exhaustive and fully reliable list of the types of compulsory insurance existing in the countries considered was not possible without a thorough study of comparative law entailing demands in terms of costs and time incompatible with the aim of this paper, it was considered that the primary task ought to be to ensure that the review of compulsory insurance in the countries considered should be such as to enable the sectors in which insurance cover was compulsory to be made plain and the way the situation had changed over time to be assessed. This goal should be achievable even if the review omitted an occasional compulsory insurance from a country or gave a doubtful date of introduction for a given compulsory cover.

In order to ensure that insurance schemes were classified in a uniform manner irrespective of country of origin, they were considered under the following headings: 1: Transport; 2: occupational accidents, health; 3: leisure, sports associations and youth movements; 4: pollution; 5: nuclear power; 6: professional indemnity; 7: others.

Since some types of insurance cover could come under more than one heading, choices had to be made. It was consequently decided to put insurance cover relating to sports events into the category 3 even though some were related to means of transport; liability insurance covering the health professions has been included under professional indemnity cover and not placed in category 2; liability insurance for travel agencies and campsite operators will be found among leisure insurance and not in category 6.

A succession of twenty-six lists detailing the insurance cover compulsory in twenty-five countries will inevitably be tedious to peruse, but its purpose is to provide background information to which reference may be made when following the discussion in subsequent chapters, which treats the subject in a more comprehensive and analytical manner.

II. Review of compulsory insurance cover

In the following account of compulsory insurance cover prevailing in 25 countries, the countries inside and outside Europe have been treated successively. The former[1] are

---

[1] Established sources, at least with regard to European countries, were examined by LEGRAND, B., (1993) "Les assurances de la responsabilité civile obligatoires en Europe", *Risques,* No.12, *Dossier*, pp. 38-41 and (1993) *Updating the study on compulsory liability insurance*, EIC document; H. DE RODE and M. COLLIGNON, Les assurances obligatoires en Europe - Etat de droit comparé, *Bull. Ass.* Dossier n° 7, 2001, *op.cit.*, pp. 47-78. In the case of some individual countries, other published sources will be given.

listed in roughly descending order of the number of compulsory types of insurance in force.

A. *France* [1]

France is considered to hold the record for the largest number of types of compulsory insurance, having about 100 in all.[2]

Transport

Third party liability arising from use of motor vehicles must be insured by the persons subject to such liability (1958).

There is a guarantee fund to meet victims' claims when the driver responsible for an event leading to a claim is unknown, has stolen the vehicle, is uninsured or whose insurance company is unable to meet the claim (bankruptcy or liquidation). Should insurers contest liability to indemnify a victim, they are still compelled by law to make payment on behalf of their client but will be reimbursed by the fund if their objection is upheld. The fund takes the place, with respect to victim's rights, of the persons responsible for events giving rise to claims, or their insurers, when it pays indemnity.

Since 1985, indemnity for damage suffered by pedestrians, cyclists and passengers has been paid by the insurer of the owner of the vehicle involved in the accident, regardless of proof of negligence on the part of the driver or of the victim, provided the latter has not displayed gross negligence. Some vulnerable road users (victims under 16 or over 70 years of age, or suffering from incapacity or disability greater than 80%) receive indemnity even if they have shown gross negligence. An accelerated procedure for paying indemnity to such victims has been provided by the law.

In the event of dispute between an insurer and a would-be policy holder, a request to set premium or deductibles may be referred to a special administrative body, the Central Tariff Bureau. By means of this body, any person required to take out insurance cover may be enabled to find an insurer; the Bureau, by its decision, may compel the insurer to accept the risk subject to its usual conditions or subject to payment of an extra premium.

The liabilities to which persons running driving schools are exposed must be covered by insurance (1970). Such insurance shall cover damage to third parties and to persons in the vehicle used for teaching purposes. Cover must be unlimited. Such insurance is a necessary requirement for the establishment to receive a license to operate.

---

[1] See LAMBERT-FAIVRE, Y., *Droit des Assurances*, Paris, Dalloz, 11th ed., 2001, pp. 12-16.

[2] Though precise counting is difficult, France may now have been taken over by Belgium and/or Portugal (see below, Sections 2 and 3).

Public carriers of persons and goods must have third party liability cover (1935). Such compulsory cover must extend to property carried.

Air transport is subject to a number of compulsory types of insurance. Carriage by military aircraft must be insured (1985) to cover persons carried, baggage and freight. Airport operators must be insured against liability for damage arising from work at and operation of the airport. Operators of aircraft must carry insurance (1962) to cover them against damage to third parties at ground level and to persons on board. The operators or owners of helicopters must carry insurance covering liability for damage or injury to third parties (1971). They must also carry insurance against liabilities arising from work at and operation of a heliport (1971) Proof of such cover is a necessary condition for issue of a license to operate a heliport.

Third party liability cover is compulsory for inland waterway carriers with respect to damage to cargo (1942).

Occupational accidents, health

The risk of occupational disease or accident in given occupations has been the target of special laws. For example, medical and pharmaceutical staff employed in public hospitals must be insured against the risk of occupational accident (1943); employers of war correspondents must insure them against occupational accident and the risk of death (1944); voluntary firemen at commune level must be insured against risk of accident or disease while on service (1953). Such insurance must cover the cost of treatment, prostheses, rehabilitation and a pension in the event of complete disability. Similarly, students at schools of nursing must be insured against occupational accident (accidents occurring during in-service training or at the school, commuting accidents and occupational disease) and against third party risks (during in-service training or at the school) (1981).

Leisure, sports associations and youth movements

Organisation of sports events has given rise to various insurance requirements. Organisers of sports events and competitions taking place on the public highway must be covered by insurance (1954) Organisers of events in the air must also carry insurance covering property damage or injury to spectators and third parties and against liabilities incurred by competitors other than persons subject to public law (1964). The same applies to events held in areas not open to road traffic in which motor vehicles compete (1958). Organisation of public entertainment also involves compulsory insurance cover (1964).

In hunting, the principal insurance requirement is third party liability cover for activities involved in the shooting of game or destruction of vermin (1955); such compulsory insurance must provide unlimited cover for accidental damage to third parties. No forfeiture of liability to victims or persons with claims upon them is permissible. Such insurance must also cover any liabilities associated with dogs.

Indemnity for damage for which an uninsured sportsman is liable will be paid by the guarantee fund.

Another compulsory insurance is required to cover third party liabilities incurred by those engaged in sport fishing at sea (1968). Federations of underwater fishing associations must also carry insurance (1960). Authorised hunters' associations organised at communal and inter-communal level must also carry insurance cover (1964).

The third party liability of those operating mountain lifts (funicular railways, cable cars, ski lifts etc.) must be covered by insurance. Cover must be unlimited in the case of personal injury, and minimum cover, depending on the means of transport in question, has been set for damage to property.

The premium and excess for the contract in question may be set by the Central Tariff Bureau.

Travel agencies must carry third party liability cover against damage caused to their customers, service providers or third parties (1975). The third party liabilities of non-profit-making associations organising travel activities must also be covered by insurance (1975).

Those running dancing schools must be insured against third party liability, including liability incurred by teachers, employees and pupils (1989). Insurance cover is a precondition for opening such establishments. Any breach of this requirement carries penal sanctions.

Various types of insurance are compulsory in other sports. Boxers not affiliated to a Federation who take part in a public boxing event must carry accident cover (1963). Sports groups, organisers of sports events and promoters of sports events must carry third party cover and also provide third party cover for licensees, employees, and participants (1955).

Pollution

Operators of ships carrying oil must carry insurance cover against third party liability for damage resulting from pollution resulting from carriage of oil (1977). Such cover may be replaced by a financial guarantee provided by the operator.

Nuclear power

Operators of nuclear-powered ships must carry insurance cover against third party liability for damage caused by the radioactive properties of nuclear fuels or by radioactive products or waste (1965). The operator may provide a financial guarantee in lieu of insurance cover. Third party insurance is also required from operators of nuclear installations (1968).

Professional indemnity

Many types of insurance covering medical and paramedical liabilities have been made compulsory.

Thus, blood transfusion centres must carry cover against their liabilities with respect to blood donors (1963). They are also required to carry unlimited cover against third party liabilities with respect to donors (1961); penal sanctions are also provided.

Promoters of biomedical research must be insured against damage arising, even where no negligence is involved, from biomedical research carried out for no direct therapeutic purpose, and for any damage caused by negligence in the case of research for direct therapeutic purposes (1988).

More generally, since 2002, health professionals and institutions and any legal person other than the State active in prevention, diagnosis and care, as well as producers, users and providers of health products must carry liability insurance.

There are a number of areas in the building industry where insurance cover is compulsory. To start with, a two-fold cover was introduced in 1978, one part of which comprises construction damage cover, to be taken out by the person for whom the building is being erected, which covers the ten-year guarantee and unsuitability of the building for its intended purpose. The other part requires the builders to carry insurance cover against third party liabilities. The insurer holding the construction damage cover first indemnifies the person for whom the building is being erected, and is then reimbursed by the third party insurer of the builder concerned. The Central Tariff Bureau may be given the task of setting the premium and excess for the contract.

Next, the third party liability of land surveyors and appraisers must be insured (1985), as must that of land surveyors and appraisers in professional partnerships (1976). Architects too must carry professional indemnity cover (1977): such cover extends firstly to their contractual liability, for work not exceeding a given sum, in relation to the risk of collapse in course of construction, ten-year liability and cost of clearing the site, and secondly to their third party liability. Insurance cover is also required from architects in professional partnerships (1977) the requirement applies both to the individual partners and to the partnership itself.

The legal and paralegal professions have not escaped the attention of the lawmakers. Liability incurred by receivers, authorised agents and liquidators as a result of negligence in carrying out their duties must be covered by insurance (1985). Lawyers and law firms must carry professional indemnity cover (1971): such contracts must also make provision for financial guarantees to cover funds paid to a lawyer on behalf of third parties. Breach of the requirement carries penal sanctions. Notaries must carry professional indemnity cover (1965). The same applies to notaries working in partnerships (1967).

Other examples are auctioneers and appraisers, which must carry professional indemnity cover (1966) and bailiffs in professional partnerships (1989).

In the world of finance, trade and services, insurance cover must be carried by brokers and insurance brokerage firms (1990): in addition to professional indemnity such insurance must cover reimbursement of funds paid out by the insured.

Third party liability of business agents, estate agents, property administrators and trustees, and administrators of property held in co-ownership must also be insured (1970). The same applies to building societies authorised to advertise publicly for savings in the case of damage caused by buildings in their ownership (1970). Penalties for breach of the requirement to carry insurance cover must be met by the managers.

Bookkeepers and accountants must also carry insurance cover, failure to do so carries penal sanctions (1945). Insurance cover is also required of auditors (1966) and from accredited management centres (1975).

Industrial property and patent consultants must also carry insurance cover against third party liability. Such insurance cover is a precondition for enrolment on the list of patent consultants.

Motor vehicle testers must carry professional indemnity cover (1972). Such insurance shall cover negligence during the guarantee period.

Professional indemnity cover is required in a wide range of other fields: for farmers with respect to damage caused when one farmer helps out another (1962); for partnerships (1966); for groups set up to prevent industrial problems (1985); care services for the elderly must carry insurance cover against the third party liability of persons authorised to provide such services (1989) and the third party liability of persons receiving such care (1989); child care staff must carry insurance cover against damage suffered by children in their care or caused by such children.

Others

One of the major areas of compulsory insurance under this heading is schools, which must carry accident cover with respect to their pupils (1943).

Another example is compulsory insurance to cover agricultural mutual funds against misappropriation, theft, loss or destruction of funds (1962); the requirement for a civil service department granting a loan to an official for purchase of a motor vehicle to take out fire and theft cover for that vehicle in an amount not less than that of the loan (1947); a similar provision applies in the case of loans to persons working for communal administrations (1947); bonded warehouses are required to carry fire insurance cover for goods covered by a warrant (1945), the cost of such insurance must be met by the depositor; cold storage depots must carry fire insurance cover for goods in store and cover against breakdown of machinery in the event of fire (1948); national museums must take out insurance against the theft, loss or deterioration of articles on loan (1981); social security benefit officers are required to be covered against theft, misappropriation, fraud, embezzlement and loss of funds (1966).

Beneficiaries of a State loan for acquisition of moderately priced housing are required to take out life insurance (1894). Grant of such a loan is conditional on such cover, which is intended to secure payment of any outstanding annual instalments due at time of death.

Bodies providing vocational training based on a system of alternate in-service training and course work are required to take out third party insurance to cover trainees during course work and in- service training, and also accident insurance (1980). The same holds for bodies providing in-service training for minors (1982).

Establishments caring for mentally deficient or handicapped children are also required to carry insurance cover (1989).

Insurance against natural disasters is compulsory (1982), taking the form of a requirement to include such cover in property insurance policies (fire, theft, etc.). The Central Tariff Bureau may set the amounts for premiums and excesses.

B. BELGIUM [1]

After France, the country with the largest number of compulsory types of insurance is undoubtedly Belgium. The extent of the practice was already apparent by the 1960s, to the point that the Belgian Minister for Economic Affairs commissioned a university study on the subject[2]. Since then a large number of new insurance requirements have been introduced. The Insurance Supervisory Office publishes a list of compulsory types of insurance in its annual report, also available on the Internet[3]; the latest list (2003) adds up to well over 100 types of insurance; in 1994, there were only around 50 types[4].

---

[1] See CLAASSENS, H. (1977-78) "Verplichte verzekering: een nieuwe verschijnsel in België?", *Rechtskundig Weekblad*, 1977-78, col, 145-180; FONTAINE, M. & PAULUS-DE RODE H., (1979) *Les assurances obligatoires. Droit belge, droit comparé, de lege ferenda*, Centre de Droit des Obligations, Université Catholique de Louvain, Louvain-la-Neuve, 2 volumes of 287 and 123 pp. ; L'obligation d'assurance - Analyse économique et juridique, *Bulletin des Assurances* (Brussels), 2001, Dossier n° 7, 201 pp. ; H. CLAASSENS, Les obligations d'assurance en Belgique présentées en un premier essai de typologie, *Bull. Ass.*, Dossier n° 7, 2001, *op. cit.*, pp. 29-46.

[2] FONTAINE, M. and PAULUS-DE RODE H., (1979) *Les assurances obligatoires. Droit belge, droit comparé, de lege ferenda*, Centre de Droit des Obligations, Université Catholique de Louvain, Louvain-la-Neuve, 2 volumes of 287 and 123 pp.

[3] *http.//www.cdv-oca.be/fr/assurances/reglementations/assuranceobligatoire.htm*

[4] The exact number is difficult to determine since some regulations make more than one form of

In the last decades, following the federalisation of Belgium, the largest number of new types of compulsory insurance has appeared at the Regional or Community level (Flanders, Wallonia, the French and German Communities, the Brussels Region).

The expansion of compulsory insurance in Belgium does not seem to have followed any particular plan. In many cases an insurance requirement has been built into new regulations for no particular reason or justification. Objections to this state of affairs are frequently voiced, but the introduction of new forms of compulsory insurance has become a sort of habit that it would be difficult to break.

The following enumerations are far from being exhaustive. Some of the requirements derive from regional or community regulation and are thus only applicable in their scope of competence.

Transport

Means of transport, motor vehicles in particular, have been the spur for a first group of compulsory types of insurance. Third party cover is compulsory for motor vehicles in general (1989)) and for liability relating to carriage of persons (1947). Driving schools must have coverage for their students' own liability as well as personal and property damage (1988, 1998); third party cover for aircraft operators is also compulsory (in the absence of a sufficient financial guarantee) in relation to damages to third parties at ground level (1966).

Occupational accidents, health

Occupational accidents and a number of health-related activities form a second group: insurance against occupational accident in general (which remains private insurance in Belgium) (1971), accidents suffered by pupils of technical schools (1934), persons undergoing vocational training (1985), voluntary firemen (1985), members of electoral boards (personal accident and third party liability) (1991, 1994) and blood donors (1997).

Leisure, sports associations and youth movements

There are many compulsory requirements for insurance in the sports and leisure sector. Although the list is not exhaustive, the following may be noted:

A large number of regulations, most often non-federal, require insurance cover for youth organisations, sporting and culture and similar associations, ecological associations, sports camps and charitable and voluntary organisations. In many cases, insurance cover is a precondition for granting subsidies.

---

cover compulsory, such as liability insurance and personal insurance. In addition, there are often parallel regulations in different regions or communities making up federal Belgium

Operators of camping sites must carry insurance (1971, 1991, 1995)

Organisers of bicycle races (1967, 2000), and organisers and competitors in motor racing events (1989) must carry insurance against their liabilities.

Third party insurance for hunting is also compulsory (1963).

"Stewards" in charge of controlling supporters in football games must be insured against personal accidents and third party liability (1996).

Zoos must insure their liability for damages caused by animals (1998).

The same applies to insurance cover for the liabilities of travel organisers and intermediaries (1994, 1995).

Holders of concessions related to river tourism infrastructure must take insurance against fire, explosions, damages caused by water, third party liability and all special risks linked to their activities (2002).

Pollution

Liabilities related to pollution (wastes, oil pollution) make up a further group, since regulations relating to pollution proliferate, particularly at regional level (since 1976).

Nuclear Power

Insurance cover for the liabilities of operators of nuclear power installations and transporters of nuclear wastes is compulsory in the absence of any other form of financial guarantee (1966, 1985).

Professional indemnity

Professional indemnity insurance must be carried by establishments working with therapeutic substances based on human blood 1968), consulting physicians and services dealing with mental health and toxicomania (1996).

In the construction sector, insurance cover is compulsory for architects (1985), public tender adjudicators (1977) and security co-ordinators (2001).

Third party insurance for insurance brokers has been made compulsory (1995).

Other professional indemnity risks for which insurance cover is compulsory are those relating to container accreditation bodies (1984), slag heap operators (1985), persons in charge of child care (1988 and 1995), surveillance firms (1990), institutions responsible for approving toys (1991), retirement homes for the elderly (1993), real estate agents (1999), accountants (1991) and certifiers of electronic signatures (2001).

Third party no-fault fire cover is required by Belgian law of operators of certain public places (1991). The spectacular fire that broke out at a hotel in Antwerp in early 1995 focused attention on the importance of such insurance.

Others

A number of types of property insurance are compulsory, such as the fire cover required for rest homes (1994), for residential establishments for the handicapped (1988), and for buildings where application has been made for a grant for construction or acquisition in the Walloon region (1990).

Municipalities and provinces must carry liability and legal expenses insurance for mayors, town councillors and provincial executives (1999).

Town treasurers must provide either security or fidelity insurance (2000).

Other compulsory types insurance may be cited, without being exhaustive, such as insurance cover relating to animal production (1976) and protected monuments (1993); offices for recruitment, replacement and selection services (1993); youth protection organisations (1987). Some of these regulations were taken at the sub-federal level.

Without being compulsory in themselves, cover against risks of terrorist attacks (1988), storms (1995) and floods (2003) must be included in fire insurance, which is not compulsory but is widely held.

Similarly, a draft bill envisaged the compulsory inclusion of minimal legal expenses coverage in private liability policies (which themselves are wide-spread but non compulsory) (2002).

C. PORTUGAL

Portugal also has many areas where insurance is compulsory. The most recent list available to the authors contains over 100 items. Attention is drawn to the dates: compulsory insurance seems to have become a high growth area in this country in recent years. This was already mentioned in the edition of 1997 but the pace seems to be accelerating. The following enumeration gives representative illustrations but is not exhaustive.

Transport

Third party motor insurance is of course compulsory (1985) as is third party insurance for driving schools (1982), air transport enterprises, both scheduled airlines and others (1982, 1989), transport operators (1999) and firms assisting in transit at national airports (1999).

Occupational accidents, health

Workmen's compensation insurance is compulsory (1997, 1999), including self-employed workers (1999) and professional sportsmen (2003).

Several regulations provide for compulsory insurance for athletes, whether professional or non-professional (1984, 1993, 1995, 1998), as well as for voluntary sports directors (1995).

There is compulsory life insurance for peace-time soldiers involved in military or humanitarian missions outside Portugal (1996)

Personal accident insurance is required for many professions or activities, such as firemen (1994 and 1999), bullfighters (1991), blood donators (1990), mayors (1987), students (1985, 1986, 1988), apprentices (1996), workers on board fishing vessels (1997),

Leisure, sports associations and youth movements

As in many countries, third party insurance is compulsory in Portugal for hunters (1999 and 2000) but also for enterprises organising big game hunting programs (2000).

Liability insurance is compulsory for owners and pilots of pleasure boats (1995 and 2001) and ultra-light aircraft (1990).

Third party insurance is also compulsory for travel and tourist agencies (1997), organisers of water-slide parks (1997), recreational grounds (1997), leisure activities (2000), and tourist maritime programs (2002).

Pollution

Liability insurance against damage to the environment or injury to public health is compulsory (1987); such cover is also compulsory for accredited enterprises working in the environment sector (1992) and enterprises licensed to operate and manage municipal systems for the treatment of urban solid wastes (1994).

Portugal is particularly concerned about liabilities arising from handling of gas products. In this area, insurance is compulsory against liability for damage caused by the internal networks of agencies distributing gaseous fuels (1985), operators of liquefied natural gas terminals and natural gas pipelines, operators of regional distribution networks for natural gas (1989), enterprises mounting gas installations or assemblies, enterprises holding concessions for the import of liquefied natural gas or natural gas (1989 and 2003) and businesses engaged in the assembly or repair of kits for conversion of vehicles for operation on liquefied petroleum gas (1991).

Nuclear power

There is compulsory insurance in connection with installations, equipment and materials for the production of radiation and ionisation (1989), for the professional transport of radioactive waste (1996), for activities dealing with sealed radioactive sources (1996) and ionising radiation areas (2002).

Professional indemnity

In the medical sector, hospitals must be insured against damage suffered by tissue or organ donors (1993). Insurance cover for those carrying out clinical trials on human beings is also compulsory (1994), as well as for private health units practising physical medicine and rehabilitation (1999) and dialysis (1999) or using ionising radiation, ultrasounds or magnetic fields (1999). Private dentists must also insure their liability (2001).

Solicitors must have liability insurance (2003).

Liability insurance must be carried by firms servicing lifts (2002), by gas stations (2002) and by test laboratories (1999).

There is compulsory insurance for construction materials (1993) and pressurised equipment (1999).

Insurance must be carried by private security firms (1999), insurance brokers (1991), real estate agents (1999), accountants (1999), money-lenders (1999), exchange rate agencies (2001) and enterprises certifying digital signatures (1999).

Third party liability insurance is obligatory for firms involved in the production, distribution and transportation of electricity (1995), in the treatment and distribution of water for public consumption (1994), or in the exploitation of gas warehouses and distribution to consumers (2001), as well as for inspectors of the gas distribution system (2000).

Other examples, without giving an exhaustive list, are compulsory liability insurance for stevedoring firms (1993), film producers (1993), art galleries (1991), fire-fighting services (1993), and businesses promoting voluntary youth service activities (1993). There is also compulsory third party liability insurance linked to the exercise of a class action (1995).

Others

Fire and theft insurance is compulsory in several sectors in Portugal, such as co-operative housing (1974), art galleries (1991), handling of goods at docks (1994), casinos (1995), forests (1996) and private security firms (1998).

Insurance is compulsory for owners of potentially dangerous animals (2001).

The Civil Code provides for compulsory property insurance of flats and apartments.

D. ITALY

There is a long list of compulsory types of insurance in Italy; according to information received it contains about 70 items, including compulsory insurance related to certain regions or provinces. Liability insurance represents the lion's share.

Transport

Firstly, third party cover is compulsory in relation to vehicular traffic and utilisation of motorboats (1969).

Other subjects of compulsory cover are driving schools (1959), transport of postal items (1939), carriage of property for third parties (1974), liability cover for airlines with regard to damage to third parties at ground level and demonstration of aeronautical equipment (1985), non public inspection bodies of the EC marking of simple pressure vessels (1997).

Occupational accidents, health

Italy has a number of cases of compulsory personal insurance, for instance, for aircraft passengers and crew, for staff of the National Insurance Institute (life cover) (1926), for voluntary workers in developing countries (life, accident and sickness cover) (1979), sports professionals (accident cover) (1981), Italian workers employed in countries outside the European Union (accident cover) (1987) and volunteers, as well as conscientious objectors, in the alternative civilian service sent abroad (accidents, sickness, third party liability)(2001). Insurance is also compulsory against the risks connected with the alternative civilian service (2002).

Compulsory life insurance and loss of employment cover is compulsory for employees in a number of public service departments as security for salary cessions (1950).

Leisure, sports associations and youth movements

Third party cover is compulsory for hunting (1977).

The same applies to flying for pleasure or sport (1969).

Pollution

Liability arising from oil pollution of the sea must be covered by insurance (1978).

There is compulsory insurance for non-public certification bodies of the EC marking equipment and protective systems intended for use in potentially explosive atmospheres (1998).

Nuclear power

Operators of nuclear installations must carry liability insurance (1962).

Compulsory insurance cover is also required for transport of fissile material (1962).

Professional indemnity

Liability insurance must be carried by hospitals (1969), blood transfusion and blood product production centres (1971), by dental students and trainee dental technicians (1984) and by certification bodies of in vitro diagnostic medical devices (2000).

Third party insurance is compulsory for insurance brokers (1984), stockbrokers (1991) and tax consultants (1991). Brokers must carry liability and employee infidelity insurance.

The same applies to voluntary organisations, mail-order or door-to-door sales agencies (1971), bottled gas distributors (1973), non-public inspection bodies of the EC security marking of toys (1997), agricultural advice centres (2001) and non-public testing laboratories for radio and terminal equipment (2002).

Others

With regard to property insurance, compulsory cover is required for social housing (fire, explosion, lightning strike) (1938) and the takings from bingo games (theft, fire) (1990).

Insurance cover is compulsory in a number of cases where property is offered as security: furniture in pawn (1939), mortgaged buildings (1991), ships and other property offered as security against fishing credits (1982).

E. SPAIN

Spain is also a country where compulsory insurance is widespread. The Insurance Contracts Act of October 8, 1980 makes third party insurance cover compulsory in cases decided by the government; public authorities may not authorise the relevant activities without proof of such cover; administrative penalties are provided for any breach (art. 75).

According to our Spanish sources, in general, the causes to set up mandatory insurance are the following:

Individual activities in which negligence may produce serious damages (hunting, pollution....)

Activities in which a single event may cause many victims (camping, entertainment...).

Activities that may cause many damages even to broad groups of people (travel agencies, real estate agents...)

Other unclassifiable motives which may produce civil liability (surveyor....).

In the last years, the Spanish legislation has established many types of mandatory insurance. The main types have been regulated by national law as well as by regional law.

Transport

Third party motor insurance cover is compulsory (1968) as is third party insurance for carriage of property (1987).

In the case of passenger transport accident insurance cover for passengers has long been compulsory (1928).

Insurance is also compulsory in air navigation to cover risks to aircraft, passengers and goods, and liability for damage and injury to third parties on land, sea or in flight (1960).

Occupational accidents, health

Many collective agreements make provision for insurance against damage resulting from occupational accidents.

Insurance is compulsory against damage suffered by blood donors (1985).

Leisure, sports associations and youth movements - volunteer services

Third party insurance cover is compulsory for fishing and hunting (1970).

Travel agencies are required to insure against third party risks (1974).

Those practising sports governed by federations must be covered against accident; the details are specified in the regulations governing each particular sport (1990)- Organisers of bullfight games are required to subscribe accident and third party liability insurance (1986).

Third party insurance cover is compulsory for owners of recreational or sports boats (1999).

The social volunteer organisations are obliged to contract sickness insurance and accident insurance to cover the volunteers (1996).

Pollution

Insurance is compulsory against liabilities arising from the production and handling of toxic and hazardous wastes (1986).

The same applies to damage caused by oil pollution of the sea (1975).

Third party insurance cover is compulsory to obtain a licence to keep hazardous waste (2000).

Nuclear power

Third party cover against nuclear risks is compulsory (1964). Such cover may, however, be replaced by deposit of a sum as a guarantee.

Professional indemnity

Third party cover is compulsory for lawyers (1982).

Third party cover is compulsory for private security companies (1994).

The same applies to mortgage registrars, public notaries, auditors, insurance brokers and bodies managing pension schemes and investment funds (2001).

Housing developers and builders must contract insurance cover to guarantee the damages caused by defects or hidden faults in the building due to certain causes, for a period of ten years (1999).

Professional indemnity cover is also compulsory for manufacturers (1984), a number of bodies responsible for monitoring compliance with safety standards in industry, firms involved in issuance of certificates of quality (mine safety, environment, vehicle inspection) (1979), firms installing, maintaining and repairing various equipment and machinery.

Many collective agreements make provision for insurance cover for workers against damage to third parties resulting from their activities.

Others

Housing developers must take out insurance cover to secure payments made by purchasers in the event that building has not begun or has not been completed by the due date (1976).

In multiple property the following types of insurance are compulsory (1998): third party cover in force during the promotion until complete transmission of the right, third party cover of the occupants, fire insurance and insurance on building and guarantee insurance to cover the payments made during the construction of the building.

Owners of dangerous animals –certain races of dogs- are obliged to contract a third party cover against damages caused by those animals (1999)

Cover must be provided by the *Consorcio de Compensación de Seguros* against a number of "extraordinary" risks (disasters), such as flooding, earthquake or terrorism, in insurance policies in some fields (accident, motor insurance, train insurance, natural risks, property, fire, accident linked pension schemes and damages in nuclear industries). The cover is not compulsory in itself but forms a necessary part of those policies by means of payment of a tax included in the premium.

A guarantee fund built into the *Consorcio* comes into operation in the case of forest fires.

The *Consorcio de Compensación de seguros* has established a guarantee fund also with regard to nuclear risk insurance, agricultural insurance, mandatory motor insurance, mandatory travel insurance and mandatory hunting insurance.

F. GERMANY[1]

In our study of 1997 we had noted that Germany had a number of compulsory types of insurance, but that the practice did not appear to be spreading. Comparison of a report from the 1960s [2] with a new list we had obtained then [3] showed that although

---

[1] See the review by PRÖSSL-MARTIN, *Versicherungsvertragsgesetz*, 25th ed., pp.36-37.

[2] *Ibid.,* 21st ed., pp.23-25.

[3] *Ibid.,* 25th ed., pp.36-37.

many regulations had been amended or renewed in the meantime, the number of sectors in which insurance cover was compulsory had remained remarkably similar: after a lapse of almost twenty years the same 18 compulsory types of insurance were found.

In more recent years, however, there seems to have been acceleration in the creation of new types of compulsory insurance. Our most recent list contains many additions to that compiled in 1997.

A peculiarity of the German situation is that there is compulsory insurance not only at the Federal level, but also at the State level, a circumstance that makes it very difficult to present an exhaustive catalogue. The following survey is certainly not comprehensive.

German law is peculiar in including in contract insurance law a number of rules relating to compulsory liability insurance in general (V.V.G. of 30 May 1908, §§ 158-158h); the principal aim of these provisions is to strengthen the rights of third party victims in relation to the insurer.

Transport

Third party motor insurance is of course in the forefront (1956).

Other compulsory types of third party insurance apply in air transport (in addition to accident insurance for passengers) (1981), third party risks relating to transport of goods by road and private railroads.

The state of Bavaria has compulsory insurance for inland navigation transport.

Leisure

Hunters must carry third party insurance cover (1934).

Insurance is compulsory for funfair operators and other trades in the leisure sector (1984).

Pollution

Insurance is compulsory for installations representing a hazard for the environment (1991).

Nuclear power

In the nuclear power sector, a number of establishments and activities must carry insurance cover (1962).

Professional indemnity

Liability insurance must be carried by nursing and midwifery schools (1938), as well as medical doctors.

Notaries (1961) and barristers (1994) must carry insurance cover.

The same is true of estate agents and builders (1990).

Architects must insure their liability in many states. There is also compulsory insurance for drafters of stability studies.

Compulsory cover is also required of chartered accountants (1961), tax advisers (1961), security firms (1976) and certifiers of digital signatures.

Several states provide for compulsory liability insurance of experts.

Development aid bodies must take out third party and sickness insurance for their voluntary workers (1969).

Pharmaceutical manufacturers must take out insurance against user accidents (1978). Insurance is also compulsory for pharmaceutical research on men.

Others

Dog owners must insure their liability in several states.

Various types of property insurance are compulsory: fire insurance for warehouse operators (1931), fire insurance for buildings used as collateral for loans (1942), insurance cover for a life tenant with respect to the building concerned, fire, theft and water damage insurance for pawnbrokers (1987).

Chimney-sweepers must carry life insurance (1969).

Dependants' insurance is compulsory in Germany (1994).

G. *AUSTRIA*

About twenty-five different types of insurance are compulsory in Austria.

Transport

Third party insurance for motor vehicles is of course compulsory, as well as for air carriers and ground services at airports.

Operators of horse carriages also have to have insurance.

Leisure

There is compulsory liability insurance for hunters, mountain and ski guides and ski-lifts operators.

Pollution

Operators of pipe line and natural gas nets, as well as environment controllers must carry liability insurance.

Nuclear power

Third party liabilities must be insured in the nuclear sector (installations, transport, and damages due to radioactivity).

Professional indemnity

Several types of professional indemnity insurance are compulsory. This applies to advocates, mediators, notaries, insurance brokers, providers of certification of digital signatures, experts, fiduciaries, different kinds of financial controllers, assets advisors, sponsors, verification, surveillance and certification firms.

Insurance must also be carried for liabilities relating to pharmaceuticals and the use of genetic techniques.

Others

Dog owners must have third party liability insurance.

H. ICELAND

The list concerns types of insurance that are mandatory in Iceland under national legislation.

Transport

Compulsory motor insurance: third party liability and accident insurance for drivers of motor vehicles (traffic law no. 50/1987). Damages caused by uninsured or unknown vehicles are indemnified by the International Motor Insurance in Iceland.

Aircraft liability (law on aviation n° 34/1964).

Accidents insurance for pilots and passengers in private aviation and flying schools (law on aviation n° 60/1998).

Hull and liability for motor boats between 8 and 100,49 tons (law on boat insurance companies no. 18/1976 and regulation on mandatory fishing boat insurance no. 673/1994).

Occupational accidents, health

Accidental ships and boats crew insurance against war (law n° 43/1947).

Seamen's accidents at work (navigation law n° 34/1985).

Accidents compensated by the Social Security (law on social security n° 117/1993).

Accidents of workers (provided for in contracts on the labour market).

Leisure, sport associations and youth movements

Professional liability for travel agents and carriers (law n° 34/1985).

Professional indemnity

Liability insurance for health care institutions (law on insurance for patients n° 111/2000).

Professional liability for lawyers (law regarding solicitors and lawyers no. 61/1942, 24/1995).

Professional liability for construction managers and certified designers (law on design and construction n° 73/1997).

Professional liability for marine and real estate agents (law on marine and real estate agents n° 34/1986).

Professional liability for stockbrokers (law on stockbrokers n° 9/1993).

Professional liability for securities brokerage (law on securities transactions n° 13/1996).

Professional liability for insurance brokers (law on insurance activity no. 60/1994 and regulation on insurance brokering n° 473/1994).

Professional liability for certified public accountants (law on certified public accountants n° 18/1997).

Professional liability for used car dealers (law on car dealers n° 69/1994).

Professional liability for renters (law n° 36/1994 on house rental).

Others

Fire insurance for buildings (law on insurance against fire no. 48/1994).

Insurance of buildings and some other construction against natural catastrophe (law on Icelandic Emergency Organisation no. 55/1992).

It is required for all homeowners to insure against volcanic eruptions, earthquakes, mudslide, avalanches and flood.

Livestock (law on livestock insurance n°. 20/1943).

War risks (law on war risks n° 2/1994).

Liability insurance for dog owners (regulated at the municipal level).

I. NORWAY

Norway has some twenty compulsory types of insurance.

Transport

Compulsory third party insurance, which is required of owners of automotive vehicles (apart from those running on rails) covers the no-fault liability of the insured person. Damage caused by uninsured or unknown vehicles are indemnified by the Motor Insurers Bureau.

Air transport is subject to a number of compulsory types of insurance. Acquisition of an air transport license is conditional on proof of insurance covering injury to passengers travelling by air (1933). Third party liability relating to use of an aircraft must be covered by insurance with regard to both property damage and physical injury (1993). This refers to damage caused outside the aircraft. Each insurer must deposit a document of guarantee with the Norwegian Civil Aviation Authority, which until and unless it is withdrawn requires the insurer to provide coverage.

Occupational accidents, health

Employer liability for employees is a no-fault insurance and must be covered (1989). Since any uninsured injury will be covered by the Workers' Compensation Bureau, lapse of insurance will have no repercussions for the victim.

Insurance against physical injury caused by a pharmaceutical product or by the testing of new pharmaceutical products is compulsory (1988). Such cover is provided by a national pool. However, this pool has been considered, by the EFTA surveillance

Authority, to be in breach with the EU/EEA competition rules. As a consequence, the pool will (from the next renewal) no longer offer this compulsory type of insurance. The law of 1988 requires all producers or importers to be members of an association buying collective liability insurance cover for them. The law says this can also be arranged through a pool. Regulatory authorities will wait to see if the association manages to find cover from individual insurance actors in the private market.

Leisure

Organisers of fairs and owners of amusement parks must insure their liabilities with respect to the public (1991). No protection is provided for victims should the insurance lapse. The obligation to insure third party liability has been recently extended to operators of "bump cars".

Operators of ski-lifts and cable cars must carry third party insurance (1949). Such cover is a precondition for obtaining an operating license. No rules have been laid down in the event of lapse of cover.

Travel agencies must carry liability insurance (1985).

Nuclear power

Operation of nuclear installations must be covered by liability insurance (1972). No protection is provided for victims should the insurance lapse.

Professional indemnity

Health professions are subject to a number of compulsory types of insurance. Public hospitals and hospitals financed by public bodies must carry liability cover in relation to certain forms of damage to patients; this is a no-fault insurance. No provision is made for lapse of insurance cover; which is not necessary since public bodies are involved.

In addition, owners of pharmacies must be covered against third party liability with respect to their customers (1963). There are no rules relating to lapse of insurance.

Third party liability of physicians with respect to injury to their patients must be secured by deposit of a sum as security or by insurance cover (1980). License to practice may be withdrawn by the ministry if such security lapses.

Liability of dentists for injury to their patients must be insured (1980). Such insurance may be replaced by a deposit of a sum as security. License to practice may be withdrawn if such security lapses.

A new act on patients' rights regulating compensation for injury/damage to patients was implemented on January 1, 2003.

The new act will also apply to all private health contributors/medical clinics/physicians etc, which now must purchase liability insurance. The liability is based on a no-fault rule. However, due to protests from the private insurance market, the act will not apply to the private sector before 2004. More than likely, a bureau will be established to cover uninsured injuries. Earlier, only the public sector was obliged to purchase liability insurance, and these claims will still be handled by the Norwegian patients liability organisation – NPE - (owned and ran by the public hospitals).

In the construction industry, architects are obliged to carry liability insurance (an agreement-based requirement: 1971).

Lawyers must carry liability insurance or offer equivalent financial security (1993).

In occupations in the field of trade and financial or other services, debt collectors must carry liability insurance (1964 and 1989), as must estate agents (1989), consulting engineers (agreement-based requirement: 1973), insurance brokers (1989), and pharmaceutical manufacturers (1989).

Others

Fire insurance necessarily includes insurance against natural disasters (1989). The insurance company must pay a fixed proportion of the premium to the Natural Disaster Reparation Fund.

J. SLOVAK REPUBLIC

There are a little more than twenty compulsory types of insurance in the Slovak Republic. The competitive market, organised with contractual insurance, is recent, as in the other Eastern countries[1].

Transport

Motor third party liability insurance is compulsory. It was formerly provided by the monopolistic Slovak insurance company (the *Slovenská poistovna*); a successful transformation process created a market mechanism in the insurance sector and a competitive environment. This process has had a positive impact in improving the quality of insurance services and products and this compulsory insurance is now contractual (Act No. 381/2001).

---

[1] Cf. also, about the development of insurance market in Slovakia, P. FALUSH, "The development of reinsurance market in the economies in transition", in *Insurance regulation and supervision in economies in transition, OECD proceedings,* OECD, 1997, pp. 278-279.

In connection with the process of full compliance of the Act n° 381/2001 with the EU directive 2000/26/ES, amendment of this law is now in the legislative process.

Other compulsory types of third party liability insurance cover air transport, inland marine and river vessels, road carriers and aircraft.

Leisure, sport associations and youth movements

Hunters are required to have liability insurance (law of 1962).

Travel agencies have a duty to conclude compulsory contractual insurance against travel agency bankruptcy (Act No. 281/2001).

Professional indemnity

Compulsory professional liability insurance is required in the following professions: commercial lawyers, authorised construction engineers, patent attorneys, auditors, authorised designers, tax advisers, notaries, dentists, medical doctors, attorneys, veterinary surgeons, insurance brokers, intermediaries and auctioneers.

Compulsory professional liability insurance is required also in the field of clinical psychology, against damage caused by non-state medical establishment, against damage caused by non-state pharmacy, against damage occurred during the verification of medical experiments on human being.

Others

Some particular legal regulations provide that performance of some special activities is submitted to the underwriting of insurance contract covering damages caused to others persons (clients, employees, public ...).

K. DENMARK

Danish law makes provision for some fifteen to twenty compulsory types of insurance. The problem of ensuring that the insurance requirement is respected has been a particular concern (more so than in any other of the countries reviewed), and in many cases complex monitoring procedures have been put in place (not all compulsory types of insurance in the country entail the same depth of monitoring). This interesting characteristic of the Danish system is worth noting, although all the relevant procedures will not be considered in detail.

Transport

To start with, third party motor insurance is compulsory. The Danish (green card) Bureau covers damage caused by unidentified or uninsured vehicles. Should insurance lapse or not be paid, the firm concerned notifies the police, who will confiscate the vehicle license plates.

Insurance cover against damage to hired vehicles is also compulsory (1963).

With regard to aviation, third party insurance is compulsory for the owners of aircraft used for normal air traffic or for test purposes; such cover must extend to liabilities of aircraft owners and users.

Breach of the insurance requirement is punishable by a fine or in some cases by a prison sentence.

Occupational accidents, health

Employers are required to insure their employees against occupational accident. In the case of failure to insure, any indemnity due to an injured employee is provisionally paid by the Occupational Accidents Department, which then seeks reimbursement from the employer. Breach of the insurance requirement is punishable by a fine.

Insurance cover is not required for domestic staff working short hours; indemnity for occupational accidents suffered by such workers is paid by the Health Insurance Department, whose costs are reimbursed by all occupational accident insurers pro rata to the premiums they collect.

Leisure

Third party liabilities of hunters must be covered. Insurance cover is a necessary part of the license required for hunting. Such insurance also covers damage or injury caused by uninsured or unknown persons. However, victims are not entitled to compensation if injured by persons known or ascertainable by them not to have a license, or if they have taken part in a hunting party without holding the required license.

Nuclear power

Liabilities arising from operation of a nuclear installation are laid to the charge of the owners (1962). Permission to operate such installations is conditional on proof on insurance. The State will pay compensation for any loss not covered by the insurer or the other guarantees offered by the insured.

Professional indemnity

Liability insurance is required by law for public or private hospitals (1992). Hospital authorities may cover the risk themselves without seeking insurance cover. Uninsured damage will be indemnified by the Ministry of Health, which may reclaim such payments from the negligent party.

173

Lawyers are required to carry professional indemnity cover. In order to practice, lawyers must be members of the Law Society, whose regulations require professional indemnity cover. The Law Society will indemnify damage caused by an uninsured lawyer.

Chartered accountants are required to carry professional indemnity cover (1989). Such insurance is a precondition for registry. The insurer must notify the Accountants' Association in the event of a lapse of policy. Permission to practice, or registration, will be withdrawn should the insurance requirement fail to be observed.

Energy consultants must carry liability insurance, as must certified weighers and measurers (1989).

Firms working within the "domestic help system" must carry liability insurance to cover damage or injury to customers or their property during domestic help.

Professional indemnity insurance is also compulsory for real estate agents, insurance agents and brokers and for authorised building experts.

Others

Liability insurance must also be carried by dog owners (1969 and 1984). A Fund (constituted by an association of firms insuring this risk) meets any indemnity due as a result of damage caused by unknown or uninsured dogs.

A number of property types of insurance- are compulsory. Thus, the employer of a domestic worker living in the employer's home must insure the worker's property against fire (1980). The employer will be held personally liable should such insurance not be carried. Similarly, traders must carry fire insurance to cover goods entrusted to them for sale or bought by them for their customers (1986). Housing built on agricultural land must be insured against fire.

L. POLAND

Compulsory insurance in Poland comprises:

Transport

Third part liability insurance of motor vehicle owners arising from the use of such vehicles (Act on insurance activities, 1990)

Leisure

Third party liability insurance is compulsory for organisers and agents of tourism services (1997)

Nuclear power

Liability insurance for operators of nuclear installations (2000).

Professional indemnity

Third part liability insurance for farmers on account of having a farm (Act on insurance activities, 1990).

Regulation of many activities and professions requires third part liability insurance. This includes lawyers (1982), legal advisors (1982), notaries (1991), health care institutions (1991), expert auditors (1994), tax advisors (1996), real estate agents, managers and experts (1997), organisers of mass events (1997), court officers (1997), architects and building engineers (2000), patent agents (2001), detectives (2001), certifiers of electronic signatures (2001), insurance brokers and agents (2003).

Others

Farm buildings must be insured against fire and other perils (Act on insurance activities, 1990).

M. GREECE

Mandatory insurance is an expanding phenomenon in Greece, where some nineteen sorts of insurance are now enforced.

Transport

Civil liability for motor accidents (codified law n° 489/76).

Compulsory third party insurance for cyclists.

Civil liability of international land carriers (law n° 559/77).

Compulsory insurance of ship-owners of passengers vessels (law n° 2575/98).

Compulsory third party insurance for aircraft operators.

Compulsory insurance against a number of risks concerning ocean-going vessels (hull insurance, war risks, pollution, legal expenses, etc...), as prerequisites regarding the listing of stock exchange equities in ship companies of certain investment companies (law decree n° 2843/00).

Compulsory insurance of the flying personnel of the national airline company (law decree n° 4262/62).

Local and international air carriers' civil liability (art. 137 Code of air law).

Occupational accidents, health

Compulsory insurance of the flying personnel of the national airline company (law decree n° 4262/62).

Leisure, sports associations and youth movements

Civil liability of organisers of speed sporting events (law n°489/76).

Civil liability, as well as personal accident insurance of hunters (ministerial decision 79570/2968/1.7.92).

Tour operators' professional civil liability (presidential decree n° 339/96).

Civil liability arising from professional and private pleasure crafts; also from professional pleasure crafts whose ship register is no longer in force, when they sail to shipyards (law n° 2743/99);

Pollution

Civil liability for sea pollution by commercial vessels (law n° 314/76).

Civil liability of natural gas management institutions (law n° 2364/97).

Civil liability of large consumers of natural gas (law 2364/97).

Civil liability of the ship-owners regarding the expenses of shipwrecks salvage (law 2881/01).

Professional indemnity

Engineers and of construction firms liability (law n°1418/84).

Insurance broker's professional civil liability (law n° 1569/85).

Attorneys' civil liability acting in Greece with a license issued by another member State (presidential decree n° 152/00).

N. CZECH REPUBLIC

There are some sixteen types of compulsory insurance in the Czech Republic. The first ones were introduced in the sixties. The largest part of them became compulsory in the nineties.

Transport

Third party liability insurance for motor vehicles is compulsory. Originally it was provided by one state insurance company, without an individual insurance contract.

It has been adapted in 1999 and the insurance cover now corresponds to EU Motor Third Party Liability Insurance Directives (Act No.168/1999 Coll.). The insurance is provided by 13 insurance undertakings. They are organised in the Czech Bureau of Insurers which holds among others the guarantee fund to meet victims' claims when the driver responsible for the accident is not insured, is unknown or when its insurance company is insolvent.

Third party liability insurance is also compulsory for aircraft operators (Act No. 49/1997 Coll.) and inland waterway transport providers (Act No. 114/1995 Coll.).

Occupational accidents, health

Employers' liability insurance for damages caused by occupational accidents and diseases is mandatory according to the Labour Code (No. 65/1965 Coll.). The cover is provided by two insurance companies.

Private institutions providing health care must be insured against third party liability for damages arisen to their patients or employees (Act No. 160/1992 Coll.).

Leisure, sports associations and youth movements

Travel agencies must carry third party cover against damage caused by their bankruptcy to their customers (Act No.159/1999 Coll.).

Hunters are required to have liability insurance (Act No. 23/1962 Coll.) as well as providers of sport flying equipment (Act No. 49/1997 Coll.).

Nuclear power

Operators of nuclear installations must underwrite third party liability insurance or provide a financial guarantee in place of insurance cover (Act No. 18/1997 Coll.).

Professional indemnity

Many professions are required to underwrite professional indemnity cover. It is the case for lawyers (Act No. 358/1992 Coll.), architects (Act No. 360/1992 Coll.), auditors (Act. No. 524/1992 Coll.), tax advisors (Act. No. 523/1992 Coll.), insurance brokers (Act. No. 363/1999 Coll.), veterinarians (Act. No. 381/1991 Coll.), medical doctors, dentists and chemists (Act. No. 220/1991 Coll.).

O. SWITZERLAND

Consideration of compulsory insurance in Switzerland is attended by a problem peculiar to federal or confederate States. In addition to types of insurance compulsory at federal level, which are few in number, a wide variety of insurance coverage is required under cantonal provisions; Switzerland, as everyone knows, is composed of 23 cantons. Unless indicated to the contrary, the types of insurance listed below are compulsory at the federal level.

In some cases, insurance can be replaced by an adequate financial guarantee.

Transport

Third party insurance for motor vehicles is compulsory, as well as for enterprises engaged in the automobile business. Such insurance is also compulsory for cyclists, aircraft operators, inland shipping and users of the infrastructure of another railroad company.

Occupational accidents, health

Private insurers are involved in the compulsory insurance of workers against accident along with the Swiss National Accident Fund (CNA) and a number of other funds. The private sector is also involved, in addition to recognised sickness insurance funds, in compulsory sickness insurance.

Insurance against occupational accident and disease is required for the crews of Swiss ships

Leisure, sports associations and youth movements

Owners of Swiss yachts must carry third party insurance, as well as hunters and cable cars operators.

Pollution

Liability associated with the transport by pipeline of liquid or gaseous fuels or combustible substances must be insured. Owners of businesses or installations can be required to take environmental coverage.

Nuclear power

Third party risks from nuclear power must be insured (nuclear plants, transport, activity involving ionising radiation).

Professional indemnity

To practice law in a court, lawyers must contract professional liability insurance with appropriate coverage.

Others

A wide range of compulsory cantonal types of insurance provide fire cover for buildings and moveable property; they may be provided by private insurers or by the cantonal authorities. Under a federal provision, institutions providing fire cover for buildings and moveable property in Switzerland must also provide cover for damage caused by natural disasters.

P.   UNITED KINGDOM

Transport

Liability insurance for motor vehicles is compulsory (1930). This is the only compulsory insurance for which protection of victims is specifically provided in case of lapse of cover: the insurer generally remains liable to the victim until the insurance certificate has been returned by the insurance holder.

Insurers in this sector must be members of and contribute to the funds of the Motor Insurers' Bureau, which pays compensation to the victims of uninsured or unknown drivers.

Insurance cover is required for third party liabilities incurred by space activities, such as the launch of a space object.

Licensed carriers must carry third party liability insurance.

Occupational accidents, health

Employers must carry liability insurance to cover injury to employees in the course of their employment.

The regulations to which this compulsory insurance is subject differ in Great Britain and in Northern Ireland.

Leisure, sports associations and youth movements

Those running riding schools must carry liability insurance to cover injury to riders or other persons.

Pollution

Boat owners' liabilities relating to oil pollution must be covered by insurance in conformity with the Brussels Convention on Civil Liability for Oil Pollution Damage (1969).

Nuclear power

Liability insurance must be carried by operators of nuclear installations to cover property damage or physical injury to persons other than the operator, irrespective of whether the accident occurs at the site or elsewhere, in specified circumstances, and arising from the radioactive properties of the materials used, or caused by the emission of ionising radiation (1965).

Professional indemnity

Third party insurance is compulsory for insurance brokers (1986), solicitors (it is noteworthy that different regulations govern such insurance cover in England and Wales, in Scotland (1980) and in Northern Ireland (1976)) and credit unions (for losses resulting from fraud or malpractice by an employee - different regulations govern this insurance in Great Britain and in Northern Ireland).

Others

Fire insurance is required for farm buildings and various other buildings in specified circumstances.

Insurance must be carried by owners of dangerous wild animals against damage or injury to third parties (1991) (dogs bred for fighting).

Q. THE NETHERLANDS

There are few compulsory types of insurance in this country : third party motor vehicle insurance (1963) (Transport), insurance for medical experiments involving humans subjects (1999), certain forms of occupational retirement schemes (Occupational accidents, health), third party insurance for hunters (1954) (Leisure, sports associations and youth movements), third party insurance relating to pollution by oil tankers (1975) (Pollution), liability of operators of nuclear installations (1979), and operation of nuclear-powered ships (1973) (Nuclear power); liabilities relating to pipeline operation (1972); liabilities relating to storage in underground tanks (Professional indemnity). Insurance is also required of usufructuaries to cover the object of the usufruct against the usual risks (Others).

The professional associations of notaries and advocates require their members to hold third party insurance.

R. LUXEMBOURG

The Grand Duchy of Luxembourg has somewhat over ten compulsory types of insurance.

The main such insurance is third party motor vehicle insurance (Transport). Other types of liability insurance relate to third party risks in sports activities: hunting (1956), parachute jumping (1986), pleasure sailing and boating (1987), organising and participating in sports competitions held on the public highway (Leisure, sports associations and youth movements), and some professional indemnity cover: architects (1989), travel agents and insurance brokers; hotel-keepers against fire, theft and third party risks (Professional indemnity). Civil servants and state employees on duty travel are required to carry baggage insurance; when travelling by air, insurance against risks not covered by compulsory social accident insurance is required. Stockbreeders and butchers must carry insurance against loss resulting from confiscation of meat from the country's slaughterhouses (Others).

S. TURKEY

There are six types of compulsory insurance in Turkey:

Third party liability insurance for motor vehicles (Transport)

Passenger insurance for buses (Transport)

Insurance made in accordance with the Civil Aviation Act (Transport)

Third party liability insurance related to the LPG trade (Pollution)

Third party liability insurance related to dangerous materials (Pollution)

Earthquake insurance (Others)

T. IRELAND

The only compulsory insurance is third party insurance related to the use of motor vehicles (1961 and 1962) (Transport).

U. KOREA

There are many areas in which insurance is compulsory in South Korea. The following is a list of twenty items requiring insurance, primarily liability insurance. Compulsory insurance has become increasingly emphasised in recent years.

Transport

Third party motor vehicle insurance in the form of no-fault coverage (1963).

Third party insurance for aircraft operators covering not only damage to a third party at ground level but also to passengers (1971); for freight carriers (1992); port operators (1993); fishing boat operators (1995); and driving school operators (2001).

Occupational accidents, health

Life, accident and sickness insurance for crew members at sea (1984).

Leisure, sports associations and youth groups

Insurance coverage for youth organisations, sporting and cultural associations, and sports camps (1991).

Third party coverage for the operators of large athletic facilities (1994); hunters (1997); and water-leisure sports facilities (1999).

Pollution

Liability insurance covering oil spills at sea are mandatory (1992).

Nuclear power

Operators of nuclear installations must carry liability insurance (1969).

Professional indemnity

Gas distributors (1983), elevator operators (1996), constructors (in the case of government orders) (1999), architects and public tender adjudicators (2001), as well as multi-level marketing distributors (2002) must have professional liability insurance.

Liability insurance is compulsory for Korean expatriates working abroad (1997).

Other insurance coverage

Fire insurance is compulsory for public places and for buildings above a defined scale (1973).

V.   MEXICO [1]

Transport

Highway insurance (1993).

Insurance for civil aviation (1995).

Boat insurance (1994).

Traveller insurance. Any person or company dedicated to the economic exploitation of railroads, street cars, navigation, aviation, buses and automobiles of federal public service must carry traveller insurance. This insurance covers medical and hospital expenses in case of accidents as well as compensation in case of death. It also covers baggage and belongings losses reported by the traveller in the moment of the boarding of the transport (1976, 1994, 1995, 1996).

Insurance of Public Transport (taxis and microbuses)(1995); insurance for public transport users (1997).

Insurance for transport of goods (1997).

Occupational accidents, health

Health insurance for workers employed in a ship (sea people) in a territory where the decree is in force (1984).

Health and accidents insurance for participants contemplated in an Agreement of scientific co-operation with Guyana (1997).

Leisure, sports associations and youth movements

Tourist insurance covering diving activities (1992).

Tourist insurance covering medical expenses as well as an indemnity in case of death. This applied to tourists transported in a vehicle whose responsibility rest in a tour guide (1988).

Insurance for tourists and hotelkeepers contracting with tourist services operators regulated by an Official Mexican Norm (1996).

Pollution

Insurance for transport carriers covering environmental damages (1993).

---

[1] The information provided is updated until 2001.

Environmental insurance covering damages governed by several regulations, concerning e.g. sea contamination by oil (1994), transport and import of toxic waste (1996), or the Bylaw of Urban and load transport in Mexico City (1993).

Others

Life insurance is compulsory for scholarship holders learning medical practice in a hospital under supervision (1982).

Life Insurance is also compulsory to cover commercial credit liabilities (the premium is paid by the consumer designating as beneficiary the supplier of the good).

Another case of compulsory insurance is the Products and supplies Insurance, based on a concession granted by the *Secretaría de Comunicaciones y Transportes* (1991) to the company *Servicios Siderúrgicos, S.A de C.V.* for the exclusive use of a load maritime terminal.

Fire, earthquake and other catastrophic risks are insured pursuant to the Social Housing insurance (1992).

W. AUSTRALIA

Transport

Owners of motor vehicles must hold third party cover (compulsory third party insurance). Compulsory third party is regulated under State and Territory laws and the arrangements for underwriting and the amounts of damages that can be paid differ between States. Such insurance is a precondition for registration of the vehicle. The insurance covers personal injury.

The insurer, depending on the State concerned, may be a government insurance bureau or an authorised private insurer. Proceedings involving uninsured or unidentified vehicles must be brought against the nominal defendant.

Occupational accidents, health

Under Australian law, employers' liabilities with respect to their employees must be insured with an authorised insurer (workers' compensation insurance). The Commonwealth, States and Territories have different laws governing this requirement, but all schemes are based on the 'no fault' principle. Insurance is by way of annual premiums or by self-insurance, where the employer is required to meet certain prudential requirements.

Leisure, sports associations and youth movements

Accredited travel agencies are required, by their professional associations, to take out third party insurance [1].

Pollution

There are requirements applicable to transportation vehicles for carrying hazardous waste, and to firms engaged in the storage, treatment and removal of hazardous waste.

Firms exporting or importing hazardous waste must be reasonably insured against risks; in general, this means they should be covered by public liability insurance with a limit of liability of at least AUD 5 million;

Ships that have a gross tonnage of 400 tonnes or more, visiting Australian ports and carrying oil as cargo or bunkers are required to carry an insurance certification that they have in place adequate insurance cover against pollution risks.

Professional indemnity

Under the Corporations Act, from March 2004, all holders of financial services licences, which include insurance brokers, stockbrokers and financial planners, will be required to have in place adequate compensation arrangements, which could include holding professional indemnity insurance. However, this requirement is currently being re-examined, partly due to the difficulties in obtaining professional indemnity cover in the Australian market.

Certain professions require members to have professional indemnity insurance if they are to be allowed to practise e.g. barristers, solicitors, medical practitioners in private practice.

Other professions require a minimum level of professional indemnity cover for membership of professional bodies e.g. accountants, auditors.

In the State of Victoria, professional builders must take out professional indemnity insurance before they can be registered. In other States e.g. New South Wales, other professions in the building industry, such as building consultants, are required to have professional indemnity insurance cover.

Recently there has been a move towards the adoption of professional standards legislation in Australia. Professional associations are permitted to set limits, either by setting liability ceilings, or in the form of multiples of the cost of service, or a

---

[1] Our Australian source also mentions that in practice, most providers of leisure activities carry public liability insurance.

combination of the two which effectively limits professional indemnity if it can be shown that the person in question has insurance cover for this amount or owns corresponding property that may serve as security. Such limitations do not apply in the case of physical injury, fraud or malpractice. In order to obtain the benefits of these limits, professional associations must implement standards of conduct which include risk management processes, professional training, complaints handling mechanisms and appropriate disciplinary procedures. Professional standards legislation is already in place in two States, and a national approach is being considered by all other States in an attempt to deal with the rapidly increasing costs of professional indemnity insurance in Australia.

X. JAPAN

Japan has very few compulsory types of insurance. Apart from third party motor vehicle insurance (Transport), the only requirements are for liability insurance in the nuclear field (Nuclear power) and fire insurance for goods in storage, the cover for which must be taken out by the depositors (Professional)

Transport

Compulsory Automobile Liability Insurance (CALI)

The Automobile Liability Security Law was enacted on December 1, 1955, in order to provide protection and financial security to traffic accident victims and to ensure that the driver at fault can meet his financial liability. In accordance with the law, any person who puts an automobile into operation is obliged to take out a Compulsory Automobile Liability Insurance (CALI) policy. Operating an automobile without CALI is illegal.

The outline of current CALI scheme is as follows:

The coverage for a victim; Death: JPY 30 million, Permanent Disability: JPY 30 million – JPY 0.75 million (After-effect requiring care: Grade 1 JPY 40 million, Grade 2 JPY 30 million), Bodily Injury: JPY 1.2 million.

Limited exclusions of coverage (only in case of wilful acts and double insurance)

Limited application of contributory negligence (reduction of the sum of the claim payment by 20%, 30% or 50% only in case that the victim has been grossly negligent)

Victims' right to claim for damages directly against the insurer

Obligation of insurers to assume CALI.

Operation of the CALI based on what is called the "no-loss and no-profit rule".

Note: As a result of revision of the Automobile Liability Security Law, the CALI government reinsurance scheme, where CALI contracts were reinsured en bloc with the government on 60% of quota share basis, was abolished on April 1, 2002. The entire CALI premium portfolio is reinsured with the CALI Reinsurance Pool, in which all insurers operating in CALI business in Japan participate.

Nuclear power

Nuclear energy liability insurance

Article 6 of the Law on Compensation for Nuclear Damage obliges nuclear operators, including an approved installer of nuclear reactors, to take one of the following three measures against third party liability for nuclear damage.

The first is to take out one of the following three insurance policies with a private non-life insurer: 1) Nuclear Site Liability Insurance, 2) Nuclear Transport Liability Insurance, or 3) Nuclear-Powered Vessel Operators' Liability Insurance. In addition, the nuclear operators are obliged to conclude an indemnity agreement with the government in order to compensate for nuclear damage (whereby the losses which are not covered by private insurers are indemnified).

The second measure is to deposit a specified amount with the government. Because this requires the freezing of large amounts of funds for a long period of time, there has been no precedent of operators taking this measure.

The third measure is an open-ended option, which requires the operator to take a measure equivalent to the former two and be approved by the Ministry of Education, Culture, Sports, Science and Technology. However, there has been no precedent of this either.

Professional indemnity

Warehouseman's obligation to take out fire insurance on the goods in his custody

Article 14 of the Warehousing Business Law stipulates that every warehouseman ought to take out fire insurance to protect the goods placed in his custody by the depositor. However, this shall not apply in cases where the depositor raises an objection against such cover or where the warehouseman entrusts such goods in his custody to another warehouseman.

Y. CANADA

Transport

Third-party liability insurance for private and commercial vehicles is mandatory in Canada, although the required minimum levels of insurance vary from province to province. This insurance provides financial protection in the event that policyholders are held liable for injury or loss sustained by others arising from the operation of their vehicle(s). In addition, there are requirements for passenger hazard coverage and cargo coverage for commercial vehicles.

Many provinces have implemented "no fault" coverage in their automobile insurance systems. Such a system permits accident victims, regardless of fault, to claim compensation from their own insurers for injuries. However, many provinces have an additional "tort" component, allowing individuals to sue for excess expenses under certain circumstances.

Insurance against damage to a vehicle is available on a voluntary basis. If this insurance is not purchased and the driver of the vehicle is at fault in an accident, there will be no recovery at all for vehicle damage.

Depending on the province, automobile insurance is provided by private insurers or by provincial government insurance companies. In the provinces where a provincial government insurance company provides automobile insurance, both private and government insurers compete for optional additional coverage.

In the maritime sector, Canada is currently developing compulsory insurance requirements for commercial and public-purpose passenger vessels. Ship owners are also required to maintain insurance coverage or other types of financial security to cover their liability arising from the carriage of passengers and cargo (*Marine Liability Act*, 2001).

Occupational accidents, health

Insured health services in Canada include all medically necessary hospital services and medically required physician services, as well as medically or dentally required surgical-dental services necessitating a hospital for their proper performance. The plan is administered and operated on a non-profit basis by a public authority, responsible to the provincial government and subject to audit of its accounts and financial transactions. The plan must insure all insured health services provided by hospitals, medical practitioners or dentists. All insured persons of a province are entitled to the insured health services provided for by the plan, and residents moving to another province continue to be covered.

Each province and territory has its own legislated Workers' Compensation Act that, along with the various regulations, defines and describes the rules and benefits available to eligible employee groups. Each province, in its respective Act and regulations, designates the industries in which workers must be covered under the workers' compensation plan. Employers must carry liability insurance to cover injury to employees in the course of their employment. Based on the principles of collective liability and no-fault, the workers' compensation system is funded by employer assessments. The amount of the employer's contribution is determined by a payroll assessment rate that reflects the accident risk of similar firms within the industry.

Leisure, sports associations and youth movements

Most recreation and leisure facilities are insured under a comprehensive general liability policy. Although this type of insurance coverage is not compulsory, most organisations are covered by this type of policy.

Nuclear power

The Nuclear Liability Act establishes that the operator (and only the operator) of a nuclear installation is liable for bodily injury and property damage caused by nuclear material in the installation or in transit. The Act currently limits operator liability to $75 million, though pending changes to the legislation will increase the limit to $650 million. Mandatory insurance is provided to operators through the Nuclear Insurance Association of Canada (NAIC), an association underwritten by several large Canadian insurers. Through a reinsurance agreement with the NAIC, the federal government provides coverage for certain types of injury (stress, trauma) and certain incidents (terrorist acts). The Act also stipulates that the federal government can provide additional compensation, e.g., beyond the statutory limit of $75 million, soon to be increased to $650 million.

Professional indemnity

All lawyers are required to have coverage. Some provinces require architects, engineers, and chartered accountants to have coverage. In addition, some professional associations require members to have insurance in order to obtain a license.

Others

There are many situations, varying between provinces, where insurance is necessary as a condition of obtaining a licence, for example, private investigators, guard dog operators, day-care operators, pesticide operators etc.

Z. UNITED STATES

No exhaustive list of types of insurance compulsory in the United States is available to our knowledge.

It would be very difficult to draw one up in view of the very large number and diversity of regulations applicable not only at the federal level but also within the 50 States of the Union. Comments will therefore be restricted to a number of general indications on the major sectors in which compulsory insurance is found.

Transport

Third party motor vehicle insurance is not required everywhere. It is compulsory only in some 40 States, sometimes in the form of conventional liability insurance, more rarely in the form of no-fault cover.

Occupational accidents, health

Compulsory occupational accident insurance is also found in some States.

Pollution

The environmental damage sector has been the area in which many forms of compulsory insurance have appeared in recent years. At the federal level such requirements apply for instance to ships and trucks carrying oil and to firms engaged in the storage, treatment and removal of toxic wastes. Most States have also introduced insurance requirements in these fields.

Professional indemnity

Many states require the purchase of medical malpractice coverage and where there is no state requirement, hospitals generally make health care providers obtain medical malpractice coverage as a condition for obtaining access to hospital facilities.

CHAPTER 2

COMMENTS

Section I will present a number of general comments arising from the review of compulsory insurance in OECD countries. After a look at the historical antecedents of the practice, attention will focus on the grounds given for introduction of compulsory insurance; the advantages and disadvantages of the practice will be discussed. Criteria for determining the desirability of making insurance compulsory will then be sought, and in the light of the criteria a critical look will be taken at the principal forms of compulsory insurance reviewed in the paper.

Section II will discuss the principal mechanisms available to ensure effective compliance with a requirement to hold insurance.

I. Comparative summary – desirability of compulsory insurance

Following an outline of the history of compulsory insurance (A), a look will be taken at the grounds used to justify such a requirement (B) and the latter's advantages and disadvantages (C). In the final part of the chapter, this discussion will be brought to a close by considering which categories of insurance are worth making compulsory and which it would be better to leave voluntary (D).

A. *History of compulsory insurance*

The concept of compulsory insurance[1] arose in the eighteenth century, in a number of German principalities in which fire insurance was made compulsory. In nineteenth century France, the concept of insurance as a means of guaranteeing a minimum of security to the most deprived took hold and led to the adoption of compulsory insurance to cover the outstanding portion of loans made for acquisition of dwellings at moderate rent and compulsory insurance for pensioners. A fierce debate between partisans of laissez-faire policies, who were opposed to forced insurance, and partisans of more socially-oriented policies, who upheld the virtues of compulsory cover (even perhaps nationalised cover), went on throughout the century but ultimately led to a new approach to sharing the burden of social problems by the adoption in 1898 of compulsory insurance to cover employers' liability in relation to occupational accidents.

Social problems, as a general rule, in particular occupational accidents, provided the spur to the development of compulsory insurance. The next major problem, which attracted the attention of lawmakers in the first half of the twentieth century, arose as motor vehicle traffic began to proliferate. As the price of motor cars became more accessible their numbers increased and the question of compensation for traffic accidents became increasingly important. Compensation for damage suffered had to be

---

[1] See for example EWALD, F. (1993) "Politiques de l'assurance obligatoire", *Risques, op. cit.*, pp. 59 *et seq.*

provided for the growing number of victims; drivers too had to be protected against mounting liabilities, which could endanger their assets. Drivers had a duty to provide compensation for the harm they caused, but also a duty to remain solvent; the State had an obligation to ensure the latter was respected. For that reason, in almost all the countries considered, insurance against liabilities arising from motor vehicle risks was made compulsory in the mid-twentieth century.

In most countries, introduction of this new form of compulsory insurance went hand in hand with establishment of a guarantee fund, a new kind of body to which every insured person contributed (in the form of a percentage of premium paid). The purpose of such a fund is to compensate victims for damage caused by unidentified or uninsured drivers, or by vehicle thieves. The system relies on sharing the burden of such cover among the whole community of drivers in order to secure compensation for victims unable to serve a claim against any specific insurer.

The proliferation of compulsory types of insurance seen in some countries began in the second half of the twentieth century and grew exponentially thereafter until the late 1980s. In the first edition of this study, published in 1997, a tendency to restrain excessive further developments of compulsory insurance seemed to appear here and there. Six years later, the authors are under the impression that this tendency did not prevail. In those countries and in several others, the recent years have seen new significant expansions of the numbers of compulsory types of insurance.

The development of compulsory insurance relates principally to liability insurance. The legal and financial professions (lawyers, accountants, insurance brokers, patent consultants, etc.) and the health-related professions were the principal targets of such developments. Compulsory types of personal insurance, generally to cover occupational accident, have been in existence for longer but are less numerous. On the other hand, compulsory property insurance has remained relatively rare, fire being the risk most often covered (see also below with respect to construction insurance in France and to insurance cover against natural disasters, which is found in a number of countries). Instances of compulsory fidelity (Belgium, municipal treasurers; Italy, brokers) and legal expenses insurance (Belgium, local officials) will be reported.

Some of the fields most recently added to compulsory insurance include dependants' insurance (Germany, 1993) and liability of certifiers of digital signatures (Germany; Austria, 1999; Portugal, 1999; Belgium, 2001; Poland, 2001).

It is noteworthy that in no country does the provision of compulsory insurance seem to be the outcome of consistent legislative policy. Laws are adopted in response to social or political pressure, seemingly provoked by events that have caught public attention, which may explain the considerable differences in date sometimes found in laws introducing compulsory insurance in different countries (for instance, motor vehicle insurance became compulsory in the United Kingdom in 1930, but did not do so in Italy until 1967; liability insurance for hunting was made compulsory in Germany in 1934, but was not introduced in Denmark until 1987). A contagious effect is sometimes seen, at least in some countries, adoption of compulsory insurance in one field leading to legislation to introduce it in related sectors.

The disparate nature of compulsory insurance is also displayed in the origin of the requirement for cover. Generally speaking compulsory insurance is introduced by legislation, whether national, regional or local. In some cases, the obligation arises as a result of agreement, in other words by means of regulations which professional associations make binding on their members (but such professional rules are sometimes made compulsory by public regulation). In France in particular, many types of compulsory insurance are introduced by ministerial decree or even by ministerial circulars, which as a general rule have no legal force.

In addition to growth in the number of compulsory types of insurance, developments in the countries concerned have also changed perceptions of the conditions under which such categories of insurance should operate.

In many fields fault liability insurance has been superseded by no-fault liability cover, in which the victim need no longer prove negligence on the part of the person implicated in the damage caused in order to receive compensation; thus the Brussels Convention on Civil Liability for Oil Pollution Damage of November 29, 1969 imposes a system of no-fault liability under which the owner of the ship giving rise to the claim may only disclaim liability if he can provide proof of certain outside circumstances (this principle was conserved in the London Protocol of November 27, 1992 and the new London Convention of March 23, 2001); in France "vulnerable" traffic accident victims receive compensation regardless of whether the driver involved has been negligent (1985); a similar system has applied in Belgium since 1994; in Norway, public hospital insurance is also based on no-fault liability.

A notable development in the evolution of compulsory insurance has been the provision in France of compulsory insurance against damage to buildings under construction (1978). This has a number of distinguishing features. Firstly, although liability cover is required of builders (the potential negligent party), property cover is also required of the person for whom the building is being constructed (the potential victim). Recognition of damage done enables the victim's claims to be met, whereupon the onus is upon the insurer to seek recovery from the negligent party. Secondly, the dual insurance requirement serves more than one purpose: the legislation is intended not only to accelerate and ensure settlement of the victim's claim, but also seeks to encourage builders (whose insurance costs will rise in proportion to the number of claims proved against them) to improve their methods of work and adopt preventive measures. In this sense, compulsory insurance plays a regulatory role in the technical and economic spheres[1].

Other types of property insurance now compulsory in some countries relate to natural disasters (France, 1982; Norway, 1989; Spain, 1990; Turkey; Belgium has

---

[1] EWALD, F. (1993), *op. cit.*, pp. 75 and 76.

recently made storm (1995) and flood (2003) cover compulsory components of fire policies, which remain optional; the same approach has been adopted with respect to labour disputes and terrorist attacks, cover against such risks has been a compulsory component of fire insurance since 1988).

Apart from the Paris Convention on Third Party Liability in the Field of Nuclear Energy, July 29, 1960, few types of compulsory insurance operate on a Europe-wide basis. A major development, however, was the European directive 71/166 of April 24, 1972, which made third party motor liability insurance compulsory in the member States.

More recently, the European Directive on insurance intermediaries has introduced a requirement of professional indemnity insurance for insurance and reinsurance intermediaries (Dir. 2002/92 of December 9, 2002, art. 4, 3°). A draft directive is currently under discussion that would impose compulsory insurance related to the prevention and repair of damages to the environment caused by sea pollution by oil.

On another level, the non-life insurance directives of June 22, 1988 (article 8) and June 18, 1992 (article 30), have excluded compulsory insurance from their general rules on conflict of laws, stipulating that the laws of the country imposing the requirement shall as a rule prevail[1].

B. The bases of compulsory insurance

The major types of compulsory insurance, which are also the most widespread, have given rise to much explanatory comment on the reasons why such cover has to be compulsory. This is especially true in the case of third party motor vehicle insurance - the number of road traffic accidents and the severity of the injuries that may result make it imperative to protect victims by ensuring, through compulsory insurance, that they will be indemnified. Compulsory insurance also protects the negligent party against the risk to assets to which such party may be exposed[2].

In the case of third party liability for hunting, the large number of accidents is also the reason given to justify this victim protection measure[3].

In general, compulsory personal insurance or compulsory liability insurance is intended, even where this is not explicitly stated, to protect victims against the risk of accidents that are especially frequent or serious, and (in the case of liability insurance) to protect the assets of the negligent party. The priority given to protection of victims is sometimes evident from the measures designed to address it, such as provision for direct proceedings (*"action directe"*) by the victim against the insurer, accompanied by a

---

[1] LEGRAND, B. (1993) *op. cit.*, p. 43.

[2] FONTAINE, M. & PAULUS-DE RODE H., *op. cit.*, p. 202; EWALD, F. *op. cit.*, pp. 68 *et seq.*

[3] FONTAINE, M. & PAULUS-DE RODE H., *loc. cit.*

procedure whereby defences the insurers may assert against the insured may not be raised against the victim (such direct proceedings form part of third party motor vehicle cover in most of the countries considered except the United Kingdom)[1].

Another justification for making insurance cover compulsory is the extended liability attached to some risks. If the law increases the liability of any given economic agent, it is reasonable to provide measures to enforce such liability otherwise it will remain a dead letter (an example is the Paris Convention on Third Party Liability in the Field of Nuclear Energy of July 29, 1960, which attaches no fault liability to the operator of a nuclear installation coupled with a requirement for insurance cover).

Compulsory property insurance is rare. Fire is the risk most frequently covered by such insurance (Switzerland, Germany, Denmark and Norway; and Italy in the case of social housing). The reasons for such cover are not generally explicitly stated. Although compulsory insurance for property held for a third party as a professional service could be considered justified in the same way as liability insurance, the same cannot be said of property belonging to the insured.

C. Advantages and disadvantages of compulsory insurance

There is one obvious advantage to compulsory insurance: it prevents citizens from becoming careless about risks they underestimate which may occasion severe damage. Furthermore, by making insurance cover compulsory a State also protects itself by reducing the need for action on its part[2]. Compulsory insurance also discourages exclusion of risks and promotes balance in the insurance market. Nevertheless insurers have mixed views on compulsory insurance.

They consider that the minimum cover requirements of compulsory insurance are often too high, which causes difficulties with reinsurance. Compulsory insurance also means that public authorities can exert greater pressure on rates[3]. Insurers have not made enough effort to combat unlimited cover in compulsory insurance, which in some cases has had a disastrous effect[4]. Insurers also consider that compulsory insurance removes or at any rate greatly reduces the opportunities voluntary insurance give them to promote measures to prevent damage: in voluntary insurance, the insurer can demand preventive measures, adapt the amount of premium or deductibles to the preventive action taken by the insured, etc. - all of which is generally not possible in compulsory insurance. The inflexibility of compulsory insurance also precludes the case-by-case

---

[1] International Insurance Law Association (AIDA) (1994), *Motor insurance in the world*, p. 59.

[2] GOLLIER, Ch. & ROCHET, J.Ch. "Les économistes face à l'assurance obligatoire. Un débat contradictoire.", *Risques*, op. cit., pp. 48 *et seq.*

[3] FONTAINE, M. & PAULUS-DE RODE H., *op. cit.*, p.277.

[4] BARROUX, J., FLORIN, P., MARGEAT, H. & THOUROT, P. "Une maladie française. Débat" *Risques*, *op.cit.*, p.12. The case of transmission of AIDS by blood transfusion is given as an example.

assessment of risk that in voluntary insurance allows appropriate cover to be precisely determined. Supervision of compliance with insurance requirements entails additional costs for insurers whenever they are expected to notify the authorities that a policy has been cancelled or to furnish proof of annual renewal of cover. Furthermore, the existence of compulsory insurance leads to increasingly harsh assessment by courts and tribunals of the extent of liability of the insured, since any sums involved will inevitably be paid[1]. This trend in case law to take account of possible insurance cover has come in for much criticism: in France, Professor Chabas has said *"... the existence of insurance cover has become the reason for an adverse verdict: liability is now no more than the end to be achieved in any eventuality"*[2].

Other untoward effects of compulsory insurance have been pointed out. The fact that compulsory insurance is anchored in law makes it less flexible: for example, the amount of cover set is not reviewed and in time becomes inadequate. Supervision of compliance with the requirement for cover is also a major problem; without such supervision enforcement is impossible. However, absolute supervision is difficult to achieve and is expensive. Lastly, compulsory insurance may diminish the sense of personal responsibility. One of the results of this has been to increase fraud in the areas covered by compulsory insurance. Economists point for example to *"... the American savings and loan debacle, largely attributable to compulsory deposit insurance. Compulsory insurance managed by a remote agency weakens any incentive to prevention on the part of the economic agents exposed to risk. In some cases, it encourages fraud. Compulsory insurance can thus only be beneficial if ... monitoring of the risks insured is carried out with as much care as is employed in the private sector"*[3].

The results are therefore not all on the plus side. Two conclusions are already apparent: firstly, that compulsory insurance should be restricted to those areas where a need is genuinely felt. Secondly, it should only be introduced in sectors where supervision is possible at reasonable cost.

D. Desirability of compulsory insurance

The complete absence of compulsory insurance is unquestionably bad for a society and its citizens, but so is a proliferation of such insurance. It is therefore evident that consideration of the subject calls for a coherent political and economic approach. The studies of the subject conducted in France and Belgium, which incidentally gave very similar results, may serve as a starting point for such an approach[4].

---

[1] LEGRAND, B., *op. cit.*, p.45.

[2] (1993) "L'assurance de personnes au service du droit de la responsabilité civile", *Risques*, n° 14, pp.83 *et seq.* An insurers' viewpoint is also given by J. ROGGE, *Bulletin des Assurances* (Brussels), 2001, Dossier n° 7, *op. cit.*, pp. 121-123; also see the reply of an insurance public supervisor presented by H. CONRUYT, *ibid.*, pp. 133-138.

[3] See GOLLIER, Ch. & ROCHET, J.Ch., *op. cit.*, pp.51 and 52.
[4] See above, notes 2 and 3, p.147.

1. General criteria [1]

The most widespread types of compulsory insurance are third party motor vehicle cover and occupational accident cover (the latter cover is universal but in some countries forms part of the national social security system and in others is provided by the private insurance market). The gravity of the risks involved in these two areas, and the frequency with which they occur, makes compulsory insurance essential.

The prevalence of other types of compulsory insurance varies from country to country. It is therefore worth looking at whether they are really needed. In view of the attendant disadvantages, compulsory insurance should only be provided if deemed indispensable on the basis of the following criteria:

- compulsory insurance is justified whenever a grave risk is involved, one that is sufficiently widespread to represent a major social problem. Insurance against third party risks entailed by the use of motor vehicles and occupational accidents are the most evident examples.

- compulsory insurance is also justified in cases where the risk involved is very serious even though less widespread. This criterion applies to hunting, and to accident cover for motor racing.

- compulsory insurance is necessary when the law increases the extent of liability, since without obligation such provisions would be unenforceable. This of course raises the question of whether liability really needs to be extended. This will be considered later.

2. Application of the criteria to various types of compulsory insurance found in OECD countries

The different categories of compulsory insurance existing in the various countries will now be looked at, under the headings used in the first chapter of the paper and in the light of the criteria given above.

Transport

Third party cover related to the use of motor vehicles unquestionably meets the first criterion above for justified compulsory insurance. A question which may arise in the case of such insurance is whether extended liability is a necessary addition.

In France, Belgium and Denmark, a system of no-fault accident liability is provided for accidents suffered by vulnerable victims (pedestrians, cyclists, passengers; in Denmark, protected victims are pedestrians, cyclists and horse riders). In some other

---

[1] See FONTAINE, M. & PAULUS-DE RODE H., *op. cit.*, pp.278-279; LEGRAND, B., *op. cit.*, p.41.

countries no-fault liability is provided in all cases (Norway; Spain in the case of physical injury). Partisans of no-fault liability point to the frequency of accidents, the fact that motorists are persistently negligent at the wheel and the length and cost of proceedings to establish liability. Opponents of the system claim that it saps the sense of personal responsibility and increases costs for all insured persons.

Vulnerable victims (pedestrians, cyclists, passengers) are obviously in a weak position with respect to drivers: the risk of severe physical injury is greater in their case. They are also in a more unfavourable situation as regards evidence relating to the circumstances of the accident, since they are more often injured and thus unable to seek witnesses to an accident forthwith. A solution to these difficulties might be to amend the rules of evidence in the case of accidents involving injury: presumption of liability on the part of a driver until proved innocent would redress the balance between the two protagonists and prevent the loss of sense of responsibility provoked by no-fault insurance (such a system is applied in the Netherlands, for example)[1].

Liability insurance for aircraft owners and/or operators exists in most countries, such as Austria, Belgium, the Czech Republic, Denmark, France, Germany, Greece, Korea, Iceland, Italy, Norway, Portugal, Slovakia and Switzerland. Such insurance responds to the second desirability criterion. Such compulsory insurance should be made universal and cover not only damage to third parties at ground level but also damage to persons carried.

The same arguments apply to compulsory insurance for helicopter operators and heliports (France).

On the other hand, there appear to be no convincing grounds for making compulsory cover for damage to hired vehicles compulsory (Denmark).

Occupational accidents, health

Compulsory insurance in this sector generally refers to occupational accidents.

Since the social problem posed by the frequency and gravity of occupational accidents is universally acknowledged, no objection can be made to compulsory cover for this risk irrespective of the procedures selected for the purpose (social security or private insurance).

There are more specific requirements for accident insurance in certain especially dangerous professions, such as firemen (Belgium, France, and Portugal), bullfighters (Spain, Portugal) or even "stewards" trying to prevent violence at football games (Belgium). This may be justified. But are there solid reasons explaining the need for

---

[1] International Insurance Law Association (AIDA) (1994), *Motor insurance in the world, op. cit.*, p. 50.

compulsory accident insurance to cover mayors (Portugal) or members of electoral boards (Belgium)?

Leisure, sports associations and youth movements

In the leisure arena, the most common compulsory insurance is liability cover for hunters (Austria, Belgium, the Czech Republic, Denmark, France, Germany, Greece, Korea, Italy, Luxembourg, the Netherlands Portugal, Slovakia, Spain, and Switzerland). The risk of severe accident entailed by this sport justifies the requirement for cover.

Compulsory third party cover for operators of motor racing events (Belgium, France, Greece and Luxembourg) and air shows (France) is necessary, as is cover for those competing[1]. Such events carry a high risk of serious accident. Nevertheless, as far as competitors are concerned, third party cover does not solve all problems in that it is often difficult to determine whether negligence of another participant is involved. This is a case in which accident cover, taken out either by participants on an individual basis or by the organiser on their behalf, is justified and should be made compulsory.

Travel agents in several countries must carry liability cover (Belgium, the Czech Republic, France, Iceland, Norway, Portugal, Slovakia and Spain). The relative rarity of such compulsory cover would indicate that there is no real social need for it. Nevertheless, in countries where such cover is compulsory, there has been a very high level of litigation in the sector. Assessment of whether such cover should be compulsory will therefore depend on the economic circumstances prevailing in the country concerned.

Ski-lift or cable-cars operators are often required to take third party liability insurance (Austria, France, Norway and Switzerland).

Some compulsory types of insurance of this category raise questions. For instance, is there any need, as in France, to make accident cover compulsory for boxers, and liability cover compulsory for dancing schools? French insurance experts recommend the removal of such requirements, and in fact there does not seems to be any social problem arising from the risk that would justify it[2].

Should camp site operators be required to take out liability cover, as happens in Belgium? The authors do not feel that the level of risk involved in this activity justifies the requirement; the fact that this is the sole example of such compulsory cover would seem to prove it.

---

[1] In Belgium, such cover is also compulsory for bicycle racing. The death of a participant in the 1995 *Tour de France* was a reminder that this sport may also cause fatalities.

[2] DEFRANCE, G. (20 August 1993) "Le mal français", *Argus*, p. 14; "Comité de liaison de l'assurance, Assurances obligatoires. Rapport du groupe de travail", *Risques, op. cit*, p. 34.

Sports other than those considered above, and youth movements, should remain areas where insurance cover is voluntary since such activities represent no major social risk. It would therefore be preferable to leave sports associations and youth organisations to determine their own insurance needs and to be responsible for their own cover[1].

Pollution

Historically, the first instrument making insurance cover against a pollution risk compulsory was the International Convention on Civil Liability for Oil Pollution Damage (done at Brussels on November 29, 1969). It has been ratified by many of the countries covered in this study. This Convention provides an option for replacement of insurance cover by equivalent financial security such as a bank guarantee or a certificate issued by an international indemnity fund. Further international instruments on this matter are the London Protocol of November 27, 1992 and the new London Convention on Civil Liability for Oil Pollution Damages of March 23, 2001, currently in the course of ratification.

The disastrous nature of the risk involved in this type of pollution clearly justifies the adoption of such an instrument by all countries with vessels registered or licensed for the carriage of oil and for countries whose ports or territorial waters are a point of departure or arrival for such vessels.

Other types of compulsory insurance related to pollution can also be mentioned: insurance for pipeline operators (Austria, the Netherlands, and Switzerland), insurance against environmentally-hazardous activities (Germany, Portugal, and Switzerland), insurance for activities dealing with waste disposal (Australia, Belgium, Mexico, Portugal, and Spain), natural gas (Greece) or LPG (Turkey). The gravity of the risk involved and likelihood of its affecting a large area of national territory or even several States also warrants making such insurance compulsory.

Nuclear power

On July 29, 1960, the Convention on Third Party Liability in the Field of Nuclear Energy was signed in Paris (a convention that was followed by a number of supplementary conventions and additional protocols). National legislation to make third party liability cover compulsory for the operators of nuclear installations has been adopted in many countries (Austria, Belgium, Canada, the Czech Republic, Denmark, France, Germany, Italy, Japan, Korea, the Netherlands, Norway, Poland, Portugal, Spain, Switzerland, the United Kingdom), whether or not they have ratified the Convention.

The disastrous nature of the risk involved also makes compulsory insurance cover in this area a necessity in all countries where such installations exist.

---

[1] This is also the case with French insurers: see "Comité de liaison de l'assurance", *op. cit.*, p. 33.

Professional indemnity

In view of the wide range of professions subject to compulsory insurance cover in the countries considered, it is advisable to group them by category. Consideration will be given in turn to the health professions (i), professions related to the building industry (ii), legal professions (iii), commercial and financial professions (iv), and other professions not belonging to any of these categories (v).

i. Health professions

Compulsory liability cover for health care providers cannot be considered as just another compulsory professional indemnity cover. To take but one example, that of the French hemophiliacs infected by AIDS following blood transfusion, it is evident that such liabilities may entail grave social problems.

Not all health professions, however, represent a high degree of risk to third parties. In this connection, it would not appear essential to make insurance cover compulsory for professions such as dentistry (as in Norway).

Members of the medical profession and hospitals are required to carry insurance cover in many countries (Australia, Belgium, the Czech Republic, Denmark, Germany, Iceland, Italy, Norway, Portugal, and Slovakia). Sometimes the requirement has been reorganised in connection of a major reform of the liability system (France, 2002).

Although the risk involved in curative procedures is a major one, it is no way evident, in our opinion, that imposing compulsory insurance by law is the best way of dealing with the problem. A legal requirement to carry insurance cover may, in the case of professions governed by a professional association, be replaced by a system embodied in an agreement whereby the professional association makes insurance cover compulsory. However, in the case of health professions not subject to regulation by a professional association, compulsory insurance is clearly the only solution.

Account needs to be taken of the customs prevailing in the professions concerned in each country. In many of the OECD countries considered in this paper, liability cover is very widespread in the health professions; provision of compulsory cover is not justified since the intervention of the professional associations allows a much more flexible approach to insurance. On the other hand, if liability insurance is rare then it would be advisable, as a first step, to make it compulsory, leaving the professional associations to take over responsibility for such insurance later when the insurance habit has become the norm.

Two untoward effects of the general spread of insurance in this field are worth noting: the fact that insurance exists provokes claims and means that liability is assessed more severely by the courts, with the inevitable result of driving premiums up to very high levels. This disturbing trend is apparent for example in the United States, France and Belgium. Another consequence has been seen in the United States, where the proliferation of medical liability cases has changed treatment practices among many medical practitioners; therapy presenting no opportunity for a medical liability suit is preferred to medical acts that give better results but are open to charges of negligence. Medical risk is sometimes considered to be so high that, in Belgium for example, some insurers refuse to cover it.

Pharmaceutical manufacturers are liable to risks so disastrous as perhaps to justify compulsory insurance cover. Such insurance is required in Germany and Norway.

ii. Professions associated with the building industry

Compulsory third party cover is common for architects: it exists in Belgium, the Czech Republic, some German States, France, Korea, Luxembourg, Norway, Poland and Portugal. It may be accompanied by compulsory insurance cover for builders (France and Portugal) and land surveyors and appraisers (France). Different variations of compulsory insurance related to construction appear in many countries, such as insurance for security co-ordinators (Belgium), building experts (Denmark), engineers and construction firms (Greece), construction engineers (Slovakia), public works (Korea), housing developers and builders (Spain), construction managers and designers (Iceland).

France has introduced a compulsory dual insurance system, damage being compensated first by the property insurer of the person for whom the building is being erected, who then brings a claim against the insurers of the negligent party, as was described earlier.

The large number of claims and suits in this field has been the prime mover in the introduction of compulsory insurance. Such liability insurance is undoubtedly very necessary. French insurers, who in other circumstances deem that professional indemnity insurance should no longer be required by law but should be regulated within the professions themselves, nevertheless consider that insurance should remain compulsory in the building industry because of its special importance to the economy (in the case of liability insurance for architects, the approach recommended is to retain only the requirement for ten-year liability cover)[1]. The authors consider this approach justified.

iii. Legal professions

The law requires liability cover for lawyers (advocates, solicitors, barristers, depending on the country) in Australia, Austria, Canada, the Czech Republic, Denmark, France, Germany, Iceland, Norway, Poland, Portugal, Slovakia, Switzerland and the United Kingdom. Greece required insurance from lawyers licensed in another State.

---

[1] "Comité de liaison de l'assurance", *op. cit.*, pp.29 and 34.

Liability insurance is compulsory for notaries in Austria, France, Germany, Poland, Slovakia and Spain.

Liability insurance is also compulsory in France for bailiffs, appraisers and auctioneers, administrators appointed by the courts and appointed liquidators.

Such insurance is very desirable but does not seem to meet the criteria justifying compulsory cover. It could be provided through professional associations and societies, as is the case for example in Belgium.

iv. Commercial and financial professions

During the past ten years, a number of countries have made liability insurance compulsory for insurance brokers (Australia, Belgium, the Czech Republic, France, Greece, Iceland, Italy, Norway, Poland, Portugal, Slovakia and the United Kingdom). It has been said that in the European Union, such insurance has been made compulsory by the Directive of 2002 on insurance intermediaries.

Liability insurance is also compulsory for accountants in several countries, but the original legislation in this field is older (Austria, Germany, France and Denmark). Other examples are auditors, industrial property and patent consultants, building societies and property managers (France), experts (Austria, Germany, Poland) and real estate agents (Belgium, Denmark, France, Iceland, Norway, Poland and Portugal).

More recently, certifiers of digital signatures have been subject to a requirement of third party liability insurance in several countries (Austria, Belgium, Germany, Poland, and Portugal).

These are the principal professions subject to regulations in this respect.

The authors consider that in the case of these professions there is no convincing justification, in the light of the criteria they have given, for insurance cover to be made compulsory by law; insurance in such sectors should be controlled by the professional associations[1].

v. Other professions

Other examples of professions for which liability cover is compulsory are veterinary surgeons (France), energy consultants (Denmark) and consulting engineers (Norway). According to the criteria established, we feel that such insurance cover should remain voluntary and not compulsory.

Other insurance covers

---

[1] On this point, see "Comité de liaison de l'assurance", *op. cit.*, p.34.

In some countries dog owners must carry liability insurance (Austria, Denmark; Spain, Portugal and the United Kingdom for dogs of dangerous breeds). The hazards represented by such animals do not seem to the authors to constitute a social problem justifying compulsory insurance. The Belgian approach to the matter is of interest: in 1984 a Royal Order provided compulsory areas of cover to be included in personal liability insurance (which is voluntary); such insurance includes liability associated with dogs. But Belgium imposes specific compulsory insurance for zoos.

Several countries have made insurance cover for natural risks (storm damage, flooding, etc.) a compulsory part of fire insurance (France, Spain, Norway and Belgium). Such cover meets the criteria justifying compulsory insurance. In some cases, moreover, compulsory insurance is the only way of avoiding exclusion of a risk (such as of flooding). Earthquake insurance is compulsory in Mexico and Turkey.

Fire insurance is sometimes made compulsory for some activities or some forms of property; this applies e.g. to farms in Denmark and Poland, to warehouses in Germany and Japan, to public and large buildings in Korea, to flats in Portugal and to multiple property in Spain. In Belgium, compulsory insurance for operators of various public places is linked to a regime of no-fault liability in case of fire.

When involving property attended by large groups of people, such compulsory fire insurance would appear to be justifiable in view of the high level of risk involved.

Finally we would like to comment on the Belgian draft to make legal expenses cover a compulsory element of private liability insurance, itself widely weld but not compulsory. The social preoccupation behind this draft is to facilitate access to justice, certainly a major social problem. However the implementation of such insurance at a reasonable cost proves to be a most difficult task. The draft has drawn much criticism, and its future is uncertain.

II. Technicalities of compulsory insurance

In different countries, examination of the texts providing compulsory insurance shows them to be drafted with very varying degrees of complexity. Some systems are set out in great detail. This is often the case with third party motor vehicle insurance where a series of laws and regulations may make provision for the insurance requirement, control procedures, penalties, the rights and obligations of the parties, the rights of third party victims, a guarantee fund and other aspects. At the other extreme, in the case of some compulsory insurance cover, a text may simply state that such and such a person is obliged to carry liability cover without further detail.

A requirement to carry insurance may, however, remain a dead letter without indication of a minimum of rules not only governing content and cover (see, for example, the problem of excepted risks) but also organising the requirement itself (see, for example, the problem of monitoring compliance with the requirement).

The relevant problems will be dealt with one by one and the principal solutions available indicated.

A. *Definition of Cover*

Should public authorities wish to make a type of insurance compulsory, it is not enough to express the requirement in general terms (e.g. "Every medical practitioner must carry professional indemnity cover").

The text must set out the principal features of the cover required, otherwise the cover may be practically eluded when a contract is drawn up, by means such as insertion of many exclusions and restrictions.

All details, however, must not be provided by the law that creates the obligation. Delegation can be given to regulatory authorities to specify the various specific aspects, sometimes in co-operation with professional associations[1].

In any case, it is particularly important that the following should be clearly indicated in the law or the implementing regulations:

1. *Persons insured*

These are not necessarily the persons compelled to subscribe the cover (see below). Compulsory cover may protect the interests of other persons, and this mechanism is widely used. In such cases the beneficiaries of the cover must be correctly identified.

Example: in compulsory third party motor vehicle insurance, the liabilities covered are generally not confined to those of the policy holder, but also comprise those of the owner of the vehicle, any driver, passengers, holders of the vehicle, etc.

2. *Risks covered*

Texts should clearly specify what risks are to be covered. In the case of liability insurance, for example, should cover be restricted to tort third party liability or should it also include contractual third party or other liabilities? Should it be dependent on occurrence of an accident?

Example: In Belgium, third party motor vehicle cover comprises both tort and contractual liability.

---

[1] On this, cf. J. KULLMANN, L'accompagnement juridique de l'obligation d'assurance en France, *Bulletin des Assurances* (Brussels), 2001, Dossier n° 7, *op. cit.*, pp. 82-87.

3. Excluded risks

This is a particularly sensitive aspect of cover, which should not be left undefined. Risks whose exclusion is allowable must be explicitly stated. Account must be taken of exclusions covered by general insurance contract law (such as wilful acts or war risks) and those that may result from practices prevalent in given sectors (for example nuclear risks or dangerous sports). Attention must also be paid to possible duplication of cover by other compulsory types of insurance (such as professional indemnity cover and third party motor vehicle cover) in order to eliminate this by means of exclusion clauses. In the case of liability insurance, a decision must be made whether to render some exclusion clauses ineffective against the victim; in such cases the insurer must be enabled to seek remedy against the insured.

4. Damage and indemnifiable persons

Where necessary, texts should specify whether the cover should extend to both property damage and physical injury; they might also state the position with regard to moral damage.

In liability insurance, some persons may be excluded from benefiting from the cover extended to victims, either to prevent any collusion or to avoid overlap with another compulsory insurance.

Example: before elimination of the problem by a European directive, the spouse and other relatives of the negligent party were frequently excluded from benefiting from any indemnities due under motor vehicle insurance.

5. Extent of cover

Texts relating to compulsory cover may allow the insurer to restrict its liability to given amounts: minimum capital sums in the case of personal insurance (in which a distinction may be made between death benefit and permanent disability benefit), minimum guarantees or, what comes to the same thing, authorised capping of liability insurance (in which cover for damage to property may be distinguished from that for physical injury, and where different minimum levels may be set by victim and by claim).

Such sums would be set not only in consideration of the cover required but also in terms of the technical features of the risk (degree of risk, calculation of premium, opportunity for reinsurance, etc.).

Example: in Denmark, dog owners' insurance must cover damage to property up to two million DKR and physical injury up to 5 million DKR.

Introduction of deductibles may be permitted, or required, if carelessness on the part of the insured is a possibility and/or the statistics in the field show a large proportion of small claims. In liability insurance, a decision must be made whether or not to make deductibles enforceable against the victim.

Example: in France maximum deductibles are provided in the case of insurance relating to care services for the elderly and in the case of professional indemnity insurance for lawyers.

6. Geographical limits

It is important that texts should provide an answer to the various questions that may arise with respect to the geographical limits of cover. Is compulsory cover incumbent only on persons or bodies native to or domiciled in the country concerned or may it in some cases be applicable to foreigners? Are the risks covered restricted to those occurring on national territory (where necessary it must be specified whether it is the generating event or the occurrence of the loss that is to be considered)? What is the situation of persons liable to benefit from the cover, either because of inclusion in the cover or as third party victims?

Example: the Belgian Act applying the Brussels Convention on Civil Liability for Oil Pollution Damage of 29 November 1969 makes its provisions applicable to all ships licensed or registered in Belgium regardless of whether they are sailing in territorial waters or not.

In some cases, in particular with regard to insurance cover for vehicles, a "frontier insurance" system may be applied. If the same compulsory insurance is provided abroad, a co-operative international scheme may be set up whereby the powers of special bodies are jointly recognised (such as the Bureaus that exist in third party motor vehicle insurance) in order to facilitate any compensation procedures.

7. Claims by victims

In property or personal insurance, the victims themselves are insured and therefore may seek remedy against the insurer on the basis of the contract. This may be strengthened by making defences ineffective.

Example: in Belgium, the law on compulsory occupational accident insurance (personal insurance) does not permit the insurer to reject a victim's claim by reason of gross negligence or wilful act on the part of the employer.

In liability insurance, if it is wished to place the emphasis on protection of victims rather than on protection of negligent parties, a direct claims procedure should be provided for the former with a relatively wide ban on assertion of defences. It is important that the texts should be explicit and specific with respect to the direct claims principle and the extent of the ban on defences. Where necessary, the insurer may reserve the right to seek remedy against the insured.

A special procedure may be applied to victims with regard to some aspects of disputes: competence, limitation, etc.

8. *Mandatory aspects*

Where special texts have set out the principal features of compulsory cover, they must be made mandatory, since they are intended to prevent contractual provisions from emptying the compulsory cover of its content.

Such mandatory force is to be understood as a barrier to provision of less extensive cover. It does not prevent provision of more extensive cover.

In liability insurance, some restrictions of cover may be permitted provided they do not apply to the victims.

B. *Organization of Compulsory Insurance*

Where insurance cover is to be made compulsory, care must be taken to ensure the technicalities are correct otherwise it may loose some or all of its effectiveness. If, for example, the person subject to the requirement of taking insurance is not accurately identified, or supervisory measures are not provided, then the requirement may remain a dead letter. A number of problems must be dealt with.

1. *Person subject to the requirement of compulsory insurance*

The person or persons required to take out the cover must be clearly identified. This is all the more important when failure to meet the requirement involves penal sanctions.

Example: in Belgium, payment of third party motor vehicle cover is incumbent on the vehicle owner; in Denmark, payment of liability cover for operation of a nuclear power station is incumbent on the owner of the installation.

2. *Insurers*

It seems unnecessary to recall that the contract must be taken out with an insurer authorised for the purpose in accordance with the supervisory regulations, since such authorisation is the general rule.

However, in some cases it may be specified that the insurer must be one authorised to cover certain risks.

Where necessary, the text should state the position relating to involvement of mutual credit associations or co-insurance pools.

3. Supervision

No requirement for compulsory cover will be respected without effective supervisory measures.

When the activity for which compulsory insurance cover is required is itself subject to prior authorisation, proof of insurance cover must be required as a precondition for such authorisation. In all cases, provision may be made for insurers to issue a special certificate attesting that the contract has been taken out, which document may have to be produced at the request of the supervisory authorities.

For example: in France, a sticker attesting to insurance cover must be displayed on vehicles.

Measures must also be provided to supervise continuance of the original contract. Arrangements to provide proof of regular payment of premiums may be provided. It would be preferable, however, to designate an authority to be responsible for receiving notification from insurers of the various acts affecting continuation of cover: suspension of cover or contract, expiry, cancellation, etc. As a matter of legislative policy, such notification might be directed to a single body, such as the insurance supervisory authority. When the activity concerned requires authorisation, such authorisation may be given for a temporary period only in order to allow for regular checks.

Example: in Denmark, insurers must notify the accountants' association of the expiry of policies belonging to its members; authorisation to practice the profession is withdrawn if insurance cover is not renewed.

Texts may also designate the agents and officials competent to investigate breaches of the requirements.

4. Penalties

Possession of insurance cover may be only one of the requirements to be met in order to practice a given activity, breach of any of which may be liable to penal sanctions.

Example: in France, breach of the requirement for lawyers to hold professional indemnity cover is subject to penal sanctions.

In other cases, where general penalties appear insufficient, the insurance requirement may be made the subject of specific penalties. These are primarily penal sanctions. Where necessary, authorisation may be refused or revoked. In some circumstances, confiscation of the property subject to the insurance cover may be envisaged.

5. Alternatives to compulsory insurance

The practice prevalent in some sectors whereby insurance cover may be replaced by other forms of security, such as a bank guarantee, should be approached with caution, particularly in cases where claims may proliferate to an extent that can be properly handled only by insurance procedures.

Example: in France, insurance cover for nuclear-powered ships and oil tankers may be replaced by alternative guarantees.

6. Compulsory inclusion of cover in a voluntary insurance

In some cases it is worth considering the technique which consists in not making insurance compulsory as a separate form of cover but to require the relevant cover to be included in a voluntary insurance policy. This system is used in some countries to cover natural disasters and certain acts of violence.

Provided that the host policy is widely sought on its own account (as in the case of fire insurance), the intended aim of spreading the burden of some risks open to selective exclusion is attained at low cost.

Example: in Spain, cover against natural disasters and terrorist acts are included in some types of property insurance.

7. Guarantee funds

A guarantee fund, capable of being funded in whole or in part by contributions from insurance firms operating in the sector concerned may remedy any inadequacies of the system resulting from failure to comply with the insurance requirement or from failure of the insurer.

Example: in France, guarantee funds have been set up for third party motor vehicle cover and cover for hunters.

Sometimes such funds may also cover a number of eventualities falling outside ordinary cover.

Example: in Belgium, the motor vehicle guarantee fund provides compensation for damage caused by unidentified vehicles

8. Cover for "bad risks"

Where insurance cover is compulsory, anyone engaging in the activity concerned must be able to find such cover on the market. However, bad risks are likely to be refused by all the insurers in the sector concerned. Such a situation may be considered healthy, since it prevents practice of the activity concerned in particularly hazardous conditions. Nevertheless there are cases where this extreme result in unacceptable and private insurers must be compelled to accept bad risks in exchange for a number of conditions (higher premiums, larger deductibles, etc.).

This aspect is sometimes automatically included in the technical procedures for providing insurance cover, with insurance firms setting up systems for covering bad risks. If absent, it may have to be made compulsory in the case of insurance for activities the practice of which is difficult to prevent and the insurance market for which is relatively restricted.

Example: in France, the Tariff Bureau takes such action in the several cases such as insurance against natural disasters, third party motor vehicle insurance and property damage insurance in the building industry.

C. A Compulsory Insurance Act?

Would it be a good idea to adopt legislation to govern compulsory insurance as a whole, in other words to provide a general legal framework for the practice?

No OECD country has gone down this road for understandable reasons. The arguments put forward in the two preceding sections may serve as a check-list of the points to be taken into consideration when introducing any specific insurance requirement, but the items covered will vary from case to case. Compulsory insurance covers too varied a field for any useful purpose to be served by subjecting it to a common regulatory system.

That at least is the authors' view with respect to overall regulation. More specific aspects could well be subject to a common regime. A given system of law may find it useful to provide measures to regulate the manner in which compulsory insurance is initiated, supervised or penalised (see Spanish law).

Less liberal rules for dealing with conflict of laws may be provided for compulsory insurance (see E.U. law). The rights of the victim against the insurer may be strengthened in all cases of compulsory insurance (see German and Belgian law). The same body may act as a guarantee fund for various types of compulsory insurance.

However, a legal instrument that seeks to provide a general and detailed framework applicable to all forms of compulsory insurance would appear to be neither useful nor practicable.

* *
*

The above represents a list of the principal technical problems associated with compulsory insurance, from the aspects of both definition of cover and organisation of the insurance requirement. All these problems must be tackled if the system introduced is to work properly. In less important sectors, some of the items covered may be omitted in view of the relatively high cost of including them. Provision of a centre to which notification of lapse of contract or guarantee must be sent, or establishment of a guarantee fund, are certainly not necessary in every case.

CHAPTER 3

COMPULSORY INSURANCE AND
THE COUNTRIES OF CENTRAL AND EASTERN EUROPE

Review and comparison of compulsory insurance in 25 OECD countries shows how complex and extensive the practice is. A number of useful pointers may be taken from it for countries of Central and Eastern Europe concerned to provide their insurance sector with a proper legal framework (Section I). Special attention will be given to the Baltic countries (Section II).

I. Compulsory insurance in Central and Eastern Europe

To start with, the contractual nature of compulsory insurance must be stressed. Next, consideration must be given to the desirability of such insurance and the technicalities of providing it.

A. *Contractual Status*

The compulsory types of insurance in question are generally made compulsory by laws or regulations.

However, as is the case with voluntary insurance, actual cover is provided on the basis of a contract between the insurer and the insured, which is subject to insurance contract law in all aspects where specific provision is not made.

This concept, which is the rule in OECD countries, was not always understood during the phase of transition undergone by the countries of Central and Eastern Europe, where compulsory insurance was often synonymous with insurance only regulated by the law and not based on a private contract.

Thus, the former 1992 Insurance Act of the Russian Federation contrasted *"voluntary"* insurance, based on a contract between insurer and insured, and *"compulsory"* insurance, whose *"types, conditions and procedures are governed by the laws of the Federation ..."* (art. 1). The Belarus Law on Insurance of June 3, 1993 still provides that on the one hand *"Forms, conditions and order of compulsory insurance are determined by the Republic of Belarus legislation acts concerning compulsory insurance"*, while *"Conditions of voluntary insurance are determined by an agreement of the parties in accordance with the legislation"* (art. 4). The 1997 Ukraine law on insurance still contains similar provisions: comp. art. 6 on voluntary insurance and art. 7 on obligatory insurance.

A better understanding has developed. The Insurance Act of the Republic of Kazakhstan, for instance, makes a distinction between compulsory and voluntary insurance cover, but provides that in the case of the former, *"the holder must enter into an insurance contract with an insurer on the basis of conditions established by the law regulating this type of insurance"* (art. 6). The Civil code of Russia, in its Chapter on insurance, now provides that compulsory insurance will be implemented *"by means of the conclusion of contracts in accordance with the rules of the present Chapter"* (art. 927,2°).

It is important that options should be selected in full knowledge of their implications. The relationship between law and contract are not always made sufficiently clear.

Admittedly, in many Western countries, the term "insurance" is sometimes used to describe forms of cover based on purely legal foundations. This is the case with the "social insurance" that comes under the heading of social security; for instance, mention is made of sickness, disability or unemployment "insurance". Such compulsory cover is frequently funded by salary deductions, employers' contributions and State interventions, the amount of which are determined by law. The benefits payable are also determined by the law. Beneficiaries acquire that status under conditions determined by the law, not through any contract with the body making payment. The latter has no similarities with a private insurance firm. In such cases, the term "insurance" is merely being used in a metaphorical sense. The cover offered by social security bears no resemblance to true insurance.

The insurance cover offered by the private sector, in cases where the law has made such cover compulsory, is entirely different. The best example is that of third party motor vehicle insurance, but any of the many cases of compulsory insurance described earlier would also serve.

In this case, the law requires a contract to be concluded and determines in greater or lesser detail what the requisite cover must include. Nevertheless, the object is to enter into an insurance contract with a private insurer, as in the case of a voluntary insurance, which contract is subject to the law on insurance contracts in all aspects not covered by the specific rules pertaining to the compulsory type of insurance in question. The legislation making third party motor vehicle insurance compulsory will necessarily define the liabilities for which cover is to be provided, but it will probably leave to ordinary law matters such as description of risk when the contract is taken out, or the penalties to which failure to pay a premium is subject.

It should be noted that the fact of giving compulsory insurance the status of a contract does not mean it is freed from all restrictions, since contracts themselves are subject to insurance contract law, which currently contains many mandatory provisions intended to protect the consumer.

Legislation imposing compulsory insurance cover may be more or less detailed in setting out the different requirements. Attention will be drawn below to the need for at least a minimum of provisions to ensure that the system is effective. However, there is no need for the same degree of detail in a minor sector such as insurance cover for hunters as in a major sector such as third party motor vehicle insurance. In any event, there is no need to provide compulsory insurance with rules governing the relationship between insurer and insured which have no special relevance to the reasons for making the insurance compulsory.

Other aspects of the problem are more political than technical. For example, should premiums be set by the law or should they remain subject to market forces, or be subject to some form of regulation?

Such questions may be asked in relation to any insurance, but they are sometimes pressed more strongly in relation to compulsory insurance. This is clearly associated with the notion that compulsory insurance is regulated by law and not by contract. The authors consider that setting premiums by law is incompatible with the technical requirements of insurance and with the requirements of a market economy. Some supervision must however be exercised by the authorities, in particular to prevent premiums from falling below a level threatening the cost-effectiveness and solvency of insurance firms.

In the interest of achieving economy of means and the associated advantages attendant on uniform fundamental rules, the authors recommend that compulsory insurance should remain based on contracts subject to the provisions of general insurance contract law in all areas not specifically concerned with the regulations making the insurance compulsory.

B. Desirability

Comparative review has shown the very variable and sometimes chaotic development of compulsory insurance in member countries of the OECD. France has almost a hundred types of compulsory insurance, Ireland only one. In closely linked countries such as the Benelux countries, Belgium is distinguished by a very high number of types of compulsory insurance, whereas the Netherlands and Luxembourg have a very moderate number. The prevalence of the practice is not easily reducible to geographical or cultural divides. Other countries with a relatively extensive range of compulsory types of insurance include not only Italy, Spain and Portugal, but also Norway and Austria.

Analysis of distribution by sector, although showing some constants, gives an impression of great heterogeneity. Third party motor vehicle insurance is compulsory everywhere, but liability cover for other means of transport varies greatly from country to country. Professional indemnity cover of various sorts of figures frequently on the lists, but why should such cover be compulsory for notaries in some countries only, architects in others, and travel agencies elsewhere still? Some compulsory cover is very specific indeed, such as the cover required in France for dancing schools. The comparative review given earlier in the paper furnishes many other subjects for speculation of this type.

Another impression is that few countries have given any general thought to the subject of compulsory insurance. Such systems have sprung up haphazardly, often provoked by an event that has caught public attention. In some countries, the practice has spread by a sort of knock-on effect, but without any comprehensive view as to the sectors where compulsory cover would be justified, or the technicalities governing its provision. The grounds for providing compulsory cover, which may be stated when a new system is introduced, rarely discuss the matter in any general context.

A golden opportunity exists for the countries of Central and Eastern Europe now in the process of providing appropriate regulations for their insurance sector, to draw lessons from these vagaries.

Compulsory insurance can be introduced in an ordered manner, based on a considered review of what has been done in other countries. This action should apply both to the selection of which types of insurance to make compulsory and to the technical features to be included.

With regard to selection of sectors, the criteria we consider as providing justifiable grounds for making an insurance compulsory are restated below:

- existence of a serious risk, sufficiently widespread to represent a major social problem (e.g. third party motor vehicle insurance; occupational accident insurance where this is not included in social security);

- existence of a very high degree of risk, even though not widespread enough to constitute a social problem (e.g. third party insurance for hunters);

- some situations where the law increases the extent of liability (e.g. in cases of pollution).

Attention must also be drawn to the usefulness of the technique of making a specific type of cover a compulsory part of a voluntary but very widely carried insurance policy covering a broader range of risk, in order to spread the burden of a risk open to exclusion (e.g. flood cover provided by fire insurance policies).

The comparative review provided allows opinions to be formed in the light of these criteria with regard to most kinds of compulsory insurance found in the countries considered. These are the authors' opinions and may not be shared by all. It is however strongly recommended that the countries of Central and Eastern Europe should approach the introduction of compulsory insurance by subjecting the grounds for such a requirement to comprehensive consideration. Several Western European countries have been taken aback to realise the anarchic situation they have created and would like to reduce their lists of compulsory insurance to more appropriate proportions. The impact of compulsory cover is, moreover, weakened when the practice becomes too widespread. In addition, the provision of such insurance requires accompanying measures (see below), the costs of which must not be allowed to get out of hand.

Priority must be given to the introduction of certain forms of compulsory insurance; examples are third party motor vehicle insurance, occupational accident insurance where this remains in the private sector, liability insurance in the nuclear industry, and a number of other forms of cover.

However, there are many cases where compulsory cover has been decreed by countries with very little justification.

Between these two extremes, there is frequently room for hesitation, and it is normal for national lists to differ from country to country. The main point is that decisions should be taken in a considered manner on the basis of stringent criteria, and that compulsory cover should remain the exception.

C. Technicalities

A restrained approach to the introduction of compulsory insurance should be matched by the pains taken over the implementation of such a requirement.

The discussion in the earlier section on technicalities relating to compulsory insurance should be kept in mind, in particular the fact that a requirement to hold cover may remain a dead letter if the details of its operation have not been set out sufficiently clearly.

The various aspects of the cover provided must be clearly specified: persons insured, risks covered, risks excluded, damage and persons to be compensated, extent of cover (in both financial and geographical terms), victims' rights in the case of liability insurance, the mandatory nature of the relevant rules. Provision must also be made to ensure compliance with the insurance requirement: by specifying who must take out the cover, which insurers may offer cover, how compliance with the insurance requirement is to be supervised, and what penalties will apply. A guarantee fund may be established, as well as a system for covering bad risks.

These various points have already been the subject of detailed discussion. They are recalled in these recommendations to the countries of Central and Eastern Europe because every time an insurance requirement is made compulsory at least some regulatory provisions have to be made. As has been said, however, the degree of detail of the relevant rules will depend on the importance of the compulsory cover concerned. It is also recalled that it is neither necessary nor desirable to regulate matters that may be left to general insurance contract law and that a general law relating to compulsory insurance does not appear to be either useful or practicable.

II. Compulsory insurance and the Baltic States

The study published in 1997 presented general observations concerning the countries of Central and Eastern Europe. This additional part includes observations and recommendations more specifically meant for the Baltic States.

A. Status of Compulsory Insurance

It has been explained that compulsory insurance, even though it is required by law, still implies the conclusion of an insurance contract between the policyholder and an insurer. Misconceptions had appeared on this subject in some early legislation in certain countries of Central and Eastern Europe; they were mentioned before.

For that matter, the Lithuanian Law on insurance of July 10, 1996 still appears to be unsatisfactory. It states that in compulsory insurance the main provisions are established by law, whereas voluntary insurance is carried out by an agreement between a policyholder and an insurance company (art. 4). This seems to create an opposition where compulsory insurance would appear not to be governed by a contract, but only by law, which is incorrect. This should be amended at the occasion of a future revision of the law.

On the other hand, the situation is satisfactory in this respect in the other two countries.

An Estonian bill of 1995 on insurance contracts still excluded its application to "contract clauses and conditions in compulsory types of insurance", a formula which seemed to indicate that such insurance was governed by a contract, but a contract not subject to general insurance contract law. But the provisions on insurance contained in the Law on Obligations of 2002 now make clear that insurance made compulsory by law implies entering into an insurance contract (art. 422, 2°).

In Latvia, the law of 1998 on insurance contracts correctly provides that " In the case of compulsory insurance, the insurance contract shall include the requirements prescribed for the relevant class of insurance by regulatory enactments of the country in which this insurance is compulsory " (art. 2, 6°).

B. Review of Existing Compulsory Insurance Laws

In the past ten years, the Baltic States have developed various types of compulsory insurance. It is especially the case in Latvia, where 27 types of insurance are mandatory, and in Lithuania, where 22 types are concerned.

It is not surprising that most of these are types of liability insurance. The legal texts concern notaries, auditors, owners and possessors of motor vehicles, insurance brokers, aircraft owners (Estonia, Latvia, Lithuania), waste management enterprises, tourism operators (Estonia, Latvia, Lithuania), nuclear equipment operators, constructors, bailiffs, (Latvia, Lithuania), certification services, insolvency administrators, commercial carriers, activities dangerous for environment, public services regulators (Latvia), solicitors, medical researchers, customs brokers, health care institutions, electricity producers, transmitters or suppliers, assets appraisers, dangerous cargo carriers and special cargo transports by railways (Lithuania).

There are also compulsory types of health insurance, completing the national security system (for instance, in Latvia, health and life insurance organised for judges, public prosecutors and the Central Electoral Commission, health and accident insurance for the State Audit Office, diplomats living abroad, certain members of the National Opera staff).

Mandatory property insurance is not common; Latvia has organised such insurance concerning property of public undertakings, property pledged to secure mortgage loans and property of a public undertaking in the case of its lease. Lithuania has organised obligatory insurance for bank deposits (and liabilities to investors).

Comments

It is somewhat surprising that the list of compulsory types of insurance received from Estonia is shorter than these of the two others Baltic States, for these pieces of legislation were adopted in the same period of time in the three countries, and followed the same influences.

On the other hand, there is quite an analogy between legislation about mandatory insurance in Latvia and Lithuania: the similarity between the number of categories of obligatory insurance (27 in Latvia, 22 in Lithuania) is symptomatic.

The most common types of compulsory insurance appear in the three countries: third party motor insurance, air transport insurance, occupational accident, nuclear activities. Strangely, another of the most frequent mandatory types of insurance - insurance of hunters - is not regulated in the Baltic States. We consider that this type compulsory insurance is especially justified.

The list of professional activities submitted to compulsory liability insurance is different in each country, although the hazards linked with the professions of notaries and auditors are equally recognised in the three Baltic countries.

The three national legislators should compare the different legal texts and re-examine their lists of obligatory types of insurance. Such comparison should induce new mandatory insurance laws, concerning particularly hazardous transports, environmentally dangerous activities and most risky medical activities such as medical research, considering the importance of damages that these activities can cause.

C. *Organization of Compulsory Insurance*

According to some comments received by the authors, the report published in 1997 is still of interest and the Baltic Authorities take into account the principles exposed in it. This makes it unnecessary to re-examine into details the positions and suggestions exposed in that report.

An essential factor of evolution is, of course, the future integration of the Baltic States in E.U., which should lead the Baltic Legislators to review their legislation, so as to implement the various European regulations concerning insurance. The authors note that some legal revisions were already made in Latvia, aiming to adjust insurance law to these regulations, and that nowadays Lithuania is revising third party motor insurance law. The revised law will not regulate premiums; the authors had insisted strongly on this solution.

As other countries, the Baltic States organised their regulations in various manners. In some cases, the law provides only the principle of insurance obligation. In other cases, a detailed regulation exists. The authors have explained that the regulation should organise different essential questions; if it is not the case, compulsory insurance could remain as a dead letter.

The following regulations will now be examined as examples, in order to suggest principles of reasoning for their improvement or the improvement of other types of compulsory insurance: liability insurance for bailiffs (Lithuania); liability insurance for notaries (Estonia); liability insurance for sworn auditors (Latvia).

1. Liability insurance of bailiffs (Lithuania)

It should first be noted that this legislation is precise on different important questions, such as the minimum amount of compulsory insurance, which is LTD 200,000 for each insurance event. Such a precision is important; but the Act should also specify that this amount is indexed, for obvious reasons.

The law does not sufficiently organise the control of the obligation. Such control is in the hands of the Bailiffs Chamber of Lithuania, which has to obtain payments of premium from every member. This solution is very interesting, but the law does not organise the right for the National Chamber to exclude members, who do not pay the premium. If this problem is not solved somewhere, it should.

2. Professional liability insurance for notaries (Estonia)

The Notaries Act provides an insurance obligation for notaries. Many important questions are clearly organised in this Act; for instance a minimum amount of coverage is prescribed not only by event, but also by year, which is a rare precision. However, the law should also provide that the amounts are indexed.

The control of the insurance obligation is in the hands of the Minister of Justice, who can delegate supervision to the Chamber of Notaries. An easy solution is to include the premium in the annual fees notaries have to pay to their Chamber. The Act does not organise sanctions in case of breach of the obligation; penalties could be organised by a ministerial decree or a regulation of the Chamber of Notaries.

The Act provides that the insurance does not cover intentional faults. This solution is not favourable to the victims, who could remain without indemnity in case of intentional damages! This problem could be solved by imposing payment of the indemnity to the insurer, who could then obtain reimbursement from the notary.

Another solution is to create a Fund, financed by the notaries' contributions; the Fund would indemnify the victims in case of intentional damages and also require reimbursement from the notary. Such a Fund would also insure the payment of indemnities in case of absence or insufficiency of the compulsory insurance. This is of great interest for the victims; damages caused by notaries' faults are often very costly.

3.   Professional liability insurance of sworn auditors (Latvia)

The law on sworn auditors is lengthy but only one section deals with the insurance obligation. There are no provisions concerning rights of victims, excluded risks, penalties, supervision. These questions should be regulated.

The legislator focused its concern on the minimum coverage. It is of course an important matter, but a coverage corresponding to the annual revenue could be insufficient, as the risk of damages can be quite larger.

BIBLIOGRAPHY

BARROUX, J., FLORIN, P., MARGEAT, H. & THOUROT, P. "Une maladie française. Débat" *Risques,* 1993, pp. 12 et seq.

CISSE, I., Assurances obligatoires en Afrique, Risques, 1998, pp. 101-110.

CHABAS, F., "L'assurance de personnes au service du droit de la responsabilité civile", Risques, 1993, n° 14, pp. 83 et seq.

CLAASSENS, H. (1977-78) "Verplichte verzekering: een nieuwe verschijnsel in België?", Rechtskundig Weekblad, 1977-78, col. 145-180.

CLAASSENS, H., Les obligations d'assurance en Belgique présentées en un premier essai de typologie, Bulletin des Assurances, Dossier n° 7, 2001, pp. 29-46.

CONRUYT, H., "L'autorité publique face au problème de l'obligation d'assurance", Bulletin des Assurances, 2001, Dossier n° 7, pp. 133-138.

DEFRANCE, G. "Le mal français", Argus, 20 August 1993, p. 14.

DEFRANCE, G., "Comité de liaison de l'assurance, Assurances obligatoires. Rapport du groupe de travail", Risques, 1993, p. 34.

DE RODE, H., and COLLIGNON, M., "Les assurances obligatoires en Europe - Etat de droit comparé", Bulletin des Assurances, Dossier n° 7, 2001, pp. 47-78.

EWALD, F., "Politiques de l'assurance obligatoire", Risques, 1993, pp. 59 et seq.

FALUSH, P., "The development of reinsurance market in the economies in transition", in Insurance regulation and supervision in economies in transition, OECD proceedings, OECD, 1997, pp. 278-279.

FONTAINE, M. and PAULUS-DE RODE H., (1979) Les assurances obligatoires. Droit belge, droit comparé, de lege ferenda, Centre de Droit des Obligations, Université Catholique de Louvain, Louvain-la-Neuve, 2 volumes of 287 and 123 pp.

FONTAINE, M., (1993) "Le droit du contrat d'assurance dans les pays de l'OCDE: étude comparative, orientations de lege ferenda", In Aspects fondamentaux des assurances, OECD, Paris, pp. 259-301.

FONTAINE M. and DE RODE H., Mandatory insurance in OECD countries, in OECD Proceedings, Insurance Regulation and Supervision in Economies in Transition, Paris, 1997, pp. 73-138.

GOLLIER, Ch. & ROCHET, J.Ch. "Les économistes face à l'assurance obligatoire. Un débat contradictoire.", Risques, 1993, pp. 48 et seq.

KULLMANN, J., L'accompagnement juridique de l'obligation d'assurance en France, Bulletin des Assurances, 2001, Dossier n° 7, pp. 82-87.

L'obligation d'assurance - Analyse économique et juridique, Bulletin des Assurances, 2001, Dossier n° 7, 201 pp.

International Insurance Law Association (AIDA), Motor insurance in the world, 1994.

LAMBERT-FAIVRE, Y., Droit des Assurances, Dalloz, 11th ed., 2001, pp. 12-16.

LEGRAND, B., (1993) "Les assurances de la responsabilité civile obligatoires en Europe", Risques, 1993, No.12, Dossier, pp. 38-41.

LEGRAND, B., Updating the study on compulsory liability insurance, EIC document, 1993.

PAVELEK, E., " Seguros obligatorios y obligacion de asegurarse", Rev. esp. de seguros, 2001, pp. 235-275.

PRÖSSL-MARTIN, Versicherungsvertragsgesetz, 25th ed., pp. 36-37.

ROGGE, J. "Les assurances obligatoires. Opportunités et menaces pour l'assureur", Bulletin des Assurances, 2001, Dossier n° 7, pp. 121-123.

THE TAXATION OF LIFE INSURANCE POLICIES IN OECD COUNTRIES

IMPLICATIONS FOR TAX POLICY AND PLANNING WITHIN THE BALTIC COUNTRIES

Harold D. Skipper

Abstract

This study explores tax policy as it relates to the ownership of life insurance products sold by life insurers. Other products and services sold by life insurers, such as accident insurance, health insurance, administrative services, guaranteed investment contracts and the like are not covered here. In addition, the study does not cover the tax treatment of private pensions, although making a clear demarcation between private pensions and life insurance products can be problematical.

Some attention is also accorded life insurer taxation, because governments should not consider life insurance product taxation in isolation from life insurance company taxation. For purposes of this study, it will be assumed that the effective tax burden of life insurers within the Baltic countries is similar to that of other businesses of equivalent profitability. By invoking this assumption – which, in any event, is a desirable trait of a tax system – the study may more rationally emphasize product (consumer) tax issues.

TABLE OF CONTENTS

INTRODUCTION

This study provides an overview of current tax policy regarding life insurance products within the OECD countries.[1] The study's purpose is to provide some insight into how best to structure life insurance product taxation for the Baltic countries.[2]

Scope of the study

The study explores tax policy as it relates to the ownership of life insurance products sold by life insurers. Other products and services sold by life insurers, such as accident insurance, health insurance, administrative services, guaranteed investment contracts and the like are not covered here. In addition, the study does not cover the tax treatment of private pensions, although making a clear demarcation between private pensions and life insurance products can be problematical.

Some attention is also accorded life insurer taxation, because governments should not consider life insurance product taxation in isolation from life insurance company taxation. For purposes of this study, it will be assumed that the effective tax burden of life insurers within the Baltic countries is similar to that of other businesses of equivalent profitability. By invoking this assumption – which, in any event, is a desirable trait of a tax system – the study may more rationally emphasize product (consumer) tax issues.

Study overview

Following this introduction, the first section provides an overview of the economic and social role of life insurance. Any tax concessions accorded life insurance should be justified because of a perceived special economic or social role. The next section presents a discussion of the principles of taxation. Life insurance product taxation should be consistent with these principles. The tax treatment accorded life insurance products among selected OECD countries is presented in the third section, followed by a set of considerations in establishing life insurance tax policy and the elements of such a policy. The study ends with a summary and conclusions section.

---

[1] I acknowledge with appreciation the help of my research assistant, Veena Raman.

[2] This study is an updated version of Harold D. Skipper, "The Taxation of Life Insurance Products in OECD Countries," in *Policy Issues in Insurance: Investment, Taxation, and Solvency* (Paris: OECD, 1996).

CHAPTER 1

THE ECONOMIC AND SOCIAL ROLE OF LIFE INSURANCE

Life insurance is important worldwide. It is found in the most economically advanced economies and the least developed. Generally, the more economically developed a country, the greater the role of life insurance as an economic security device. The question arises as to why life insurance is so pervasive and why government policy makers might want to encourage its purchase. Tax incentives can be justified if *society* derives benefits from incented *individuals* purchasing more insurance; i.e., if positive spill-over effects (externalities) result from the incentive. We examine whether such spill-over effects exist.[1]

Life insurance provides at least three categories of services important to economies. We discuss each below.

I. Partial substitute for government security programs

Life insurance can serve as a partial substitute for government security programs. An OECD study highlighted this important point:

> *"The fact that so many life insurance policies are purchased undoubtedly relieves pressure on the social welfare systems in many states. To that extent, life insurance is an advantage in the context of public finance, and, as a result, is generally viewed with favor by governments. A number of governments acknowledge this in tangible form by granting tax relief to policyholders."*[2]

A study by Swiss Reinsurance Company reinforces the view that privately purchased life insurance can substitute for government-provided benefits and vice versa. For a group of 10 OECD countries, the study found a significant negative relationship between social expenditures and life insurance premiums. The researchers attributed the high growth in life insurance premiums, in part,

---

[1] This section draws from Kenneth Black, Jr. and Harold D. Skipper, Jr., *Life and Health Insurance*. 13th ed. (Englewood Cliffs, NJ: Prentice-Hall, Inc., 2000), Chap. 3; R. Levine "Foreign Banks, Financial Development, and Economic Growth," in *International Financial Markets*, Claude E. Barfield, ed. (Washington, D.C.: The AEI Press, 1996); and Harold D. Skipper, "Risk Management and Insurance in Economic Development," in *International Risk and Insurance: An Environmental-Managerial Approach* (Boston: Irwin McGraw-Hill, 1998).

[2] Organization for Economic Cooperation and Development, *Consumers and Life Insurance* (Paris: OECD, 1987).

". . . to the growing financial difficulties of the social old-age pension systems. . . . Life insurers thus take an increasingly important role in relieving the burden of social pension schemes."[1]

II. Mobilizes savings

The general financial services literature emphasizes the important role of savings in economic development. Countries that save more tend to grow faster. Savings can be either financial or non-financial. Non-financial savings take the form of real assets such as land, jewelry, buildings, etc. Financial savings are held in financial assets such as savings accounts, bonds, shares, and life insurance policies. Generally, the more economically developed a country, the greater the proportion of its total wealth in financial savings. This result is consistent with the view that financial development and overall economic development move in tandem.

Life insurers offer the same advantages as other financial intermediaries in channeling savings into domestic investment. Financial intermediation of all types decouples the savings and investment functions. By doing so, investment is no longer confined to the sector in which the saving takes place. Funds can flow to the most productive sectors in an economy, which, in turn, implies the possibility of larger productivity gains. Insurers enhance financial system efficiency in three ways.

As financial intermediaries, ***insurers reduce transaction costs*** associated with bringing together savers and borrowers. Thus, thousands of individuals each pay relatively small life insurance premiums, part of which typically represents savings. Insurers then invest these amassed funds as loans and other investments. In performing this intermediation function, direct lending and investing by individual policyholders, which would be time consuming and costly, is avoided.

Insurers create liquidity. They borrow short term and lend long term. "Borrowing" for insurers means that they use funds entrusted to them by their policyholders to make long-term loans and other investments. Life insurers stand ready to provide policyholders with instant liquidity if an insured event occurs. Additionally, they stand ready to provide policyholders with the savings accumulated within their policies. The creation of liquidity allows policyholders to have immediate access to loss payments and savings while borrowers need not repay their loans immediately. If all individuals instead undertook direct lending, they likely would find unacceptable the proportion of their personal wealth held in long-term, illiquid assets. Insurers and other financial intermediaries thereby reduce the illiquidity inherent in direct lending.

Insurers facilitate economies of scale in investment. Some investment projects are quite large, especially in relation to available financial capital in many transition economies. They require correspondingly large amounts of financing. Such large

---

[1] Swiss Reinsurance Company, "A Comparison of Social and Private Insurance, 1970-1985, in Ten Countries," *Sigma.* Zurich, 1987.

projects often enjoy economies of scale, promote specialization, and stimulate technological innovations and therefore can be particularly important to economic development. By amassing large sums from thousands of smaller premium payers, insurers can often meet the financing needs of such large projects, thereby helping the national economy by enlarging the set of feasible investment projects and encouraging economic efficiency.

The more developed (complete) a country's financial system, the greater the reliance on markets and the less the reliance on intermediaries. Financial markets are more developed in developed market-economy countries and, therefore, are of greater importance in such countries than in transition economies. Even so, financial intermediaries are more likely to be providers of investment funds to the typical business than are financial markets. Only firms of a certain minimum size can easily tap into securities markets. Because of this fact and because financial markets are more complete in developed countries, one would expect financial intermediaries, such as insurers, to play a relatively greater role in investment finance in emerging markets than in developed market-economy countries.

A well-developed financial system will have a myriad of financial institutions and instruments. The greater the variety, other things being equal, the more efficient the system and the greater its contribution to economic development. Contractual savings institutions, such as life insurers and private pension funds, can be especially important financial intermediaries. Their longer-term liabilities and stable cash flows are ideal sources of long-term finance for government and business.

III. Fosters more efficient capital allocation

Insurers gather substantial information to conduct their evaluations of firms, projects, and managers in their roles as lenders and investors. Although individual savers and investors may not have the time, resources, or ability to undertake this information gathering and processing, insurers have an advantage in this regard and are better at allocating financial capital. Insurers will choose to provide funds to the most attractive firms, projects, and managers.

Because insurers have a continuing interest in the firms, projects, and managers to whom they provide financial capital, they monitor managers and entrepreneurs to reduce the chances that they engage in unacceptable risk-increasing behavior. Insurers thus encourage managers and entrepreneurs to act in the best interests of their various stakeholders. By doing so, insurers tangibly signal the market's approval of promising, well-managed firms and foster a more efficient allocation of a country's scarce financial capital.

Life insurance premium growth was particularly strong for many countries during the 1990s. Figure 1 shows the average annual real growth rates of life insurance premium income by region for the period 1991 through 2000. It also shows the growth rate for the year 2001 separately. The ten-year compounded average growth rates have been especially strong for emerging markets.

The 2001 growth rate of 24.4 percent for Central and Eastern Europe is skewed by a 44 percent growth rate for Russia, itself inflated because of use of short-term policies taken out for tax reasons. Even so, the growth rate omitting Russia is a strong 8.1 percent. For comparison, real 2001 growth rates for Estonia, Latvia, and Lithuania – not included in the above figures – were 10.5, -7.5, and 20.2 percent, respectively.[1] These high growth rates have resulted in life insurance representing an increasing share of personal sector financial assets in many countries.

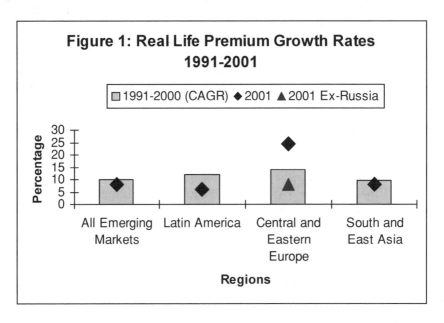

Figure 1: Real Life Premium Growth Rates 1991-2001

Source: Swiss Reinsurance Company, "World Insurance in 2001: Turbulent financial markets and high claims burden impact premium growth," *Sigma*. Zurich, 2002.

---

[1] *Insurance Markets in the Baltic States*, 2001.

CHAPTER 2

THE PRINCIPLES AND EFFECTS OF TAX POLICY

This section presents an overview of taxation principles through discussions of the general purposes of taxation, desirable traits of tax policy, and systems of taxation.[1] The section ends with a brief discussion of tax policy's impact on national savings.

I.   General purposes of taxation

Three general purposes of a tax system can be identified:

- To raise revenue

- To promote economic goals

- To promote social goals

That taxation is intended *to raise revenue* for government needs little explanation. Government requires revenue to provide the services demanded of it by its citizens.

Governments often design tax systems also *to promote economic goals*, although this purpose is usually subservient to the revenue-raising objective. The economic goals may be national, or they may relate to some specific industry or even to individual economic activity. Certain industries may enjoy tax concessions because government wants to stimulate productive activity of those sectors. For example, some governments have provided significant tax concessions to stimulate research and development by businesses.

Many developing countries impose high tariffs – a type of excise tax – on imported manufactured goods. This is another example of government believing it is promoting economic goals, even if the actual effects may hinder development. The intended goal may be to discourage the outflow of foreign exchange reserves or to shelter a domestic industry from the fullness of foreign competition. Of course, such tariffs also raise revenue for the government.

Policy makers also design tax systems *to promote social goals*. Many such examples can be found in virtually every tax system. These social goals may relate either to discouraging or to encouraging certain social behavior. Thus, the typically heavy taxation imposed on tobacco and alcohol products reflects not only a desire to raise revenue from the sale of such products but also an attempt by government to discourage their use or to impose a social levy for the perceived societal harm (negative

---

[1] This section draws from Harold D. Skipper, "State Taxation of Insurance Companies: Time for a Change," *Journal of Insurance Regulation*, Vol. 6 (Dec. 1987), pp. 122-128.

externalities). On the other hand, governments may permit tax deductions and credits for certain activities in an attempt to encourage those activities. Tax rates, deductions, exemptions, and credits are the tax-related tools that government policy makers use to craft a tax system to promote specific economic and social goals.

II. Desirable traits of tax policy

An ideal tax policy is one that possesses these traits:

- Equity

- Neutrality

- Simplicity

A. Equity

The intent of *equity* in taxation (also referred to as *vertical equity*) is to have each taxpayer contribute his, her, or its fair share in taxes. The difficult part is determining the "fair share." Most countries judge this fair share as related to ability to pay taxes; those with greater ability should pay more taxes. Net income is widely used as a proxy for ability to pay.

B. Neutrality

A tax system or provision ideally should possess *economic neutrality* (also referred to as *horizontal equity*), meaning that economically equivalent entities, products, and services should be taxed equivalently. In the absence of overriding economic or social goals to be served by the tax system, the system should not influence economic decisions of individuals, businesses, or other taxpaying entities.

Thus, lacking the existence of some market failure, the tax system should avoid benefiting one industry compared with any other; within a single industry (e.g., financial services), should accord no advantage to one set of competitors relative to others; and, within a given firm, should not influence the firm's choice of production inputs or outputs. The principle underlying the economic neutrality concept is that overall national welfare is enhanced if market forces, not the tax system, drive individual and business decision-making.

C. Simplicity

A tax system should be *simple* meaning that it is not complex administratively, its costs of collection are low, it is not easily evaded, and taxpayers can comply with the law without undue expenditure of time and money. Implicit within this trait is that the tax system is appropriate for the country's level of development and the sophistication of its administrative apparatus. This goal often conflicts with the goals of equity and neutrality. How these conflicts are resolved depends on the economic circumstances and conditions of the country at the time the tax system is implemented. A tax system not attuned to its environment is an invitation to avoidance and inefficiency.

III. Systems of taxation

Many tax systems have evolved over time. The common ones are highlighted below. The focus is on the various bases for applying the tax; tax exemptions, deductions and credits; and tax rates. Together these items define a system of taxation.

A. Tax bases

A tax system must begin with the tax base, from which deductions or exemptions may be allowed to derive taxable income. The broader the tax base, the better. No completely satisfactory scheme exists for classifying tax bases but, for presentation purposes, three categories may be used:

- Income

- Consumption

- Wealth

Income is the most widely used tax base internationally. Many policy makers consider net income to be the best measure of ability to pay and so the most equitable means of taxing both individuals and businesses. Significant deductions and other tax concessions are typically provided to derive net taxable income (see below).

Payroll taxes, such as those to finance social insurance schemes, are a type of income tax. Unlike broad-based net-income tax systems, however, payroll taxes apply to earnings from labor only. Interest, rents, dividends, and other income derived from capital are not subject to payroll taxes. Moreover, payroll taxes often apply only to a ceiling income level.

A second important tax base is *consumption*. Consumption taxes may take two forms: where consumers themselves are taxed, as with an expenditure tax, or where the goods or services purchased by consumers are taxed. The latter form is more common. Consequently, further discussion will focus on it. Here the subject of taxation is not the income of the taxpaying entity but some measure of the turnover or amount of transactions.

Sales, excise, and value-added taxes are probably the best-known examples of transactions-based taxes. Sales taxes are levied on the consumption expenditures of goods and (sometimes) services. Excise taxes are levied on specific commodities such as gasoline, tobacco, and alcoholic beverages. Value-added taxes are levied at each stage of production.

A consumption tax is an identifiable burden on a financial transaction itself, as contrasted with an income tax levied on a taxpaying entity. Unlike income taxes, most consumption taxes are impersonal and therefore often clash with the equity goal. Consumption taxes can be designed to modify social behavior. Excise taxes are well known in this regard, being the tax-of-choice with respect to consumption of goods that entail negative externalities for society (i.e., society at large pays a price for the individual's consumption of the good).

Consumption taxes also can be designed to modify economic behavior. Thus, import duties and tariffs discourage the purchase of foreign-made goods. The insurance premium tax in most countries is not a tax on consumption. Yet, because the tax is levied on insurers' premium revenues, it can have the same economic effect as a consumption tax.

Lately, some policy makers have advocated an explicit consumption tax on insurance premiums (and other financial services). Such taxation seems inconsistent with the purpose of such a tax. Insurance services are not consumption items. Rather, they constitute the basis for smoothing consumption over time – as with annuities, pensions, and other life insurance savings products – or across different states of nature – as with policies that pay on the insured's death. Thus, as an intermediate financial service whose payoffs are used to purchase fully taxable consumption goods, life insurance premiums theoretically should be exempt from such taxation.[1]

Governments often implement the benefit principle of taxation through a consumption tax. This principle holds that certain recipients of government services should provide the revenue to fund the services. Thus, states levy a tax on fuel, the purpose of which is to help pay for road construction. Those persons who purchase fuel – the beneficiaries of a state's road system – pay the tax.

The third common basis for taxation is *wealth*. Many countries tax a person's wealth, of which property is one element. Estate duties are a type of wealth tax. The objective of such taxes is to minimize great concentrations of wealth, although some countries have eliminated or are in the process of eliminating such taxation.

B. Tax exemptions, deductions, and credits

Tax exemptions, deductions, and credits are the most important mechanisms for modifying a tax system to accomplish social and, to a large extent, economic goals. Their use can be justified on economic grounds if they address a market failure (i.e., when competition fails to achieve an efficient result, the most notable being

---

[1] The exemption need not apply to policy fees. For discussions about the issues associated with such taxation, see Harry Grubert and James B. Mackie III, "Must Financial Services be Taxed Under a Consumption Tax?" *National Tax Journal* vol. 53 (March 2000); and William Jack, "The Treatment of Financial Services Under a Broad-Based Consumption Tax," *National Tax Journal* vol. 53 (Dec. 2000).

externalities). Without appropriate use of these incentives, a tax system cannot be fine-tuned to target specific behavior.

Thus, if government wants to promote certain activities, it may provide a complete exemption from taxation for those entities that provide the desired services or goods. Qualified educational organizations, charities, and other nonprofit organizations are typical examples of tax-exempt entities – the theory being that their good works benefit society as a whole, not just immediate recipients.

Most tax systems permit deductions to be taken in deriving taxable income. Many governments have determined it to be socially desirable to encourage individuals to save for their retirement. Tax deductions for savings through qualifying products are the route typically taken to promote this goal.

Tax credits are another mechanism to encourage individuals and businesses to alter their social and economic behavior. Thus, an investment tax credit can encourage capital expansion by businesses. A research and development tax credit is rationalized on the theory that the additional private research spurred by the credit provides benefits to society broadly, not just to the firms that qualify for the credit.

C. Tax rates

The tax rates that government chooses to apply to taxable income determine the tax impact on the taxpaying entity. Other things being equal, the higher the marginal tax rate, the greater the effect that the tax rate itself has on economic behavior, as individuals avoid the highly taxed activity. For this reason economists advocate low marginal tax rates.

IV. The impact of tax concessions on national savings

In considering the important economic and social role of life insurance, one may too easily accept the proposition that significant tax concessions are desirable as a means of enhancing national savings. This case may seem facially compelling, but several considerations bear on the issue.

First, neither theoretical nor empirical research has investigated the effects on national savings of life insurance product tax concessions. Related research on Individual Retirement Accounts (IRAs) in the United States and Registered Retirement Savings Plans (RRSPs) in Canada offers ambiguous results.[1] Savers, to some degree, substitute tax-preferred savings for taxable savings; thus not necessarily increasing aggregate national savings but merely changing its allocation.

---

[1] For a survey of research on these and other tax-preferred instruments, see B. Douglas Bernheim, "Taxation and Saving" in A. J. Auerbach and M. Feldstein, eds., *Handbook of Public Economics: Fourth Edition* (Amsterdam: North Holland, 2002).

Second, more general empirical research on the effects of the real interest rate on savings has proven ambiguous. Some studies lend credence to the idea that higher interest rates provoke higher savings rates whereas others have done the opposite.[1]

The ambiguity is associated with opposing substitution and income effects. A higher effective interest rate (for example, because of tax concessions) can be expected to encourage consumers to substitute savings for consumption, as the relative price of consumption is raised. On the other hand, a higher effective interest rate provides savers with greater future income. Other things being the same, this could lead to a reduction in overall savings for target savers. The net effect of these two opposing tendencies is not obvious.

Third, it must be recognized that enhanced national savings can arise from three sources.

1. Individuals and businesses can increase savings, thus leading to enhanced national investment. The preceding discussion touches on this source.

2. Foreigners can be induced to save more within the country. This study does not address this source directly, but notes that foreign capital to establish domestic insurers can be an additional source of national investment. Endogenous theories of economic growth hold that high levels of growth require high levels of national investment, but the theories do not suggest that the savings to finance the investment need be national.

3. Governments can increase their net savings. Tax concessions that lead to increased household savings, however, can result in lower government savings because of a decrease in tax revenues. Thus, it is not clear that tax preferences would increase overall national savings. They may merely change its allocation.

Many economists argue that, even if tax concessions do not lead to increased national savings, they could lead to a more efficient allocation of savings. Thus, even if tax concessions fail to increase the overall level of national savings, the resultant shift in savings from the government to the private sector could lead to a more efficient allocation of resources, thus benefiting the national economy.

---

[1] See Auerback and Feldstein (2002).

CHAPTER 3

TAX TREATMENT OF LIFE INSURANCE IN OECD COUNTRIES

As financial instruments, life insurance products are subject to national tax policy in all OECD countries. Besides an examination of life insurance product taxation, a brief overview of life insurer taxation is presented.

I. Life insurance product taxation

Perhaps every OECD country provides some tax preference in connection with the purchase, ownership, or execution of life insurance policies. The extent and nature of these concessions vary from being relatively minor and designed to simplify tax administration, to being substantial and designed to promote life insurance purchase or maintenance because of its perceived worthwhile social role. This exploration of the tax treatment of life products is structured around life product cash flow components: premiums, living benefits, and death benefits. The information is believed to be current as of 2000.

The tax treatment of the components ideally should be internally consistent. Thus, that which is deductible to one party in a transaction should be income to the other party, and that which receives tax preference now should be taxable later. As we will see, however, such internal consistency is the exception, not the rule among OECD countries.

A. *Premiums*

Many countries grant some form of tax relief for premiums paid on qualifying life insurance, although the trend internationally is away from such concessions, consistent with the neutrality principle. Perhaps the first country to grant an income tax deduction for life insurance premium payments was the United Kingdom. It was introduced in 1799, although removed some years later when the income tax was abolished. It was reintroduced in 1853 and remained in effect until 1984. Its repeal was said to have been prompted by the government's desire to introduce tax neutrality among all forms of savings and investments plus a growing governmental irritation with certain abusive tax avoidance schemes associated with life insurance contracts.[1]

As Table 1 shows, of the 24 OECD countries examined here, some relief is provided in 14 countries. Ten states provide no tax relief on premiums paid for life insurance. Tax concessions more commonly apply to policies whose predominant purpose is to provide living benefits. Concessions are less commonly extended to policies whose purposes are predominately to provide death benefits. Also, tax concessions are frequently denied when consumers purchase otherwise qualifying policies from unlicensed insurers. Of course, taxation principles suggest that life insurance premiums should be accorded no special tax preference because they represent savings (future consumption) and protect against loss.

---

[1] "LAPR Killed after 131 Years," *Post Magazine and Insurance Monitor* (22 March 1984).

**Table 1: Selected OECD countries' laws
on tax relief for premiums paid for qualifying life insurance policies**

Country	Tax treatment of premiums for purpose of policyholder tax liability
Australia	Not deductible except for key-man insurance taken out by businesses.
Austria	Deductible to a maximum of €2,900 a year for premiums for voluntary health, life, and accident insurance as a special expense depending on taxable income. The higher the income, the lower the allowance; over €50,900 no allowance. From the lower of the calculated or actual premium paid, a quarter is tax-deductible.
Belgium	Deductible if certain conditions are met.
Canada	Not deductible.
Denmark	Deductible if certain conditions are met.
Finland	Not deductible.
France	Limited tax relief on qualifying premiums.
Germany	Deductible to specific amounts and depending on the circumstances of the policyholder.
Ireland	Not deductible respecting premiums written before 2001. Deductible 2001 and later subject to certain limits.
Italy	A tax credit of 19% of the premium paid, not exceeding €1,291 allowed on contracts executed prior to 2001. No tax deduction allowed on contracts executed thereafter.
Japan	For individual policyholders, deductible up to a maximum of –50,000.
Korea	Deductible to ω700,000.
Luxembourg	Deductible to maximum amount.
Mexico	Not deductible.
Netherlands	Not deductible except for annuity considerations.
New Zealand	Not deductible.
Poland	Not deductible.
Portugal	Deductible for qualifying premiums, to defined limits.
Spain	Not deductible.
Sweden	Not deductible.
Switzerland	Deductible to a limit that varies by canton.
Turkey	Deductible to a limit.
United Kingdom	Not deductible.
United States of America	Not deductible.

Sources: PriceWaterhouseCoopers, International Comparison of Insurance Taxation (2002) and Taxing Insurance Companies (Paris: OECD, 2001).

1. Living benefits

In most and perhaps all OECD countries, payments by life insurers for so-called living benefits exceed payouts because of insured deaths. Living benefit payouts or accruals may be classified broadly into three categories. The first category relates to policy cash values and maturity (capital sum) amounts. The second category comprises dividends (bonuses) under participating (with profits) contracts. The third category constitutes payouts under annuity contracts. Each is covered below.

2. Cash values

OECD countries generally do not directly or indirectly tax interest credited on policy cash values – the so-called inside interest build up, as Table 2 shows. A few countries provide that certain policies with high cash values in relation to the policy's death benefit or with unacceptably short durations may provoke taxation of the inside interest build up. In addition, some countries deny the inside interest build up exemption to policies purchased from unlicensed insurers.

Some countries tax the inside build up indirectly by taxing that portion of insurers' investment incomes considered attributable to the taxpayer/policyholder's internal policy interest accruals. This tax is in addition to the regular corporate tax, although it may be taken as a deduction. Denmark, for instance, taxes the interest buildup by laying the responsibility of deducting a flat tax of 15 percent on the life insurer. Similarly, the UK places the tax collection responsibility on the life insurer. In France, the interest buildup is subject to social security contributions.

Debate continues whether sound public policy should permit the tax-advantaged inside interest buildup within life insurance policies. Tax neutrality principles would have such interest taxed like other interest income. Critics claim that favorable tax treatment distorts the savings market, making life insurance products artificially more attractive than other savings instruments. They also note that the government loses tax revenues because of this tax favoritism.

Proponents of this tax preference argue that socially worthwhile spillover benefits attach to life insurance, in that it allows families to make provision for their financial security while aiding economic development. They also note that the income may not actually be received by the policyholder unless the policy is surrendered, much as the homeowner does not actually receive his or her home's appreciated value without selling the home. (Tax economists would counter that this value also should be taxed.)

One reason for the generally favorable tax treatment of the inside build up relates to the complexity involved in trying to do otherwise. Rather than attempt to tax policyholders on interest earnings within a policy, the more common approach in OECD countries – see Table 2 – is to tax a policyholder, if at all, only on the maturity or surrender of the policy and then only to the extent that the benefits received (the maturity amount or the cash value plus the sum of all dividends received) exceed the sum of the premiums paid under the policy. This difference, if positive, might be subject to income tax. If the difference is negative, no deduction is usually permitted against income on the theory that the procedure understates taxable income because it effectively allows a deduction for the policy's cost of insurance and assessed expense charges.

Table 2: Income taxation of life
Insurance values in selected OECD countries

Country	Taxation of inside interest buildup?	Taxation on gain on surrender?	Death proceeds subject to income taxation?
Australia	No	No, unless the policy terminates in less than 10 years	No
Austria	No	No, unless the policy terminates in less than 10 years	No
Belgium	No	No, except for policies with tax relief on premiums	No, except for policies with tax relief on premiums
Canada	Yes, indirectly at 15% via insurer plus directly for annuities and high savings-oriented policies	Yes	No, unless savings policy
Denmark	Yes, indirectly at 15%	Yes for tax deductible policies, otherwise no	Yes for tax deductible policies, otherwise no
Finland	No	Yes	No
France	No	Yes, for some policies	No, except for large policies
Germany	No	No, except partial annuity taxation	
Ireland	No for new business	Yes via insurer	Yes via insurer
Italy	No	Yes	No
Japan	No	Yes, on gain over −500,000 at ½ ordinary rate	No
Korea	No, except for high savings-oriented policies	No, except for high savings-oriented policies	No
Luxembourg	No	No	No
Netherlands	Yes	Yes	Yes
New Zealand	Yes, indirectly via insurer	No	No
Poland	No	No, except unit linked	No
Portugal	No	Yes, on gain subject to certain relief	No
Spain	No	Yes	No
Switzerland	No	No, if certain conditions met	Yes, at special rates
Turkey	Yes, indirectly via insurer	Yes, indirectly via insurer	No
United Kingdom	Yes, indirectly via insurer	No, with exceptions on non-qualified policies	No
United States	No, except for high savings-oriented policies	Yes	No

Sources: PriceWaterhouseCoopers, *International Comparison of Insurance Taxation* (2002) and author.

3. Dividends

The general rule in OECD countries is that dividends paid do not cause current taxable income.[1] To the extent that premiums are not deductible and the inside interest buildup is taxed, this treatment is consistent with good tax policy. However, if either of the two conditions fails to apply – as with most OECD countries – some or all of dividends paid to policyholders should be taxable income. The logic offered for this failure to tax is that dividends represent mainly a return of the policyholder's money and because of the administrative complexity in trying to tax some or all dividends.

4. Annuities

Payments under annuity contracts are the third category of living benefits. The inside interest build up of annuities during their accumulation period usually receives the same tax treatment as other life insurance products and is the object of similar tax controversy (see above). Most OECD countries tax annuity payouts to some degree. In a few countries – such as France, Italy, and Spain – a prescribed, fixed portion of each payment is subject to tax. In most countries, various mechanisms are prescribed in which the excess of payments received over premiums paid is taxed, usually on some type of prorata basis over the annuity payout period.

5. Death proceeds

Most OECD countries exempt death proceeds paid under qualifying life insurance policies from income taxation, as Table 2 shows. In fact, taxation is the exception rather than the rule.

A cash value policy's death proceeds can be viewed as comprised partly of the cash value. If the interest component of the cash value was not taxed during the insured's lifetime, it thereby can escape income taxation completely on the insured's death. This tax treatment may be more favorable than that accorded to other savings media, thus distorting the savings market.

Governments commonly levy inheritance taxes or other estate duties, measured on the value of property that a decedent owned, controlled, or transferred. Life insurance death proceeds are subject to estate duties in many OECD countries, including Belgium, France, Germany, Japan, Korea, Spain, Turkey, the UK, and the US. In most instances, however, provision is made for special circumstances wherein the proceeds are excluded, in whole or in part, from assessment.

---

[1] Tax law in the United States provides that dividends paid in cash are taxed if the policy contains a savings orientation greater than a defined maximum. The great majority of policies do not exceed the maximum.

II. Life insurance company taxation

We should not divorce consumer taxation from supplier taxation. Tax concessions extended to either the consumer or the supplier can have similar economic effects. By extending tax concessions to consumers for the purchase of a specific product, government is effectively lowering the product's price. Depending on the product's demand elasticity, government theoretically could achieve the same price-reducing result by extending a tax concession to the supplier. Consistent with this logic, government should recognize that the desired beneficial effects of a tax concession extended to the consumer can be negated by an increase in the supplier's tax burden. We thus cover the subject briefly here. Life insurer taxation typically is of two types: premium taxation and net income taxation.

A. Premium taxation

Several OECD countries levy taxes on insurers' premium revenues. Table 3 shows some countries that do so along with their tax rates. Premium taxes are the most common, but some countries levy stamp duties and other assessments. The insurer is responsible for tax payment in the great majority of countries, although the broker or insured may be responsible when business is placed with an unlicensed insurer. Even with the insurer responsible for payment, such taxation is closely related to policyholder taxation.

Under the typical premium tax structure, the tax base is the simple total of the insurer's premium revenue, with certain alterations. Premiums received from assumed reinsurance are usually excluded from the tax base, as the original insurer that wrote the business would have already been subjected to tax on its direct premiums. Most jurisdictions permit a deduction from the tax base for dividends paid to policyholders. The premium tax base may include premiums received for personal accident and health insurance, but more commonly they are taxed separately, often at a higher rate. Insurers' investment income is not included in the tax base.

Most countries do not levy premium taxes on annuity considerations paid to insurers. Even those states that tax annuity considerations typically exempt contributions to qualified retirement plans or tax them at a lower rate.

B. Income taxation

OECD governments typically tax life insurers on some variation of net income, in much the same way as other companies are taxed. Table 3 shows the general approaches followed and the maximum marginal tax rates for selected OECD countries. In the past, several countries taxed life insurers on their investment income only, but the trend is toward a tax base composed of total (investment and premium) income. Australia and the United Kingdom follow the so-called I-E (investment income minus expenses) approach.

Table 3: Taxation of life insurance companies in selected OECD countries

Country	Premium taxation?	Basis for net income tax?	Maximum income tax rate?
Australia	Yes, at 10% of first year's premium depending on state and type of policy	Investment income less expenses	30% except pensions at 15%
Austria	Yes, at 4% except 11% for policies of less than 10 years duration	Total income	34%
Belgium	No, except group at 4%	Total income	39%
Canada	Yes, 2-4% depending on province	Total income	39-46% depending on province
Denmark	No	Total income	30%
Finland	No	Total income	29%
France	No	Total income	36.43%
Germany	No	Total income	38.5%
Ireland	No	Total income	12.5%
Italy	No	Total income	35%
Japan	No, except limited prefectual taxation	Total income	36.21%
Korea	Yes, 0.5%	Total income	16.5% on first ω100 million, 27.9% on excess
Luxembourg	No	Total income	30%
Netherlands	No	Total income	29% on first €22,6895, 34.5% thereafter
New Zealand	No	Total income	33%
Norway	No	Total income	28%
Poland	No	Total income	28%; lower in future
Portugal	Yes, 0.33%	Total income	33%
Spain	No	Total income	35/25% stock/mutual insurer
Switzerland	Yes, 5% except single premium at 2.5%	Total income	17-31% depending on canton
Turkey	No	Total income	33%
United Kingdom	No	Investment income minus expenses	20 or 22%/30% policyholder/shareholder funds
United States	Yes, 1-3% depending on state	Total income	35%

Sources: PriceWaterhouseCoopers, International Comparison of Insurance Taxation (2002); OECD Taxing Insurance Companies (2001) and author.

Determining life insurer profit is a challenge. The challenge arises from the difference in timing between premium payments and claim payments.[1]

The typical tax base for purposes of calculating taxable income is the sum of investment and premium income. The yearly increase in policy reserves, acquisition and administrative expenses, policy dividends paid, and premiums paid on ceded reinsurance usually are deducted from this sum. Other deductions may be permitted and special rules may exist for loss carryovers and (domestic and foreign) branch income.

---

[1] See *Taxing Insurance Companies*, Paris; OECD, 2001 for an analysis of these and other issues associated with life insurer taxation.

CHAPTER 4

ESTABLISHING TAX POLICY TOWARD LIFE INSURANCE

In establishing its tax policy toward life insurance products, government should ask itself whether special concessions should be extended to them and, if so, what form these concessions should take. This section explores these two issues, drawing on the information presented in the earlier sections.[1]

I. Considerations in establishing life insurance tax policy

In deciding its tax policy toward life insurance products, government should consider thoughtfully the policy's purpose, effect on tax revenues, compatibility with the level of development, compatibility with the insurance regulatory structure, alignment with the desirable traits of tax policy, and compatibility with other countries' tax systems. Each of these is discussed below.

A. Purpose of tax policy

The purpose of most tax systems is to raise revenue. Tax policy toward life insurers and their products ordinarily shares this purpose. The issue, however, becomes complex because life insurers and their products are complicated, and governments often view life products as intertwined with their economic security systems and social welfare. If a government extends some tax concessions to life products, it should be clear as to the purposes it seeks to accomplish by doing so (and conduct studies to learn whether the purposes are being accomplished).

Usual rationales for extending tax concessions to life products flow from the belief that life insurance carries meaningful positive externalities (i.e., benefits for society). These were discussed earlier. These benefits and considerations relate to the role of life insurance both as a savings instrument (and the accompanying role of life insurers as financial intermediaries) and as a financial protection instrument.

Governments use tax policy to encourage national savings. The effectiveness of such policies remains unclear. First, tax concessions for savers will probably result in decreased tax revenues and, therefore, government savings will decrease. Second, consumers often shift from taxable to tax-preferred savings, thus not necessarily increasing total national savings but merely changing its allocation. General studies have supported the concept that taxes shape household asset portfolios.[2] Third,

---

[1] This section draws on *Establishing Life Insurance Tax Policy in Developing Countries* (Geneva: UNCTAD, 1985).

[2] For a survey of the literature on this point, see, James M. Poterba, "Taxation and Portfolio Structure: Issues and Implications," in Luigi Guiso, Michalis Haliassos, and Tullio Jappelli, eds., *Household Portfolios* (Cambridge; MIT Press, forthcoming).

although tax concessions increase the effective yield on savings, overall savings will not necessarily increase as target savers may save less.

Tax concessions toward life products conceivably could have effects different from those found with other savings media, as most life products combine death protection with savings. Regrettably, research on this issue is sparse. If government decides to try to spur national savings by extending tax concessions to life insurance, it should recognize that such a policy's effects cannot be predicted, except for one observation: preferential tax concessions extended to life insurance products can be expected to cause a reallocation of national savings from non-tax-preferred financial instruments, from non-insurer financial intermediaries to life insurers, and from government to life insurers.

Of course, such a policy violates the principle of neutrality. Government may, nonetheless, decide that potential benefits outweigh neutrality concerns. For example, government may conclude that life insurers' long-term liabilities and stable cash flows are preferred sources of term finance. Government also may prefer private sector savings to public sector savings because of a belief that the private sector uses resources more efficiently.[1] At the same time, government policy makers should be mindful that sectors seeking preferential tax treatment always assert the existence of positive spillover effects for society from the preference.

Other social benefits of life products flow from their protection function. In this sense, life insurance can substitute partially for government-provided survivor benefits. Government, therefore, may wish to encourage citizens to arrange for their families. Special tax concessions for life insurance purchases could, in effect, lower the price of life insurance and thereby should stimulate demand.[2] The few studies that explore the extent to which favorable tax treatment affects life insurance demand reveal conflicting results.[3] Anecdotal evidence suggests that countries that have eliminated elements of

---

[1] Achievement of this goal would not require violation of the neutrality principle; that is, tax preferences could be extended to all savings products.

[2] The extent of the stimulation is a function of the price elasticity of life insurance demand, a little explored subject. Life insurance products could have a relatively elastic demand if substitutes abound or an inelastic demand if substitutes are rare. Cash value life insurance products may exhibit dual demand traits – one type of demand for savings and another for death protection.

[3] In, Tullio Jappelli and Luigi Pistaferri, "Tax Incentives and the Demand for Life Insurance: Evidence from Italy," discussion paper no. 2787, Centre for Economic Policy Research (May 2001), the authors conclude that lowering tax concessions for the purchase of life insurance by high income individuals and raising concessions for low income individuals had no effect on life insurance purchases. This result was attributable to information asymmetries and lack of needed commitment to long-term savings.

By contrast, the working paper by Jan Walliser and Joachim K. Winter, "Tax Incentive Motives and the Demand for Life Insurance: Evidence from Germany," (June 1998), concludes that taxes affect life insurance demand.

favorable tax policies have generally witnessed at least a temporary decline in life insurance sales.[1]

Governmental policy makers should be clear about whether any favorable life insurance tax policy is designed to promote savings, protection, or both. If the promotion of savings is the objective, qualifying policies should be heavily savings oriented (*e.g.*, annuities and endowments). If the promotion of death protection is the primary objective, qualifying policies should be predominately protection oriented (*e.g.*, term life products). If they seek the promotion of both protection and savings, policy qualification requirements can be broad.

Taken together, the protection and savings functions of life products have been judged by most countries to offer sufficient economic and social benefit to warrant some tax concession. At the same time, the desirability of maintaining an economically neutral fiscal environment should be emphasized.

B. Effect on tax revenues

In deciding the best mix of tax concessions, government will want to explore carefully which concessions can be expected to achieve their intended purpose at minimal tax loss and administrative complexity (see below). Government policy makers hardly need reminding that tax concessions mean decreased revenues, which can mean decreased public-sector investment for roads, bridges, public utilities, education, and the like. Such public-sector investment is a necessity for economic success by transition economies, in general, with this observation seeming to be especially relevant for the Baltic countries. Tradeoffs between the desire to promote private-sector investment and the need for public-sector investment should be weighed carefully.

C. Compatibility with the level of development

Whatever tax structure is developed, it should be compatible with the country's economic and political circumstances. The administrative systems in some emerging markets may be insufficiently attuned to the many necessary nuances that a more developed market-based economy demands. Opportunities for mistake and fraud abound, and the life insurance tax system must function in such an environment. This means that the system should be crafted to reduce opportunities for error and noncompliance by focusing on direct, simple administrative and compliance mechanisms.

Priorities naturally will differ from one country to another, and life insurance tax policy should align with the country's particular priorities. Thus, for example, if the life market is developing more slowly than a country believes desirable, tax incentives could spur development – even in preference to other financial institutions and products.

---

[1] "LAPR Killed after 131 Years," *The Post Magazine and Insurance Monitor*, 22 March 1984.

An appropriate tax system for life insurance should not be designed in isolation from the structure of the existing tax system. For example, if government relies heavily on consumption taxation (*e.g.*, value added or excise taxes) rather than on income taxes, attempting to develop a sophisticated net income tax system for insurance could be inappropriate.

The approach to using incentives or disincentives in the tax system should be consistent with the government's general attempt to influence economic and social behavior through the tax system and by other means such as expenditure programs, grants, discretionary undertakings to private industry, and direct intervention in the economy through government operations. Policy makers should remember, however, that use of the tax system to influence behavior ordinarily is a second-best approach to more direct approaches.

Tax rules applicable to life insurers should be coordinated with the form of corporate taxation followed in the country. These can vary from separate taxation of corporate income with full taxation of shareholder dividends, to a completely integrated system under which full credit for corporate tax is given to shareholders, with a variety of compromises between. Once the unique issues in the life insurance industry are resolved, the appropriate form of coordination is usually apparent.

D. *Compatibility with the insurance regulatory structure*

The overriding purpose of insurance regulation is to minimize insurer insolvencies and by that to protect the public from unsound operators. The main purpose of insurance taxation is to raise revenue for the government. Herein lies the potential for intra-governmental conflict.

Regulation typically requires pricing, reserving, and investment conservation. Therefore, insurers must behave in a correspondingly conservative manner. The designers of a life insurance taxation system must be sensitive to these regulatory requirements, use them as appropriate, and try to avoid measures that inadvertently or unfairly penalize life insurers that must function in such a conservative environment.

A country's insurance legislation and regulation provide a reference point and framework for tax planning. Tax designers should, therefore, make well-informed decisions before imposing their own, different requirements on life insurers and their products. Also, both taxation and regulatory authorities should be sensitive to the fact that a tax system can inadvertently encourage life insurers to attempt to avoid some statutory requirements to save taxes. With these facts in mind, countries would be well advised to ensure that an adequate and clearly defined system of insurance legislation and regulation is set up before embarking on any extensive revision of the life insurance tax system.

E. Alignment with the desirable traits of tax policy

As discussed earlier, tax systems should be equitable, neutral, and simple. Life insurance product taxation should be compatible with these traits.

1. Tax equity

Tax equity holds that taxpayers who earn more should pay more in taxes. It is not clear, *a priori*, how individual life product taxation should be crafted to fit with this principle. Certainly, if special tax concessions are extended to life products, they should be fully applicable to lower-income persons.

A tax equity question is whether concessions also should be extended fully to higher-income earners. Upper-income taxpayers have greater opportunities to practice tax arbitrage (and thereby shift from taxable to tax-preferred savings) and, of course, have greater opportunities to take advantage of tax concessions. At the same time, upper-income persons save more than lower-income persons, thus having a greater potentially positive effect on national savings.

If tax equity is a major consideration in deciding upon life product taxation, any tax preference could be weighted in favor of lower-income persons. For example, use of a tax credit rather than a tax deduction carries relatively more benefit for lower- than higher-income persons. Placing an upper limit on the amount of premium or insurance that qualifies for tax concession also can promote equity. On the other hand, system simplicity suffers with each attempt to promote individual equity.

2. Tax neutrality

Tax neutrality is perhaps the most important consideration in establishing tax policy toward life insurance products. The objective of tax neutrality is to establish balance within a country's fiscal environment. This means that tax policy should not cause one industry, type of product, or supplier to have an economic advantage over another. Neutrality requires that government raise revenues in ways that interfere as little as possible with the economic choices of consumers and businesses.

- *Financial intermediaries versus other businesses*. To minimize interference with the choices that entrepreneurs, investors, and employees make, government ideally should establish a regime in which the taxation of financial institutions is neither advantaged nor disadvantaged compared with the taxation of non-financial businesses. The tax neutrality trait, of course, is subject to compromise if judged essential to promote social or economic goals or if necessitated by concerns about complexity.

- *Life insurers versus other financial intermediaries*. The above neutrality logic ideally should apply also at the corporate level among financial institutions. Thus, in the absence of compelling social or economic policy reasons, government should provide no tax advantage to life insurers that is not also provided to banks and other financial institutions (and *vice versa*). To provide any such advantage is to encourage greater investment and employment within the advantaged sector and thus to distort the financial services market.

- **Life insurance products versus other savings media.** The *a priori* position of neutrality-minded tax planners should be that life insurance products enjoy no special tax concessions not extended also to other savings products and *vice versa.* Sound tax policy holds that a compelling economic or social benefit distinction must be made to justify a difference in tax treatment among such competitor saving instruments. This study takes no position about whether such a compelling distinction exists. This is a decision for each country's policy makers. This study has pointed out that one or more of the following objectives might provide a rationale for tax treatment more favorable for life insurance than for other financial instruments:

- A desire to encourage citizens to arrange for their dependents so as to relieve taxpayers of part of the burden.

- A desire to encourage personal savings via insurance (in preference to other savings media) because:

    - the local life insurance industry is underdeveloped compared with other domestic financial service industries, and it is desired quickly to have a variety of financial intermediaries and instruments to promote economic growth;

    - economic development requires more long-term finance, and contractual savings institutions such as life insurers (and pension funds) can be particularly important sources of such finance because of their typically long-term liabilities;

    - populations accustomed to substantial government-provided economic security may need special encouragement to provide for themselves.

Lacking one of the above or other distinguishing goals, any tax concessions extended to one class of financial products should be extended to all. As noted earlier, most OECD countries apparently believe some distinctions exist, although the trend is toward greater neutrality among competing financial products.

- **Stock versus mutual insurers.** In some life insurance markets, stock (shareholder-owned) life insurers predominate. Mutual life insurers dominate other markets. In a survey of several countries' tax systems, only Spain accorded special tax concessions to mutuals and not to stock insurers. Other countries essentially tax stocks and mutuals in the same manner, except for the element of dividends to policyholders.

A strong argument can be made that a tax system should tax all life insurance companies and their products equivalently. Ordinarily, government should not advantage one corporate form over another, so as to avoid rendering products sold by one form less costly than those sold by insurers of a different legal structure.

- **Domestic versus foreign insurers.** The issue of how to tax foreign-domiciled life insurers that conduct business via cross-border sales within a country will be closely linked to the country's general policy regarding foreign insurer operations within the country. Given that tax harmonization does not exist, the principle of *tax territoriality*, adopted by the European Union, probably should apply. Under this principle, cross-border services are subject to the taxes of the country where the service is exercised. No economic reason exists for taxing locally established, foreign-owned insurers any differently from that of locally owned insurers. Indeed, sound economic policy argues for adoption of a national treatment standard as regards insurer taxation; i.e., foreign-owned insurers should be accorded tax treatment no less favorable than that accorded domestically owned insurers.

- **Participating versus nonparticipating insurance.** Life insurance policies are generally classified as participating (with profits) or nonparticipating (without profits).[1] Participating policies provide that part of the surplus funds generated by the policies will be distributed among the policies as dividends (bonuses). With nonparticipating policies, the insurer does not distribute any part of surplus funds to policyholders. Usually, premiums for participating policies are higher than those of nonparticipating policies. Thus, part of the surplus funds generated by participating policies is derived from a deliberately conservative pricing structure.

The concept of tax neutrality would accommodate the two classes of life insurance through an appropriate recognition of policy dividends under participating policies. This recognition would apply both to the taxation of the insurance company and to that of the policyholder. This issue is covered more fully later in this study.

3. Tax simplicity

Tax systems should be simple. The goal of simplicity often conflicts with the goals of equity and neutrality.

---

[1] This distinction has blurred as life insurers offer non-participating products that permit the pass-through to policyholders of investment, expense, and mortality experience.

Life insurers and their products are complex. Because of this complexity, extensive tax rules typically are required. These tax rules become even more complex when one attempts to shape them to accomplish specific economic or social goals.

Thus, at least a part of the reason that most countries extend tax concessions to the inside interest build up, policy dividends, and other policy values is because of the administrative challenges faced in implementing a system to tax such interest. Much of the analysis in the following area suggests a need to permit the simplicity goal partially to override equity and neutrality goals for some countries.

F. Compatibility with other countries' tax systems

Countries revising their life insurance tax systems are wise to consider the tax regimes of other countries, including their neighbors and major trading partners – countries that might have already grappled with life insurance taxation issues. Indeed, a premise of this study is that countries can gain insight for developing their own tax regimes by examining the tax regimes of other countries. This admonition is of obvious relevance to the Baltic countries as they join the European Union.

As more markets liberalize, the issues of tax differences and convergence assume greater importance, although their discussion is beyond the scope of this paper. Countries revising their tax systems may afford themselves a marketplace advantage by patterning their tax systems closely after those of their major trading partners. Similarly, they should consider other countries' tax systems to avoid placing their own domestic financial intermediaries at a competitive disadvantage.

II. The elements of life insurance product tax policy

With the preceding considerations as background, we can now explore the elements that the Baltic countries might incorporate into their tax systems for life insurance products. This section parallels the earlier tax treatment overview.

A. Tax policy relative to premiums

Many approaches exist to granting tax concessions but all have common features. First, each approach defines qualifying policies. The definition may be exceedingly narrow or quite broad, depending upon the overall objective in granting such relief. For example, both Canada and the United States follow a narrow approach. They grant no general tax relief on life insurance premium payments, but each provides that payments by certain classes of individuals can qualify as tax deductible under individually established retirement plans. Several other countries follow a broad approach, granting general tax relief for certain broad categories of policies.

The second common feature is that each approach defines eligibility according to the life insured under the policy. All countries granting relief provide it to the policyholder and, in some manner, to his or her spouse. A few countries also provide relief for premium payments made for insurance on a child's life. If the objective of tax relief is to promote the protection aspects of life insurance as opposed to the savings aspect, little logic exists for relief for insurance on children. Moreover, if savings promotion is the primary goal, the logic for limiting tax concessions to such products sold only by life insurers weakens considerably.

The third common feature is that all systems have some limitation as to the maximum amount of premiums paid for which a tax deduction may be taken. In most countries, the usual procedure is to state the ceiling as a percentage of income or a fixed amount.

As to operational procedures, one approach is to have taxpayers show the qualifying amount as a deduction on their income tax returns. With a progressive tax system, this means that the higher the policyholder's income, the greater is the tax benefit. Having modest ceilings tempers this in most countries. Another approach is to permit a direct credit against income tax owed. This approach is of relatively greater benefit to lower-income earners.

Yet another procedure is to allow policyholders to gain tax relief by taking a deduction directly from the premium remitted to the life insurer. The insurer then obtains reimbursement from the government by taking a credit through its corporate tax return. This was the procedure adopted in 1979 in the United Kingdom. For such a system to be viable, the same implicit tax rate should be used for everyone. The United Kingdom permitted a credit against the premium of one-half the basic income tax rate. Such an approach benefits lower-income persons relatively more than upper-income taxpayers. This procedure has the further advantage of reducing the administrative burden on taxpayers and tax authorities.

The tax policy adopted by government concerning life insurance-funded employee benefit plans can have a major impact on the demand by employers for such coverages. Payments made by employers on behalf of employees often are not taxable income to the employees. Of course, this treatment is inconsistent with good tax concepts, but, nonetheless, common. Certain conditions, however, must be met if the payments are not to be considered as taxable income to employees, and limits may be placed on the exempted amount of coverage. These conditions are intended to minimize the chances that higher paid employees receive a disproportionately large share of the benefits. Employers are permitted to deduct payments for such plans as legitimate business expenses for purposes of determining taxable income.

Given the trends within the EU respecting tax relief on premiums, one could imagine a certain reluctance by the governments of the Baltic countries to embrace such tax policy. Moreover, avoiding this tax preference keeps administration less complex while being consistent with good tax policy.

B. Tax policy relative to living benefits

This section discusses possible tax policy approaches that the Baltic governments could adopt with respect to benefits payable during life.

1. Policy cash values

The tax neutrality principle would have interest credited to policy cash values taxed as any other interest income. However, few countries tax policyholders directly on the inside interest build up. This is evidence of administrative difficulty and perhaps an implicit recognition of a social value ascribed to life insurance savings.

As a compromise between simplicity and neutrality, the usual tax approach is to measure gain only on policy maturity or surrender. This net gain approach overstates the cost basis (total premiums paid). To be conceptually correct, only that portion of the premium that represents policy savings should form the tax basis. The charge for mortality risk and expenses should not form a part of the tax basis. As the basis is overstated, taxable income is understated. Also, by postponing tax payment until policy surrender, the policyholder is deferring taxation – an obvious advantage – especially during periods of high interest rates. If tax relief has been granted on premium payments, the cost basis should be reduced accordingly.

Even with these problems, it may be wise for the Baltic countries to make no attempt presently to tax the annual interest credited to policy cash values. The administrative complexities and resultant compliance costs might outweigh tax revenue generated. The net gain approach could be adopted as a reasonable compromise between neutrality and simplicity. Alternatively, a tax based on the insurer's investment income could be levied on the insurer.

Usually, taxation of endowment policies involves the same considerations as in the cash value discussion above. This suggests that an appropriate tax policy upon maturity is the net gain approach under which the amount subjected to tax is any positive difference between the maturity proceeds plus all dividends received and the sum of all (after-tax) premiums paid.

Other tax rules related to cash values exist. For example, some countries tax a person's wealth. This tax is levied annually on a person's adjusted net worth (*i.e.*, assets minus liabilities), except that special allowances are permitted in recognition that certain assets are essential for an individual's livelihood. Life insurance cash values are often excluded from such taxation, with certain minor exceptions.

Even if a country has a wealth tax and an estate duty, the total tax revenue generated by applying these taxes to life insurance values is often small. They are mentioned here for the sake of completeness, not because of their importance as revenue sources.

2. Policy dividends

Policy dividends represent in part a return to the policyholder of a deliberate premium overcharge. Logically, therefore, the mere return to policyholders of monies they had previously provided the insurer should not produce a taxable event, assuming no tax preference within the contract. Moreover, for mutual insurers, some portion of investment income allocated through dividends can be considered an implicit return on the policyholder's ownership interest in the insurer. Conceptually, this portion should be subject to the same tax treatment as that accorded dividends on shares.

Taxing policy dividends could be administratively difficult. Also tax revenues generated likely would be small from doing so. The usual treatment of not taxing policy dividends – even in the face of other tax preferences – might be reasonable, particularly if life insurance promotion is considered desirable.

3. Annuities

For purposes of policy analysis, annuity tax issues can be divided into those that arise during the accumulation and liquidation phases. The accumulation phase is that period during which contributions are made and before payments commence to annuitants.

The main issues that arise during the accumulation phase are whether tax relief should be granted for contributions to the annuity and whether interest credited to annuity cash values should be taxed currently. If government's policy is to encourage private savings via tax policy, the granting of tax relief on annuity considerations and the deferral of current income taxation on the annuity's inside interest build up might be effective, although note is made of the earlier discussion concerning the opposing substitution and income effects.

During their accumulation phase, annuities are closely akin to other long-term, private savings media. A policy of tax neutrality argues for other such media being taxed equivalently to annuities, for better or worse. Many countries grant tax relief for payments into annuities. Those that do not grant tax relief for payment usually do not tax the annual interest credited to annuity cash values. Rather, they subject the cash value to tax only at time of liquidation or if a cash value withdrawal is made before the liquidation phase.

If it is determined that some tax preference should be accorded annuities during the accumulation phrase, the approach that would create less distortion to the countries' savings market would be to treat all similar, long-term savings instruments equivalently. For example, provision could be made for creation of some type of individual pension funding via annuities or other instruments. This matter relates actually to the countries' private pension funding and taxation and, as such, is beyond the scope of this paper.

The tax issues related to the liquidation phase of annuities are less varied than those of the accumulation phase. When the life insurer begins to make periodic annuity payments (typically monthly or quarterly) to the annuitant, each payment is composed of part principal and part interest. If the interest accretions have escaped taxation during the accumulation phase, economic neutrality calls for each annuity payment to be subject to tax to the extent that it represents untaxed interest earnings. Moreover, if tax relief has been granted for premium payments during the accumulation phase, that portion of each annuity payment that represents tax-advantaged principal also should be taxed. Of course, the converse applies in each case.

4. Employee benefit plans

The premiums paid by employers for life or health insurance coverage for employees sometimes are not taxed as income to employees. Benefits received by employees from employer-funded retirement plans are usually subject to income tax upon receipt but only to the extent of each payment. This tax treatment presumes that contributions by the employer toward the retirement plan were taken as tax deductions and the contributions were not taxed to employees. This approach to retirement benefit taxation has been considered reasonable by most governments, although it violates the tax neutrality principle.

The tax treatment of individually purchased retirement annuities (and other qualifying savings media) could be coordinated with that of employer-provided retirement benefits, thereby enhancing equity among citizens. For example, in Canada, any citizen with earned income may establish and contribute to an individual, tax-deductible, retirement savings plan. This maximum sum is deductible only for those who do not participate in an employer-provided, tax-favored retirement plan (or for whom employer contributions or benefits are low). The deduction maximum phases out as employer-funded amounts or benefits increase, eventually being zero for those participating in generous employer-funded plans.

C. Tax policy relative to benefits payable on death

Many policyholders purchase life insurance because of a recognition that their death could cause financial hardship to dependents, and they wish to minimize this hardship. The purchase and retention of a life insurance policy, therefore, often rely on noble human motivations that probably have positive spillover effects for society.

In recognition of the motives behind life insurance purchases, the typically great financial need of surviving dependent individuals, and sympathy for the bereaved survivors, few countries impose income taxation on death proceeds. Of course, this practice means that any previously untaxed interest on cash values escapes income taxation. This practice can be inconsistent with the neutrality goal but many countries apparently believe that it represents reasonable public policy. In an environment of tax neutrality, death proceeds would be received income-tax free because no special tax concessions would have been extended to life insurance during the insured's life.

Governments do not hesitate to subject life insurance death proceeds to wealth and estate duties. This subject, however, is outside the scope of this study.

III. The elements of life insurer tax policy

As noted throughout this study, life insurance *product* taxation should not be viewed in isolation from life *insurer* taxation. This section briefly covers life insurer premium and income taxation.

A. *Evaluation of premium taxation*

Premium taxation has both desirable and undesirable attributes.[1] A system of taxation based on an insurance company's premium income is a simple approach to taxation. Administration by both insurers and tax authorities is easy. Compliance verification is not particularly difficult. This taxation produces a steady and usually increasing revenue flow to the state.

Insurance companies have been subjected to premium taxation for more than 150 years. This method of taxation arose at a time when governmental tax administration needed great simplicity and ease in administration. As a United Nations' study pointed out, however, "its simplicity is the source of potentially great inequity."[2] Commentators have noted several objectionable aspects of premium taxation:

- It is a direct tax on savings that is applicable only to insurers and not other, competing financial intermediaries

- It is inequitable (regressive) in that it burdens lower-income persons who purchase life insurance relatively more than higher-income persons, as unit costs of insurance are higher for small policies than larger ones and low-income customers purchase small policies

- It discriminates unfairly against higher-premium (and cash-value) forms of life insurance, as its assessment is based on the premium

- It discriminates unfairly against those who must pay higher premium rates, such as the elderly and insureds who must pay higher than standard premiums because of health or other difficulties

- It must be paid irrespective of insurer profitability

---

[1] This section draws from Skipper (1987).

[2] *Establishing Life Insurance Tax Policy in Developing Countries* (Geneva: UNCTAD, 1985), p. 13.

While premium tax rates of 2.0 or 3.0 percent may seem low, they are applied to a large tax base and few tax concessions are provided. The net result can be a high effective tax burden. Studies have found that the effective tax burden on insurers arising from premium taxation is consistently higher than that on other financial and non-financial institutions. With increasing competitiveness within the financial services community, economically neutral tax systems become more critical.

For the above reasons, premium taxation generally should be avoided. As a practical matter, a premium tax at a modest level (*e.g.*, less than 1.0 percent) could be used as a short-term substitute for a broad-based life insurer income tax system or as a simple, temporary alternative tax. It should be recognized, however, that a premium tax distorts the financial services marketplace and falls short of the goals of equity and neutrality.

B. *Evaluation of income taxation*

A life insurer tax system based on an insurer's total income probably offers the greatest practical opportunity to address equity and economic neutrality issues meaningfully. Such a tax system, however, can be complex, as the enormous variations in system details among OECD countries attest. For example, in some OECD countries, tax deductible actuarial reserves are calculated using the same assumptions as those laid down for regulatory purposes. In other countries, special tax-prescribed assumptions must be used.

Ideally, a country should tax all corporations, including life insurers, under the same general approach. If some variation of the net income approach is adopted, the system applicable to life insurers could be simplified, at least initially, as relates to reserve and policyholder dividend deductions.

The range of variations found in OECD countries for calculating the reserve deduction attests to the view that there is no perfect method. Although the reserves determined for regulatory purposes are calculated conservatively (and, therefore, are intended to be higher than necessary), the simplest approach would be for the taxing authorities to adopt the supervisory authority's standards. If no published standards exist, the reserve position as reported in the company's financial statement could be used. As tax authorities develop expertise in this technical area, the tax reserve deduction could be changed. Use of the same standard simplifies the administrative burdens on both tax authorities and life insurers. Life insurers would not need to prepare different reserve calculations for tax and regulatory authorities. The tax authorities, in turn, could place greater reliance on the accuracy of the computation since the regulatory authorities might be charged with verifying it.

The effect of using statutory reserves for tax purposes is to overstate the reserve deduction and, hence, to understate taxable income. This need not be considered as a major problem if the country is dedicated to the promotion of life insurance. It can be viewed as one aspect of a favorable tax policy.

Dividends paid on participating life insurance policies are usually deductible in whole or in part in determining taxable income under a total income tax system. In fact, a separate accounting of the income attributable to participating business is usually required in OECD countries. If the insurer is a stock company, the shareholders may be entitled to a small percentage only of the profits from the participating business. If the insurer is a mutual company, policyholders effectively own the company, in which case profits of any nonparticipating business plus those from the participating business may be distributed to the participating policyholders as policy dividends.

As noted earlier, policy dividends represent both a return of excess premiums and a distribution of income. Distinguishing between the two elements is difficult. To allow a full deduction for policy dividends may reduce the tax base of a life insurer below the comparable corporate tax base of other businesses. Within the industry itself, to do so may give mutual companies an unfair advantage over stock companies.

Most countries allow a full deduction for policy dividends. However, Canada limits the deduction to the amount of the participating income. This tends to place stock and mutual companies on a similar basis. The deduction for policy dividends in Japan is limited to a deemed minimum return of 7.0 percent on insurer surplus. Under the United States' system, deductions for policy dividends paid by a mutual company are limited to reflect a return on net worth, but full deductibility is allowed stock companies.

CHAPTER 5

SUMMARY AND CONCLUSIONS

The purpose of this study has been to examine life insurance product taxation in OECD countries and thereby to provide insight for the Baltic States as they develop or revise life insurance tax policies. Life insurance plays important economic and social roles for both individuals and societies. Life insurance affords individuals, families, and businesses the opportunity to hedge against the adverse financial consequences of death and to save in a convenient, perhaps quasi-compulsory manner.

As important financial intermediaries, life insurance companies help mobilize national saving to support greater national investment. Enhanced investment is a prerequisite to stronger, long-term economic growth. Additionally, individually purchased life insurance undoubtedly relieves pressure on social welfare systems, thus minimizing taxes.

The financial sector – including the life insurance industry – is believed to have a special role to play in the transformation and development of economies. This is because of the need for a more efficient allocation of savings, for strong stabilization policies and structural reforms, for overall confidence building, and for particularly strong sources of external finance for non-financial businesses.

Because of these beneficial spillover effects, a case can be made for using tax policy to encourage citizens and businesses to purchase life insurance. However, research to date neither supports nor refutes the premise that a favorable life insurance tax policy will be effective from a macroeconomic perspective. The ambiguity on the impact of tax policy on national savings adds little to our confidence that life insurance tax concessions will prove to be a panacea.

Tax provisions applicable to life insurance ideally should be consistent with general tax principles. These principles include the general purposes of taxation (to raise revenue, to promote economic goals, and to promote social goals), the desirable traits of tax policy (equity, neutrality, and simplicity), and the various systems of taxation.

All OECD countries provide some tax concessions in the purchase, maintenance, or execution of life insurance policies. Most grant modest tax relief for premiums paid for qualifying life insurance policies. Policies that are primarily survivorship contracts (*i.e.* endowments and whole life) are more likely to enjoy tax preferences. The trend internationally is away from such tax concessions.

OECD countries generally do not tax life insurance policy dividends nor do they directly tax the inside interest build up under cash value contracts. Rather, any excess of a policy's maturity or cash value (and dividends) over premiums paid is typically taxable, but only at policy maturity or surrender. Death proceeds ordinarily do not incur income tax, but are typically subject to estate duties.

All OECD countries tax life insurers on either their total income or investment income. Life insurers in a minority of OECD countries also are taxed on their premium income. Life insurance product taxation should not be considered in isolation from the taxation of life insurers.

Several considerations should apply as the Baltic countries establish their life insurance product tax policy. First, policy makers should have a clear view of the purposes they seek to accomplish via any life product tax concessions and of the expected effects on revenues of tax concessions. The importance of life insurance tax policy being compatible with the country's level of development, with the insurance regulatory structure, and with other countries' tax policies is noted. A life insurance product tax system should align with the desirable traits of tax policy. Of the traits of equity, neutrality, and simplicity, the latter two are perhaps key to a successful life product tax system. Neutrality requires that government tax decisions minimize interference with the economic choices of individuals and businesses. Thus, lacking a compelling argument to the contrary, tax policy should not create an economic advantage for one industry, supplier, or type of product compared with all others.

The elements of a possible life product tax system for the Baltic States could omit any tax concessions on premiums paid for life insurance policies issued to individuals, whether term or cash value insurance. Premiums paid by employers for reasonable life-insurance-funded employee benefits should be deductible to employers as a regular business expense, if the country has a net income tax system in which expenses of conducting business can be taken against gross income. Premiums paid for these benefits should constitute taxable income to employees, based on the tax principle that what is deductible to one party must be income to the other. If the Baltic governments want to provide a special encouragement to businesses to offer employee benefits, however, such payments – perhaps limited to some formula maximums – could escape taxation to employees.

Living benefits paid under life policies generally could be accorded some tax concessions, as much to avoid the administrative complexities of doing otherwise as to promote life insurance. Thus, both policy dividends and the interest credited on policy cash values could enjoy typical OECD country treatment. Any gain on policy surrender or maturity might be taxable income. Annuity payments, being composed of part principal and part interest, should invoke taxation on any untaxed interest portion only or, if contributions were deductible, on both portions. Death benefits of life insurance policies could be excluded from income taxation.

Life insurance company taxation logically should not be separated from life product taxation. Governments ideally should tax insurers and other financial intermediaries equivalently.

Premium taxation is simple administratively for both tax collection authorities and the taxpayer. On the other hand, its application creates substantial inequity among life products and is not competitor neutral given that it must be paid irrespective of profitability. The premium tax approach should be used only if the need for administrative simplicity dominates the goals of equity and neutrality.

The corporate income tax is a logical, if potentially complex, means of taxing life insurers if other corporations are also subject to such taxation. It can be crafted to reduce inequities and to achieve reasonable neutrality. By permitting policy reserve deductions based on statutory reserves and full policy dividend deductions, such a system can be simplified without great sacrifice of either tax revenues or neutrality.

Thus, a complete life insurance tax system would be composed of two parts. The taxation of the insurer itself would be consistent with taxation of other financial intermediaries, with certain concessions to tax simplicity for some markets. Except for concessions to simplicity, life insurance product taxation also would be consistent with the taxation of non-insurance financial instruments, unless government policy makers believe that life products deserved special tax concessions, as discussed earlier.

In crafting the details of the above tax policy, the Baltic countries will want to afford particular attention to tax policy and practice within the EU countries. With increasing financial services liberalization and integration, the desirability of having at least minimal tax-system harmonization grows.

BIBLIOGRAPHY

Bernheim, B. Douglas (2002). "Taxation and Saving" in A. J. Auerback and M. Feldstein, eds., *Handbook of Public Economics,* North Holland, Amsterdam.

Black, Kenneth, Jr. and Harold D. Skipper, Jr. (2000). *Life and Health Insurance*, 13th ed., Prentice-Hall, Inc., Englewood Cliffs, NJ.

Grubert, Harry and James B. Mackie III (2000). "Must Financial Services be Taxed Under a Consumption Tax?" *National Tax Journal* vol. 53 (March).

Insurance Markets in the Baltic States (2001).

Jack, William (2000). "The Treatment of Financial Services Under a Broad-Based Consumption Tax," *National Tax Journal* Vol. 53 (Dec.).

Jappelli, Tullio and Luigi Pistaferri (2001). "Tax Incentives and the Demand for Life Insurance: Evidence from Italy," discussion paper no. 2787, Centre for Economic Policy Research.

Levine, R. (1996). "Foreign Banks, Financial Development, and Economic Growth," in *International Financial Markets,* Claude E. Barfield, ed. AEI Press, Washington, D.C.

"LAPR Killed after 131 Years" (1984). *The Post Magazine and Insurance Monitor*, 22 March.

OECD (1987). Consumers and Life Insurance, OECD, Paris.

OECD (2001). *Taxing Insurance Companies*, OECD, Paris.

Poterba, James M. (forthcoming) "Taxation and Portfolio Structure: Issues and Implications," in *Household Portfolios,* Luigi Guiso, Michalis Haliassos, and Tullio Jappelli, eds. MIT Press, Cambridge.

PriceWaterhouseCoopers (2002). International Comparison of Insurance Taxation, PWC.

Skipper, Harold D., Jr. (1998). "The Nature of Government Intervention into Insurance Markets: Taxation," in *International Risk and Insurance: An Environmental-Managerial Approach,* Irwin McGraw-Hill, 1998.

Skipper, Harold D., Jr. (1998). "Regulatory Harmonization and Mutual Recognition in Insurance," in *International Risk and Insurance: An Environmental-Managerial Approach,* Irwin McGraw-Hill, 1998.

Skipper, Harold D., Jr. (1998). "Risk Management and Insurance in Economic Development," in *International Risk and Insurance: An Environmental-Managerial Approach,* Irwin McGraw-Hill, 1998.

Skipper, Harold D., Jr. (1987). "State Taxation of Insurance Companies: Time for a Change," *Journal of Insurance Regulation*, Vol. 6.

Skipper, Harold D., Jr. (1996). "The Taxation of Life Insurance Products in OECD Countries," in *Policy Issues in Insurance: Investment, Taxation, and Solvency*, OECD, Paris.

Swiss Reinsurance Company (1987). "A Comparison of Social and Private Insurance, 1970-1985, in Ten Countries," *Sigma*, Swiss Reinsurance Co., Zurich.

Swiss Reinsurance Company (2002). "World Insurance in 2001: "Turbulent financial markets and high claims burden impact premium growth" *Sigma*, Swiss Reinsurance Co., Zurich.

UNCTAD (United Nations Conference on Trade and Development) (1985). *Establishing Life Insurance Tax Policy in Developing Countries*, UNCTAD, Geneva.

Walliser, Jan and Joachim K. Winter (June 1998). "Tax Incentive Motives and the Demand for Life Insurance: Evidence from Germany." Working Paper.

LIBERALIZATION OF THE INSURANCE MARKETS:

ISSUES AND CONCERNS

Harold D. Skipper

Abstract

This paper addresses several issues that may be relevant to the Baltic insurance markets and governments as they continue their transition to liberal, market economies. The study approaches liberalization issues from two perspectives. First, it sets out the role and importance of government policy in insurance. The main issue is that government intervention into insurance markets is essential but should be carefully targeted to minimize undue interference.

Next, the study explores the role of foreign insurers, with particular emphasis on the concerns that have been expressed historically about their roles in national insurance markets of emerging economies. In this respect, the major underlying idea is that such insurers should be expected to play an important role in market evolution and development.

TABLE OF CONTENTS

INTRODUCTION

The Meaning of Liberalization

This paper addresses several issues that may be relevant to the Baltic insurance markets and governments as they continue their transition to liberal, market economies.[1] The paper approaches liberalization issues from two perspectives. First, it sets out the role and importance of government policy in insurance. The essential point here is that government intervention into insurance markets is essential but should be carefully targeted to minimize undue interference. To some, this discourse might appear a bit academic, but it is the most important in this treatise, because it lays the foundation for the circumstances under which government should and should not intervene into insurance markets.

Next, we explore the role of foreign insurers, with particular emphasis on the concerns that have been expressed historically about their roles in national insurance markets of emerging economies. The essential point here is that such insurers should be expected to play an important role in market evolution and development.

Liberalization cannot be separated from regulation – hence, both are covered. **Liberalization** means the process by which government takes actions to move toward liberal markets in which, subject only to economically justifiable government restrictions, the market determines:

1. who should be allowed to sell insurance,

2. what products should be sold,

3. how products should be sold, and

4. the prices at which products should be sold.

The first item, who should be allowed to sell insurance, deals with issues such as market access and equality of competitive opportunity, including national treatment. In turn, market access issues encompass prudential regulation. Items 2 through 4 commonly deal with issues such as product, price, and market conduct regulation. All four items subsume competition regulation.

---

[1] Earlier versions of this paper were presented at the *Roundtable on Insurance in Russia*, Moscow, 15-16 May 2000 and the *Seminar on Insurance Markets in Transition: Balancing Competition, Fairness, and Soundness,* at the Indian Institute of Management Bangalore, 13 July 2000.

CHAPTER 1

THE ROLE AND IMPORTANCE OF GOVERNMENT POLICY

Liberal insurance markets are in states' national interests because they offer businesses and individuals greater choice and better value than alternative approaches.[1] A central point about liberal markets, however, should be clear at the outset. A liberal insurance market is not a market devoid of regulation. Indeed, a liberal market demands government intervention if it is to function appropriately. The challenge for government is to craft just the right degree of intervention.

Many governments have undertaken liberalization and deregulation efforts. At the same time, some seem tentative — facially endorsing competitive markets while retaining elements of restrictive regulatory systems. Thus, many governments continue to deny their citizens and businesses access to low-priced, high-quality insurance policies and services. These actions suggest either that regulation exists more to protect established private interests than the overall national interest or policymakers remain skeptical that liberal markets will deliver the benefits to the national economy as suggested above. Both issues are analyzed below.

I. Different Regulatory Approaches Reflect Different Interests

Government intervention into insurance markets takes many forms; some direct, some indirect. Its stated purposes are always noble — to protect consumers, to raise revenue to support worthwhile social objectives, or to ensure orderly, well functioning markets. However, in reality, regulation does not always serve noble purposes.

Various factors influence regulatory policies and behavior. These factors include market problems that regulators are seeking to rectify, ideology, special interests, and regulatory resources. Other factors sometimes distort regulation. Often, private interests or special interest groups exert undue influence on regulation to serve their own interests at the expense of consumers and the overall national welfare. For example, established insurers might support government action that limits entry and diminishes competition from new insurers — both national and foreign. The resulting restrictions might be cloaked in the guise of "protecting the consumer," "protecting the national interest," or "protecting domestic jobs" but consumers and the national economy are harmed by such restrictions. Special interest groups typically are better informed, financed, and organized than consumers, so their views often predominate. Additionally, the economic justification for liberal insurance markets – while sound – is not one that can be explained simply, whereas opponents of liberal markets can tout facially appealing, simplistic slogans.

---

[1] This section draws in part from Harold D. Skipper and Robert W. Klein, *Insurance Regulation in the Public Interest: The Path Towards Solvent, Competitive Markets*, Working Paper no. 99-4, Center for Risk Management and Insurance Research, Georgia State University (1999).

Regulation unduly influenced by such special interests is characterized by:

- restrictions on entry of new national and especially foreign insurers;

- suppression of price and product competition;

- control of inter-industry competition from those selling similar or complementary products.

Insurance regulation that exhibits these characteristics is likely subject to "capture" by the local industry, resulting in both individual and commercial insureds being penalized through high prices, lack of product innovation, and poor product choice. That private interests sometimes take precedence over the greater national good remains an obvious challenge confronting policymakers. Citizens and businesses — through dedicated government representatives and through publicity — must be ever vigilant in exposing such abuses of the public trust and should support measures that expose and thwart such abuses. The glaring light of truth coupled with transparency in all relevant government decisions and processes provide the strongest, most effective means of preventing and detecting abuse.

II. Competition Enhances Choice and Value

Some policymakers seem skeptical about the benefits of competition. The case for liberal insurance markets, while clear to those schooled in economics, can be a confused array of conflicting claims to those charged with making policy decisions.

A. The Case for Liberal Insurance Markets

The objective that a market-oriented economy has for its insurance industry is the same as that which it has for other industries — an efficient allocation of society's scarce resources. Furthermore, society desires an economic system that leads to continuous innovation and improvement. These objectives are most likely to be achieved through reliance on competitive markets.

Competition not only leads to economic efficiency, it provides an automatic mechanism for fulfilling consumer needs and wants and for creating a greater variety of choices. Additionally, competition compels insurers to improve their products and services, thus further benefiting buyers. A *perfectly* competitive market – one in which new suppliers enter and exit the market with ease, buyers and sellers are perfectly informed, and all sellers offer identical products at the same prices – requires no government direction or oversight to accomplish these desirable social goals. Perfect competition, however, is an ideal not realized in practice.

Even so, this economic ideal provides a useful construct against which we can compare actual market functioning. We know that the closer a market is to this competitive ideal, the more efficiently it functions. Indeed, a market that is workably

266

competitive functions well and provides most of the benefits of perfect competition. Markets characterized by *workable competition* generally have low entry and exit barriers, numerous buyers and sellers, good information, governmental transparency, and the absence of artificial restraints on competition. The markets for numerous products satisfy these conditions sufficiently such that little government intervention is required for the market to function well.

For insurance markets to be workably competitive, however, substantial government intervention is necessary in key areas because important imperfections exist in such markets. Because of these market imperfections (also called market failures), government intervention into these areas is required to ensure healthy competition and good performance.

B. Empirical Evidence in Favor of Liberalization

Until recently, we have had scant empirical evidence about the practical effects of insurance liberalization itself within emerging markets. A doctoral dissertation at Georgia State University might be the first to explore this important issue empirically. In her research, Dr. Thitivadee Boonyasai – now a professor at Chulalongkron University in Thailand – examined the effects on life insurer efficiency of insurance market opening (defined as liberalization in her study) and deregulation efforts undertaken by Korea, the Philippines, Taiwan, and Thailand.[1] All four countries undertook some market opening during the past decade, with Korea and the Philippines undertaking modest deregulation as well. In neither instance could these deregulation efforts be characterized as substantial. Nonetheless, these two markets can be contrasted with those of Taiwan and Thailand, which undertook virtually no deregulation during the study period.

Dr. Boonyasai found that liberalization and deregulation of the Korean and Philippine life insurance industries seem to have stimulated increases and improvements in productivity. In addition, liberalization and deregulation of these markets created more competitive markets as witnessed by life insurers' improving efficiency; e.g., achieving cost savings and adjusting their scale of operations. Merely allowing greater market access without dismantling restrictive regulatory regimes – as was the situation with Taiwan and Thailand – seems to have had little effect on increases and improvements in productivity.

Thus, her study findings are consistent with the view that market access is a necessary but not a sufficient condition for contestable markets. Study findings also are consistent with the view that, in a restrictive regulatory environment, welfare gains will be minimal if deregulation does not closely follow market opening.

---

[1] Thitivadee Boonyasai, *The Effect of Liberalization and Deregulation on Life Insurer Efficiency*, unpublished Ph.D. dissertation, Georgia State University, 1999.

Another study focused on the relationship between liberalization commitments under the GATS and overall market factors. The authors confirm that a greater propensity to make liberalizing commitments is correlated with greater macroeconomic stability, better prudential regulation, and greater existing market penetration by foreign firms.[1] This study suggests that liberalization is associated with greater stability.

III. Competition has Limitations

Unlike the perfectly competitive market that underpins economist analysis and thought, the real marketplace is a jungle of imperfections. Competition is always threatened and threatening. It is threatened because businesspeople, without governmental oversight, are prone to undermine it through various anti-competitive activities and to promote government restrictions that unduly limit competition. Businesses are committed to making profits, and the more restrictive is a market the greater the opportunity for high profits.

Liberal markets are also threatening for competitors because it is tough to compete – better to avoid it if you can, because you might lose if you are not good enough. Merely existing – not to mention prospering – in a competitive world is not easy.

If market imperfections did not exist, insurers – if they existed at all – would be mere pass-through mechanisms akin to mutual funds, and no regulation would be necessary as all customers would have complete information. The existence of imperfections in insurance markets explains and justifies the great majority of both insurer operations and insurance regulation. An understanding of these imperfections, therefore, is essential if one is fully to appreciate both the need for government intervention into insurance markets and, importantly, the desirability for appropriate intervention. Four major classes of imperfections are presented below.

A. Information Problems

A critically important assumption of the competitive model is that both buyers and sellers are well informed. As a practical matter, we know otherwise regarding insurance. Information problems abound in insurance, and arguably are the industry's most important market imperfection.

Insurance is a complex business, with buyers having superior information to sellers in certain instances (e.g., buyers have better information about their relative risk when they apply for insurance) and vice versa in others (e.g., insurers know more about their financial condition than do buyers). *Asymmetric information problems* exist when one party to a transaction has relevant information that the other does not have.

---

[1] Harms Philipp, Mattoo Aaditya, and Schuknecht Ludger: "Expanding liberalization commitments in financial services trade," World Bank Policy Research Working Paper 2999 (March 2003).

The nature of the insurance transaction involves a contract that makes a present promise of future performance upon the occurrence of stipulated events. Individuals and businesses purchase policies in good faith, relying on the integrity of the insurance company and its representatives. Even assuming that insureds could be induced to take an interest in the financial condition of their insurers, few are sufficiently knowledgeable to do so without some assistance. Insurance is necessarily a technical, complicated subject, and the true financial condition of an insurance company can be determined only by expert examination. Also, some individuals may have difficulty understanding the complex nature of insurance contracts. These observations are less applicable to sophisticated buyers, such as large businesses, than to individuals.

Information problems for insurance customers – especially the so-called *"lemons" problem* of the buyer being less informed than the seller – provide the rationale for the great majority of insurance regulation. Insurers and their representatives have little incentive to disclose adverse information to potential customers. Doing so hurts sales. Governments seek to rectify the unequal positions between insurance buyer and seller by mandating certain disclosures for insurers, by monitoring insurer financial condition, by regulating insurers' marketing practices, and through other means.[1]

Because insurance is a financial future-delivery product tied closely to the public interest, governments judge the "lemons" problem to warrant substantial oversight of the financial condition of insurers. The widely accepted view is that the public, especially poorly informed consumers, must be protected.

The market has evolved some solutions to these problems. Financial rating agencies monitor insurers' financial condition, rendering opinions as to their solidity. Their services are widely used in North America, Europe, and elsewhere. Also, insurance intermediaries, especially independent agents and brokers, often provide evaluations of insurers. Even so, government often must provide consumer information for the public good.

Of course, the insurance buyer is often better informed than the seller on certain matters. Adverse selection and moral hazard problems exist for insurers. *Adverse selection* occurs when customers use their superior knowledge to secure insurance at lower prices than is actuarially justified. Insurers underwrite (evaluate) proposed insureds principally to deter and detect adverse selection. It plagues insurers worldwide and is the principal reason that insurers seek such extensive information about proposed insureds. They want to know as much as practical about the loss potential of those to whom they issue insurance. In this way, they can charge equitable prices that reflect the expected value of the proposed insureds' losses.

---

[1] Another way government may address this problem is by providing consumer information and education. Private for-profit and non-profit organizations also can provide consumer information and education, but government may play a valuable role in this area as well.

Moral hazard is the tendency of individuals to alter their behavior to take less vigilance *because* they are insured. Moral hazard problems are of concern in all types of insurance. Insurance contract design and insurer claims settlement departments seek to discourage moral hazard. The extreme versions of adverse selection and moral hazard are addressed through laws that limit recovery under policies obtained through misrepresentation or where insureds purposefully cause losses.

In many aspects of insurance processes, neither the buyer nor the seller has complete information because the desired information simply does not exist. Insurers cannot know the future. Environmental factors — such as the economy, inflation, new laws and regulations, and changing consumer attitudes and preferences — present great uncertainty to both insurance buyers and sellers.

Because of these problems and other market imperfections, private insurers will not supply every type of insurance that consumers demand. Insurers may perceive excessive adverse selection or moral hazard problems, or they may be unable to diversify their loss exposures. Thus, the private insurance mechanism generally offers little unemployment insurance and faces some difficulty in insuring catastrophic events such as terrorism acts, earthquakes and other natural disasters, and nuclear disasters that could cause huge, concentrated losses in a particular area. In each instance, insurers perceive too much uncertainty occasioned by a change in the state of nature or state of the world, coupled with prospects for severe adverse selection. If such exposures are to be insured, government itself or some government-subsidized private arrangement often provides the insurance.

Asymmetric information also can lead to *principal-agent problems* in insurance markets. Such problems arise, for instance, when policyholders have difficulty in monitoring and controlling the behavior of their insurer. The insurer might incur additional financial risk that is hazardous to its policyholders' interests or fail to meet its obligations to policyholders. If the insurer becomes insolvent or refuses to pay claims, policyholders may find it very costly or impossible to recover funds or force the insurer to fulfill its obligations. Unequal resources and bargaining power between the insurer and an individual policyholder can exacerbate the problem.

B. Market Power

Insurers can acquire market power that, under some circumstances, permits them to limit competition. *Market power* is the ability of one or a few sellers (or buyers) to influence the price of a product or service. Under the competitive model, sellers and buyers are price takers — meaning that they are so small compared with their market that they cannot exercise any meaningful influence over the price and quantity of a good or service, either individually or collectively. If some players in the market can affect price and quantity significantly to serve their interests, the allocation of resources generally will be inefficient.

Without appropriate government oversight, insurers – like other profit-seeking businesses – would be prone to engage in anti-competitive activities that result in their gaining market power through such practices as marketing sharing arrangements, pricing collusion, and exclusion dealings. Government's responsibility is to prevent or punish such activities that otherwise could thwart the benefits of a competitive market.

Insurers often attempt to gain market power through *price discrimination*. For example, an insurer may offer identical insurance through its agents, through brokers, and through the Internet, with each carrying a different price. With increasing competition, insurers seek ways to segment their target markets to charge different prices in each. Insurance regulators become concerned about price discrimination when the insurer's underlying loss experience or expenses do not justify price differences on otherwise identical policies.

If an insurer can differentiate its products from those of its competitors in the minds of its customers, it gains market power and can secure higher profits. *Product differentiation* exists when buyers prefer one firm's products over those of its rivals. This preference may stem from perceived differences in product quality, service, reputation, convenience, or other attributes.

Like other firms, insurers routinely try to differentiate their products from those of their competitors. This is one of the reasons that insurers seek to establish and maintain good reputations. Some products — such as automobile insurance and term life insurance — are more difficult to differentiate than others, such as cash-value life insurance. In general, the more complex the insurance product or, at least the more complex the product is perceived to be in the minds of customers, the greater the likelihood of a successful product differentiation strategy. Regulators are concerned about product differentiation only if the effect is to mislead purchasers. Otherwise, product differentiation can lead to enhanced consumer choice and value and to continuous product improvement.

National tax regimes can create market power. Some countries assess higher premium taxes on the local business of foreign insurers than they do on the local business of national insurers. Such practices are analogous to trade tariffs and have similar adverse economic consequences.

Explicit or implicit collusion historically has been common in many insurance markets internationally, especially concerning pricing. Tariff markets, in which all sellers charge similar or identical prices, remain common in many countries and for certain insurance lines in some OECD countries.

National licensing requirements technically are entry barriers, although they are justified on consumer protection grounds. Some entry restrictions are appropriate to ensure that insurers are financially sound and their owners and managers are honest and competent. However, some governments go beyond this legitimate objective and will grant new licenses only under circumstances that have little to do with prudential concerns. Other countries require local equity participation. Transparency in the licensing process is less than desired in many markets, with numerous unwritten rules.

In the absence of undue government restrictions, insurance markets are structurally competitive. Entry and exit barriers and economies of scale and scope are not of a nature that would allow a small number of insurers to acquire meaningful market power. Even in highly concentrated markets, the ever-present threat of new entry can impose competitive discipline; i.e., the concept of contestable markets. If insurers enjoy meaningful market power within a country, the cause usually can be traced to restrictive government control over entry and competition. The solution in such instances is not more regulation, but rather the removal of the government restrictions on entry and competition.

C. Externalities

Externalities cause markets to be imperfect. An *externality* exists when a firm's production or an individual's consumption has direct and uncompensated effects on others, either negatively or positively. With negative externalities (e.g., air or water pollution), too much of the good or service will be produced or consumed, the price will be too low, and too little effort and resources will be devoted to correcting or reducing the externality. With positive externalities (e.g., one firm learns about a new way of marketing by observing another firm), too little of the good or service will be produced, and its price will be too high; also, too little effort will be devoted to enhancing the externality.

Perhaps the most significant insurance-related negative externality is the deliberate destruction of property and the occasional murder that occur to collect insurance proceeds. From 5 to 15 percent of all nonlife insurance claims in some markets (e.g., in Europe and North America) are believed to involve fraud. Such destruction is a deadweight loss to society that is a cost associated with insurance.

Another example of a negative externality flows from the important systemic roles played by financial intermediaries, such as banks, securities firms, and insurers. *Systemic risks* exist if the difficulties of financial institutions cause disruptions elsewhere within an economy. Two types of systemic risks exist. The first — *cascading failures* — exists when the failure of one financial institution is the cause of the failure of others. The potential for cascading failures exists in insurance through risk pooling and reinsurance. Some reinsurer failures have led to direct-insurer failures. To date, these instances have been rare and their economic effects limited. They have been within the nonlife branch only. The prevention of these types of cascading failures is within management control through careful selection of reinsurers and business diversification.

The second type of systemic risk is a *run* in which many policyholders or other creditors demand their money at once. A loss of confidence stemming from the real or imagined fear of insolvency usually causes runs. Runs have occurred in insurance. For example, policyholders of the two largest US life insurer failures — Executive Life and Mutual Benefit Life — initiated runs by placing exceptionally high demands for policy loans and policy savings, as have policyholders of smaller failed insurers. To date, runs on life insurers have been limited to insurers already in financial difficulty. They have not caused the failure of sound insurers. The possibility of such contagion effects exists, however, and, with the continued move by life insurers to offer bank-life products, we should not ignore the risk.

D. Free Rider Problems

When goods or services are available to others at no cost, they are said to suffer from a *free rider problem*. After all, who among us would not be content to enjoy a good or service and have someone else pay for it. Some collectively consumed goods or services carry extensive positive externalities. Examples include police and fire protection, national defense, the court system, public health, and education. By contrast, a private good is one in which one person's consumption precludes it being consumed by another. A *public good* is characterized by non-rival consumption – meaning that one person's consumption of the good or service does not reduce its availability to others.

The desirability of public goods provides a rationale for government regulatory and risk management actions. With public goods, societal benefits exceed private benefits, so the market will produce too few of the affected goods because of the free rider problem. Having government provide the public good improves efficiency.

National defense and police protection are classic examples of public goods. The military protects everyone, even those who pay no taxes. Police do likewise, and also help preserve order in society, which is essential to efficient markets. The law and its fair interpretation by courts also are essential public goods, especially as they establish clear and enforceable property rights. This reduces uncertainty, providing an environment conducive to economic prosperity. When rules are transparent and enforced impartially, transactions and monitoring costs can be kept low.

Loss control resources often have elements of public goods. Thus, reducing the likelihood of flooding for one person by appropriate water management practices reduces the risk for others in a flood plain. Indeed, numerous aspects of community disaster preparedness have elements of public goods.

When many people face similar hazards, risk assessment and information dissemination often are public goods. Thus, if government provides risk management information to one member within a group, other members can benefit at little or no additional cost. Without government involvement in risk information dissemination, too little of it would be produced.

IV. Insurance Regulation Should Rectify Market Imperfections

Government's role in crafting insurance regulation should be limited to rectifying imperfections that can cause significant harm. Therefore, governmental intervention into the insurance market is economically justified only with respect to matters that meet three conditions:

- an actual or potential market imperfection exists,

- the market imperfection causes or can reasonably be expected to cause meaningful consumer or public harm, and

- government action can ameliorate the harm.

Conversely, if any one of the three conditions is not met, no government intervention is warranted. Thus, no government intervention is justified with respect to any insurer operation that does not cause demonstrable or reasonably expected harm. Even if some aspect of insurer operations might adversely affect some individuals, no intervention is warranted if the intervention would be ineffectual or might actually exacerbate the problem. Just as there is no perfectly competitive market, so too is there no perfect government regulation.

All existing and proposed insurance regulations should be tested against these three conditions. Some existing and proposed regulations will meet all three conditions. Others will not and should be abandoned or modified.

The likelihood of consumer abuse because of market imperfections will vary from country to country. Thus, countries with a long history of competitive insurance markets have already resolved many of the complex issues concerning appropriate government intervention. Transition economies, such as the Baltics, on the other hand, must exercise a certain degree of caution to ensure that abusive practices do not undermine confidence in an embryonic, competitive insurance market. The building of consumer trust is essential for insurance.

Justifiable government intervention should be as minimally intrusive as necessary to accomplish its purpose and should be as efficient as possible. For example, one way to minimize consumer harm occasioned by insurer insolvencies is to allow insurers to collude to set prices so high that even the most inefficiently operated insurer is guaranteed a profit and, therefore, survival. Such an approach, however, results in high priced insurance and excessive profits for insurers — all at the expense of consumers and businesses and, therefore, at the expense of the national interest. The superior approach is to allow price competition but to establish reasonable capital standards while closely monitoring insurer financial condition. This approach yields lower priced insurance — thus benefiting the national economy — while minimizing the possibility of consumer harm that would otherwise arise from excessive insurer financial risk and insolvencies.

CHAPTER 2

THE APPROPRIATE ROLE OF FOREIGN INSURERS

Concern persists that certain dimensions of liberalization may carry unacceptable risks and drawbacks. One such concern relates to the appropriate role of foreigners in the provision of financial services generally and insurance in particular.[1] Before exploring these concerns, we need to be clear about how insurance aids economic development, for foreign insurers can have a vitally important role here.

I. How Insurance Aids Economic Development

Insurance companies are financial intermediaries. As such, they perform the same types of functions and provide similar generic benefits to a national economy as other financial intermediaries. At the same time, their role in individual and corporate risk management means that their contributions to economic development will not precisely overlap with other financial intermediaries.

Financial services generally and insurance in particular, of course, are of primordial importance to economic development. Another doctoral dissertation at Georgia State University established this importance in a way that no one has done before. In his research, Dr. Ian P. Webb investigated the mechanisms by which insurance and banking jointly stimulate economic growth.[2] At first, economists considered that economic growth was driven mainly by labor and capital inputs. When it was found that, in fact, these two factors alone left much of economic growth unexplained, economists added technology to their equations, thereby increasing their explanatory power but with troubling gaps remaining. Dr. Webb asked whether banking and insurance, when added to existing economic growth models, might further explain economic growth.

His research showed that nonlife insurance, life insurance, and banking all have significant roles in explaining national productivity gains. The results indicated that the exogenous components of banking, life insurance, and nonlife insurance are important predictors of economic productivity. Additionally, he found evidence of synergies among financial intermediaries. Thus, each sector fuels economic growth independently, but they collectively provide greater growth impetus than suggested by merely summing their component contributions. Financial institutions may both share some common role in stimulating economic growth and function better collectively than separately. Thus, the more efficient banks' payment systems are, the lower attendant insurer administrative costs. Property/liability insurance protects bank collateral. Also,

---

[1] This section draws from Harold D. Skipper, *Foreign Insurers in Emerging Markets: Issues and Concerns* (Washington, D.C.; International Insurance Foundation, 1997).

[2] Ian P. Webb, *The Effect of Banking and Insurance on the Growth of Capital and Output*, unpublished Ph.D. dissertation, Georgia State University, May 2000.

the growth of one type of financial intermediary in a society can have positive spillover effects on the demand for services offered by other financial intermediaries as consumer sophistication grows. Dr. Webb's research provides tangible support for what has been to date largely reasoned economic suppositions.

Thus, the more developed and efficient a country's financial market, the greater will be its contribution to economic prosperity. It is for this reason that governments should foster greater competition among financial service providers, while ensuring that the market is financially sound.

It is wrong to view insurers as simple pass-through mechanisms for diversifying risk under which the unfortunate few who suffer losses are indemnified from the funds collected from many insureds. Laudable though it is, this function masks other fundamental contributions that insurance makes to prosperity. Countries that are best at harnessing these contributions give their citizens and businesses greater economic opportunities. Insurance provides seven categories of services that collectively constitute the mechanisms by which insurance contributes to economic growth, as found in Dr. Webb's research.

A. Insurance Can Promote Financial Stability

Insurance helps stabilize the financial situation of individuals, families, and organizations. It accomplishes this task by indemnifying those who suffer loss or harm. Without insurance, individuals and families could become financially destitute and forced to seek assistance from relatives, friends, or the government. Businesses that incur significant uninsured losses may suffer major financial reverses or even fail. Besides the loss in value of the owners' stake in the business occasioned by an uninsured loss, the firm's future contribution to the economy is foregone. Employees lose jobs, suppliers lose business, customers forgo the opportunity to buy from the firm, and government loses tax revenues. The stability provided by insurance encourages individuals and firms to create wealth with the assurance that their resources can be protected.

B. Insurance Can Partially Substitute for and Complement Government Security Programs

Insurance, especially life insurance, can substitute partially for government security programs. Private insurance also complements public security programs. Thus, it can relieve pressure on social welfare systems, reserving government resources for essential social security and other worthwhile purposes, and allowing individuals to tailor their security programs to their own preferences. Studies have confirmed that greater private expenditures on life insurance are associated with a reduction in government expenditures on social insurance programs. This substitution role is especially important because of the growing financial challenges faced by many national social insurance systems.

C. Insurance Can Facilitate Trade and Commerce

Many products and services are produced and sold only if adequate insurance is available. Insurance coverage is a condition for engaging in some activities. Because of the high risk of new business failure, venture capitalists often make funds available only if tangible assets and the entrepreneurs' lives are adequately insured. Entrepreneurs are more likely to create and expand their business ventures if they can secure adequate insurance protection. Insurance underpins much of the world's trade, commerce, and entrepreneurial activity.

This fact is unsurprising. Modern economies are built on specialization and its inherent productivity improvements. Greater trade and commercial specialization demand, in turn, greater financial specialization and flexibility. Without a wide insurance product choice and constant service and pricing innovations, insurance inadequacies could stifle both trade and commerce. It is in these ways that insurance serves as a "lubricant of commerce."

D. Insurance Can Help Mobilize Savings

Studies have shown that, on average, countries that save more tend to grow faster.[1] Insurers play an important role in channeling savings into domestic investment. Insurers enhance financial system efficiency in three ways. *First*, insurers reduce transaction costs associated with bringing together savers and borrowers.

Second, insurers create liquidity. Insurers invest the funds entrusted to them by their customers to make long-term loans and other investments.

Third, insurers facilitate economies of scale in investment. By amassing large sums from thousands of smaller premium payers, insurers often can meet the financing needs of large projects, thereby helping the national economy by enlarging the set of feasible investment projects and encouraging economic efficiency.

Other things being the same, the greater the variety of financial institutions and products, the more efficient the system and the greater its contribution to economic development. Contractual savings institutions, such as life insurers and private pension funds, can be especially important financial intermediaries in emerging markets. In contrast with commercial banks, which often specialize in collecting short-term deposits and extending short-term credit, contractual saving institutions usually take a longer-term view.

---

[1] IMF (1995). *World Economic Outlook*, May, pp. 69-70. Of course, this finding does not suggest that every country with a high savings rate will have a high growth rate. Countries whose financial systems are inefficient are less likely to achieve high growth rates even with high savings rates.

E. Insurance Can Enable Risk to be Managed More Efficiently

Financial systems and intermediaries price risk and provide for risk transformation, pooling, and reduction. The better a nation's financial system provides these various risk management services, the greater the saving and investment stimulation and the more efficiently resources are allocated.

Risk Pricing. A competitive market's success depends on pricing. The pricing of risk is fundamental to all financial intermediaries and is no less important to their resource allocation than to any other supplier of goods or services.

Insurers price risk at two levels. *First*, through their insurance activities, insurers evaluate the loss potential of businesses, persons, and property for which they might provide insurance. The greater the expected loss potential, the higher the price. In pricing loss potential, insurers quantify the consequences of risk-causing and risk-reduction activities and, thus, allow investors and managers to deal with risk more rationally. Investors in projects judged too risky for insurance at any price are put on notice and should rationally expect commensurate returns. When governments interfere with accurate insurance pricing, their actions can distort the allocation of insurance and, therefore, other resources.

Second, through their investment activities, insurers evaluate the creditworthiness of those to whom they extend loans and the likely business success of those in whom they invest. By these activities, business owners, potential investors, customers, creditors, employees, and other stakeholders can be better informed about the firm's overall risk characteristics and thereby make better informed decisions.

Risk Transformation. Insurance permits businesses and individuals to transform their risk exposures to suit their own needs better. Many property, liability, loss of income, and other risk exposures can be transferred to an insurer for a price and, in the process, the insured's risk profile changed. Moreover, life insurers, by tailoring contracts to the needs of different clients, help individuals and businesses transform the characteristics of their savings to the liquidity, security, and other risk profile desired.

Risk Pooling and Reduction. Risk pooling and reduction lie at the heart of insurance and, as with risk pricing, occur at two levels. *First*, in aggregating many individual risk exposures, insurers can make reasonably accurate estimates as to the pool's overall losses. The larger the number of insureds, the more stable and predictable is the insurer's experience. This fact leads to a reduction in volatility and, by that, permits insurers to charge smaller risk premiums for uncertainty and maintain more stable premiums.

Second, insurers benefit from pooling through their investment activities. In providing funds to a broad range of enterprises, individuals, and others, insurers diversify their investment portfolios. The default of a few borrowers is likely to be offset by the many sound investments. The more stable and predictable an insurer's investment experience, the less it can charge for loans.

F. Insurance Can Encourage Loss Mitigation

Insurance companies have economic incentives to help insureds prevent and reduce losses. Moreover, their detailed knowledge about loss-causing events, activities, and processes can afford them a competitive advantage in loss assessment and control. If pricing or availability is tied to loss experience and risky behavior, insureds, in turn, have economic incentives to control losses.

Insurers support many loss control programs, typical of which are fire prevention; occupational health and safety activities; industrial loss prevention; reduction in automobile property damage, theft, and injury; and dozens of other loss control activities and programs. These programs and activities reduce losses to businesses and individuals and complement good risk management. Society as a whole benefits from the reduction of such losses.

G. Insurance Can Foster Capital Allocation Efficiency

Insurers gather substantial information to conduct their evaluations of firms, projects, and managers both in deciding whether and at what price to issue insurance and in their roles as lenders and investors. While individual savers and investors may not have the time, resources, or ability to undertake this information gathering and processing, insurers have an advantage in this regard and are better at allocating financial capital and insurance risk-bearing capacity. Insurers will choose to insure and to provide funds to the soundest and most efficient firms, projects, and managers.

Insurers have a continuing interest in and monitor the firms, projects, and managers to whom they provide financial capital and risk bearing capacity. They encourage managers and entrepreneurs to act in the best interests of their various stakeholders (customers, stockholders, creditors, etc.). By doing so, insurers tangibly signal the market's approval of promising, well-managed firms and foster a more efficient allocation of a country's scarce financial capital and risk bearing capacity. National financial systems that impose minimum constraints on insurers' abilities to gather and evaluate information in this way should realize a more efficient allocation of capital and therefore stronger economic growth.

II. The Costs of Insurance

Insurance offers societies great social and economic benefits, but it also carries certain costs. Government, insurers, and insureds have an interest in minimizing these costs. *First*, insurers incur sales, servicing, administration, and investment management expenses. These expenses are an indispensable part of doing business, but increase the cost of insurance. Such expenses may account for 10 to 40 percent or more of a policy's premium, with the loss payment portion accounting for the balance. The more competitive is an insurance market, the more efficient insurers should become, thereby permitting lower expense loadings in premiums, thus offering better value for insureds.

Second, the existence of insurance encourages moral hazard. Some insureds inflate otherwise legitimate claim payment requests. Moral hazard can manifest itself in mere carelessness, with attendant higher losses than otherwise. Occasionally, individuals deliberately cause the destruction of or damage to property to collect insurance proceeds. From 5 to 15 percent of all non life claims are believed to be fraudulent in Germany, Spain, Italy, Austria, Finland, and the US. Each year, some insureds are murdered for life insurance proceeds. All such behavior causes premiums to be higher than they would be otherwise, represents a deadweight loss to society, can lead to disruptions in otherwise well functioning markets, and truly is a cost of insurance.

III. Arguments Favoring Greater Foreign Insurer Involvement

Briefly, the specific arguments favoring greater foreign insurer participation are that countries could realize one or more of the following benefits: [1]

- improvements in customer service and value;

- increased domestic savings;

- transfers of technological and managerial know-how;

- additional external financial capital;

- improvements in the quality of insurance regulation;

- creation of beneficial domestic spillovers, including the addition of more and higher quality jobs, quality-enhancing backward and forward linkages, and societal loss reductions.

Each of these items was examined in detail in a 1997 study by the author. The conclusion was that each is potentially relevant.

IV. Concerns about Foreign Insurer Involvement

Policymakers have expressed numerous reservations about foreign insurer participation in their domestic markets. In the 1997 study, such reservations were classified around seven common themes, five of which were found to have little or no justification or the associated issues can be addressed more adequately and with less welfare loss through alternative means. The validity and importance of a sixth theme cannot be established *a priori*. The seventh reservation theme was judged to warrant policymaker concern.

---

[1] This section draws from Skipper (1997).

The five classes of reservations either lacking factual justification or for which more efficient, viable alternatives exist are as follows:

First, foreign insurers might dominate the domestic market and thereby precipitate adverse microeconomic (less consumer choice and value) or macroeconomic (failure to contribute adequately to economic development) effects.   If a market offers great potential and if domestic insurers are inadequate and unsophisticated, market liberalization could lead to foreign domination.   In such a case, however, no rational basis exists to support a parallel belief that the nation's consumers and businesses will suffer harm or that the national economy will be harmed.   On the contrary, that the market offered great potential, was unsophisticated, and had an inadequate capacity suggests that the status quo was stifling microeconomic and macroeconomic improvements.

The *second* reservation class for which factual justification is lacking or for which more efficient means exist to address the concern than denial of market access is that foreign insurers might market insurance selectively, thereby leading to adverse microeconomic or macroeconomic effects.   This selectivity may be because of concern that foreign insurers will market insurance only to the most profitable segments, to multinational corporations, or to the commercial sector, ignoring the retail market.

Governmental efforts to discourage selective marketing can be harmful. Specialization and market segmentation lead to efficiency improvements, as suggested earlier.   It is true that segmentation could cause some market segments to be under served.   If it does and if these under served segments are judged critical, policymakers would be wise first to examine whether repressive regulation (such as price suppression) is at fault.   If not, insurers can be enticed into neglected segments through less distorting subsidies or other positive means.

The *third* class of reservations is that foreign insurers might fail to make lasting contributions to the local economy.   In the study, no reasonable factual basis to support this belief could be identified.

The *fourth* class of arguments for limiting foreign insurer market access is that the domestic market is already well served by locally owned insurers or through reinsurance.   Again, no reasonable factual basis to support this belief could be established.

The *fifth* reservation category is that the national industry should remain locally owned for strategic reasons, such as national security concerns or because of the desire for economic diversification.   To the extent that these goals are valid and not driven by special interests, less market-distorting means exist for accomplishing them than limits on foreign insurer participation.

The *sixth* reservation class is that foreign insurers may provoke a greater foreign exchange outflow.   The validity of this concern cannot be ascertained *a priori*.   Over the short-term, of course, foreign exchange would flow into the country in the form of capital to establish or purchase insurers. More importantly, as the UNCTAD has noted, any loss of foreign exchange may not be substantial enough to justify the opportunity cost involved in running and upgrading national insurance corporations.

The *final* reservation relates to the belief that full market liberalization should await insurance and possible macroeconomic regulatory reforms so as to minimize the chances of micro- or macroeconomic disruptions. This concern is valid, particularly regarding adequate prudential supervision, competition regulation, and market conduct oversight. Reasonable insurance laws and regulation are essential. They should exist prior to full market liberalization to avoid abuse by the unscrupulous.

The study concludes that opening insurance markets to appropriate foreign insurers is likely to aid economic development, enhance overall social welfare, and carry few unresolvable negative possibilities. Countries that maintain unjustifiable market access barriers and that fail to extend national treatment to foreign-owned insurers likely are doing their citizens, businesses, and national economies a disservice.

CHAPTER 3

THE PATH TOWARDS LIBERAL, SOLVENT INSURANCE MARKETS

In today's globally competitive financial services world, the nature and specific features of each government's intervention into its insurance market should be reassessed to ensure that every aspect is essential and is accomplishing its goal with minimum market disruption in light of the country's economic, political, and social situation. The most common rationale for government intervention into insurance markets is to protect buyers — in economic terms, to rectify market imperfections. To do this, insurance regulation should seek to ensure that *quality, reasonably-priced* products are *available* from *reliable* insurers.

A well-structured liberal market will ensure that the *quality, reasonably-priced,* and *availability* goals are attained. Hence, an important role of government is to promote fair competition to achieve these goals, while protecting buyers from misleading, collusive, and other anti-competitive practices. At the same time, arguably the most important governmental role is to ensure that insurers are *reliable.*

To promote these twin goals of having a liberal *and* solvent insurance market, insurance regulation should have the following traits:

- adequacy

- impartiality

- minimal intrusiveness

- transparency

In structuring insurance markets that better serve each country's interest, regulatory reform should reflect certain principles that are designed to ensure competitive, solvent, and fair markets. As members of the International Association of Insurance Supervisors (IAIS), the Baltic countries have access to IAIS regulatory standards, research, and background papers. The Baltic States have also benefited from the OECD experiences in terms of liberalization through its codes in particular and the OECD Baltic regional program on insurance and pension reforms. Moreover, as these countries continue along the path toward full European Union (EU) membership, they will be led by EU insurance directives as well as by useful documents and technical assistance. Together, these worthwhile sources should provide the basis for establishment of a sound regulatory regime.

CONCLUSION

The globalization of financial services promises to continue. Many critics express concern about this trend, which is fostered by liberal markets. They favor greater government restrictions on international competition. Of course, more restrictive regulation, with its natural consequence of less competition, yields higher prices for customers and higher profits for businesses. This result fails to maximize the benefits of liberal markets for the national economy, and, perversely, is more or less the same as that which businesses would realize by engaging in anti-competitive practice. Government would have done for businesses that which they would have done for themselves were it not illegal.

The lack of clear, enforced government policies and rules, of transparency, and of competitive markets, punishes economic development. Greater market access and involvement by foreign financial services firms is associated with less economic volatility. Indeed, as noted earlier, a recent World Bank study on financial services trade found a greater propensity to make liberalizing commitments was correlated with greater macroeconomic stability and better prudential regulation. The lesson for governments is to craft laws and enforce regulations that promote more transparent markets supported by fair competition unfettered by government direction, favoritism, and unwarranted interference. This statement is not an invitation for a *laisser faire* role by government, but rather an invitation for carefully considered regulation. Liberal markets are much more difficult to regulate than restrictive markets.

Liberal insurance markets serve each country's interest. Governments that deny their citizens and businesses such markets lessen consumer choice and value and needlessly hinder national economic development. This simple message is as relevant for the Baltic countries as any other nations.

ENVIRONMENTAL RISKS AND INSURANCE:

A COMPARATIVE ANALYSIS OF THE ROLE OF INSURANCE IN THE MANAGEMENT OF ENVIRONMENT-RELATED RISKS

Alberto Monti LL.M.

Abstract

This report is devoted to an in-depth comparative analysis of the role of insurance and reinsurance companies as well as financial markets and governments in the management of environmental risks – environmental pollution risk and natural catastrophe risk in particular. It finally seeks to draw the attention of law and policy makers in the Baltic States on the proper role that the private insurance sector might be called upon to play in the future management of environment-related risks.

While the first chapter of the report introduces the general issue of insurability of environment-related risks, chapter 2 deals with the risk of liability for environmental pollution, taking into account both factual and legal variables that may affect risk insurability. Chapter 3 in turn is devoted to the management of natural catastrophe risks, i.e. the risk posed by the potential occurrence of such extreme natural events as hurricanes, floods and earthquakes. The author underlines the role of insurers as well as the limits of private insurance solutions for the coverage of such extreme risks, due to the magnitude of their economic consequences and the difficulties faced in pooling risks. The last chapter provides some recommendations for both policy makers and insurance managers in the Baltic States when dealing with these issues.

TABLE OF CONTENTS

ACKNOWLEDGMENTS

In the course of preparation of this report, I greatly benefited from discussions with members of the OECD Directorate for Financial Fiscal and Enterprise Affairs and, in particular, with André Laboul, Cécile Vignial and Stephen Lumpkin, whose thoughtful comments and criticisms challenged me to strengthen and refine several arguments. Extremely helpful feedback was also offered by OECD Member Countries and by the CEA, with whom I had the opportunity to discuss Chapters 1, 2 and 3 of this report on the occasion of the 70th session meeting of the OECD Insurance Committee, held in Paris on December 12-13, 2002. With reference to the status of the environmental insurance market in Latvia and Lithuania, kind information has been provided by the Financial and Capital Market Commission of the Republic of Latvia and by the Lithuanian State Insurance Supervisory Authority. This final report is considerably improved thanks to their input.

INTRODUCTION

In the recent times, the complex relationship between human activities and the environment has become a major public concern, raising issues of legal, political and economic relevance.

The adverse impact of industrial activities on natural resources and biodiversity, as well as the need for sustainable development, stimulated a debate on appropriate policies and techniques aimed at improving the current level of environmental protection and preservation. Conversely, a growing concern has developed over the effects of such extreme natural events as hurricanes, typhoons, floods and earthquakes which pose a serious threat to human life and property, being able to disrupt local communities and to affect the economic stability and growth of entire nations.

From the increasing incidence of environmental pollution and soil contamination, to natural disasters occurring on seasonal to inter-annual time scales, the risks posed by the constant interaction between human activities and the environment are diverse, manifold and often catastrophic in their consequences. Therefore, the elaboration of effective risk-management plans, aimed at formulating viable response strategies, requires the pro-active contribution of all the economic actors involved: governments, public officials, international organizations, financial institutions and private parties are all called upon to take part in this endeavour.

Against such backdrop, this report focuses upon the role of insurance and reinsurance companies in the management of environmental risks. In particular, according to the proposed research plan, the analysis concentrates on issues related to two different kinds of environment-related risks:

the **environmental pollution risk** and

the **natural catastrophe risk**

For the purposes of this report,

1. the **environmental pollution risk** is the risk associated with industrial and commercial activities that may adversely affect the environment, cause human health problems, damage property, contaminate natural resources and affect biodiversity. From the standpoint of the owners and operators of such activities, in most, if not all, OECD countries it can be framed as the risk of incurring legal liability for the consequences of environmental pollution phenomena. The scope and nature of environmental liabilities are changing over time and they may greatly vary from jurisdiction to jurisdiction. At present, the most important categories are:

   a. liability for bodily injury, property damages and economic losses caused by pollution to third parties;

   b. liability for the costs of preventive and remediation measures, including the cost of cleaning up the polluted site;

   c. liability for ecological impairment, including reduced biodiversity and other natural resources damages (NRDs).

while

2. The **natural catastrophe risk** is the risk associated with the occurrence of natural disasters, such as earthquakes, floods, hurricanes or other extreme environmental conditions: such catastrophic events often cause large-scale material damages, as well as severe economic losses.

Both these environment-related risks, as mentioned, are characterized by the potential for catastrophic consequences. However, even if they may share some common features, they are structurally different from the standpoint of the insurer and, therefore, they deserve to be treated separately in this report.

After a brief overview (Chapter 1) of the traditional functioning of the insurance and reinsurance mechanisms and an introduction to the general problems affecting the insurability of certain risks, Chapter 2 of this study deals with the risk of liability for environmental pollution, taking into account both **factual and legal variables that may affect risk insurability**. Environmental pollution risk, in fact, is highly influenced by the underlying legal and regulatory framework. **Identifying the major trends in the development of environmental liability regimes in OECD countries, therefore, constitutes the basis for any discussion concerning the role of the insurance sector in this field.**

In this perspective, a **theoretical discussion** of the most relevant features of an environmental liability regime is complemented by a comparative overview of the main evolutions of environmental legislation in some OECD countries, as well as by the **evaluation of the most recent developments** that are taking place at the European Community level.

To this purpose, particular attention is devoted to the recent proposal for a "Directive of the European Parliament and of the Council on environmental liability with regard to the prevention and remedying of environmental damage" presented by the Commission of the European Communities on January 23, 2002 [COM(2002) 17 final]. The proposal aims to establish a framework whereby environmental damage would be prevented or remedied; the main benefits expected include improved enforcement of environmental protection standards, in line with the "Polluter Pays Principle"[1], and efficient levels of prevention. According to the text of the proposal (article 16), EU Member States should encourage:

---

[1] The polluter-pays principle, stated in Article 174(2) EC (*ex* art. 130r of the EC Treaty), is acknowledged in the 1972 OECD GUIDING PRINCIPLES CONCERNING INTERNATIONAL ECONOMIC ASPECTS OF ENVIRONMENTAL POLICIES:

"a) *Cost allocation: the Polluter-Pays Principle*

2. Environmental resources are in general limited and their use in production and consumption activities may lead to their deterioration. When the cost of this deterioration is not adequately taken into account in the price system, the market fails to reflect the scarcity of such resources both at the national and international levels. Public measures are thus necessary to reduce pollution and to reach a better allocation of resources by ensuring that prices of goods depending on the quality and/or quantity of environmental resources reflect more closely their relative scarcity and that economic agents concerned react accordingly.

3. In many circumstances, in order to ensure that the environment is in an acceptable state, the reduction of pollution beyond a certain level will not be practical or even necessary in view of the costs involved.

4. The principle to be used for allocating costs of pollution prevention and control measures to encourage rational use of scarce environmental resources and to avoid distortions in international trade and investment is the so-called "Polluter-Pays Principle". This principle means that the polluter should bear the expenses of carrying out the above mentioned measures decided by public authorities to ensure that the environment is in an acceptable state. In other words, the cost of these measures should be reflected in the cost of goods and services which cause pollution in production and/or consumption. Such measures should not be accompanied by subsidies that would create significant distortions in international trade and investment.

5. This principle should be an objective of Member countries; however there may be exceptions or special arrangements, particularly for the transitional periods, provided that they do not lead to significant distortions in international trade and investment."

See: RECOMMENDATION OF THE COUNCIL ON GUIDING PRINCIPLES CONCERNING INTERNATIONAL ECONOMIC ASPECTS OF ENVIRONMENTAL POLICIES, 26th May, 1972, Council Document

- the use by operators of any appropriate insurance or other forms of financial guarantee, in order to provide effective cover for obligations under the Directive;

and

- the development of appropriate insurance or other financial security instruments and markets by the appropriate economic and financial operators, including the financial services industry.

In response to the above, the insurance industry is developing new strategies and techniques aimed at tackling the peculiar insurability problems posed by ecological damage phenomena and it made strong commitments at an international level [1].

This report presents an **overview of the different environmental insurance products** currently available on the international market and suggests that modern ecological insurance may serve **different purposes**: in addition to contributing in the solution of the **"judgment proof"** (or "insolvency") problem, in fact, it would guarantee the *ex ante* **internalization of pollution costs** posed by the industry and it might also be able to work as a **surrogate regulation mechanism**, providing appropriate incentives for increased levels of prevention and precaution.

With a view to throwing some brighter light on the role that the insurance sector is expected to play in the near future, the interaction among regulation, liability, funds and insurance is briefly discussed.

Chapter 3 of this report, in turn, is devoted to the analysis of the **role of insurance in the management of natural catastrophe risk**, i.e. the risk posed by the potential occurrence of such extreme natural events as hurricanes, floods and earthquakes.

Starting from the observation that natural disaster risks pose severe problems to the traditional functioning of insurance and reinsurance – mainly because the risks associated with these events are not independent and because of the **magnitude of their economic consequences** –, this chapter of the study discusses alternative risk management solutions already tested in different institutional contexts.

Since the law of large numbers does not apply – at least at the primary market level[2] –, aggregating risks is unproductive and the natural comparative advantage of

---

no. C(72)128. Paris: OECD. See also: The Rio Declaration on Environment and Development of June 1992 (Principle 16).

[1] See, especially, the United Nations Environmental Programme - UNEP Statement of Environmental Commitment by the Insurance Industry, signed in Geneva, on 23 November, 1995.

[2] With respect to the international reinsurance market, some professional risk carriers affirm that natural catastrophe risks can be relatively well diversified on a global scale, since

insurance may be lost when dealing with natural catastrophes[1]. This factor, together with the size of expected losses, explains why the **partnership between governments and the private sector** is crucial in developing effective natural catastrophe risk management strategies.

This chapter of the study, therefore, describes and analyzes the main features of several governmental disaster schemes and other institutional arrangements that have been designed and tested around the world in order to supplement or replace traditional reinsurance.

Moreover, since capital markets have developed new **financial instruments** such as **catastrophe bonds**, **weather derivatives** and other complex **risk securitization** devices aimed at providing funding and economic protection against large losses from natural disasters, the present analysis will also take into account the current role of such financial techniques.

Finally, the last chapter of this report (chapter 4) is devoted to an overview of the current situation in the Baltic States with respect to environmental risks and insurance. The aim of this fourth chapter is to draw the attention of law and policy makers in Estonia, Latvia and Lithuania on the proper role that the private insurance sector might be called upon to play in the future management of environment-related risks.

As a conclusion, this report suggests that, while **private insurance** may not be considered as a straightforward and ready-to-use solution to the complex problems posed by the "environmental pollution risk" and by the "natural catastrophe risk", it **certainly has the potentials to play a decisive role** in this field and, therefore, it should be regarded by governments and policy makers as a **key instrument** in the available array of risk management tools.

---

natural disasters are independent from each other, provided sufficiently broad terms of reference are defined. See: Swiss Reinsurance Company (2002), Natural Catastrophes and man-made disasters in 2001, Swiss Re SIGMA series 1/2002. Zurich, Swiss Reinsurance Company, 11.

[1] Priest, G.L. (1996), The Government, the Market, and the Problem of Catastrophic Loss, Journal of Risk and Uncertainty 12 (Number 2/3): 219-237

CHAPTER 1

RISK, INFORMATION AND INSURANCE

I. Different attitudes towards risk and the traditional functioning of insurance and reinsurance mechanisms

Economic actors have different attitudes towards risks. It depends on several factors, including the nature of the risk, the probability of loss, the potential magnitude of the loss and the ability to absorb its economic consequences. Assuming rationality and perfect information, economic actors are able to calculate the actual value (present discounted value) of a given risk by discounting the magnitude of the loss by the probability of its occurrence (PxL).

Once the risk is properly identified and evaluated, however, risk management decisions still need to be taken. In this perspective, economic actors may be:

> **risk averse**: if they are willing to pay even more than the discounted value of the risk in order to transfer its harmful consequences to someone else;

> **risk preferring**: if they prefer to retain the risk of loss, rather than transferring it by paying upfront an amount equal to its discounted value.

> **risk neutral**: if they are indifferent with respect to the alternative between *(a)* retaining the risk and *(b)* transferring it to someone else by paying upfront an amount equal to its discounted value.

Risk aversion, therefore, generates demand for insurance. Insurance companies, in turn, are willing to undertake the risk in exchange for an amount of money relatively close to its discounted value (the insurance premium), because the law of large numbers makes them able to manage such risks effectively, by making predictable, with reasonable accuracy, the claims they will pay from year to year. According to this mathematical law, the larger the number of exposures considered, the more closely the losses reported will match the underlying probability of loss. This means that insurance companies need to pool together a rather **large number of homogeneous but independent risks** in order to become risk neutral.

Against such background, the functioning of the traditional insurance mechanism can be divided into four phases:

> **risk assessment** (i.e. the overall evaluation of risk, which is usually performed through statistical and probabilistic analyses)

> **risk transfer** (i.e. the shifting of its harmful consequences by way of the insurance contract)

> **risk pooling** (i.e. the placement of the risk in a pool of homogeneous but independent risks allows the insurer to spread the risk and to benefit from the law of large numbers)

risk allocation (i.e. the pricing of the risk through premium setting techniques)

As the magnitude of expected losses increases, **the insurers' financial ability to absorb them can be severely jeopardized**. In other words, insurance capacity is limited, since over and above certain levels of financial exposure insurers themselves tend to be **risk averse**. In this context, **coinsurance** and **reinsurance** are viable options for primary carriers who are willing to cede part of the risk they undertook, in exchange for the payment of a fraction of the premiums they collected.

Reinsurance agreements may be of different types, among which:

> **quota share (proportional) treaties** (by which the reinsurer undertakes a quota of the risk transferred to the primary carrier)

> **excess of loss (or stop loss) treaties** (by which the reinsurer undertakes the upper layer of the risk, after a certain attachment point).

II. Risks predictability, generalized uncertainty and informational asymmetries

The briefly described insurance mechanism is able to perform its functions correctly under specific conditions of risk and uncertainty[1]. In a well-known contribution, Frank Knight distinguished between risk (predictable probabilities) and uncertainty (unpredictable probability of loss) and argued that insurance works best with the former[2].

In other words, the basic argument is that the insurer must possess *ex ante* accurate information on the probability that the insured event will occur, as well as on the magnitude of its economic consequences: without such information, the insurer is not able to adequately calculate the premium.

In the past decades, several **criteria for insurability** of risks have been identified and discussed by the literature[3]. Baruch Berliner[4], for instance, proposed the following nine criteria against which evaluate any risk:
1. Randomness (of the loss occurrence)
2. Maximum possible loss

---

[1] See: Abraham, K.S. (1986), Distributing Risk: Insurance, Legal Theory and Public Policy, New Haven: Yale University Press.

[2] Knight, Frank H. (1921), Risk, Uncertainty, and Profit, Boston: Houghton Mifflin Company.

[3] See: Berliner, B. (1982), Limits of Insurability of Risks. Englewood Cliffs, NJ, Prentice-Hall, Inc.; Faure, M.G., The Limits to Insurability from a Law and Economics Perspective, Geneva Papers on Risk and Insurance, 1995, 454-462; Skogh, G. (1998), Development risks, strict liability and the insurability of industrial hazards, Geneva Papers on Risk and Insurance, 87, 247.

[4] Berliner, B. (1982), Limits of Insurability of Risks. Englewood Cliffs, NJ, Prentice-Hall, Inc.

3. Average loss amount upon occurrence
4. Average period of time between two loss occurrences (i.e. loss frequency)
5. Insurance premium
6. Moral hazard
7. Public policy
8. Legal restriction
9. Cover limits

The author maintained that the above set of criteria forms a concise and almost complete evaluation system, in the sense that its use allows professional risk carriers to determine whether or not a risk is **subjectively insurable**[1]. In fact, the insurability of a risk depends on calculations made based on insurance techniques, but also a complex decision-making process by each individual insurer who takes several considerations into account. Such criteria contain subjective as well as objective aspects and they are not independent from one another; if only one of them is not fully satisfied with respect to the position of a professional risk carrier, then the risk may be considered subjectively uninsurable.

The intersection of all subjective domains of uninsurability forms the **objective domain of uninsurability**, while the intersection of all subjective domains of insurability constitutes the objective domain of insurability. Between these two domains, lies an area of separation, consisting of all risks that are insurable for some professional risk carriers and uninsurable for others.

A more concise set of criteria for evaluating the insurability of risks in general has been recently restated [2] and it consists of the following four elements:

 a. **ASSESSIBILITY**: the probability and severity of losses must be quantifiable.

 b. **RANDOMNESS**: the time at which the insured event occurs must be unpredictable and the occurrence itself must be independent of the will of the insured.

 c. **MUTUALITY**: numerous persons exposed to a given hazard must join together to form a risk community within which the risk is shared and diversified.

 d. **ECONOMIC FEASIBILITY**: private insurers must be able to charge a premium commensurate with the risk.

Risks that do not readily satisfy all of these criteria may be considered by professional risk carriers as uninsurable and, therefore, coverage may become unavailable

---

[1] See also: Berliner, B., Spühler, J. (1990), Insurability issues associated with managing existing hazardous waste sites, in 'Integrating Insurance & Risk Management for Hazardous Waste', edited by Howard Kunreuther and Rajeev Gowda, Kluwer Academic Publishers, 134 ff.

[2] Swiss Reinsurance Company (2002), Natural Catastrophes and man-made disasters in 2001, Swiss Re SIGMA series 1/2002. Zurich, Swiss Reinsurance Company, 18.

on the market. It is worth noting that, the actual availability of insurance coverage for a certain risk does not merely depend on its insurability, but also on its attractiveness in comparison to risks from other branches that are competing for the available insurance capacity. With respect to the above issues, severe problems are posed by:

    a.   Generalized uncertainty and

    b.   Informational asymmetries

    a. **Generalized uncertainty** – A condition of uncertainty is said to be generalized when both the insurer and the prospective insureds are equally affected by it. It is important to note that **generalized uncertainty** depends on both **factual and legal circumstances**; it means that the general level of uncertainty and ambiguity concerning a certain risk is often influenced by the underlying legal regime.

As said, in order to be insurable, a risk must be predictable *ex ante* to a certain extent, at least by means of past experience and statistic calculations[1]: the insurance company must possess sufficient information about the probability and magnitude of the expected loss, in order to properly assess the risk undertaken and to calculate the so-called **actuarially fair premium**. A severe condition of generalized uncertainty about the features of a certain risk may hinder its insurability. Even if uncertainty is not so critical to impede risk insurability, it still has an impact on the cost of insurance, since the premium charged to the insured contains a series of loadings, some of which (e.g. safety and fluctuation loadings) are precisely aimed at covering the residual level of unpredictability that characterizes every risk.

As this report will discuss in more details *infra*, since several features of the underlying legal framework greatly affect uncertainty, ambiguity and insurability of environment-related risks, **choices made by legislators and policy makers very often play a determinant role in this field**.

    b. **Informational asymmetries** – Whenever the insured possesses more information than the insurer about the risk (asymmetrical uncertainty), problems of **adverse selection** and **moral hazard** may occur.

The notion of **adverse selection** identifies the tendency of poorer-than-average risks to buy and maintain insurance. Adverse selection occurs when insureds select only those coverages that are most likely to have losses[2].

---

[1] Skogh, G. (1998), Development risks, strict liability and the insurability of industrial hazards, Geneva Papers on Risk and Insurance, 87, 247.

[2] "This problem may arise when the policyholder has some hidden information that is not in the possession of the insurer. Assume, for illustrative purposes, that there are two types of policyholders according to the insurer's point of view: 'good' risks and 'bad' risks. The insurer cannot distinguish between them and the policyholders do not reveal their nature - both maintain that they are good risks. In that case the market may break down. The logic is as follows: initially, the insurer charges the same premium for the

Moral hazard, instead, refers to the increase in probability of loss that results from a decrease in the preventive measures adopted by the insured following the purchase of insurance coverage. In other words, it identifies the hazard arising out of an insured's indifference to loss because of the existence of insurance [1].

These informational asymmetries generate **agency costs** [2] and, in order to cure these problems, risk carriers are forced to employ a variety of **monitoring** and **bonding devices**. Monitoring devices are mainly aimed at controlling the insured's behavior, thereby leveling the information asymmetry, while bonding devices provide incentives meant to realign the otherwise diverging interests of insurer and insureds. Common examples of these devices are the use of complex application screening processes, risk differentiation techniques, feature and experience ratings, exclusions of coverage, co-insurance clauses and deductibles.

With respect to asymmetrical uncertainty as well, choices made by legislators and regulators are extremely relevant. A legal rule that mandates compulsory coverage for a certain risk, for example, may help reducing the problem of adverse selection. Conversely, a creative interpretation of insurance policy terms (especially: exclusions and conditions of coverage drafted to prevent moral hazard) made by courts in order to favor the insured parties in the short run, may ultimately lead to unavailability of coverage for such risk.

In summary, therefore, both generalized and asymmetrical uncertainty influence **risk insurability**, since they have the potential to reduce: *(1)* the ability of risk carriers to undertake certain risks, *(2)* the scope and availability of insurance coverage on the market and *(3)* the willingness of prospective insureds to purchase coverage, which might be perceived as too costly.

With respect to uncertainty and insurability, this report will address some of the problems and difficulties that the traditional insurance and reinsurance mechanisms face when dealing with:

the **environmental pollution risk** (chapter 2) and

---

two. The premium is based on the average actuarially expected costs. Insurance will then be a good affair for the bad risk and a relatively poor affair for the good risk. Consequently, many bad risks and few good risks will purchase insurance and the insurer will incur a loss on average. It will, then, be necessary to increase the premium the next round, thus discouraging good risks, attracting bad risks and precipitating a new loss. The cycle will repeat itself. In the end there may be no market left." Skogh, G. (2000), Mandatory Insurance: Transaction Costs Analysis of Insurance, in Bouckaert, B. and De Geest, G. (eds.), Encyclopedia of Law and Economics, Volume II. Civil Law and Economics, Cheltenham, Edward Elgar.

[1] See: Shavell S. (1979), On Moral Hazard and Insurance, Quarterly Journal of Economics (QJE), 541-562.

[2] See: Abraham, K. S. (1988), Environmental Liability and the Limits of Insurance, 88 Columbia L. Rev. 946.

the **natural catastrophe risk** (chapter 3).

Environmental pollution risk is tightly connected with the **underlying legal and regulatory framework**, whose **features may generate uncertainty, or otherwise limit risk insurability.** On the contrary, well drafted and defined environmental rules and regulations yield predictable losses and may foster the development of an effective pollution insurance market. The **factual uncertainty** associated with gradual pollution risk and the effects of environmental contamination on human beings and biodiversity, however, are also problematic. Long-tail environmental risks are extremely challenging for insurers because they must be able to establish a realistic and reliable estimate of compensation to be paid over a period of a specific and reasonable duration. Relevant obstacles, moreover, are posed in this field by severe **information asymmetries**.

The traditional insurance and reinsurance mechanisms may also encounter problems in coping with the natural catastrophe risk, since **risk predictability**, the ability to **spread the risk both geographically and over time** and the **financial capacity** of the market are severely limited for such type of risks.

In both cases, moreover, the **magnitude of expected losses** and the **information problems** affecting risk predictability and assessment require joint efforts (e.g. pooling) by several insurers and reinsurers.

It is worth noting that the highlighted need for **information sharing practices** and **market concentration** – in order to increase capacity – suggests a careful approach to antitrust regulations and **competition policies** in this area[1]. Furthermore, regulatory barriers to the free determination of premium levels and conditions of coverage may hinder the willingness and ability of insurance carriers to enter the market for environment-related risks.

In light of the above, this report suggests that all institutional actors, including legislators, governments, regulators and courts, may play a crucial role in addressing and solving the problems of predictability and insurability of environment-related risks.

---

[1] As for the application of EU competition policies to the insurance sector, see: Commission Regulation 358/2003 of 27 February 2003 (OJ L53/8 of 28 February 2003) which replaces Commission Regulation 3932/92 of 21 December 1992 (OJ L398 of 31 December 1992, p.7). See also: "Report to the European Parliament and to the Council on the Operation of Commission Regulation N° 3932/92 concerning the application of Article 81 (Ex-Article 85), Paragraph 3, of the Treaty to certain categories of agreements, decisions and concerted practices in the field of insurance", issued by the Commission on 12 May 1999, COM (1999) 192 final.

CHAPTER 2

ENVIRONMENTAL POLLUTION RISK AND INSURANCE

I. Environmental pollution as a negative externality

Environmental pollution is commonly considered in the law and economics literature as an external cost of production (**negative externality**) generated by the industry[1]. The release of pollutants into the environment by commercial and industrial activities may often impair natural resources, reduce biodiversity and cause bodily injury, property damages and economic losses to third parties.

Unless full internalization of these pollution costs is imposed by the legal system, environmentally dangerous activities may receive incentives to continue doing business even if they generate socially inefficient outcomes, since part of their costs are falling on someone else.

The environment is a public good and, therefore, the impairment of such natural resources as air, water, land, flora and fauna negatively affects the society as a whole. Nowadays, environmental protection is a worldwide growing concern: natural resources are becoming really scarce on our planet and, to a greater or lesser extent, all the nations are adversely affected by inefficient uses of them[2].

II. Different legal approaches to the externality problem: ex ante regulation v. ex post liability

The goal of imposing full internalization of pollution externalities is, therefore, very important and, theoretically, it can be achieved through different legal devices.

---

[1] See e.g.: R. Posner, Economic Analysis of Law, 4th ed., 1992; R. Cooter and T. Ulen, Law and Economics, 2nd ed., 1996; A. M. Polinsky, An Introduction to Law and Economics, 2nd ed., 1989; D. Barnes and L. Stout, Cases and Materials on Law and Economics, 1992; Trimarchi P. (1961), Rischio e responsabilità oggettiva, Milano: Giuffrè.

[2] The relevance of this problem has been clearly depicted by the inspired words of the *Declaration of the Sacred Earth Gathering of Spiritual Leaders* at the UNCED Conference, Rio de Janeiro (Brazil), 1992 (*The planet Earth is in peril as never before (...) The World Community must act speedily with vision and resolution to preserve the Earth, Nature and Humanity from disaster. Time to act is now. Now or never.*) and, less dramatically, addressed by the Principles of International Environmental Law as reflected in THE RIO DECLARATION ON ENVIRONMENT AND DEVELOPMENT of June 1992 (Principles of Sustainable Development, Polluter Pays Principle, Principle of Prevention, Principle of Good Neighbourliness and International Cooperation, Precautionary Principle, Principle of Good governance, Principle of Common but Differentiated Responsibility, Principle of Sovereignty over Natural Resources and the Responsibility not to cause Environmental Damage).

A way of dealing with this problem is characterized by the strict centralized enforcement of a sophisticated net of **public law regulations**: those command-control rules, setting standards and sanctions, operate *ex ante* and reflect the results of a costs-benefits analysis already performed by the authorities.

A second possible solution is the *ex post* imposition of the external costs on the actors through a mechanism of **liability rules**[1], enforced by the courts or by other adjudication or authoritative bodies; in this perspective, the polluter can freely pursue his activity, but he is then forced to pay compensation for the damages caused to the environment and to third parties, thereby internalizing *ex post* the costs of pollution.

Of course, both these alternative theoretical approaches have already been widely analyzed and criticized: the former mainly because of its own intrinsic rigidity and the latter in light of the relevance of litigation costs and of the so-called 'judgment proof' (or 'insolvency') problem[2]. It seems well established that **a combination of the two is possibly the most efficient solution**[3].

Starting from this assumption, this report tries to go a step forward, by focusing upon **the impact of modern environmental insurance on** both the **liability system and the regulatory framework**. In particular, the advantages and the limits of the *ex post* mechanism of environmental liability and the role of professional ecological insurance in preventing the most common failures of this device are considered and discussed.

III. Environmental liability: compensation and deterrence

It is recognized that environmental liability regimes should be aimed at achieving efficient levels of **compensation** and **deterrence**.

In other words, applying economic theory to environmental policies, the enactment of a liability regime in response to the ecological emergency can be explained as an attempt to pursue two important and interrelated policy goals:

compensation for damages caused by pollution and

deterrence of inefficient activities, thereby preventing pollution that is not cost-justified.

---

[1] See: G. Calabresi (1970), *The cost of the accidents*, Yale University Press; for a comparative perspective see also: U. Mattei, *Tutela Inibitoria e Tutela Risarcitoria*, Milano, 1987; Id., "I modelli nella tutela dell'ambiente", in *Riv. dir. civ.* 1985, II, 389.

[2] See: S. Shavell, "The Judgment Proof Problem", 6 *Int. Rev. Law and Econ.* 1986, 45-58.

[3] See: M. Trebilcock and R. A. Winter, "The Economics of Nuclear Accident Law", 17 Int. Rev. Law and Econ., 1997, 215-243; S. Shavell, "Liability for Harm versus Regulation of Safety", 13 Journal of Legal Studies 1984, 357 ff.; C. Kolstad, T. Ulen, G.V. Johnson, "Ex post Liability for Harm vs. Ex ante Safety Regulation: Substitutes or Complements?", 80 *American Economic Review*, 1990, 888-901.

By focusing on compensation for the losses sustained, the position of the injured parties is mainly taken into account. The deterrence function, on the other hand, is more concerned with the need to provide appropriate behavioral incentives to the potential polluters. From a slightly different perspective, however, both these goals constitute the beneficial results of an effective mechanism of **risk allocation** that imposes **full internalization** of the pollution costs.

A. *The choice between negligence and strict liability*

In determining the features of a liability rule, the first choice that legislators face is between **strict liability** and a **negligence** standard.

While negligence can be considered as an effective mechanism of risk spreading, it has been shown that strict liability is more efficient in circumstances where the potential tortfeasor is in a better position to evaluate the costs and benefits of a particular **level of activity** than either the potential victims or the court (finder of fact)[1]. The negligence standard, in fact, provides appropriate incentives to the parties only with respect to:

> **the level of care** (the diligence in performing a given activity)

> but not with respect to

> **the level of activity** (the intensity and frequency of a given behavior or activity).

Both variables, however, affect the probability of an accident[2].

When the injured party has substantially no control over the risk of loss (**unilateral accidents**) there is little need to give him/her incentives to invest in precautions and it suffices to control the behavior of the potential tortfeasor (i.e. the potential polluter). A strict liability standard, imposing a full internalization of the negative externalities, forces the potential tortfeasor to consider both the **level of care** and the **level of activity** and, therefore, it generates incentives to behave in an efficient manner[3]. Strict liability allocates the risk of loss to the party who is better able to control it and, therefore, who is the **least cost avoider** of the harm.

---

[1] Shavell, S. (1980), Strict Liability Versus Negligence, 9 Journal of Legal Studies 1980, 1.

[2] Shavell, S. (1987), Economic Analysis of Accident Law, Harvard University Press.

[3] "The failing of the negligence rule that is under discussion can be regarded as resulting from an implicit assumption that the standard of behavior used to determine negligence is defined only in terms of care. Were the standard defined also in terms of the activity level, injurers would make sure not to engage in their activity to an excessive extent" Shavell, S. (1987), Economic Analysis of Accident Law, 25.

Environmental pollution events, in the vast majority of cases, are **unilateral accidents**. Hence, in order to achieve an efficient level of **deterrence**, strict liability proves to be more appropriate than negligence, at least with respect to dangerous activities[1].

As regards the **compensation** perspective, strict liability offers many advantages compared to a negligence standard, especially in the industrial pollution cases. In the typical pollution dispute, in fact, the proof of negligence can be perceived by the injured parties as a *probatio diabolica* - an obstacle often too difficult to overcome - given the difficulties in accessing relevant information and the technical character of the notions involved[2].

On the other hand, a strict liability rule is conceivable as a form of insurance, whose beneficiaries are the injured parties. Moreover, deprived of any punitive character, this form of liability should be more easily transferable on the commercial insurance marketplace. In this sense, environmental insurance would work as a form of reinsurance.

In light of the above, it is not surprising to find out that strict liability is established as the basis for all new environmental legislation enacted in several OECD countries in the recent years[3] and that liability is generally imposed on owners and operators of dangerous activities (i.e. the persons in better control of the environmental pollution risk).

B. *Allocation and apportionment of concurrent liabilities*

Another dilemma arises in the very usual situation in which more polluters are involved in the same environmental accident: should the liability be imposed on an **individual basis** (proportional liability) or should all the polluters be held **joint and severally liable**?

If the **compensation** function is considered alone, joint and several liability clearly offers great advantages to the injured parties. The **deterrence** goal, however, requires

---

[1] See: Trimarchi, P. (1961), *Rischio e responsabilità oggettiva*, Milano: Giuffrè.

[2] "If a fault-based liability regime is applied to environmental damage, claimants find themselves in an impossible position from an *evidentiary* point of view, for reasons not unlike those raised in connection with product liability: the acts or omissions which may have been at the origin of the damage lie fully within the sphere of control of the defendant. It would thus seem logical to put environmental damage under a regime of liability not based on fault, or at the very least to reverse the burden of proof as regards fault." Gerven, Walter van; Lever, Jeremy; Larouche, Pierre, Tort law. Cases, materials and text on national, supranational and international tort law. (Ius commune casebooks for the Common law of Europe) Oxford; Portland: Hart, 2000, 684/6.

[3] See: Clarke, C. (2000), Update comparative legal study, Follow up study commissioned by the European Commission.

that each polluter pays for the consequences of his or her own activity: if liability is not individual, the mechanism of incentives may not work properly, since the potential polluter may not be able to perform a correct costs-benefits analysis.

Moreover, if insurability issues are taken into consideration, a strict, joint and several standard should be avoided, because it impairs the ability of risk-carriers to properly evaluate and assess the risks posed by their prospective customers.

In practice, the general trend in most OECD countries appears to be towards the adoption of a system which combines elements of both options: even if joint and several liability is frequently adopted as a general rule, the polluter often has the possibility to limit his financial exposure by proving the extent of his contribution.

C. Direct v. indirect protection of the environment

A third set of options, which characterizes the process of selecting an optimal environmental liability rule, has been pointed out by scholars engaged in the comparative study of environmental laws[1] and it concerns the scope of environmental liabilities, as well as the type of damages to be covered by the special regime.

On one hand, we have the possibility to grant **direct protection** to the environment by holding the polluter liable for all the harmful consequences of his activity, including cleanup costs and damages caused to biodiversity and natural resources such as air, water, soil, flora and fauna (the so-called "**environmental damage**" or "**ecological damage**").

In case of pollution, therefore, the legal system will oblige the responsible party to pay compensation for any kind of harm caused to the environment, including site remediation and clean-up costs, natural resources damages (NRDs) and biodiversity damages, in addition to and apart from any other property damage, bodily injury or economic loss (the so-called "**traditional damages**") caused to third parties by the polluting event.

In other words, with the adoption of a direct protection scheme, the traditional boundaries of tort law are extended in such a way to comprehend the obligation to compensate for **damages to a public good**, i.e. the **environment**, which is broadly defined as to include natural resources, biodiversity, endangered species, etc.

An authority (generally, the State) will then be entitled to receive compensation for ecological damage on behalf of the citizens, or to apply for a judicial remedy, such as an injunction, that compels responsible party to undertake remediation measures in the first place. It is often the case that the special environmental liability regimes enacted in those legal systems that have opted for a direct protection scheme does not

---

[1] See e.g.: Pozzo B. (1996), The liability problem in modern environmental statutes, 4. *ERPL* 1996, 111-144.

cover traditional damages caused by pollution; in this case, compensation for such damages is governed by general tort law rules (i.e. rules contained in a civil code, or common law rules, depending on the jurisdiction), adapted by case law to the specific problems posed by environmental pollution. This peculiar choice has been made, among others, by the United States, Italy, Switzerland and Portugal[1], each to a different degree.

On the other hand, nevertheless, stands the option to introduce new and tougher liability rules aimed at covering "traditional damages" whenever they are caused by a polluting event. Even if liability for the "environmental damage" (as defined above) is excluded, the environment still receives an **indirect protection**, since environmentally dangerous activities are subject to much more severe rules concerning damages caused by pollution to human health and private property.

This view is embodied in the German *Umwelthaftungsgesetz* of 1991. As we will see in more details *infra*, under § 1 of the German Environmental Liability Act operators of facilities listed in a specific appendix to the law are strictly liable to injured persons for bodily injury and property damage due to an environmental impact that issued from said facilities, and causation is presumed, pursuant to § 6.

Imposing the obligation to compensate for natural resources damages (NRDs) and cleanup costs - compared to the indirect protection scheme - has the clear advantage to force the polluter to **internalize the negative externalities** of his activity to the full extent. However, the choice for a direct protection scheme introduces new problems, the most important of which is related to the monetary **evaluation** and **quantification** of the so-called **"environmental damage"** or **"ecological damage"**.

In particular, the issue of quantification is extremely controversial with respect to the **value of natural resources** or other environmental services that cannot be fully restored or replaced after the occurrence of a polluting event. Some of the proposed monetary evaluation criteria – such as the contingent valuation method[2] and the travel cost method[3] – can be extremely subjective and they may lead to almost unpredictable results.

---

[1] See: the US *Comprehensive Environmental Response Compensation and Liability Act of 1980*, the Italian *Law of July 8, 1986 n.349, at art. 18*, the Swiss *Federal Act on Protection of the Environment* of 1983 and the Portuguese *Environmental Act* of 1987.

[2] The contingent valuation method involves directly asking people, in a survey, how much they would be willing to pay for specific environmental services or resources. People may also be asked for the amount of compensation they would be willing to accept to give up specific environmental goods. It is called "contingent" valuation, because people are asked to state their willingness to pay, contingent on a specific hypothetical scenario.

[3] This method estimates economic values associated with ecosystems or sites that are used for recreation by assuming that the value of a site is reflected in how much people are willing to pay to travel to visit the site.

It shall be noted, conversely, that holding responsible parties liable for the remediation costs and for the costs of cleaning up impaired resources on and around the polluted site under a "limited" direct protection scheme appears to be a more practicable and viable option.

With respect to this last issue, it is extremely important to point out that, in the recent years, several OECD countries, instead of - or in addition to - civil liability regimes for environmental pollution, have enacted public law schemes consisting of specific rules aimed at **imposing the obligation to cleanup contaminated sites** under the threat of **administrative** and/or **criminal sanctions**.

In case of pollution, the operator of the facility and/or the owner or occupier of the site, in other words, may be forced by the competent public authority to immediately adopt security and preventive measures and then to decontaminate the site, under the threat of penalties, fines, or even imprisonment.

The main difference between a private law regime relying on civil liability (i.e. tort law) and a public law regime based on administrative and/or criminal liability is that, in the latter scheme, preventive and restorative measures – such as cleanup obligations – are mandated by compulsory orders of the competent public authority entrusted with regulatory and enforcement powers, without the prior need for court adjudication. Sometimes, the administrative bodies may well employ the concurrent civil liability mechanism in order to seek reimbursement of the remediation costs from the liable parties, but they generally have the power to issue compulsory cleanup orders in the first place.

Recent examples of this trend in OECD countries include:

DENMARK: The Contaminated Soil Act n.370 of 2 June 1999.

FINLAND: The Environmental Protection Act n.86 of 2000 (Chapter 12)

GERMANY: The Federal Soil Protection Act (BSG) of 1998, that came into force in March 1999.

ITALY: Ministerial Decree n.471 of 25 October 1999 and Legislative Decree n.22 of 5 February 1997 (Ronchi Decree).

NEW SOUTH WALES (AUSTRALIA): The Contaminated Land Management Act of 1997.

SPAIN: Wastes Law n.10 of 1998 (Title V).

SWEDEN: Chapter 10 of the new Environmental Code, in force from 1 January 1999.

UK: The implementation in England (1 April 2000), Scotland (14 July 2000) and Wales (14 July 2001) of Part IIA of the Environmental Protection Act 1990 on contaminated land (introduced by Section 57 of the Environment Act 1995).

This general trend towards the introduction of **public law regimes**, whose effects are to impose environmental cleanup obligations or other financial responsibilities upon certain parties (generally: the causer of the harm and the owners or occupiers of the polluted land), increases the complexity of the picture and raises important questions concerning the most appropriate types of applicable insurance coverages[1].

In those jurisdictions that have enacted a public law scheme for contaminated land remediation, in fact, liability insurance might not be suitable to cover on-site cleanup obligations or other expenses made compulsory by an administrative order issued by the competent authority. Mixed products – combining property and liability cover –, therefore, may prove important in the future developments of environmental pollution insurance[2].

In any event, from an insurability perspective, it is always very important to distinguish between liability (being it civil or administrative) for cleanup of soil or water pollution and the obligation to pay monetary damages to compensate for harm to natural resources and biodiversity (both belonging to the general notion of "environmental damage" or "ecological damage", as opposed to that of "traditional damages", consisting of third party bodily injury, property damages and economic loss).

As mentioned, the monetary evaluation of natural resources damages (NRDs) and biodiversity damages may in fact be extremely subjective and unpredictable, while technical cleanup standards could well be determined by the competent authorities with a sufficient level of clarity, stability and predictability. If this is the case, the risk of liability for environmental cleanup and remediation costs may prove to be fully manageable by the insurance sector.

IV. A comparative overview of different legal approaches

In this section, a sample of different legal responses to the environmental pollution risk is examined. Comparative tables summarizing these different approaches are available at the end of this section. The aim is not to explore the details of the selected legal systems, but rather to outline the most relevant provisions of their environmental liability regimes, taking into account the issues of insurability, according to the terms of the present analysis.

---

[1] See: Spühler, J. (2000), Environmental impairment liability insurance for landfills, Swiss Reinsurance Company, Zurich: Swiss Re Publishing; and also: Spühler, J. (1999), Environmental insurance for enterprises. An insurance concept, Swiss Reinsurance Company, Zurich: Swiss Re Publishing.

[2] This point will be addressed in more details *infra*, with an overview of the different types of environmental coverage currently available on the international insurance market.

304

To this purpose, this section addresses some of the most relevant features of: *(A)* the U.S. Comprehensive Environmental Response, Compensation and Liability Act of 1980 (CERCLA) *(B)* the German Environmental Liability Act (Umwelthaftungsgesetz) of 1991 and the Federal Soil Protection Act of 1998 *(C)* the Italian Law n. 349 of 1986 and the Legislative Decree n. 22 of 1997 (Ronchi Decree) and *(D)* the proposal for a Directive of the European Parliament and of the Council on environmental liability with regard to the prevention and remedying of environmental damage, presented by the Commission of the European Communities on 23 January 2002.

A. The U.S. Comprehensive Environmental Response, Compensation and Liability Act of 1980 (CERCLA)

In 1980 the Comprehensive Environmental Response, Compensation and Liability Act (CERCLA)[1] has been enacted in the United States. Section (§) 107 of CERCLA imposes on an extremely broad category of Potentially Responsible Parties (PRPs)[2] strict, retroactive, joint and several liabilities for response costs, including cleanup costs and natural resource damages[3].

---

[1] CERCLA has been modified by *Superfund Amendments and Reauthorization Act* of 1986 (SARA). The modified version of CERCLA is codified in 42 U.S.C. §§9601- 9674.

[2] There are four categories of potentially responsible party (PRP): current owners and occupiers, past owners and occupiers, hazardous substance generators and transporters who selected the site.

[3] 42 U.S.C.A. § 9607 (a) : " Notwithstanding any other provision or rule of law, and subject only to the defenses set forth in subsection (b) of this section -

(1) the owner and operator of a vessel or a facility,

(2) any person who at the time of disposal of any hazardous substance owned or operated any facility at which such hazardous substances were disposed of,

(3) any person who by contract, agreement, or otherwise arranged for disposal or treatment, or arranged with a transporter for transport for disposal or treatment, of hazardous substances owned or possessed by such person, by any other party or entity, at any facility or incineration vessel owned or operated by another party or entity and containing such hazardous substances, and

(4) any person who accepts or accepted any hazardous substances for transport to disposal or treatment facilities, incineration vessels or sites selected by such person, from which there is a release, or a threatened release which caused the incurrence of response costs, of a hazardous substance, shall be liable for -

(A)   all costs of removal or   remedial action incurred by the United States Government or a State or an Indian tribe not inconsistent with the national contingency plan;

(B)   any other necessary costs of response incurred by any other person consistent with the national contingency plan;

(C)   damages for injury to, destruction of, or loss of natural resources, including the reasonable costs of assessing such injury, destruction, or loss resulting from such a release; (...)"

Notwithstanding detailed regulations on assessment and valuation of lost or injured natural resources have been issued by the Department of the Interior (DOI)[1], however, § 107 (a) (1-4) (C) of CERCLA concerning NRDs – i.e. "damages for injury to, destruction of, or loss of natural resources, including the reasonable costs of assessing such injury, destruction, or loss resulting from such a release" – has been rarely enforced by courts, while the provisions related to liability for response costs have been widely litigated during the past two decades.

CERCLA is a statute that combines an almost absolute liability regime[2] with a collective funding mechanism, in order to deal with the highest priority hazardous waste sites. The federal statute, in fact, established a trust fund, better known as the *Superfund*, which is sustained by various fiscal impositions, such as a petroleum tax, an environmental income tax on major enterprises and a tax on producers of those chemicals that typically compose hazardous waste[3].

The enforcement of this act has been delegated to the U.S. Environmental Protection Agency (EPA), established in 1970. The resources of *Superfund* are mainly used by the EPA to assess necessary removal and remedial actions and to locate Potentially Responsible Parties, with a view to making them pay for the costs of cleaning up polluted sites.

CERCLA is a mixed systems containing civil liability rules as well as rules granting authoritative powers that allow the EPA to issue compulsory cleanup orders, backed by the threat of severe fines and punitive (treble) damages for noncompliance. The two main mechanisms for securing response costs from PRPs are: *(1)* unilateral administrative orders pursuant to § 106(a) and *(2)* cost recovery actions against liable parties following removal and remedial measures financed from the Superfund (§ 107). After a few years, the "enforcement first" strategy took the lead; the effects of the implementation of this strategy on PRPs is not indifferent, considering that the Act prohibits any pre-enforcement review, or hearing, on liability before completion of the remedial work. A massive phenomenon of litigation characterized the fifteen years

---

[1] On the issue of NRDs evaluation see: F. B. Cross, 42 Vanderbilt Law Rev. 1989, cit.; Cummings, Shultze (1984), Valuing Environmental Goods: A state of the Art Assessment of the Contingent Valuation Method, Washington DC; Pozzo, B. (1990) "La determinazione del quantum del danno ambientale nell'esperienza giuridica degli Stati Uniti", 2 Quadrimestre, 324; Id., Danno Ambientale ed Imputazione della Responsabilità - Esperienze Giuridiche a Confronto, cit.,187-248. See also: M. B. Rutherford, J. L. Knetsch, T. C. Brown, 22 Harvard Environmental Law Review 1998, cit.; Carol A. Jones, T. D. Tomasi, S.W. Fluke, "Public and private claims in natural resource damage assessments", 20 Harvard Environmental Law Review 1996, 111; Binger, Copple, Hoffman, 35 Natural Resources Journal 1995, 443; Thomas A. Campbell, Baylor Law Review 1993, 221.

[2] The statutory defenses to liability, namely: act of God, act of war and act or omission of a third party not connected with the defendant, have each been so narrowly construed as to be almost ineffective.

[3] See CERCLA § 111, 42 U.S.C. § 9611.

following the enactment of CERCLA: several disputes involved the EPA, Potentially Responsible Parties (PRPs) and their general liability insurers. PRPs were seeking coverage for cleanup costs imposed by retroactive CERCLA liabilities under *Comprehensive General Liability* policies (CGL) issued several decades before on an occurrence basis[1]. Courts very often ruled in favor of policyholders, thereby shifting a relevant part of the remediation costs onto the insurance industry. As a result, however, substantial amounts of money have been spent in litigation and other transaction costs, to the detriment of environmental protection.

Moreover, in consequence of the very confused and questionable development of state case law with respect to the interpretation of insurance policy exclusions and conditions[2] a crisis hit the U.S. environmental insurance market and very little pollution coverage has been available until the recent years. Both the rigorous features of the CERCLA liability regime and the early controversial case law on environmental insurance issues under CGL policies created an unbearable level of legal uncertainty, which discouraged the development of environmental pollution policies.

At present, environmental liability coverage is completely excluded from the standard CGL policy by the 1986 absolute pollution exclusion and it became available again under new specific contracts, issued on a claims made, manifestation, or discovery basis, with coverage often limited to bodily injury, property damages and response (cleanup) costs[3]. This positive trend can be explained by observing that courts' decisions are becoming more predictable, cleanup costs amounts are more steadily determined and some sort of legislative reform is expected. The provisions of CERCLA that appear to be under more serious scrutiny concern the retroactive nature of the liability regime (a feature that is not expressly stated in the Act), the limited scope of

---

[1] In several cases, the release of pollutants into the environment began in the 1950s or 1960s and continued over a long period of time. See: Abraham, K.S. (1991), Environmental Liability Insurance Law - an analysis of toxic torts and hazardous waste insurance coverage issues, Prentice Hall Law & Business; see also Monti, A. (1997), Diritto ed Economia dell'Assicurazione, n.1, 41-162.

[2] At the very beginning, courts interpreting CGL policies were imposing liabilities on insurance companies despite express exclusions of coverage, such as the 1973 qualified pollution exclusion or the owned-property exclusion. Those decisions impaired the confidence of the insurance industry, which nearly abandoned the environmental marketplace for a long time. Scholars have written extensively on the subject, see: Abraham, K.S. (1991), Environmental Liability Insurance Law - an analysis of toxic torts and hazardous waste insurance coverage issues, 1991 Prentice Hall Law & Business; I. Sullivan, T. G. Reynolds, W. J. Jr. Wright, "Hazardous waste litigation: Comprehensive General Liability Insurance coverage issues", 494 Practising Law Institute / Lit. 1994, 267, and the Symposium issue of the 28. Gonzaga Law Review, 1992-1993. See also: Abraham, K.S. (1981), Judge-Made Law and Judge-Made Insurance: Honoring the Reasonable Expectations of the Insured, Virginia Law Review 67:1151-1191.

[3] Those policies are too new to fully evaluate their effectiveness; no significant disputes on issues related to those new coverages have been decided by U.S. courts.

available defenses and the very severe joint and several standard. Moreover, since the U.S. environmental regulatory framework is extremely sophisticated and strictly enforced, the insurance industry is able to offer to the regulated activities pollution insurance at reasonable prices[1], by excluding coverage in case of violation of administrative standards. Except for *Resource Conservation and Recovery Act*'s (RCRA)[2] financial requirements imposed on TDSFs (Hazardous treatment disposal and storage facilities)[3] and for the mandatory insurance coverage for underground storage tanks and marine damages caused by oil pollution, environmental insurance is generally not compulsory in the United States.

B. The German Environmental Liability Act of 1991 and the Federal Soil Protection Act of 1998

The Environmental Liability Act (*Umwelthaftungsgesetz*) was enacted in Germany in 1991. This statute imposes strict liability upon certain categories of industrial and commercial enterprises, listed in two appendixes to the Act[4], for bodily injury and property damages caused by pollution incidents[5]. The environment, therefore, receives indirect protection in the German civil liability regime and only specified types of listed activities are subject to the provisions of the 1991 Act[6].

---

[1] Relying on the effective enforcement of regulatory standards, fewer resources are invested by the insurance companies in monitoring the insured plant. A completely different situation characterizes the European insurance marketplace. See J. Spühler, Environmental Liability Risks: a global view on present problems and their assessing and covering by insurance, Recycle '95 - Environmental Technology Global Forum & Exposition, Davos - May 15-19, 1995; A. Gambaro (ed.), *Responsabilità delle imprese in campo ambientale*, Milano, IPA, 1997, 68 ff., 111 ff..

[2] This Act of 1976 is codified as part of the Solid Waste Disposal Act in 42 U.S.C. §§6901-6992k.

[3] Subtitle C of RCRA. To comply with these financial requirements, TDSFs frequently use a mixed form of financial insurance.

[4] Listed in another appendix are those plants that are not subject to the Act.

[5] Umwelthaftungsgesetz § 1. **Liability for installations having an impact on the environment:** "Where an installation mentioned in Annex I produces an impact on the environment such that someone dies or suffers injury to the body or health, or that property is damaged, the owner of the installation shall make good the ensuing damage to the injured person." In the literature, see: Hager, "Das neue Umwelthaftungsgesetz", *NJW* 1991, 136; Landsberg and Lülling, *Umwelthaftungsrecht*, Stuttgart, 1991; B. Pozzo, "La responsabilità civile per danni all'ambiente in Germania", *Riv. Dir. Civ.* 1991, I, 619; most recently, M. Hünert, "Rechtliche Bewältigung der Haftung für Massenschäden im Deutschen Recht", *ERPL* 7 (4):459-480, 1999, in particular at 466 ff.. General liability for bodily injury and property damages was already imposed by § 823 BGB (the German civil code), but under different standards.

[6] All the enterprises falling in the listed categories are subject to the liabilities imposed by the Umwelthaftungsgesetz, even if they are not yet or not any more in operation.

Liability standards under the *Umwelthaftungsgesetz* are extremely severe: § 6 introduced a presumption of causation, which practically works - under certain circumstances - as a reversion of the burden of proof in favor of the plaintiff[1]. Liability is triggered also for damages caused during normal operations (*Normalbetrieb*) of a plant that is fully authorized and which is complying with all regulatory requirements[2]. In this case, however, the presumption of causation stated in §6 does not operate[3].

Enterprises falling under the regime are also liable for the development risk (*Entwicklungsrisiko*). Besides, with a view to assuring the effectiveness of the system, the 1991 Act granted rights of information in favor of the injured parties (§ 8 Rights of Information versus plant owners - § 9 Right of Information versus the public authority), as well as in favor of the plant owners (§ 10)[4]. Environmental liabilities under the Act

---

[1] Umwelthaftungsgesetz § 6 **Presumption of causation**: "(1) If, according to the circumstances of the case, an installation is inherently suited to cause the damage suffered by injured person, that damage shall be presumed to have been caused by the installation in question. Inherent suitability is assessed in each case according to the course of operation [of the installation], the equipment employed, the type and concentration of the substances that were used and released, the weather conditions, the time and place of the occurrence of damage, the nature of the damage as well as any other fact which in a given case might tend to prove or disprove causation. (2) The first paragraph is not applicable when the installation was correctly operated, that is to say when specific operational duties were respected and the operations were not disrupted. (…)"

[2] See Landsberg and Lülling, *Umwelthaftungsrecht*, 82

[3] In case of damages deriving from normal operations of a plant which complied with all regulatory standards, moreover, § 5 states that no compensation is required for property damages of marginal entity or to be considered usual under local circumstances; Umwelthaftungsgesetz **§ 5 Limitation of liability for property damage**: "If the installation was operated correctly within the meaning of the second sentence of § 6(2), no liability arises for property damage where the property was insignificantly affected or affected in a manner which is reasonable according to local conditions)."

As for bodily injuries, in these cases liability is capped at 50.000 DM for each person.

[4] Umwelthaftungsgesetz **§ 8. Right of the injured person to obtain information from the owner of the installation**: "(1) If there are reasons to assume that an installation caused the damage to the injured person, that person can require the owner of the installation to disclose the information necessary to determine whether that person has the right to recover damages under the present Act. Disclosure extends only to information on the equipment employed, the type and concentration of the substances that were used or discharged and other effects produced by the installation, as well as information on the specific operational duties within the meaning of § 6(3) (...)"

Umwelthaftungsgesetz **§ 9. Right of the injured person to obtain information from the administration**: "If there are reasons to assume that an installation caused the damage to the injured person, that person can require the authorities that granted a permit to the installation, that are responsible for supervising the installation or that are responsible to collect information on impacts on the environment to disclose the information necessary to determine whether that person has the right to recover damages under the present Act (...)"

are capped by § 15 at Euro 85 million for death and bodily injuries and Euro 85 million for property damages deriving from each release of pollutants[1].

The plants belonging to the categories listed in Appendix II to the Act (i.e. the most dangerous installations), eventually, must meet certain financial requirements, pursuant to §19. The compulsory insurance program for high-risk activities has not yet been fully implemented; however, following the enactment of the Act, a new environmental liability policy (HUK-Umwelthaft-Modell) has been offered on the German pollution insurance marketplace by the *Verband der Haftpflichtversicherer, Unfallversicherer, Autoversicherer und Rechtsschutzversicherer e.V.* (Huk-Verband), the German Association of Casualty Insurers[2]. Coverage is provided on a manifestation basis and tailor made on the prospective insured's needs: many different 'bricks' of pollution coverage are offered under the policy, so that the insured can build up the wall of environmental protection more suited to fulfill his/her own particular needs (*Bausteinsystem*).

New rules concerning soil contamination and remediation have been enacted with the Federal Soil Protection Act (BSG) of 1998, entered into force on 1 March 1999. This federal statute provides uniform provisions concerning clean-up of contaminated sites in Germany. The Act introduced a public law regime based on strict liability which

---

Umwelthaftungsgesetz **§ 10. Right of the owner of the installation to obtain information**: "(1) If a claim is brought against the owner of an installation on the basis of the present Act, that owner can require information, or the examination of documents, from the injured person and from the owner of another installation, and can require information from the authorities mentioned at § 9, in so far as necessary to determine the scope of its liability towards the injured person or the scope of its claim for contribution from that other owner (...)"

[1] Umwelthaftungsgesetz **§ 15. Maximum liability**: "The liability of a person for all the damage arising from death or injury to the body or to health which followed from one and the same instance of impact on the environment is limited to a maximum of Euro 85 million. Liability for property damage is similarly limited to Euro 85 million. Where the sum-total of the individual awards flowing from one and the same instance of impact on the environment exceeds the maximum fixed in the previous sentences, then each award is reduced according to the proportion of the said maximum to the sum-total of the individual awards."

[2] On the Huk-Umwelthaft-Modell see: G. Küpper, "Anmerkungen zu dem genehmigten Umwelthaftpflicht-Modell und Umwelthaftpflicht-Tarif des Huk-Verbandes", in *Die Versicherungs Praxis*, February 1993; B. Pozzo, "La responsabilità per danni all'ambiente in Germania e i connessi problemi di assicurabilità del rischio ambientale: il progetto per una nuova polizza R.C"., in *Diritto ed Economia dell'Assicurazione*, 1994, 3, particularly at 23 ff.; W. C. Hoffman, "Environmental Liability and its insurance in Germany", 43 *FICC Quarterly* 1993, 147; B. Hoffman, "A gradual consideration", in *The Review*, April 7, 1993; R. Woltereck, "New environmental impairment liability policy introduced into the german market", 5 *Int. ILR Case Comment*, 1994, p. 202; W. Pfennigstorf, "Germany: the New Model policy and the difficulty of defining compulsory insurance", 8 *AIDA Pollution Insurance Bulletin*, May 1994, p. 6.

covers harm to land and associated damage to ground and surface waters. Liability for preventive and remediation measures falls on the causer of harm, his successor and current or past owners or occupiers. Apportionment involves joint and several liability in the form of a right of compensation or contribution from other liable parties.

The BSG introduced a mechanism for identifying, and monitoring hazardous sites, allocating responsibilities between the competent public authorities and liable parties. Special provisions, moreover, allow a form of contractual clean-up agreement to be submitted by the responsible parties for approval by the authorities. In case of approval, the authority withholds any administrative order.

C. The Italian Law n. 349 of 1986 and the Legislative Decree n. 22 of 1997 (Ronchi Decree)

Law n. 349 of 8 July 1986 (*Istituzione del Ministero dell'Ambiente e norme in materia di danno ambientale*) introduced in Italy a private law regime aimed at granting direct protection to the environment. In fact, article 18 L. 349/86 imposes civil liability on the causer of pollution for damages to natural resources and the State is entitled to receive compensation on behalf of the citizens[1].

Liability for "environmental damage" is based on negligence and its scope is not limited to dangerous activities or classified installations. The release of pollutants or the other wrongful action that causes environmental damage must occur in violation of administrative rules and standards aimed at protecting the environment. The choice for a negligence standard, in spite of the dissenting opinion of legal scholars[2], may be considered as a legacy of the "criminal" origins of the liability regime introduced by art.18 L. 349/86 [3]. At the very beginning, in fact, the Italian response to the ecological emergency followed the traditional criminal law approach to public policy issues[4]. Relying substantially on the enforcement of previously determined administrative

---

[1] Art. 18 comma I, L. 349/86: "*Qualunque fatto doloso o colposo in violazione di disposizioni di legge o di provvedimenti adottati in base a legge che comprometta l'ambiente, ad esso arrecando danno, alterandolo, deteriorandolo o distruggendolo in tutto o in parte, obbliga l'autore del fatto al risarcimento nei confronti dello Stato*".

[2] See e.g.: A. Gambaro, "Il danno ecologico nella recente elaborazione legislativa letta alla luce del diritto comparato", in 19 *Studi parlamentari e di politica costituzionale*, 1986 n.71, 1 trim., 73; P. Trimarchi, "Responsabilità civile per danno all'ambiente: prime riflessioni", in *Amministrare*, 1987, 189; L. Bigliazzi-Geri, "Quale futuro per l'art. 18 Legge 8 luglio 1986, n.349?", in *Rivista Critica del Diritto Privato*, 1987, 685.

[3] See A. Gambaro and B. Pozzo, in *Consumatore, Ambiente, Concorrenza - Analisi Economica del Diritto* cit., 57 ff.

[4] For the general argument that legal systems in distress tend to react according to a pre-determined sub-optimal path, see: Mattei, U. (2001), Legal Systems in Distress: HIV-contaminated Blood, Path Dependency and Legal Change, Global Jurist Advances: Vol. 1: No. 2, Article 4.
http://www.bepress.com/gj/advances/vol1/iss2/art4.

standards, the environmental liability provision contained in article 18 L. 349/86 resembles the sanctioning part of a centralized regulatory framework. In this perspective, it is not difficult to understand why liability is imposed on an individual basis[1]. Art. 18 comma VIII states that restoration of impaired resources (i.e. *restitution in integrum*) shall be granted as a remedy whenever it is materially possible, without the limit of "excessive hardship" set forth by art. 2058 of the Italian civil code. For the residual cases in which restoration is technically unfeasible, art. 18 comma VI sets forth several criteria to be employed by judges in the monetary evaluation of natural resource damages (NRDs). In light of the hybrid background of art. 18 L. 349/86, it is not surprising to find out that the degree of fault[2] and the profit earned by the polluter from the violation of environmental norms shall be taken into account in determining the size of the monetary damages award[3].

Since 1986, Italian courts have rarely applied article 18 L. 349/86 and when they decided to do so, they managed to confuse even more an already troublesome situation[4]. Some courts have said that liability under this rule is triggered by the mere violation of environmental standards, even if there is no actual proof of damage to the environment[5]. The only two reported court decisions concerning the monetary evaluation of NRDs, rendered by *Pretore di Milano, sez. Rho* in 1989 [6] and by *Tribunale di Venezia* in 2002[7], do not provide much guidance in the application of the quantification criteria provided by the law. Most recent decisions of the Italian Supreme court of cassation, eventually,

---

[1] While, on the contrary, article 2055 of the Italian civil code states that the general tort law principle is joint and several liability.

[2] An echo of what is set forth by art. 133 of the Italian criminal code.

[3] The quantification criteria are: 1) seriousness of the fault; 2) the remediation costs; 3) the profit earned by the polluter as a result of its misconduct. See: Art. 18 comma VI L. 349/86: "*Il giudice, ove non sia possibile una precisa quantificazione del danno, ne determina l'ammontare in via equitativa, tenendo comunque conto della gravità della colpa individuale, del necessario costo del ripristino e del profitto conseguito dal trasgressore in conseguenza del suo comportamento lesivo dei beni ambientali.*"

[4] See: Villa, G. (2002), Il danno all'ambiente nel sistema della responsabilità civile, in Pozzo B. (ed.), La nuova responsabilità civile per danno all'ambiente, Milan: Giuffré, 123 ff.

[5] Cass. 9 aprile 1992 n°4362, Pretore Monza 8 ottobre 1990, Pretore Rho 4 dic. 1990, Cass. pen. 31 luglio 1990 (in Nuova Giur. comm.,1991, I, 535), Pretore di Rovigo 4 dic. 1989, Pretore di Lecco 29 sett. 1989, Cass. pen. 11 gennaio 1988 (in *Riv. pen.*,1989, 515, m.); but see D. Feola, *L'art.18 l.349/86 sulla responsabilità civile per il danno all'ambiente: dalle ricostruzioni della dottrina alle applicazioni giurisprudenziali*, in *Quadrimestre* 1992, 547.

[6] Pretore di Milano - sez. distaccata di Rho, June 29, 1989, in Foro it., 1990, II, 526; notes and comments on this decision are available in English in 6 *AIDA Pollution Bulletin*, July 1991, 7.

[7] Tribunale di Venezia, Ufficio del giudice monocratico, Sez. Penale, 27 novembre 2002, n. 1286, in Rivista giuridica dell'ambiente (n.1/2003), p. 164.

stated that art. 18 L. 349/86 shall apply retroactively[1] and according to a strict liability standard[2]. As a result, the level of legal uncertainty affecting environmental pollution risk in Italy became quite relevant and problematic.

In the recent years, moreover, Legislative Decree n.22 of 5 February 1997 (Ronchi Decree) and the implementation guidelines enacted by Ministerial Decree n.471 of 25 October 1999 introduced new important provisions on liability for soil contamination.

Pursuant to article 17 of the Ronchi Decree, in fact, anyone who causes land, surface or groundwater to exceed statutory contamination limits, or a significant and imminent threat of such harm, is obliged to pay for remedial action, to make the site safe, to clean up the pollutants and to restore the environment. Liability is strict and the polluter is also required to notify the local authorities immediately, who have the power to issue compulsory cleanup orders. Site owners who are not directly involved in the polluting activity bear the liability if the causer can not be made to pay, with the authorities imposing a first charge on the land if they are forced to carry out the work themselves[3]. It shall be noted, furthermore, that article 58 Legislative Decree n.152 of 11 May 1999 introduced similar obligations on the causer of water damage. It shall be noted that, in both cases, compulsory cleanup orders are backed by criminal sanctions (art. 58 Legislative Decree n.152 of 11 May 1999 and art. 51 *bis* of the Ronchi Decree).

The various liability regimes concerning "environmental damage" in Italy (i.e.: Law n.349 of 1986, Legislative Decree n.22 of 1997 and Legislative Decree n.152 of 1999) appear to be overlapping to some extent, as well as poorly coordinated and this generates additional legal uncertainty.

At present, the environmental liability policy offered by the Italian Environmental Insurance Pool (Pool R.C. Inquinamento) does not provide any coverage for on-site cleanup obligations imposed by the Ronchi Decree, nor for the "environmental damage", as identified by art. 18 L. 349/86, with the limited exception of the costs of cleaning up impaired properties belonging to third party claimants. The Italian Pool, however, is currently working on a new draft policy, in order to provide coverage also for on-site remediation costs.

---

[1] See Cass. civ., sez. III, 3 February 1998 n. 1087, in *Foro Italiano*, 1998, I, 1142 with a case note by B. Pozzo, "La retroattività della responsabilità civile per danno ambientale: alla ricerca delle ragioni di un <obiter> della Cassazione", *Foro Italiano*, 1998, I, 1143.

[2] See Cass. civ., 1 September 1995 n. 9211.

[3] See Cons. Stato (Ord.), Sez.V, 03/04/2001, n.2114; T.A.R. Veneto, Sez.III, 02/02/2002, n.320; T.A.R. Friuli-V. Giulia, 27/07/2001, n.488, Foro Amm., 2001.

D.   The proposal for a "Directive of the European Parliament and of the Council on environmental liability with regard to the prevention and remedying of environmental damage" presented by the Commission of the European Communities on January 23, 2002 [COM(2002) 17 final]

Following the White Paper on Environmental Liability of February 9, 2000 [1], the Commission of the European Communities presented on January 23, 2002 a proposal for a Directive of the European Parliament and of the Council on environmental liability with regard to the prevention and remedying of environmental damage [COM(2002) 17 final]. With this proposal, the Commission started to implement an action foreseen by the Sixth Environmental Action Programme[2].

The proposal is aimed at preventing and remedying "environmental damage", defined for the purpose of the Directive as:

a. biodiversity[3] damage, which is any damage[4] that has serious adverse effects on the conservation status of biodiversity;

b. water damage, which is any damage that adversely affects the ecological status, ecological potential and/or chemical status of the waters[5] concerned to such an extent that this status will or is likely to deteriorate from one of the categories defined in Directive 2000/60/EC with the exception of adverse effects where Article 4(7) of Directive 2000/60/EC applies;

c. land damage, which is any damage that creates serious potential or actual harm to public health as a result of soil and subsoil contamination[6];

Pursuant to article 4 of the Directive, where environmental damage has not yet occurred but there is an imminent threat of such damage occurring, the competent

---

[1] White Paper on Environmental Liability, COM(2000) 66 final, Brussels, 9 February 2000; see also: the Green Paper, COM (93) 47, Brussels, May 14, 1993, and the Lugano Convention of June 21-22, 1993.

[2] See: Article 3(8) of the Common position adopted by the Council on 17 September 2001 with a view to the adoption of a Decision of the European Parliament and of the Council laying down the Sixth Community Environment Action Programme.

[3] "biodiversity" means natural habitats and species listed in Annex I to Directive 79/409/EEC, or in Annexes I, II and IV to Directive 92/43/EEC, or habitats and species, not covered by those Directives, for which areas of protection or conservation have been designated pursuant to the relevant national legislation on nature conservation.

[4] "damage" means a measurable adverse change in a natural resource and/or measurable impairment of a natural resource service which may occur directly or indirectly and which is caused by any of the activities covered by the Directive.

[5] "waters" mean all waters covered by Directive 2000/60/EC.

[6] "land contamination" or "soil and subsoil contamination" means the direct or indirect introduction, as a result of human activity, of substances, preparations, organisms or micro-organisms harmful to human health or natural resources into soil and subsoil.

authority shall either require the operator[1] to take the necessary **preventive measures** or shall itself take such measures; without prejudice to any further action which could be required by the competent authority, Member States shall provide that, when operators are aware of an imminent threat or ought to be aware of such an imminent threat, those operators are required to take the necessary measures to prevent environmental damage from occurring, without waiting for a request to do so by the competent authority. Member States shall provide that where appropriate, and in any case whenever an imminent threat of environmental damage is not dispelled despite the preventive measures taken by the relevant operator, operators are to inform the competent authority of the situation. If the operator fails to comply with his obligations, the competent authority shall take the necessary preventive measures.

According to article 5, moreover, where environmental damage has occurred the competent authority shall either require the operator to take the necessary **restorative measures** or shall itself take such measures. If the operator fails to comply with a request issued, the competent authority shall take the necessary restorative measures. The necessary restorative measures shall be determined in accordance with Annex II [2].

---

[1] "operator" means any person who directs the operation of an activity covered by this Directive including the holder of a permit or authorisation for such an activity and/or the person registering or notifying such an activity.

[2] Pursuant to Annex II to the Directive, remedying of environmental damage, in terms of biodiversity damage and water pollution, is achieved through the restoration of the environment as a whole to its baseline condition. Restoration is done through rehabilitating, replacing or acquiring the equivalent of damaged natural resources and/or services at the site originally damaged or at a different location. Remedying of environmental damage, in terms of water pollution and in terms of biodiversity damage, also implies that any serious harm or serious potential harm to human health be removed should such a harm be present. Where polluted soil or subsoil gives rise to a serious harm to human health or could pose such a risk, the necessary measures shall be taken to ensure that the relevant contaminants are controlled, contained, diminished or removed so that the polluted soil does not pose any serious harm or serious potential harm to human health which would be incompatible with the current or plausible future use of the land concerned. Plausible future use shall be ascertained on the basis of the land use regulations in force when the damage occurred. Once the competent authority has developed a reasonable range of restorative options, it shall evaluate the proposed options based on, at a minimum:

(1) The effect of each option on public health and safety;
(2) The cost to carry out the option;
(3) The likelihood of success of each option;
(4) The extent to which each option will prevent future damage, and avoid collateral damage as a result of implementing the option; and
(5) The extent to which each option benefits to each component of the natural resource and/or service.

If several options are likely to deliver the same value, the least costly one shall be preferred.

Operators of certain dangerous activities listed in Annex I having caused an environmental damage are **strictly liable** for the costs of preventing and remedying the **environmental damage**. Operators of other activities are liable for the costs of remedying **bio-diversity damage** (a component of the "environmental damage"), but only when they are found to be **negligent**.

Contrarily to the environmental liability regime previously envisaged by the White Paper of 2000, the current proposal for a Directive does not contemplate liability for "traditional damages" (i.e. bodily injuries, property damage and economic loss) caused by pollution; such damages, therefore, would continue to receive protection under the existing national laws.

As for the allocation of concurrent liabilities, the proposal states that where the competent authority is able to establish with a sufficient degree of plausibility and probability that one and the same instance of damage has been caused by the actions or omissions of several operators, Member States may provide either that the relevant operators are to be held jointly and severally liable for that damage or that the competent authority is to apportion the share of the costs to be borne by each operator on a fair and reasonable basis. Operators who are able to establish the extent to which the damage results from their activities shall be required to bear only such costs as relate to that part of the damage.

It is very important to note that several limits to the scope of the environmental liability regime are clearly recognized and emphasized in the proposal. Such regime, in fact, **would not cover** environmental damage or imminent threats of such damage caused by **pollution of a widespread, diffuse character, where it is impossible to establish a causal link between the damage and the activities of certain individual operators**. Moreover, biodiversity damage, as defined above, does not include adverse effects which result from an **act by the operator which was expressly authorized** by the competent authorities.

The Directive shall also not cover environmental damage or an imminent threat of such damage caused by (a) an act of armed conflict, hostilities, civil war or insurrection; (b) a natural phenomenon of exceptional, inevitable and irresistible character; (c) an emission or event allowed in applicable laws and regulations, or in the permit or authorization issued to the operator; (d) emissions or activities which were not considered harmful according to the state of scientific and technical knowledge at the time when the emission was released or the activity took place (i.e. the development risk). The operators, moreover, shall not be liable for the cost of preventive or restorative measures taken when the environmental damage or imminent threat of such damage occurring is the result of (a) an act done by a third party with intent to cause damage, and the damage or imminent threat in question resulted despite the fact that appropriate safety measures were in place; (b) compliance with a compulsory order, instruction or other legally binding or compulsory measure emanating from a public authority[1].

---

[1] Finally, the proposed liability regime shall not apply to nuclear activities, to activities the sole

In order to assure an effective environmental protection mechanism even outside the scope of the liability regime, article 6 specifies that Member States shall ensure that the necessary preventive or restorative measures are taken (a) where it is not possible to identify the operator who caused the damage or the imminent threat of damage; (b) where the operator can be identified but has insufficient financial means to take any of the necessary preventive or restorative measures; (c) where the operator can be identified but has insufficient financial means to take all of the necessary preventive or restorative measures; or (d) where the operator is not required under the Directive to bear the cost of the necessary preventive or restorative measures.

The competent authority shall be entitled to initiate cost recovery proceedings against the operator who has caused the damage or the imminent threat of damage in relation to any measures taken in pursuance of the Directive during a period of five years (limitation period) from the date on which the measures in question were affected.

Without prejudice to any investigation initiated by the competent authority of its own motion, persons adversely affected or likely to be adversely affected by environmental damage and qualified entities shall be entitled to submit to the competent authority any observations relating to instances of environmental damage of which they are aware and shall be entitled to request the competent authority to take action.

The proposed Directive does not contemplate any specific requirement to provide proof of insurance or other forms of adequate financial security. EU Member States, however, are generally requested to encourage:

- the use by operators of any appropriate insurance or other forms of financial guarantee, in order to provide effective cover for obligations under the Directive

    and

- the development of appropriate insurance or other financial security instruments and markets by the appropriate economic and financial operators, including the financial services industry.

---

purpose of which is to serve national defense and to environmental damage or to any imminent threat of such damage arising from an incident in respect of which liability or compensation is regulated by any of the following agreements: (a) the International Convention of 27 November 1992 on Civil Liability for Oil Pollution Damage; (b) the International Convention of 27 November 1992 on the Establishment of an International Fund for Compensation for Oil Pollution Damage; (c) the International Convention of 23 March 2001 on Civil Liability for Bunker Oil Pollution Damage; (d) the International Convention of 3 May 1996 on Liability and Compensation for Damage in Connection with the Carriage of Hazardous and Noxious Substances by Sea; (e) the Convention of 10 October 1989 on Civil Liability for Damage Caused during Carriage of Dangerous Goods by Road, Rail and Inland Navigation Vessels.

Table 1. Environment pollution risk and insurance: a comparative overview of different legal approaches.

	STRICT LIABILITY VERSUS NEGLIGENCE	ADDITIONAL FEATURES OF THE CIVIL LIABILITY REGIME	NATURAL RESOURCES DAMAGES AND BIODIVERSITY DAMAGE	CONTAMINATED SITE CLEANUP COSTS OBLIGATIONS	POTENTIALLY RESPONSIBLE PARTIES	COMPULSORY ENVIRONMENTAL INSURANCE
UNITED STATES THE COMPREHENSIVE ENVIRONMENTAL RESPONSE, COMPENSATION AND LIABILITY ACT OF 1980 (CERCLA)	STRICT LIABILITY	JOINT AND SEVERAL STANDARD. RETROACTIVITY.	YES, but very rarely enforced. Traditional damages (death, bodily injury and property damage) are covered by common law (tort law) rules and not by CERCLA	YES. The competent authority (EPA) has the power to issue compulsory cleanup orders.	An extremely broad category of parties listed in CERCLA § 107(a), including the present and past owners of the site.	NO. Insurance is not mandatory for liabilities under CERCLA. Other statutes require certain financial guarantees, among others for: disposal facilities; underground storage tanks; marine damages caused by oil pollution.
GERMANY THE ENVIRONMENTAL LIABILITY ACT OF 1991 (UHG) AND THE FEDERAL SOIL PROTECTION ACT (BSG) OF 1998	STRICT LIABILITY, both under the UHG and the BSG.	JOINT AND SEVERAL (UHG and BSG). PRESUMPTION OF CAUSATION (§ 6 UHG). Liability also for damages caused during NORMAL OPERATIONS of a fully authorized activity (UHG).	NO. The UHG covers ONLY TRADITIONAL DAMAGES: death, bodily injury and property damages caused by environmental pollution. Liabilities are capped (UHG § 15).	YES. Under the 1998 BSG, the competent authority has the power to issue compulsory cleanup orders.	Under the 1991 UHG only those dangerous activities listed in the appendixes to the Act. Under the 1998 BSG: anyone who causes the harm, his successor and the current or past owners or occupiers of the site.	YES, environmental insurance is mandatory for the most dangerous activities listed in Appendix II to the 1991 Act (UHG § 19). The compulsory insurance scheme has not been fully enforced yet.
ITALY LAW N. 349 OF 1986 AND LEGISLATIVE DECREE N. 22 OF 1997 (RONCHI DECREE)	NEGLIGENCE (art. 18, L.349/86). Case law, however, enforced a stricter liability regime against operators of dangerous activities, pursuant to art. 2050 of the civil code. STRICT LIABILITY (D.22/97)	Under art. 18, L.349/86: liability for environmental harm is INDIVIDUAL and LINKED TO THE VIOLATION OF ANOTHER NORM aimed at protecting the environment. Recent Italian case law, however, enforced civil liability for environmental harm on a RETROACTIVE and JOINT AND SEVERAL basis.	YES, under L.349/86, but very rarely enforced. Traditional damages (death, bodily injury and property damage) are covered under different rules, among which: articles 2043 ff. of the civil code.	YES, both under L.349/86 and D.22/97. Under D.22/97, the competent authority has the power to issue compulsory cleanup orders.	L.349/86: anyone who causes damage to the environment in violation of another protective rule. D.22/97: anyone who causes land, surface or groundwater to exceed statutory contamination limits, or a significant and imminent threat of such harm. Site owners who are not involved in the polluting activity bear the liability if the causer can not be made to pay.	NO.
EUROPEAN UNION THE PROPOSAL FOR A DIRECTIVE ON ENVIRONMENTAL LIABILITY OF JAN. 23, 2002 [COM(2002)17/FINAL]	STRICT LIABILITY for operators of dangerous activities listed in Annex 1. NEGLIGENCE for all other parties, but in this case liability is limited to biodiversity damage.	Choice between a JOINT AND SEVERAL and an INDIVIDUAL standard. NO RETROACTIVITY. No liability for DIFFUSE POLLUTION, nor for the effects of AUTHORIZED EMISSIONS. No liability for DEVELOPMENT RISK.	YES. The definition of ENVIRONMENTAL DAMAGE includes: BIODIVERSITY damage, WATER damage and LAND damage. Traditional damages (death, bodily injury and property damage) ar NOT COVERED by the proposal.	YES. The competent authority shall have the power to issue compulsory cleanup orders, but LAND DAMAGE triggers liability ONLY IF soil contamination creates serious potential or actual HARM TO PUBLIC HEALTH	As for ENVIRONMENTAL DAMAGE: only the operators of dangerous activities listed in Annex 1. As for BIODIVERSITY DAMAGE: anyone who causes serious adverse effects on the conservation status of biodiversity.	NO. The importance of financial security is acknowledged by the Commission, but environmental insurance or other guarantees are not made compulsory by the proposed regime.

318

E. Summary of the trends in environmental legislations governing pollution risks

As announced in the introduction, for the purposes of this report the environmental pollution risk can be conceived as the risk of incurring legal liabilities for the consequences of environmental pollution phenomena.

We observed that the frontiers of environmental liabilities in OECD jurisdictions are rapidly expanding. An increasing number of potentially responsible parties are involved in private and/or public law regimes imposing the obligation to compensate for different types of harmful consequences caused by the release of pollutants in the environment.

New private law rules on civil liability for "environmental damage" (i.e. natural resources damages and remediation costs) have been enacted in a number of legal systems, in order to supplement or replace the existing rules covering "traditional damages" (i.e. bodily injury, property damages and economic losses) caused by pollution. The formal obligations to pay monetary damages as compensation for injuries to the environment (NRDs), in any event, have been very rarely enforced [1].

In modern environmental statutes, the liability of operators of potentially dangerous activities is generally strict, with limited defenses, and the burden of proving causation is often relaxed or reversed.

With respect to soil and water contamination, moreover, the general trend appears to be towards the enactment of public law schemes (or mixed schemes) within which a competent authority is entrusted with the power to issue compulsory cleanup orders against polluters, backed by the threat of severe criminal and/or administrative sanctions for non-compliance. In several jurisdictions, finally, liability for the costs of the preventive and remediation measures often falls also on the owners or occupiers of the polluted site, at least to a certain extent.

The recent proposal for a European Directive on environmental liability with regard to the prevention and remedying of environmental damage incorporates some of these trends, even if it shows some relevant distinctive features.

Allocating the risk of environmental pollution by way of liability rules enforced in civil or administrative proceedings may prove to be an effective mean:

- to fully comply with the polluter pays principle (which is one of the OECD Guiding Principles Concerning International Economic Aspects of Environmental Policies) and

- to reach efficient levels of compensation and deterrence.

---

[1] See the discussion above concerning the United States and Italy.

However, it is important to bear in mind that the efficacy of any liability mechanism may be impaired by the potential insolvency of the responsible parties. If after the environmental accident the polluter has no assets to compensate for the damage caused, the whole system of environmental liability would collapse and the overall result would be an additional waste of resources invested in litigation. In light of the above, insurance and reinsurance may be called upon to play a crucial role in the effective management of environmental pollution risks.

V. Environmental pollution risk and insurance: factual uncertainty

The environmental pollution risk, nevertheless, presents many difficulties to the insurance industry, especially with respect to the so-called **gradual pollution** phenomena characterized by:

factual uncertainty and

long-term effects (giving rise to long-tail liabilities).

As outlined in Chapter 1 of this report, insurance is able to perform its functions correctly under specific conditions of uncertainty. Environmental pollution risk is quite peculiar, since it includes components of both **factual and legal uncertainty**. This is true particularly when we consider gradual pollution events which develop slowly and secretly over a long period of time and whose damaging effects may become apparent only after several years, or even decades.

In this respect, environmental pollution risk insurability may be hindered by severe problems of **asymmetrical information** as well as of **generalized uncertainty**.

Due to the complexity of modern production technologies, problems of **adverse selection**[1] are widely present in this field, whenever the insurer is not able to perform accurate risk classification. **Moral hazard** phenomena[2] are also seriously involved with respect to the environmental pollution risk: it is easy to understand how the owners and operators of high-risk installation could erroneously perceive the insurance coverage as a sort of perpetual "license to pollute", bought in exchange for payment of an annual insurance premium.

In order to cope with these problems, professional risk-carriers need to develop and employ new **monitoring and bonding devices**.

---

[1] On the implications of this peculiar information asymmetry, see the study by Nobel Prize George A. Akerlof, "The Market for 'Lemons': Qualitative Uncertainty and the Market Mechanism", 84 Quarterly Journal of Economics, 1970, 488-500.

[2] S. Shavell, "On Moral Hazard and Insurance", 93 Quarterly Journal of Economics, 1979, 541-562.

Gradual pollution events also present relevant aspects of **generalized factual uncertainty**: in most cases, pollution develops unnoticed and insidiously over a substantial period of time and it is very difficult to determine when it began and how long it lasted.

The latency and the long terms effects characterizing gradual pollution phenomena, therefore, raise questions as to the adequacy of traditional **trigger-of-coverage** clauses, such as the "act committed" or the "loss occurrence" triggers. According to the "act-committed" formula, the wrongful act must have taken place during the period of validity of the liability policy, while under the "loss occurrence" clause, the injury or loss caused by the wrongful act must have occurred during the said period. Such clauses are able to work properly with respect to sudden events, but they are completely inappropriate with respect to the gradual environmental pollution risk.

If, for example, certain toxic substances are slowly but continuously seeping out of a tank, it might be extremely difficult - if not even impossible - to establish the exact moment in which the release began and how long it lasted; it may also be hard to establish the precise timing in which the consequent environmental harm occurred (i.e. the timing in which the threshold concentration of hazardous substances in soil or water is exceeded). Since the triggering events cannot be assigned to a particular point in time, determining the existence and validity of insurance coverage under the traditional formulas becomes quite problematic. Furthermore, even if it could be established that coverage is provided under a liability policy issued several years ago, it may well be the case that the limits of coverage properly stipulated at that time have become totally inadequate, due to the ongoing depreciation of money.

Factual uncertainty also regards the potentially damaging effects of new technologies and substances: in other words, the relevance of the so called **development risk** plays a great role in this context[1]. Synergetic pollution, finally, is a quite common phenomenon and it is often difficult to identify and separate single contributions.

These peculiar features of the environmental pollution risk are common to every legal system and they can explain why, at present, this risk is almost everywhere excluded from general liability insurance and gradual pollution coverage is provided only under very specific policies and according to limited terms and conditions.

VI. Environmental liability risk and insurance: legal uncertainty

What differentiates the situation in the various jurisdictions is the **level of legal uncertainty**. This variable represents the level of generalized uncertainty introduced by the legal system itself and basically depends on:

A. the way in which legal rules (i.e. the environmental liability regime) are

---

[1] See Skogh, G. (1998), Development risks, strict liability and the insurability of industrial hazards, Geneva Papers on Risk and Insurance, 87, 247.

designed by the legislative authorities;

B. the way in which those legal rules and propositions are interpreted and applied by legal actors (governmental agencies, local authorities, judges, scholars, etc.) in a given institutional framework.

Environmental pollution risk is, for the insurance industry, a risk of liability and the **choices made by law and policy makers greatly affect risk insurability**. The domain of risk insurability is limited. If generalized uncertainty - being it factual, or legal, or both - become excessive, then insurance will become a mere gamble: the unpredictability of losses, in fact, will prevent the prospective risk-carrier from performing effectively his/her statistical calculus of probabilities. In such a situation, insurers may change their attitude towards risk, moving from risk neutrality to risk aversion. This, of course, would undermine the very basis of the whole insurance mechanism.

As mentioned, the **level of legal uncertainty** may be detected from two different perspectives: A*)* on one hand we have to consider specific features of the environmental liability regime adopted in a given legal system and B*)* on the other we have to test the intrinsic coherence of each legal formant as well as the coherence among different formative parts of that system[1].

A. *Features of the liability regime*

As regards the first component of the **level of legal uncertainty**, the general trend towards the enactment of strict liability regimes for environmental pollution does not constitute a problem in terms of insurability; on the contrary, the use of a negligence standard could cause troubles, since it may be interpreted as reflecting a punitive character that is not immediately reconcilable with the transfer of liability to the insurer.

Retroactive regimes are incompatible both with the basic idea that environmental liabilities should be aimed at providing appropriate incentive to potential polluters and with the very nature of the insurance mechanism[2].

With respect to the criteria for allocating liabilities among multiple polluters, a joint and several standard may create excessive uncertainty, because the risk carrier would have to compute not only the risk created by the prospective insured, but also the

---

[1] The notion of legal formant refers to every legal proposition that concurs in the solution of a given legal issue. Court decisions are legal formants as well as scholarly writings, constitutional norms, regulatory standards, statutory provisions et cetera. Legal formants, therefore, are sources of law in a practical sense. See R. Sacco, "Legal Formants: A Dynamic Approach to Comparative Law", 39 *Am. J. Comp. Law* 1991, 1 ff., 349 ff.; see also, U. Mattei, *Comparative Law and Economics*, cit., 104 ff.

[2] This is fully recognized by the proposal for a Directive on environmental liability (see: article 19).

risks generated by all the other actors whose conduct may eventually combine with the one of the insured in the causation a polluting event. The insurer, moreover, would bear the risk of insolvency of these other subjects, without being able to monitor or control them. Such problem would notably increase the cost of insurance. Hence, an individual (proportional) standard would seem to be much more appropriate, if insurability issues are taken into serious consideration.

Rules aimed at waiving, alleviating or reversing the burden of proving causation are also problematic for analogous reasons and, in this perspective, liability does not seem to be an appropriate mechanism for the social allocation of risks and costs associated with diffuse and widespread pollution.

With reference to direct protection schemes and, more specifically, to environmental liability regimes that allow for recovery of monetary compensation for NRDs and/or biodiversity damage, the level of legal uncertainty is also negatively affected by the controversial criteria that are employed in order to place a value on reduced biodiversity and impaired natural resources that cannot be fully restored to the pre-existing conditions. As already mentioned, these values may be highly subjective, as well as very difficult to determine, since there are no well established and recognized economic guidelines. On the other hand, at present the costs of cleaning up polluted sites seem to be much more easily assessable and predictable than NRDs, since they depend on technical standards and operations[1].

The potential overlap between cost recovery actions under civil liability regimes and the authoritative enforcement of a public law scheme may also generate confusion and increase the level of legal uncertainty.

In this regard, the recent proposal for a Directive of the European Parliament and of the Council on environmental liability appears problematic in many aspects, since it introduces elements of increased legal complexity. The proposed regime, for example, would cover land contamination, but only those cases in which it creates serious potential or actual harm to public health, according to the definition of "environmental damage" offered by Article 2(18). The concept of biodiversity damages, moreover, is broadly conceived and the actual economic scope of the obligations falling on responsible parties, notwithstanding the relevant efforts put by the Commission, is still far from clear[2]; with respect to biodiversity damage and the issue of its full insurability,

---

[1] This seems to be confirmed by the availability, in several countries, of limited insurance coverage for first-party clean-up obligations. See: Faure, M.G., Grimeaud, D. (2000), Financial Assurance Issues of Environmental Liability – Report, Follow up study commissioned by the European Commission, 181 ff.

[2] "Insurers have to be able to calculate premiums and define adequate conditions including prevention measures. The knowledge and experience regarding biodiversity damage is in its onset in Europe and it cannot be considered currently insurable even in the light of the work done by the European Commission to clarify this question. Insurers reiterate their willingness to contribute in the process to develop this concept. (…) To meet the prerequisites of insurability, means would have to be decided to establish the

moreover, it seems that the proposal is based on assumptions[1] that do not correspond to the reality of insurance practice[2].

---

amount of compensation to be paid by the liable party. The means would need to be reliable and consistent within the European Union. Biodiversity damage as described in the proposal is not at the moment measurable and thus cannot be insured through the existing insurance solutions. There is no real experience of compensating these types of damage neither in Europe nor in the U.S. and the first attempts to develop these concepts are only in their initial stage, developed by some environmental insurance pools. Insurers are, nevertheless, willing to contribute to any development that would allow the quantification of ecological damage." See: Comité Européen des Assurances (CEA), Position paper on Environmental liability with regard to the prevention and remedying of environmental damage, May 2002.

[1] "(…) (W)hether or not liability for biodiversity damage was insurable was more controversial. This type of liability was little known in the Community, and it was sometimes argued it could not be valued and insured. Given this background, the Commission conducted a study focused on the issues associated with natural resource damage – a concept similar to biodiversity damage – liability in the U.S. Indeed in that country liability for damage to natural resources has been enacted at the same time as liability for clean-up costs, more than 20 years ago, which makes the U.S. a good test case for the insurability of biodiversity damage. The conclusions of the study show that the fears that biodiversity damage is uninsurable are misplaced. The study (...) gives two key insights. First, the liabilities created by the Commission's proposal, including biodiversity damage, can be financially assured. As a matter of fact, natural resource damage liability is currently financially assurable in the U.S. and the associated insurance markets have developed over time with little problems18. Thus there are good reasons to believe that the same will happen in the EU vis-à-vis biodiversity damage." Proposal for a Directive - Explanatory Memorandum, 7-9. The referred study is: Boyd, J. (2000), A market-based analysis of financial assurance issues associated with U.S. natural resource damage liability, Follow up study commissioned by the European Commission.

[2] "The information provided in the explanatory memorandum of the proposal concerning the US insurance system is technically speaking in most parts correct. What, however, can be disputed, are the conclusions drawn by the Commission based on this information. These conclusions are mainly based on the information on insurance for marine damage and more specifically for oil damage. In the view of CEA, the explanatory memorandum is clearly not based on an in depth analysis of the U.S. market for insurance for land based environmental damage and can therefore be seen as somewhat deceptive. The directive is incorrectly based on the presumption that insurance for the risks evolving from the envisaged regime is easily available in Europe. It is true that the number of insurers providing environmental impairment insurance in the U.S. has grown over the last decade and premiums written in the environmental insurance market presently exceed $ 1 billion annually. The number of insurance companies in the U.S. offering cover is, however, very limited and the size of the environmental insurance market is negligible compared to the whole non-life sector premium income of $ 401 billion (1999)." Comité Européen des Assurances (CEA), Position paper on Environmental liability with regard to the prevention and remedying of environmental damage, May 2002

From a broader perspective, the complex relationship that would be established between the harmonized rules and the existing national regimes raises questions as to the certainty and predictability of the resulting general legal framework.

If the **insurability of environmental pollution risks is considered as an important feature of modern environmental legislations**[1], therefore, the outlined concerns should be carefully taken into account. As long as the scope and economic consequences of environmental liabilities, be they civil or administrative, are highly unpredictable *ex ante*, in fact, the insurance industry will not be capable of assessing and managing environmental pollution risks and, therefore, it will not be willing and able to offer reasonably priced coverage[2].

B. *On legal formants and incoherence: a complex analysis*

In order to detect the second variable which affects the **level of legal uncertainty**, it is necessary to look at the way in which a given legal system actually works. The above mentioned notion of legal formants is fundamental to this layered analysis[3]. In every legal system, what is written in a statute may sometimes differ remarkably from the judgments of the courts on the same legal issue. The rule formally announced by the court in its opinion may turn out to be incompatible with the actual outcome of the case[4].

In the Italian legal system, for example, negligence is formally stated by Law 349/86 as the governing standard for environmental liabilities, but recent decisions of the Supreme Court of cassation tend to enforce a strict liability regime instead, on the argument that article 2050 of the Italian civil code, concerning strict liability for

---

[1] As the European Commission seems to recognize.

[2] "In addition to insurance mathematical calculations, insurability is the result of a complex decision-taking process by the individual insurer that involves several individual considerations. The essential precondition for any risk to be insurable is that the insurer must be able to make a realistically reliable estimate of the claim amounts to be paid out over a specific and reasonably long period. Long-tail environmental risks are problematic for insurers. Any injury, damage or loss to be compensated must be quantifiable in terms of money in line with a priori established and known criteria. The insurer has to be able to estimate the probability of any loss and also the severity of the loss. This process results in the willingness of many, few or no insurers willing to provide coverage." Comité Européen des Assurances (CEA), Position paper on Environmental liability with regard to the prevention and remedying of environmental damage, May 2002.

[3] For a discussion of the theoretical foundations of this approach, see: Mattei, U. and Monti, A. (2001), Comparative Law and Economics. Borrowing and Resistance, Global Jurist Frontiers, Vol. 1: No. 2, Article 5, 2001,
http://www.bepress.com/gj/frontiers/vol1/iss2/art5.

[4] For a sharp distinction between *definitions* and *operative rules* enforced by courts see: SACCO, cit.

dangerous activities, still applies[1]. Retroactivity is not a feature that formally characterizes the Italian environmental liability statutes, but, again, some recent court decisions affirmed the opposite principle, based on a constitutional oriented interpretation of the relevant norms. The only two reported court decisions on the issue of monetary evaluation of NRDs in Italy[2] appear to be completely arbitrary and they do not provide any clear guidance for the future implementation of the criteria set forth in art. 18 comma VI of Law 349/86. Due to analogous problems, in the United States the provision of CERCLA regarding NRDs[3], while being currently in force, has been seldom enforced by courts.

Those evidences of incoherence among legal formants greatly affect the **level of legal uncertainty**, introducing elements of destabilization that may undermine the development of a pollution insurance market.

VII. Modern environmental liability insurance approaches

A. *Integrated risk management approach through differentiation*

In response to the outlined problematic factual features of environmental pollution risk, the insurance industry has developed new techniques to cope with this peculiar phenomenon.

As anticipated in Chapter 1 of this report, the traditional insurance mechanism works on a four-phase basis: 1. risk assessment, 2. risk transferring, 3. risk pooling, 4. risk allocation. The insurer tends to remain external to the situation assessed in the first step, merely accepting or refusing to undertake a given risk. In modern environmental insurance, instead, professional risk-carriers have the knowledge and technical abilities needed to actively intervene on the risk features during a new phase, which can be named: **risk remodeling**, taking place before the transfer of risk.

At present, **pollution risk coverage** is almost completely excluded from general liability policies[4] and it is provided under separate contracts on a **site-specific** basis. The modern philosophy of ecological insurance requires an extremely **careful evaluation and classification** of the risk to be transferred. To this purpose, detailed historical information and technical data concerning the prospective insured's premises are

---

[1] See above and also: Villa, G. (2002), Il danno all'ambiente nel sistema della responsabilità civile, in Pozzo B. (ed.), La nuova responsabilità civile per danno all'ambiente, Milan: Giuffré

[2] Pretore di Milano - sez. distaccata di Rho, June 29, 1989, in *Foro it.*, 1990, II, 526; notes and comments on this decision are available in English in 6 *AIDA Pollution Bulletin*, July 1991, 7; Tribunale di Venezia, Ufficio del giudice monocratico, Sez. Penale, 27 novembre 2002, n. 1286, in Rivista giuridica dell'ambiente (n.1/2003), p. 164.

[3] See CERCLA. § 107 (1-4) (C).

[4] With some exceptions for sudden and accidental events.

collected through a preliminary questionnaire. A comprehensive inspection of the industrial installation is then performed on behalf of the insurance company by a team of qualified engineers. In addition to the evaluation of the adequacy of safety measures, protection systems and emergency plans, certain features of the surrounding area are also assessed. In this respect, several elements are taken into account, including: the density and size of population in the vicinity, the type of buildings, facilities and installations, the conditions related to emission carriers, including soil permeability, groundwater levels, the direction of winds and, in general, all the geological, hydrological and atmospheric conditions of the area.

As soon as the risk is properly assessed - if the minimal safety requirements are met - the risk carrier will cooperate, in a new phase, with the prospective insured, in order to reduce the risk and to **enhance loss prevention strategies.**

Such feature plays a very important role in this field: **prevention of environmental harm should always be among the primary goals of every ecological policy**[1]. Even if the existence of an adequate insurance coverage may give effect *ex post* to the deterrence and compensation functions of environmental liabilities, it could easily be the case that impaired natural resources are unique and not replaceable or repairable; loss prevention, therefore, acquires great importance. Moreover, it has been pointed out that *ex ante* prevention systems have the clear advantage of reducing total risk[2].

After this 'risk remodeling' phase, in which cooperation between the insurer and the insured is fundamental, **pollution coverage is tailored** on the insured's needs and it should be provided by the risk carrier on a **long term basis**. A long term contractual commitment is needed by both parties, since environmental pollution coverage is offered under new trigger-of-coverage formulas such as:

claims made[3] and

manifestation/discovery[4]

---

[1] The *Principle of Prevention*, together with the *Polluter-Pays Principle*, for example, is at the very foundations of international environmental policy announced by the European Commission.

[2] Insurance provides incentives and requirements to prevent losses. The cost and availability of insurance are often linked to specific risk-prevention measures. Application requirements and continuous monitoring tend to improve compliance with established safety standards. See: Freeman, P.K. and Kunreuther, H.C. (1997), Managing environmental risk through insurance, Boston [etc.]: Kluwer, c1997 (Studies in risk and uncertainty: 9).

[3] Under a claim made formula, coverage is triggered by the filing of a claim against the insured.

[4] Under a manifestation/discovery formula, coverage is triggered by the manifestation/discovery

Such trigger formulas have the effect to limit coverage in time[1], in order to overcome the mentioned problems concerning the latency of gradual pollution phenomena and the consequent long-tail nature of environmental legal liabilities[2]. Moreover, a stable relationship is essential to justify the reciprocal investments in cooperation. In this way, the insurer would participate with his/her **expertise and technical knowledge** in the development of each customer's risk-management strategy.

During the entire period in which the contractual relationship is in force, the risk carrier will closely monitor the insured's activity in order to prevent the negative effects of moral hazard. Moreover, additional investments in precautions and safety devices may be rewarded by the insurer with a reduction in the annual premium and/or with a broader coverage, thereby enacting and implementing a flexible mechanism of **private surrogate regulation**[3].

The point just made, therefore, lines up with the broader perspective that considers the opportunity to conceive liability insurers, in various instances, as efficient regulators of the practice of their customers[4].

Furthermore, with a view to strengthening the relationship, in addition to loss prevention consultancy and financial coverage, several insurers recently started to offer integrated services to their policyholder, the most important of which is **crisis management**. An effective crisis management service is very much appreciated by those policyholders that do not have experience in promptly reacting to the insured events (e.g. a release of toxic substance into the environment) and it may also help the insurance company to substantially reduce the total costs of covered claims.

B. *Increased market capacity through pollution insurance pools*

The current market capacity for environmental pollution risk is limited, due to the outlined peculiar factual and legal feature of the risk and because of the potential for catastrophic consequences. In this regard, it is interesting to note that in a number of European countries, insurance and reinsurance companies have formed Pools in order to aggregate capacity, develop new insurance products and share information and statistical data. The following Pools are currently in operation:

---

of pollution conditions.

[1] Extended reporting periods may be allowed, but on a limited basis.

[2] See Faure, M., Fenn, P., Retro active liability and the insurability of long-tail risks, International Review of Law and Economics, 1999, 487-500.

[3] See K. S. Abraham, Environmental Liability and the limits of insurance, cit. See also: Clifford G. Holderness, Liability Insurers as Corporate Monitors, 10 Int. Rev. of Law and Econ. 1990, 115-129.

[4] See, for example: Anthony E. Davis (1996), Professional Liability Insurance as Regulators of Law Practice, LXV Fordham Law Review, 209.

FRANCE: Assurpol

ITALY: Pool RC Inquinamento

SPAIN: Pool Español de Riesgos Medioambientales

THE NETHERLANDS: Nederlandse Milieupool

C. *Different products for different needs*

As discussed in the previous sections, the boundaries of environmental liabilities in OECD countries are expanding: an increasing number of responsible parties are called upon to comply with several remedial obligations. From an insurance point of view, therefore, a correct approach to the pollution risks entails the need for some technical distinctions. In particular, it seems important to distinguish between:

First party and third party coverages

Known and unknown pollution conditions

On site and off site contamination

Insurers are moving away from using traditional policies and conventional tools for assessing environmental exposures because they may provide inadequate cover. In the recent years, the international environmental insurance sector has developed **several types of new products** aimed at meeting different needs, taking into account that often businesses and site owners must assume **the costs of cleaning up their own polluted sites**, as well as others that may have been contaminated by their activities. The most important types of coverage are:

Environmental liability policy (EIL). Under this label, it is frequently offered a third-party coverage for damages caused to third parties claimants by pollution conditions originating from the insured plant, including mitigation costs. This type of policy, also marketed as Pollution Legal Liability policy (PLL), is written on a claims-made, manifestation or discovery basis and it generally excludes NRDs, biodiversity damages and the on-site cleanup obligations mandated by the competent authority.

Coverage for on-site cleanup liability. This type of policy offers a first-party environmental remediation coverage for the risk of incurring on-site cleanup obligations, generally excluded from the EIL policy (it shall be noted that, sometimes, EIL and PLL policies contain a first-party extension of coverage for on-site cleanup costs).

Cleanup cost cap policy (brownfield site). This type of coverage can be purchased when a claim requiring the insured to incur cleanup costs has already been made. It usually covers remediation cost overruns and other cost increases resulting from unexpected factors such as unknown or undiscovered contamination, poor remedial technology performance, regulatory changes and natural disasters, up to a limit beyond a self-insured retention. It is, therefore, designed to address the risk and uncertainty associated with beginning or continuing an environmental remediation project.

Contractors pollution legal liability. This type of policy indemnifies the insured for claims and liabilities resulting from pollution conditions arising from the insured's performance of contracting operations, including contaminated soil and hazardous waste remediation works.

Transportation coverage. This policy is aimed at covering the risks associated with accidents that may occur during the transportation of hazardous substances.

Environmental coverage for landfills. Several hybrid insurance/financial products are currently in course of development in order to meet the special needs of landfill operators: of particular concern is the fact that their responsibilities extend far beyond the time when the landfill ceases operations. Financial protection is therefore needed for the closure and post-closure phases[1].

As mentioned, some professional risk carriers offer the possibility to combine different coverages in a single tailor made insurance policy. In this respect, one of the most interesting and innovative product is the environmental coverage offered in The Netherlands by the Nederlandse Milieupool. Presented in 1998, this policy consists of an integrated environmental insurance package with several options, combining first party insurance for on-site remediation obligations and a direct coverage (not liability coverage) for damages caused by pollution to third parties, who are therefore entitled to seek indemnification directly from the insurance company that issued the policy to the polluter[2].

---

[1] See especially: Spühler, J. (2000), Environmental impairment liability insurance for landfills, Swiss Reinsurance Company, Zurich: Swiss Re Publishing.

[2] For a discussion of this policy, see: Faure, M.G., Grimeaud, D. (2000), Financial Assurance Issues of Environmental Liability – Report, Follow up study commissioned by the European Commission, 183 ff.

D. Alternative risk transfer (ART) / Alternative risk financing (ARF) methods

At present, moreover, an alternative to insurance products for the financial management of environmental pollution risks is offered by several ART/ARF products that can be tailored on the special needs of the insured. The most important are:

> **Captive insurance companies.** Captives are insurance companies formed to insure the risk of its parent corporation. A captive may be formed for a variety of reasons, including tax benefits, improved investment returns, or –as for the case of certain environmental pollution risks- the lack of other insurance alternatives. This solution, of course, is available only to large enterprises.

> **Finite risk products.** Finite risk transfer insurance is a mechanism aimed at transferring financial liabilities associated with contaminated sites from the legally responsible party (i.e. the owner or occupier) to a professional risk carrier. The insurance company agrees to assume the cleanup obligation and to conduct the remediation work on behalf of the insured. The policy addresses both known and potential unknown site conditions up to a maximum amount (limit) for predetermined period of time.

> **Loss portfolio transfers (buyouts).** A Loss Portfolio Transfer agreement (LPT) is a buyout of retained liabilities. The LPT converts unknown future liabilities to a present day fixed price. Liabilities are quantified and sold to an insurance company that assumes responsibility for future payment of the liabilities, as defined under the insurance policy. LPTs are retrospective in nature, as they involve the transfer of incurred losses.

These financial instruments are often employed to cope with the uncertainty related to the scope and extent of environmental liability exposures in corporate mergers, acquisitions and real estate transactions.

E. Statement of Environmental Commitment of the Insurance Industry

In the recent years, participants in the insurance sector began to play an eminent pro-active role in the environmental arena, voicing their concerns and interests in public and committing themselves to the Principles of Sustainable Development affirmed in the 1992 Rio Declaration on Environment and Development.

Under the auspices of the United Nations Environmental Programme[1], a "Statement of Environmental Commitment" ([1]) was signed in a ceremony at the UN

---

[1] UNEP has been working with the banking and insurance industry to try to promote greater awareness of environmental issues in the business sector to encourage sound environmental management. UNEP is dedicated to promoting sustainable development, which aims to achieve a balance between trade, development and environment.

offices in Geneva by 17 leading insurance companies on November 23, 1995. At present, 88 insurance companies (plus 3 associated members) from 26 countries joined the initiative by signing the *Statement* and the number of participants is constantly increasing.

In this significant document, the general principles of sustainable development[2] are fully recognized and translated into a commitment towards environmental protection by means of insurance practice, risk management strategies and loss prevention[3].

---

[1] **"Preamble.** The insurance industry recognizes that economic development needs to be compatible with human welfare and a healthy environment. To ignore this is to risk increasing social, environmental and financial costs. Our Industry plays an important role in managing and reducing environmental risk, in conjunction with governments, individuals and organizations. We are committed to work together to address key issues such as pollution reduction, the efficient use of resources, and climate change. We endeavour to identify realistic, sustainable solutions."

[2] **"1. General Principles of Sustainable Development**

1.1 We regard sustainable development, defined as development that meets the needs of the present without compromising the ability of future generations to meet their own needs, as a fundamental aspect of sound business management.

1.2 We believe that sustainable development is best achieved by allowing markets to work within an appropriate framework of cost efficient regulations and economic instruments. Government has a leadership role in establishing and enforcing long term priorities and values.

1.3 We regard a strong, proactive insurance industry as an important contributor to sustainable development, through its interaction with other economic sectors and consumers.

1.4 We believe that the existing skills and techniques of our industry in understanding uncertainty, identifying and quantifying risk, and responding to risk, are core strengths in managing environmental problems.

1.5 We recognize the precautionary principle, in that it is not possible to quantify some concerns sufficiently, nor indeed to reconcile all impacts in purely financial terms. Research is needed to reduce uncertainty but cannot eliminate it entirely."

[3] **"2. Environmental Management**

2.1 We will reinforce the attention given to environmental risks in our core activities. These activities include risk management, loss prevention, product design, claims handling and asset management.

2.2 We are committed to manage internal operations and physical assets under our control in a manner that reflects environmental considerations.

2.3 We will periodically review our management practices, to integrate relevant developments of environmental management in our planning, marketing, employee communications and training as well as our other core activities.

2.4 We encourage research in these and related issues. Responses to environmental

VIII.   Environmental risk and insurance: a problem of incentives

In light of this modern and innovative attitude adopted by the industry, insurance seems to be an appropriate legal and economic tool available to complement both the liability system and the regulatory framework with respect to the environmental pollution risk.

Modern environmental insurance would in fact solve, at least partially[1], the judgment proof (insolvency) problem that potentially undermines the effectiveness of any environmental liability regime and it would also increase loss prevention, by stimulating the adoption of tailored safety measures.

At present, however, it can be empirically observed that environmental insurance is not widespread at all. Gradual pollution coverage is often perceived as too costly by

---

issues can vary in effectiveness and cost. We encourage research that identifies creative and effective solutions.

2.5 We support insurance products and services that promote sound environmental practice through measures such as loss prevention and contract terms and conditions. While satisfying requirements for security and profitability, we will seek to include environmental considerations in our asset management.

2.6 We will conduct regular internal environmental reviews, and will seek to create measurable environmental goals and standards.

2.7 We shall comply with all applicable local, national and international environmental regulations. Beyond compliance, we will strive to develop and adopt best practices in environmental management. We will support our clients, partners and suppliers to do likewise.

3. Public Awareness and Communications

3.1 Bearing in mind commercial confidence, we are committed to share relevant information with our stakeholders, including clients, intermediaries, shareholders, employees and regulators. By doing so we will improve society's response to environmental challenges.

3.2 Through dialogue with public authorities and other bodies we aim to contribute to the creation of a more effective framework for sustainable development.

3.3 We will work with the United Nations Environment Programme to further the principles and goals of this Statement, and look for UNEP's active support.

3.4 We will encourage other insurance institutions to support this Statement. We are committed to share with them our experiences and knowledge in order to extend best practices.

3.5 We will actively communicate our environmental activities to the public, review the success of this Statement periodically, and we expect all signatories to make real progress."

[1] It depends, of course, on the maximum available policy limits.

---

the industry and most firms do not decide to insure against environmental risks spontaneously.

The cost of environmental insurance policies is affected by the complexity of the new techniques outlined, by the factual features of the risk itself[1] and by the level of legal uncertainty. As a general rule, the prospective insured has to bear the costs of site inspections and technical analyses, costs that could be considerable if the insured has several premises. Moreover, many companies are very reserved about their properties, since most public law schemes dealing with soil contamination made it compulsory to immediately inform the competent authorities, should the site inspection reveal any pollution on the insured's premises.

Another explanation of the difficulties experienced by most insurers in marketing environmental liability policies and other pollution coverages can be found in the fact that gradual pollution risk is often a low probability/high consequences risk (LPHC) and, generally, such risks are not rationally faced by economic actors: they can be easily underestimated or even ignored[2].

Even from a pure rational choice theory point of view, moreover, the limited liability structure of corporations introduces significant distortions in the picture and it may alter the proper incentives mechanism[3]. Given the magnitude of potential losses associated with polluting events, in fact, it might often be the case that the amount of the expected damage greatly exceeds the limited financial exposure of the liable party (i.e. the polluter).

Another phenomenon that widely occurs is the following: after the plant has passed the insurability inspection performed by the risk-carrier's engineers, the prospective insured refuses to purchase coverage because he/she feels that his/her activity is safe enough. Of course, the fact that a plant is insurable does not mean that it is completely safe and that an accident will never occur. The satisfactory results of the inspection, instead, merely indicate that the risk posed by that particular installation presents the characteristics of predictability that allow a professional risk carrier to undertake it. In any event, many firms have clearly stated that they will not buy pollution coverage unless they are obliged to do so.

---

[1] See B. Berliner and J. Spühler, "Insurability issues associated with managing existing hazardous waste sites", in *Integrating Insurance & Risk Management for Hazardous Waste*, edited by Howard Kunreuther and Rajeev Gowda, Kluwer Academic Publishers 1990.

[2] See Kunreuther & Slovic, "Economics, Psychology Protective Behavior", 68 *American Economic Ass'n Proceedings* 1978, 64; Kunreuther, "Limited Knowledge and Insurance Protection", 24 Public Policy 1976, 227; Camerer & Kunreuther, "Decision Processes for Low Probability events: Policy Implications", 8 *Journal of Policy Analysis and Management* 1989, 565-592.

[3] See Hansmann & Kraakman, "Towards Unlimited Shareholder Liability for Corporate Torts", 100 *Yale* L. J. 1879.

IX. Compulsory environmental liability insurance?

Further to the above considerations, a system of **mandatory pollution insurance** - at least for those activities that are particularly dangerous for the environment – might seem to be the appropriate solution. Even this conclusion, nevertheless, turns out to be, in practice, rather problematic.

A system of compulsory insurance can be bilateral or unilateral. In the former case, the firm has the obligation to buy coverage in order to be allowed to operate and the insurance industry has the obligation to provide coverage at pre-determined conditions, approved by the authority, to each and every applicant. Bilateral mandatory pollution insurance, however, is **incompatible with the very nature of modern environmental insurance techniques**. As mentioned, environmental policies are tailor-made and site-specific and not every plant necessarily has all those characteristics that make it insurable. Standard conditions set by legislature and applicable to every insured, moreover, would drag pollution insurance back to the traditional standardized scheme, which proved to be highly inappropriate in this context. A regime of bilateral compulsory insurance, moreover, may be quite problematic if certain defences based on the insurance contract (in particular: exclusions and conditions of coverage, such as regulatory compliance, etc.) are not opposable to the third party claimant and the insurance company is therefore forced to pay and bear the risk of insolvency of its insured.

As long as unilateral mandatory insurance is concerned, purchase of pollution coverage is still a condition to operate for the firms, but insurers do not have any obligation and they may, therefore, refuse coverage to anyone at their own discretion. In this latter case, the enhanced incentive mechanism provided by modern environmental insurance would be able to work properly, but the insurance industry would be placed in the uncomfortable and inappropriate position of **environmental policeman**. In fact, the insurer would be entrusted with the power to decide which firms can continue their activity and which should, instead, withdraw from the market[1]. This is a policy choice that the authority has to make.

The question of compulsory insurance, in any event, must be examined taking the degree of market maturity and the homogeneous character of the risk to be insured into account: products developed to date vary from one market to another and a single product at European level is difficult to envisage at the moment. It should be clear, however, that a strict environmental liability regime, without any requirement for financial security, can easily turn out to be completely ineffective and it may just lead to an increase in litigation and transaction costs.

---

[1] "Government regulation that requires insurance as a "virtual license to operate" turns insurers into regulators. This changes the focus of government regulation and makes insurers watchdogs over their customers rather than service providers." See: Freeman, P.K. and Kunreuther, H.C. (1997), Managing environmental risk through insurance, Boston [etc.]: Kluwer, c1997 (Studies in risk and uncertainty: 9).

X. Financial security: possible alternatives

Insurance is not the only way to provide adequate financial guarantee with respect to the environmental pollution risk. There exist, in fact, a variety of other financial instruments that could be employed, including:

Guarantee issued by a bank or another financial institution;

Personal or collateral security;

Deposit paid in advance on an environmental account.

Instead of establishing a compulsory environmental insurance regime, therefore, the introduction of an obligation to provide financial security in any form approved by the competent authority may turn out to be a viable way to overcome the insolvency problems[1]. In this perspective, insurance would become just one of the possible ways to comply with a flexible financial guarantee obligation and competition among different forms of financial security would be highly stimulated by such a regime.

XI. Compensation for historic pollution, diffuse pollution and orphan shares. Limits of the liability regime.

As already pointed out, the social allocation of pollution risks and costs by way of an environmental liability regime does not appear to be appropriate in certain situations. In particular, a liability regime should certainly not cover:

Historic pollution.

Pollution for which a causal relation to a responsible party cannot be established.

The cumulative effect of authorized emissions.

For residual pollution damages falling in the above categories, as well as for the cases in which a responsible party under the liability regime cannot be identified or is insolvent (orphaned liabilities), other compensation mechanisms should be designed. The public authority (i.e. the State) may be ultimately responsible for such costs, so to minimize the distortion provoked by any redistribution policy, or some sort of compensation fund may be established and maintained[2].

---

[1] An ample discussion is offered by: Faure, M.G., Grimeaud, D. (2000), Financial Assurance Issues of Environmental Liability – Report, Follow up study commissioned by the European Commission, 188 ff.

[2] On this issue see: Faure, M.G., Grimeaud, D. (2000), Financial Assurance Issues of Environmental Liability – Report, Follow up study commissioned by the European

In this respect, the significant experience with the functioning of the **Superfund** established in the **United States** by the Comprehensive Environmental Response, Compensation and Liability Act of 1980 is a prominent example of possible advantages and disadvantages.

The new **Environmental Damage Insurance Act** (81/1998), which came into force in **Finland** on 1 January 1999, is another interesting example. The act creates a fund whose aim is to guarantee full compensation for environmental damage, including the costs of measures taken to prevent or limit the damage and to restore the environment to its previous state, in cases where those liable for compensation are insolvent, or the liable party cannot be identified (i.e. the orphan shares under the Environmental Damage Act of 1994). The scheme is financed by special insurance which is compulsory for the operators of high risk activities subject to a regime of environmental operating permits.

Sweden has a similar system based on Chapter 33 (Environmental damage insurance and environmental clean-up insurance) of the new **Swedish Environmental Code**. Persons who pursue environmentally hazardous activities for which a permit must be obtained or notification submitted are required to pay contributions to the insurance scheme. If environmental damage insurance or environmental clean-up insurance contributions are not paid within thirty days of the date of demand, the insurer is obliged to report the nonpayment to the supervisory authority that may issue a compliance order backed by the threat of a fine. Compensation is paid out of the environmental damage insurance, in accordance with the relevant terms and conditions, to claimants for bodily injury and material damage, where: 1. the liable party is insolvent or the right to demand compensation has lapsed; or 2. it cannot be established who is liable for the injury or damage. Compensation is paid out of the environmental clean-up insurance for any costs for clean-up that are incurred in consequence of an authority's request, where the person who is liable pursuant to the Environmental Code is not able to pay.

XII. Policy conclusions

The theoretical analysis and the comparative overview conducted in this Chapter of the report are aimed to show some of the most problematic features of environmental pollution risk, as well as the recent and innovative responses of the international insurance industry. They are also aimed at pointing out the way in which different legal frameworks may affect pollution risk insurability and the development of effective risk management strategies.

These issues are currently of great concern, since modern **environmental insurance** seems to have the potential to become a very effective complement to liability and regulation in this field:

- ecological insurance, in fact, would give effect to the compensation function

---

Commission, 198 ff.

of any environmental liability regime, providing the injured parties with a reliable source of funds when pollution occurs;

- moreover, with a view to reducing the risk of a polluting event, the insurer may act as a private surrogate regulator, thereby aligning the interests of the insured with the most advanced environmental safety concerns;

- furthermore, by forcing the ex ante internalization of environmental costs through the payment of premiums, environmental insurance proves to be fully compatible with the deterrence goal of any liability regime and also with the polluter pays principle.

In order to encourage and stimulate the development and growth of the pollution insurance market, law and policy makers should put their best efforts in circumscribing, limiting and defining with a sufficient level of clarity and predictability the financial risks associated with environmental pollution liabilities. *Ex ante* regulation of environmentally dangerous activities also plays a fundamental role, as the public authority should be able to guarantee the enforcement of up-to-date safety and protection standards. Moreover, the enactment of rules mandating the responsibility for provision of adequate financial security, in a form to be approved by the competent authority, seems highly advisable, with a view to preventing the risk of insolvency. If pollution insurance turned out to be a competitive way to comply with this financial requirement, then the socially beneficial effects of modern environmental insurance could be appreciated to a full extent. For residual pollution damages falling outside the scope of the liability regime, as well as for the cases in which a responsible party cannot be identified, or the financial guarantees have been exhausted (orphaned liabilities), the public authority should be ultimately responsible for setting up of a complementary no-fault environmental compensation scheme, aimed at guaranteeing adequate funding for expedite pollution remediation.

CHAPTER 3

NATURAL CATASTROPHE RISK AND INSURANCE

I. The increasing risk of loss from natural catastrophes

The risk from natural disasters is increasing. Large losses created, among others, by hurricane Andrew in Florida in 1992, the Northridge earthquake in California in 1994, the Kobe earthquake in Japan in 1995, the Kocaeli earthquake in Turkey in 1999, windstorms Lothar and Martin in Europe in 1999, the Bhuj, Gujarat earthquake in India on January 26, 2001 and tropical storm Allison in the USA in 2001 put large strains on the financial capacities of the international reinsurance market and, consequently, catastrophe insurance coverage availability has substantially diminished over the past years.

The increase in the magnitude of actual and insured losses from natural disasters in the past fifteen years has significantly exceeded the predictions of the insurance industry. The size of the losses resulting from an environmental catastrophe depends on both the severity of the natural forces involved, the vulnerability of buildings and infrastructures and the efficacy of plans and emergency strategies for disaster control and mitigation implemented in the afflicted region[1]. Not surprisingly, among the several causes of this unprecedented increase in losses and risk estimates are new urbanization developments in hazard-prone areas and the lack of enforcement of building codes and land-use regulations; higher population densities, the increased concentration of values in exposed locations and the adverse meteorological effects of global climate change contribute to amplify the magnitude of the problem.

In the recent years, therefore, the threat of a mega-disaster striking a major inhabited area has dramatically altered the insurance environment. Today many insurers and reinsurers indicate that they cannot continue to provide the same level of coverage against hurricanes, floods and earthquakes, without incurring an excessive risk of insolvency or substantial losses of capital or surplus. These concerns stem from a balanced reassessment of the insurance industry's financial exposures following the severe losses cited above.

---

[1] See: Swiss Reinsurance Company (2002), Natural Catastrophes and man-made disasters in 2001, Swiss Re SIGMA series 1/2002. Zurich, Swiss Reinsurance Company; Kunreuther, H.C. and R.J. Roth (ed.) (1998), Paying the Price: The Status and Role of Insurance Against Natural Disasters in the United States. Washington DC, Joseph Henry Press; Pollner, J. (2000), Catastrophe Risk Management Using Alternative Risk Financing & Insurance Pooling Mechanisms: The Insurance Market and the Case of the Caribbean Region. Washington DC: World Bank; Kunreuther, H.C. (2000), Linking Insurance and Mitigation to Manage Natural Hazard Disaster Risk, *Handbook of Insurance,* Georges Dionne (Ed.), Kluwer Academic Publishers, Boston; Froot, K. A. (ed.) (1999). The Financing of Catastrophe Risk. Chicago, University of Chicago Press.

II. The financial burden of natural disasters

The financial burden of natural disaster is extremely large and the insurance and reinsurance industry may be able to handle a substantial part of it only within the appropriate legal and regulatory framework. With respect to natural catastrophe risk, in fact, insurers face several difficult challenges. The essential problem concerns the ability of the traditional insurance mechanism to properly manage low probability and high consequences (LPHC) events, such as natural catastrophes. As mentioned in the previous paragraph, the insurance and reinsurance capacity for natural hazards risks is currently quite limited. The financial management of natural catastrophe risk is quite costly and troublesome for the industry, mainly because of:

- the magnitude of expected insured losses (i.e. the size of aggregate claims in case of a disaster) and

- the inter-temporal mismatch between the size of annual premiums and the size of the annual expected losses.

In other words, it shall be noted that the risk of loss from natural catastrophes is **correlated both temporally and spatially** and this creates both **geographical and inter-temporal risk spreading problems**.

The **risk of accumulation** is quite high in the primary market, since the same catastrophic event can cause losses involving many different insured properties and infrastructures at the same time, giving rise to immense claims burdens in a single policy period.

Adverse selection is another problem that may negatively affect the ability of insurance company to spread the risk of loss geographically, even on a national market ([1]). Effective risk spreading, therefore, can be performed only on a global scale, through a series of international reinsurance arrangements[2].

Another problem concerns the **low level of predictability of natural hazards risk**: until recent years, in fact, there has been a general lack of reliable data and objective information concerning the economic effects of natural disasters. Considerable uncertainty is associated with the estimation of the probability of disasters of different magnitudes occurring and the size of the resulting losses. Technology and computer modeling of natural perils have only recently reached the point where the risks can be clarified. As already pointed out in Chapter 2 of this report, it has been demonstrated that the limited (bounded) rationality of several individuals may lead them to

---

[1] See, supra Part I at § 2.b.

[2] See Swiss Reinsurance Company (2002), Natural Catastrophes and man-made disasters in 2001, Swiss Re SIGMA series 1/2002. Zurich, Swiss Reinsurance Company.

underestimate or ignore LPHC risks[1]: even a reasonably priced catastrophe insurance coverage, therefore, may often be perceived by prospective insureds as too costly.

III. The importance of public-private partnership for disaster management

In light of the above considerations, it seems clear that the financial burden of natural catastrophe risk cannot be carried exclusively by the private insurance sector. Some of the major obstacles to insurability, however, may be overcome through the proactive intervention of the public sector. Besides, the general trend in OECD countries is towards some sort of co-operation between governments and the private sector in the management of natural disaster risks.

The public authority can play a fundamental role by:

- providing the requisite legal framework
- subsidizing the cost of administering the disaster management scheme
- subsidizing the cost of insurance to the beneficiaries
- being a reinsurer of last resort.

The public authority as the insurer of last resort is in a better position to deal with the extreme loss potentials than are private insurance companies with limited capital and capacity[2]: governments, moreover, have the power to enforce the adoption of appropriate risk mitigation measures and to make catastrophe insurance coverage mandatory, thereby spreading the risk throughout the entire society.

The private insurance sector, in turn, has the requisite technical expertise for providing:

- proper risk assessment and risk allocation mechanisms;
- expedite loss adjustment services;
- effective surrogate regulation.

The payment of losses through risk-based insurance policies is self-funded from premiums received. This mechanism makes insurance a reliable financial tool for managing and funding risk, because insurance specializes in reserving and investing collected funds for the purpose of claims payment. With respect to natural catastrophe risk, an insurance-based mechanism is more likely to have funds to cover losses over time than an *ex post* governmental aid disaster program, which may have to compete for

---

[1] See e.g.: Camerer & Kunreuther (1989), Decision Processes for Low Probability events: Policy Implications, 8 Journal of Policy Analysis and Management 1989, 565-592.

[2] See Swiss Reinsurance Company (2002), Natural Catastrophes and man-made disasters in 2001, Swiss Re SIGMA series 1/2002. Zurich, Swiss Reinsurance Company.

funding with other programs that are subject to changes in the political climate[1]. The solid experience of the private insurance sector in assessing risks and adjusting losses, moreover, may offer great advantages. Efficient and expedite claims settlements practices may lead to socially beneficial results. Risk-based insurance, finally, may be able to provide additional precautionary incentives for policyholders, through the mechanism of private surrogate regulation already described in Chapter 2.

The establishment of government-subsidized insurance-based schemes for disasters management is a common example of public-private partnership in OECD countries.

IV. A comparative overview of different legal and regulatory frameworks

Complex governmental risk management strategies have been implemented in several legal systems. Some of the most significant institutional arrangements involving an insurance-based public-private partnership are discussed in this section. Comparative tables summarizing these arrangements are presented at the end of this section.

> **FRANCE**: **National Disaster Compensation Scheme (CAT NAT) and the role of the Caisse Centrale de Réassurance (CCR).** In France, a national disaster compensation scheme has been established by law in 1982. Law n.82-600 of 13 July 1982 (*Loi relative à l'indemnisation des victimes de catastrophes naturelles*) provides for a compulsory natural disaster extension on all property damage policies purchased on the voluntary market[2]. Coverage under the catastrophe extension is triggered when the state of natural disaster is declared by inter-ministerial decree; the damaged property must be covered by a "property damage" insurance policy and a causal link must be established between the catastrophe declared in the decree and the damage suffered by the property insured[3].

---

[1] See: Freeman, P.K. and Kunreuther, H.C. (1997), Managing environmental risk through insurance, Boston [etc.]: Kluwer, c1997 (Studies in risk and uncertainty: 9).

[2] Pursuant to Article 1 of the Law 82-600: « Les contrats d'assurance, souscrits par toute personne physique ou morale autre que l'Etat et garantissant les dommages d'incendie ou tous autres dommages à des biens situés en France, ainsi que les dommages aux corps de véhicules terrestres à moteur, ouvrent droit à la garantie de l'assuré contre les effets des catastrophes naturelles sur les biens faisant l'objet de tels contrats. En outre, si l'assuré est couvert contre les pertes d'exploitation, cette garantie est étendue aux effets des catastrophes naturelles, dans les conditions prévues au contrat correspondant. Sont considérés comme les effets des catastrophes naturelles, au sens de la présente loi, les dommages matériels directs ayant eu pour cause déterminante l'intensité anormale d'un agent naturel, lorsque les mesures habituelles à prendre pour prévenir ces dommages n'ont pu empêcher leur survenance ou n'ont pu être prises. (...)». For the detailed legislative provisions currently in force see: Code des Assurance (Partie Législative) Titre II - Chapitre V: L'assurance des risques de catastrophes naturelles (Articles L125-1 to L125-6).

[3] "The legislators did not want to limit the 1982 Law by creating a list of the natural phenomena

Pursuant to a decree of 10 August 1982 (defining standard clauses), the catastrophe insurance guarantee must cover the cost of direct material damage suffered by the property up to the value stated in the policy and subject to the terms and conditions of the said policy at the time the risk first occurs. The natural disaster coverage is also extended to in all business interruption policies. In this case, it covers loss of gross profit and additional operating costs during the indemnity period specified in the policy. Claims are settled on the basis of the "damage" cover under the policy with the widest scope and indemnity is provided in the same way as under the basic cover. According to the rules of the scheme, the insured parties must retain a portion of the risk, by means of a statutory deductible that cannot be bought back even by means of another policy. Deductibles are compulsory – i.e. they apply even when the basic policy does not include them - and their amount is determined and updated by means of decrees issued periodically of the competent authority. Since 1 January 2001, a sliding scale has been introduced to vary these deductibles so as to encourage loss prevention measures. This scale applies to those districts, which do not yet have a prevention plan for foreseeable natural risks (PPR). In other words, when a state of natural disaster is declared in such a district as a result of the occurrence of a given peril (e.g. flood), a coefficient is applied to the applicable statutory deductibles based on the number of decrees already issued in such area, in respect of the same peril, since 2 February 1995 (date of creation of PPR's). The sliding scale ceases to apply as soon as a PPR is set up for the peril in question, but it will be reapplied if the PPR is not approved within five years. As in the case of deductibles, the rates of additional premium for the compulsory catastrophe extension are set by decree. Since 1 September 1999, the rate of catastrophe premiums for property other than motor vehicles is 12% of the premium or contribution paid for the basic property coverage. This complex scheme is able to work effectively due to the fact that the Caisse Centrale de Réassurance (CCR), a state-owned company, entered into an agreement with the authorities that allows it to offer reinsurance cover with a **government guarantee** in the field of natural disasters. CCR does not have a monopoly in natural disaster reinsurance: primary carriers, therefore, are free to seek coverage from the reinsurer of their choice, and may even take the risk of not underwriting reinsurance. In any event, CCR remains the only company within its sector of activity which offers a whole range of reinsurance solutions with **unlimited cover**. This is, of course, a great

---

covered. Nor did they want to create a list of exclusions. They limited themselves, therefore, to the idea of "uninsurable damage" (this idea was then clarified by the Laws of 25 June 1990 and 16 July 1992). The following list is not, therefore, exhaustive: floods and/or mudslides, earthquakes, landslides, subsidence (collapse of land due to a sudden fall in the ground water level, after a drought for example), tidal waves, flows of water, mud or lava, moving masses of ice or snow." Les catastrophes naturelles en France. Natural disasters in France, CCR: June 2001.

advantage for insurers, since it gives them absolute security in the event of a major loss, be it a large-scale event such as a flood occurring every hundred years or a geological problem such as subsidence, which causes all kinds of damage. CCR thus provides a guarantee of solvency and security for insureds within the French natural disaster compensation scheme[1]. CCR offers two reinsurance solutions, which are combined to provide **two-fold reinsurance cover** to primary catastrophe risk carriers. Under the first solution, known as "quota-share", the insurer cedes a certain proportion of the premiums collected to the reinsurer and the latter, in return, undertakes to pay the same proportion of losses. Quota-share reinsurance ensures that the reinsurer truly follows the fortunes of the insurer, since the latter has to cede a percentage of each of the accounts in its portfolio to the reinsurer. Thus the risk of anti-selection is avoided. The second solution, known as "stop-loss", covers the portion not ceded on a quota-share basis by the Insurer, in other words the Insurer's retention. This is a non-proportional form of reinsurance because, contrary to the "quota-share" system, the reinsurer only intervenes if the total annual losses exceed an agreed figure, expressed as a percentage of the premiums retained. In particular, this type of reinsurance enables the insurer to protect itself against the frequency or accumulation risk, i.e. the risk of many claims occurring at the same time. Although most "stop-loss" reinsurance treaties contain a limit of indemnity, CCR's cover in the field of natural disasters is unlimited thanks to the State guarantee from which it benefits. The deductible under the CCR treaty therefore represents the maximum amount which an insurer will have to bear in the course of a single underwriting year, however many losses occur[2]. Pursuant to the provisions of the Insurance Code, the Natural Disaster Central Rating Bureau (*Bureau Central de Tarification des Catastrophes Naturelles*) is entrusted with several regulatory powers with respect to the governance of the CAT NAT scheme. Articles R 250-2 and R250-3, for example, lay out the procedure for referring certain controversial matters to the Bureau, such as the refusal to grant coverage by at least two insurance companies and the failure of the insured to conform to the provisions of a disaster prevention plan.

SPAIN: Consorcio de Compensación de Seguros. Set up in 1941 as a provisional body [3] to face the needs for indemnities resulting from the Civil War (1936-1939), the Spanish Consorcio de Compensación de

---

[1] See: Les catastrophes naturelles en France. Natural disasters in France, CCR: June 2001. See also: Guy Carpenter & Co., Inc. (2001), The World Catastrophe Reinsurance Market: 2001.

[2] Les catastrophes naturelles en France. Natural disasters in France, CCR: June 2001.

[3] The original name was: Consorcio de Compensación de Riesgos de Motín - Consortium for the Compensation of Riot Risks.

Seguros was given its permanent status from 1954. After that date, the activity of the Consorcio focused on the coverage of the so-called extraordinary risks and it began to play a central role in the related indemnity system. Since the approval of its Legal Statute in 1990[1], which came into force in 1991, the Consorcio lost its legal monopoly for covering extraordinary risks in Spain and it is no longer a self-running body of the Ministry of Economy and Finance, but a state-owned company - currently a public business entity - with full powers to act. The Consorcio has its own assets and liabilities, separate from those of the State, and its activity is governed by private law. This means that the new company, when doing insurance business, apart from being governed by the terms of its own Legal Statute, is subject, like any other private insurance company, to the legal rules laid down in the Private Insurance Ordering and Supervision Act and its enacting regulations, and to the Insurance Contract Act, while its activity is governed by private law. The aim of the Consorcio is to indemnify claims made as a result of extraordinary events, such as natural disasters or other events with heavy social repercussion, that occur in Spain and cause injuries and damage to people and assets in Spain, whenever any of the following conditions are met: *a)* the extraordinary risk is not specifically and explicitly covered by another insurance policy; *b)* the extraordinary risk is covered by another insurance policy but the company that issued this policy cannot face its obligations. To sum up, the Consorcio currently acts in the Spanish system of coverage of extraordinary risks in a subsidiary way, as it only pays out indemnities when the private insurance company does not cover the risks in question, or when it does cover them but is insolvent. In case of occurrence of an extraordinary event of the type included in the system, one is only entitled to indemnity when he has a policy in certain classes of insurance, which cover persons and assets located in Spain, and if the insured is up to date with payments of the premium receipts, which include the Consorcio's surcharge for covering extraordinary risks. On the other hand, whenever insurance cover of a certain type[2] is taken out, the same assets covered for the same sums insured must be necessarily covered against extraordinary risks. In other words, the extraordinary risk coverage is compulsorily linked with a base policy. Contracting this policy with any company operating in the market is an optional choice, but it is, however, a "sine qua non" condition for entitlement to an indemnity in the event of an extraordinary claim. In respect to the cover for natural catastrophes, a change was made in 1986

---

[1] See: Law 21/1990 of 19 December 1990, amended by Law 30/1995 of 8 November 1995.

[2] With regard to personal insurance: accident coverage taken out separately or as a complement to life insurance or pension plans or funds. With regard to property insurance: fire and natural perils, motor vehicles (damage to vehicle), vehicles running on rails, theft, plate glass, machinery breakdown, electronic equipment and computers, and damage to completed civil works.

from a system of indemnities based on a prior official declaration of a disaster area which took the geographical area of the loss and the volume of losses into account to a system of **automatic indemnity**, which provides cover subject only to the prerequisite that the policies, the damage and the events giving rise to the loss meet the legally established parameters. Another qualitative change in the same year concerned the surcharge used to fund the Consorcio in order to face extraordinary claims: instead of charging a percentage on the premiums, a system of own rates is now applied on the sums insured in the policies. The Consorcio's surcharge must be compulsorily incorporated into the premium charged for every policy of insurance in the mentioned classes, irrespective of whether the said policy provides for the coverage of extraordinary risks to be effected by the private Company, or whether this is excluded (in which case the Consorcio shall be responsible).This compulsory nature lies in the principles of "compensation" and "solidarity" that govern the Spanish system, without which it would not be possible to cope with the natural anti-selection of these risks. The surcharge of the Consorcio is the result of applying its own rate on the sums insured in the policies. With respect to property damage, the indemnity paid by the Consorcio solely covers **material** losses, regarded as being the destruction or deterioration of the property insured, and **direct** losses (not including, therefore, loss of profits), so damage caused directly by the event. It should also be pointed out, furthermore, that protection against extraordinary risks is entirely separate from protection against other risks provided for in the policy. In other words, the coverage of the extraordinary risks protects the same property or persons at least for the same sum insured. The main sources of the Consorcio's funds for meeting its commitments in covering extraordinary risks are the aforementioned surcharges. Just like any other insurance company, the Consorcio applies current rules on the Solvency Margin and for setting up Technical Reserves. Besides this, given the special features of frequency and intensity of the risks that are to be faced there is a need for special funding capacity, based on an adequate and sufficient accumulation of resources and on broad compensation in time, which in the case of the Consorcio takes the form of a **stabilization reserve.** This is something rather like a loss fluctuation reserve, commonly used when insuring against disasters in many countries, which is accumulative -in some cases up to certain limits- and is tax exempt. In the Spanish system, it is a reserve with no accumulation top, which is tax deductible up to a certain limit set by law. But it should be borne in mind that, in actual fact, the aim is not to compensate unexpected deviations, but rather to accept the certainty of cyclical points of losses which occur in a fortuitous manner, and to time the funding of their costs by means of a constant premium. Taking into account the special features of this cover and the very nature of the Consorcio as a state-owned company, it is essential that the Consorcio be backed by the Government guarantee in order to meet any indemnity obligations that overrun its financial capacity. However, the adequate reserves collection have enabled the Consorcio to meet its indemnity liabilities without ever having to resort to this Government guarantee.

USA: National Flood Insurance Program (NFIP). The U.S. Congress established the NFIP on August 1, 1968 - with the passage of the National Flood Insurance Act of 1968 -, in response to the rising cost of taxpayer funded disaster relief for flood victims and the increasing amount of damage caused by floods. The NFIP makes federally-backed flood insurance available in communities that agree to adopt and enforce floodplain management ordinances to reduce future flood damage. The NFIP was broadened and modified with the passage of the Flood Disaster Protection Act of 1973 and other legislative measures. It was further modified by the National Flood Insurance Reform Act of 1994, signed into law on September 23, 1994. The NFIP is administered by the Federal Insurance and Mitigation Administration (FIMA) and the Mitigation Directorate (MT), components of the Federal Emergency Management Agency (FEMA), an independent Federal agency[1]. The NFIP is a federal program enabling property owners in participating communities to purchase insurance protection against losses from flooding. This insurance is designed to provide an insurance alternative to disaster assistance to meet the escalating costs of repairing damage to buildings and their contents caused by floods. Participation in the NFIP is based on an agreement between local communities and the Federal Government that states if a community will adopt and enforce a floodplain management ordinance to reduce future flood risks to new construction in Special Flood Hazard Areas (SFHA), the Federal Government will make flood insurance available within the community as a financial protection against flood losses. The NFIP, through partnerships with communities, the insurance industry, and the lending industry, helps reduce flood damage. The NFIP is self-supporting for the average historical loss year, which means that operating expenses and flood insurance claims are not paid for by the taxpayer, but through premiums collected for flood insurance policies.

CALIFORNIA: California Earthquake Authority (CEA). California law requires all insurers to offer earthquake insurance with every homeowner's policy. Established in 1996 to relieve pressure on private insurers, the California Earthquake Authority is a privately financed, state-run insurance program that sells a "mini-policy" with a larger deductible and more limited coverage of external structures than conventional earthquake insurance policies. The State offers no guarantee: therefore, if losses from an earthquake drain the established

---

[1] See: http://www.fema.gov/nfip/

fund, the CEA may run out of business and claims will be paid out on a pro-rated basis.

FLORIDA: Florida Hurricane Catastrophe Fund (FHCF). In 1993, the State of Florida established the Florida Hurricane Catastrophe Fund (FHCF) to allow insurers to transfer a portion of their catastrophic risk. The Fund reimburses a fraction of insurers' losses caused by sever hurricanes and it is funded by premiums paid by insurers that write policies on personal and commercial residential properties. An important provision limits the Fund's obligation to pay losses to the sum of its assets and borrowing capacity. This fund is tax-exempt, enabling it to accumulate funds rapidly. The industry is responsible for losses up to a certain level; the premiums they pay for the reinsurance can be passed onto policyholders. In addition to premiums, these programs can use bonding and other financing arrangements if they have a shortfall. The policyholders, however, would have to foot the bill for the financing through assessments on their policies. If the funds are not adequate, claims are paid on a pro-rated basis so policyholders have no guarantee claims their losses will be covered.

HAWAII: Hawaii Hurricane Relief Fund (HHRF). In 1993, Hawaii created a voluntary homeowner's catastrophe fund in order to provide hurricane insurance for customers of insurers which would no longer voluntary offer such coverage. The Hawaii Hurricane Relief Fund (HHRF), a state-run insurance company, is made up of premiums paid, loans from the federal government, bond proceeds, mortgage fees and insurer assessments. The Fund discontinued its operation by the end of 2000, in light of improved private market conditions.

NEW ZEALAND: Earthquake Commission (EQC). The Earthquake Commission (EQC) is New Zealand's primary provider of seismic disaster insurance to residential property owners[1]. The EQC is a Crown Entity, wholly owned by the government of New Zealand and controlled by a board of commissioners. Crown Entities are not Government departments or state-owned enterprises but nevertheless belong to the Government and are subject to public sector finance and reporting rules. EQC administers the Natural Disaster Fund. The Government guarantees that this fund will meet all its obligations. It does this by securing New Zealand residential property owners against the cost of these disasters and by helping organize repair and replacement after the event. The main mechanism for this is the provision of seismic disaster insurance to property owners who insure against fire. All residential property owners who buy fire insurance from private insurance companies automatically

---

[1] See: http://www.eqc.govt.nz/

acquire EQCover, the Commission's seismic disaster insurance cover[1]. EQCover premiums are added to the cost of the fire insurance and passed on to EQC by the insurance company. EQC's administration of the natural disaster insurance scheme involves: collecting premiums via insurance companies; processing and meeting claims by insured people; administering a disaster fund; investing the fund in accordance with Government directions; organizing reinsurance as a potential supplement to the fund; accounting to its shareholder (the Government). EQC also encourages and funds research about matters relevant to natural disaster damage and it educates and otherwise informs people about what can be done to prevent and mitigate damage caused by natural disasters.

JAPAN: Japanese Earthquake Reinsurance (JER). Japan has had an earthquake program covering residential properties since 1966. The Earthquake Insurance Act entered into force in such year and it had been reformed several times since its enactment. In accordance with the promulgation of this law and following the launch of sales of residential properties earthquake insurance to be written in conjunction with dwelling and shop-owners comprehensive insurance policies, Japan Earthquake Reinsurance Company (JER) was established by 20 domestic non-life insurance companies. Under the Japanese earthquake insurance program, primary carriers sell earthquake policies with large deductibles on the voluntary market and then reinsure their risk 100 percent with JER, which, in turn, retrocedes part of the risk to the private reinsurance market[2]. Since coverage costs home owners considerable amount of additional premium and is not mandatory, not so many of them purchase it[3]. JER is Japan's only specialized reinsurance company for residential properties earthquake insurance and, according to the relevant provisions of law, its solvency is supported by special arrangements with the Japanese government.

TURKEY: Turkish Catastrophe Insurance Pool (TCIP). Following 1999 earthquake disasters occurred in the Marmara Region and Duzce, earthquake insurance has been made compulsory primarily for dwellings, through a Earthquake Insurance Program. The Turkish Catastrophe Insurance Pool (TCIP) was launched by the Turkish government in cooperation with the World Bank on September 27, 2000. Earthquake insurance premiums are ceded to the TCIP, which is managed by the Natural Disasters Insurance Council, DASK in the Turkish abbreviation.

---

[1] Perils insured by the EQC catastrophe coverage are: earthquake, natural landslip, volcanic eruption, hydrothermal activity, tsunami and, in the case of residential land, also storm or flood.

[2] See: Guy Carpenter & Co., Inc. (2001), The World Catastrophe Reinsurance Market: 2001.

[3] See: Gastel, R. (ed.) (2002), Catastrophes: insurance issues, Insurance Information Institute, III Insurance Issues Update, April 2002 (available in LEXIS).

The TCIP was set up in fulfillment of the government decree-law as a separate state owned legal entity, with its Board and management, to provide compulsory earthquake insurance to all registered residential dwellings in Turkey. The pool provides earthquake coverage up to certain limits for a premium which varies across the country depending upon seismicity, local soil conditions, and the type and quality of construction. The TCIP's Board has representatives from the government, the private sector, and the academic community. The pool has no public sector employees as its management function has been contracted out to Milli Reinsurance, the oldest national reinsurance company. Local insurance companies act as distributors of the TCIP policies. Coverage in excess of the TCIP coverage could be obtained on a voluntary basis from private insurance providers. To issue policies, in addition to the insurance companies underwriting systems, the pool agents and the insurance companies can use an internet-based underwriting platform that will enable the TCIP to control its risk accumulations in real time and maintain the quality of underwriting. The TCIP operates as a catastrophe risk transfer and risk financing facility. Established as the national sole-source provider of earthquake insurance, it will raise the financial preparedness of Turkey for future disasters, reduce government fiscal exposure to major catastrophic events and will make liquidity readily available to insured homeowners affected by such future events. The TCIP is modeled after the California Earthquake Authority and New Zealand Earthquake Commission programs, which provide similar earthquake coverage for homeowners and rely mainly on international reinsurance and capital markets for their risk capital capacity.

V. Risk sharing trough capital markets

Because of the current strains on the financial capacities of the international reinsurance market and the potentially enormous size of catastrophe risks, insurance companies, governments and corporations have recently sought to spread these risks to the capital markets. In this respect, the landscape of risk transfer alternatives has evolved significantly: governments, corporations, primary carriers, as well as global reinsurers today have the option of turning to the capital markets for supplemental catastrophe protection.

Table 2. Natural Catastrophe Risk and Insurance:
A comparative overview of different legal and regulatory frameworks.

	YEAR	PERILS COVERED AND TRIGGERS	COMPULSORY NATURE	ROLE OF PUBLIC AND PRIVATE SECTORS	LIMITS
FRANCE NATIONAL DISASTER COMPENSATION SCHEME (CAT NAT)	1982	NATURAL DISASTERS IN GENERAL. Coverage is triggered when the STATE OF NATURAL DISASTER is declared by inter-ministerial decree.	Law n. 82-600 of 13 July 1982 provides for a compulsory natural disaster extension on all property damage policies purchased on the voluntary market.	Primary disaster coverage is offered and managed by PRIVATE CARRIERS, as an extension to property damage policies. Private insurers can obtain full CATASTROPHE REINSURANCE from the Caisse Centrale de Réassurance (CCR), a state-owned company.	Thanks to the GOVERNMENT GUARANTEE, CCR is able to offer catastrophe reinsurance WITHOUT LIMITS.
SPAIN CONSORCIO DE COMPENSACIÓN DE SEGUROS	1954	EXTRAORDINARY RISKS. The event is covered if it occurred in Spain and caused injuries and damage to people and assets in Spain, provided that: (a) the risk is not expressly covered by the base policy; (b) the risk is covered by the base policy, but the company cannot face its obligations.	The extraordinary risk coverage offered by the Consorcio is compulsorily linked with a base policy. The Consorcio's surcharge is automatically included in the base policy's premium.	Extraordinary risk insurance is administered directly by the Consorcio, a state-owned enterprise, whose solvency is guaranteed by the State.	Financial capacity is UNLIMITED due to a STATE GUARANTEE, but coverage does not include loss of profits.

351

	YEAR	PERILS COVERED AND TRIGGERS	COMPULSORY NATURE	ROLE OF PUBLIC AND PRIVATE SECTORS	LIMITS
UNITED STATES NATIONAL FLOOD INSURANCE PROGRAM (NFIP)	1968	FLOOD LOSSES.	Not compulsory. The NFIP makes federally-backed flood insurance available in communities that agree to adopt and enforce floodplain management ordinances to reduce future flood damage.	The NFIP is funded by the federal government.	Coverage limits offered under the NFIP depend on the community's level of qualification.
CALIFORNIA CALIFORNIA EARTHQUAKE AUTHORITY (CEA)	1996	EARTHQUAKE LOSSES.	California law requires all insurers to offer earthquake insurance with every homeowners policy.	The CEA is a privately financed, state-run insurance program.	The State offers not guarantee; if losses exhaust the CEA fund, claims will be paid out on a pro-rated basis.
FLORIDA FLORIDA HURRICANE CATASTROPHE FUND (FHCF)	1993	HURRICANE LOSSES. The Fund reimburses a fraction of insurers' losses caused by severe hurricanes, declared by the National Hurricane Center.	Contribution to the Fund is compulsory for insurers that write primary coverage on personal and commercial residential properties.	The FHCF is tax-exempt. The private industry is responsible for losses up to a certain level.	An important provision limits the Fund's obligation to pay losses to the sum of its assets and borrowing capacity.
HAWAII HAWAII HURRICANE RELIEF FUND (HHRF)	1993	HURRICANE LOSSES.	NO.	The HHRF is a state-run insurance company.	The HHRF discontinued operations in 2000.

	YEAR	PERILS COVERED AND TRIGGERS	COMPULSORY NATURE	ROLE OF PUBLIC AND PRIVATE SECTORS	LIMITS
NEW ZEALAND EARTHQUAKE COMISSION (EQC) NATURAL DISASTER FUND	1994	NATURAL DISASTER LOSSES. Including: earthquake, natural landslip, volcanic eruption, hydrothermal activity, tsunami and, in the case of residential land, also storm or flood.	Automatic earthquake coverage upon purchase of fire insurance from private market. Premiums are added to the cost of the base policy and passed on to EQC by the insurance company.	EQC, a Crown Entity, administers the natural disaster insurance scheme by: collecting premiums via insurance companies; processing claims; administering the disaster fund; organizing reinsurance.	The Government guarantees that the natural disaster fund will meet all its obligations.
JAPAN JAPANESE EARTHQUAKE REINSURANCE (JER)	1966	EARTHQUAKE LOSSES.	Not compulsory. Primary carriers sell earthquake coverage for considerable amount of additional premium with large deductibles on the voluntary market and then reinsure with JER.	JER, a private entity was established by law in 1966. JER retrocedes part of the risk to the government and the private reinsurance market.	JER's solvency is supported by arrangements with the Japanese government.
TURKEY TURKISH CATASTROPHE INSURANCE POOL (TCIP)	2000	EARTHQUAKE LOSSES.	Yes. Since 2000, earthquake insurance has been made compulsory to all registered residential dwellings in Turkey.	The TCIP is a separate state-owned legal entity, managed by a Council. Local insurance companies act as distributors of the TCIP policies. Excess coverage could be obtained on a voluntary basis from the private market.	Per policy, Turkish lira equivalent of current exchange rate of $25,000.

In light of the cyclical nature of the insurance business, when cost of reinsurance is very high, capital market solutions may become quite appealing. Catastrophe securities are a recent development in investing: by floating such bonds for specific risks over limited time periods in defined geographic regions, insurers and reinsurers reduce risk by transferring it to investors. Investors, in turn, have viewed the introduction of the insurance-linked security as an opportunity for the development of a new market, with the added attraction that so-called **cat bonds** are largely uncorrelated with other financial instruments. Investors – usually hedge funds or other major institutional investors – get a high rate of return, in exchange for the possibility of losing much of their principal or interest, or both, in the event of disasters[1]. Catastrophe bonds entail almost **no credit risk**, since the money paid upfront by the investor and put in escrow, in a trust fund or invested in liquid securities and is therefore readily available. However, the use of physical trigger cat bonds[2] entails a different risk, named **basis risk**. In contrast to traditional reinsurance, in fact, **this kind of coverage may not be a perfect hedge** for the insured portfolio, being only imperfectly correlated to the actual insured losses caused by the occurrence of the triggering event. In this respect, the reinsurance credit risk needs to be balanced against the indexed cat bonds basis risk[3]. There is little evidence yet, however, of a major increase in the use of non reinsurance options like catastrophe bonds or weather derivatives[4].

These relatively new financial products have been made possible because of relevant improvements and developments in scientific studies, engineering analyses and information technologies. Today natural hazards risks and the potential losses of future disasters can be predicted with more accuracy than in the past: new risk assessments techniques have reduced the uncertainty associated with estimating the probabilities that certain disasters will occur in specific regions, while recent engineering studies have

---

[1] "A catastrophe bond (cat bond) is an instrument whereby the investor receives an above-market return when catastrophes do not occur, but shares the insurer's or government's losses by sacrificing interest or principal when catastrophes do occur. With cat bonds or other capital market instruments, insurers (and governments as insurers) can pay to transfer catastrophe risk to investors." Kunreuther, H.C., Linnerooth-Bayer, J. (1999), The Financial Management of Catastrophic Flood Risks in Emerging Economy Countries, paper presented at Global Change and Catastrophic Risk Management, Laxenberg, Austria: IIASA, June 6-9, 1999.

[2] Examples of these triggers are: earthquake strength and wind speed.

[3] "In contrast to an indemnity contract where the entity providing protection (e.g. the reinsurer) can become insolvent if it suffers catastrophic losses, the firm does not face any credit risk from an indexed-based cat bond. The money to pay for the losses is already in hand. On the other hand, such a cat bond creates basis risk. Basis risk refers to the imperfect correlation between the actual losses suffered by the firm and the payments received from the cat bond. Insurance sold to firms or excess-of-loss reinsurance to insurers has zero basis risk because there is a direct relationship between the loss and the payment delivered by the reinsurance instrument." Kunreuther, H.C. (2001), Mitigation and Financial Risk Management for Natural Hazards, *The Geneva Papers on Risk and Insurance*, Vol. 26, n.2 (April 2001) 276-295.

[4] Guy Carpenter & Co., Inc. (2001), The World Catastrophe Reinsurance Market: 2001.

provided additional information on how structures and infrastructures perform under the stress of extreme environmental conditions[1]. Due to the growing knowledge of cat risk among institutional investors cat bonds have the potential to increase the amount of capital available for catastrophic risk, as well as alter the pricing of risk[2].

VI. Regulation and catastrophe insurance

Regulatory policies may greatly affect the development of markets for disaster risk coverages and, consequently, the availability of effective catastrophe insurance[3]. Governments' policies often imposed significant cross-subsides from low-risk to high-risk areas and sometimes even imposed cross subsidies from non-catastrophe lines of insurance to the catastrophe lines. Such policies distort incentives and undermine the ability of market forces to make necessary adjustments and operate effectively in managing catastrophe risk.

Significant effects may also be generated by:

- **Regulatory constraints.** Regulation imposes further indirect costs on insurers in complying with regulatory requirements.

- **Market entry/exit rules.** Rules imposing limitations on the ability to enter/exit the market for certain risks may discourage the willingness of the insurance industry to undertake such risks.

- **Rules on the admissibility of ART**. Regulators must be aware that alternative risk transfer mechanisms can be essential when there is a shortage in reinsurance capacity.

---

[1] See: Kunreuther, H.C., Linnerooth-Bayer, J. (1999), The Financial Management of Catastrophic Flood Risks in Emerging Economy Countries, paper presented at Global Change and Catastrophic Risk Management, Laxenberg, Austria: IIASA, June 6-9, 1999.

[2] In 2002, for example, Swiss Re has received USD 255 million of four-year protection against a series of natural catastrophe risks. As part of the transaction, Swiss Re signed a financial contract with PIONEER 2002 Ltd. ("PIONEER"), a special purpose Cayman Islands exempted company and the issuer of the USD 255 million of securities. Subsequently, Swiss Re Capital Markets Corporation, acting as sole bookrunner, privately placed the securities with institutional investors. The proceeds from the offering fully collateralize PIONEER's financial contract with Swiss Re and will serve to replenish Swiss Re's capital should any of the specified natural catastrophes occur. Source: Swiss Re. In 2001 Munich Reinsurance Company announced the successful private placement of a total of USD 300 million of risk-linked securities, the largest ever to provide protection against US hurricane, Californian earthquake and European windstorm events, based on an innovative parametric trigger structure for a package of the three perils. Source: Munich Re.

[3] See: Kunreuther, H.C. and R.J. Roth (ed.) (1998), Paying the Price: The Status and Role of Insurance Against Natural Disasters in the United States. Washington DC, Joseph Henry Press, especially at Chapter Eight (authored by Robert Klein).

Financial and fiscal issues. Monitoring the solvency of insurance companies is fundamental in order to be able to rely on insurance as an effective funding mechanism for natural hazards. Rules allowing for tax-exempt catastrophe reserves may also prove to be highly beneficial.

Regulation of claims practices. With a view to assuring expedite payments, effective rules concerning settlement practices and procedures to be followed by the insurance companies upon occurrence of the insured event (i.e. the natural disaster) may turn out to be fundamental.

Antitrust and competition policies. In some jurisdictions, the formation of catastrophe insurance pools aimed at raising adequate financial capacity and sharing data and information may be considered as incompatible with the antitrust and competition policies in force[1].

VII. Integrated risk management strategies: catastrophe bonds and insurance can be coupled with incentives and other regulatory mechanisms to reduce disaster losses.

In light of the above considerations, an effective disaster risk management strategy requires an integrated approach and the proactive involvement of all the relevant stakeholders, including:

- Homeowners and businesses at risk
- Governments
- Insurers and reinsurers
- Investors in cat bonds

The following points, therefore, appear to be quite important in the future development of catastrophe risk management strategies:

The adoption of an integrated approach[2]

---

[1] In Italy, for example, the Antitrust Authority expressed serious concerns about a pending legislative proposal aimed at setting up a national disaster scheme based on the introduction of a mandatory disaster extension on all fire policies and on the formation of a special catastrophe insurance pool. See: Decision AS168 of 12/04/1999 in Antitrust bulletin 13-14/1999.

[2] "Based on an understanding of the vulnerability of the city or region and the decision processes of the key interested parties, one needs to develop a strategy for reducing losses and providing financial protection to victims of future disasters. This strategy will normally involve a combination of private and public sector initiatives which include insurance and new financial instruments as well as well enforced building codes and land-use regulations. These measures will differ from country to country depending on the current institutional arrangements and existing legislation and laws. In summary, a combination of building codes, reinsurance and indexed cat bonds can form a useful strategy for reducing losses to property owners as well as insurers and the investment community. The implementation of this strategy requires a concerted

The development of scientific risk evaluation techniques aimed at improving:

- Risk predictability
- Expected loss estimates

The implementation of effective measures for structural mitigation and vulnerability reduction[1].

Enforcing building codes in hazard-prone areas would likely reduce future disaster losses significantly. Well-enforced building codes would reduce the magnitude of losses, enable insurers to provide additional coverage to property owners, and decrease the need for reinsurance and funds from other sources such as the capital market and state pools. It also would enable insurers to lower prices. At the same time, the costs of building code enforcement can be significant for the local community. As a result, it is important to redistribute some of the benefits from the reduction in exposure back to the local community pay for environment of codes. Thus, understanding the interdependence among property owners, insurers, and state and local agencies is critical to designing workable solutions. Well-enforced regulatory measures, such as building codes, can complement insurance and other financial instruments by forcing the adoption of **cost-effective risk mitigation measures** (RMMs)[2]. Incentives are

---

effort by both the public and private sectors. For example, the implementation of mitigation measures requires inspections by certified personnel. Banks and Financial institutions can play a role in this process by making their mortgage and related loans conditional on such an audit. Insurers can offer lower premiums for those adopting these mitigation measures." Kunreuther, H.C. (2001), Mitigation and Financial Risk Management for Natural Hazards, *The Geneva Papers on Risk and Insurance*, Vol. 26, n.2 (April 2001) 276-295.

[1] "In determining the vulnerability of a city or region one needs to know the design of each structure (e.g. residential, commercial, public sector) and infrastructure, whether specific mitigation measures are in place or could be utilized, and their location in relation to the hazard. (e.g., distance from an earthquake fault line or proximity to the coast in a hurricane prone area) as well as other risk-related factors. The ingredients for evaluating the vulnerability of a city or region to natural hazards are risk assessment and societal conditions. Ideally a risk assessment specifies the probability of events of different intensities or magnitudes occurring and the impact of the direct and indirect impacts of these events on the affected interested parties. Societal conditions include human settlement patterns, the built environment, day-to-day activities and the institutions established to deal with natural hazards" Kunreuther, H.C. (2001), Mitigation and Financial Risk Management for Natural Hazards, *The Geneva Papers on Risk and Insurance*, Vol. 26, n.2 (April 2001) 276-295.

[2] "Building codes mandate that property owners adopt mitigation measures. Such codes may be desirable when property owners would otherwise not adopt cost-effective RMMs because they either misperceive the benefits from adopting the measure and/or underestimate the probability of a disaster occurring. If a family is forced to vacate its property because of damage that would have been prevented if a building code had been in place, then this additional cost needs to taken into account by the public sector when evaluating the cost effectiveness of an RMM from a societal perspective. There are several key interested parties who can enforce building codes. Banks and financial

needed since property owners often underestimate the risks from disasters[1]: as mentioned, empirical research have shown that individuals' and firms' decisions with respect to mitigating and insuring natural hazard risks do not conform to rational models of choice[2]. In addition, effective mitigation measures may produce **positive externalities** by reducing other costs arising out of a disaster.

VIII.   Conclusions

This section of the report presents some of the insurability problems associated with the natural catastrophe risk and offers an overview of several economic and institutional alternatives to the traditional insurance and reinsurance mechanisms. It also briefly discusses the implications of an **integrated approach to disaster management** based on insurance, prevention, mitigation, compensation and a close partnership between the public and the private sectors. On the basis of the above risk partnership, it seems that the international insurance and reinsurance industry is able to play a central role in the future management of natural hazards.

---

institutions could require an inspection of the property to see that it meets the code before issuing a mortgage. Similarly insurers may want to limit coverage only to those structures that meet the building code. Inspecting the building to see that it meets the code and then providing it with a seal of approval provides accurate information to the property owner on the condition of the house. It also signals to others that the structure is disaster-resistant. This new information could translate into higher property values if prospective buyers took the earthquake risk into consideration when making their purchase decisions." Kunreuther, H.C. (2001), Mitigation and Financial Risk Management for Natural Hazards, *The Geneva Papers on Risk and Insurance*, Vol. 26, n.2 (April 2001) 276-295.

[1] "An alternative way to encourage consumers to adopt mitigation measures is to change the nature of their insurance coverage rather than reducing the premium. More specifically, the insurer could offer a lower deductible to those who adopt mitigation at the same or lower price than if they had decided not to invest in the RMM. Such a program is likely to be very attractive given the empirical and experimental evidence that suggests that consumers appear to dislike deductibles even though they offer considerable savings in premiums." Kunreuther, H.C. (2000), Insurance as a Cornerstone for Public–Private Sector Partnerships, Nat. Hazards Rev., 1, 126–136.

[2] Camerer & Kunreuther, "Decision Processes for Low Probability events: Policy Implications", 8 *Journal of Policy Analysis and Management* 1989, 565-592.

CHAPTER 4

THE CURRENT SITUATION IN THE BALTIC STATES

I. Environmental legislation reform and the Baltic States' accession to the European Union

After successfully growing from 6 to 15 members, the European Union is now preparing for its biggest enlargement ever in terms of scope and diversity. Estonia, Latvia and Lithuania (the Baltic States), together with Cyprus, the Czech Republic, Hungary, Malta, Poland, the Slovak Republic, and Slovenia, are set to join on 1 May 2004. They are currently know by the term "acceding countries". The accession treaty has been signed in Athens on 16 April 2003 and these new member states will join the EU once the accession treaty is ratified.

Baltic States' efforts to achieve accession to the European Union have brought about dramatic change in their environmental laws, many of which have been repeatedly amended during the last decade in order to keep up-to-date with the latest EU directives.

In Latvia, for instance, a new Law on Pollution has been adopted on 15 March 2001, entered into force on July 1, 2001 and has subsequently been amended. This law determines pollution prevention and control requirements on the operator of dangerous activities, as well as a procedure for pollution prevention and control. Its declared purpose[1] is to prevent or reduce damage on human health, property and the environment caused by pollution, to counteract consequences of such damage and:

1. to prevent pollution or, where that is not possible, to reduce emissions to air, water and soil arising from polluting activities;

2. to prevent or, where that is not possible, to reduce the use of non-renewable natural resources and energy for polluting activities;

3. to prevent or, where that is not possible, to minimise generation of waste;

4. to provide for inventory and registration of contaminated and potentially contaminated areas lying within the national territory;

5. to determine the measures for investigation of contaminated and potentially contaminated areas and for remediation of contaminated areas;

6. to identify the persons who shall cover the costs of investigation of contaminated and potentially contaminated areas and the costs of remediation of contaminated areas.

---

[1] See Section 2 (Purpose), Latvian Law On Pollution, text consolidated by the Ministry of Environmental Protection and Regional Development with amending law of 20 June 2002.

According to the text consolidated by the Ministry of Environmental Protection and Regional Development with amending law of 20 June 2002, a *polluting activity* is an activity that involves the use of soil and subsoil, water, air, buildings or installations and other stationary objects, which may cause any environmental pollution or risk for accidents, as well as an activity within a contaminated area that may lead to further dissemination of pollution. *Operator* is defined as any natural or legal person who operates a polluting activity or is responsible for the technical functioning of this activity or has decisive economic power over the polluting activity concerned; *pollution*, in turn, is defined as the direct or indirect impact of the emission on the environment, which may be harmful to human health, result in damage to material property, create damage on the environment, including ecosystems, impair or interfere with exploitation of natural resources or other legitimate uses of the environment.

Pursuant to Section 38 of the 2001 Law, in case of *pollution* the costs of investigation and remediation[1] measures shall be covered by:

a. the *operator*, who was operating a *polluting activity*, which resulted in creation of a contaminated or potentially contaminated area;

b. the *operator*, who runs or plans to run a *polluting activity* within a contaminated or potentially contaminated area;

c. the land owner who have had a decisive influence over the enterprise that operated a *polluting activity*, which has resulted in the creation of a contaminated or potentially contaminated area within his land;

d. the owner or user of the relevant land property or object, who volunteers for a full or partial coverage of these costs.

Where the land owner did not have a decisive influence over the enterprise that operated a *polluting activity*, he shall cover the costs of remediation measures if these measures were taken with his consent and the value of the land has increased after their application and if the remediation costs cannot be fully covered by other liable persons. The costs to be covered by the landowner may not exceed an increase in the land value caused by performed remediation measures.

According to Section 39 of the law, if several persons shall cover the costs of the investigation or remediation measures, the costs shall be divided *proportionally to the environmental damage caused by each person*. The costs shall be divided taking into account the volume and type of emissions and the operation period of the polluting activity. If costs can not be divided the responsible parties shall be held jointly and severally liable. The relevant Regional Environmental Board shall evaluate the division of costs. The Regional Environmental Board shall also supervise and control investigation and remediation of contaminated or potentially contaminated areas, except

---

[1] Pursuant to Section 1 of the Law on Pollution, remediation is defined as: "clean-up and rehabilitation of a contaminated area to the level where, as the minimum, human health or the environment is no longer endangered and where the area can be used for the certain economic activity."

for contaminated and potentially contaminated areas in the possession of the Ministry of Defense. The Ministry of Defense or its authorised institution shall supervise and control investigation and remediation of contaminated or potentially contaminated areas in its possession.

If the responsible authority possesses information about the contaminated area that endangers or may endanger human health or the environment, it shall decide that the remediation is necessary. Where it has been decided that that the remediation is necessary, the responsible authority shall, in accordance with Section 38, identify persons that shall cover respective costs and their degree of liability. Where the persons that shall cover remediation costs cannot be identified or where sufficient funds for the remediation cannot be obtained, the responsible authority shall estimate funds necessary for the remediation and inform the Ministry of Environmental Protection and Regional Development or the Ministry of Defense concerning the areas in its possession. The Ministry of Environmental Protection and Regional Development or Ministry of Defense shall consider whether funds from the State budget or other sources can be raised to conduct the remediation. If the funds have been obtained, the responsible authority shall decide on the conduction of the remediation.

The above mentioned provisions of the recently enacted and amended Latvian Law on Pollution of 2001 constitute a first example of legislative enactment of the Polluter Pays Principle[1] in the Baltic States.

Together with Latvia, Estonia and Lithuania seem to be moving in the same direction with respect to the legal reform of their environmental sector.

In Estonia, two governmental regulations have been recently adopted in the field of industrial pollution control and risk management, transposing a substantial part of the Seveso II Directive.

In Lithuania, the framework Law on Environmental Protection was amended in December 2001 and entered into force in January 2002, while in the field of industrial pollution control and risk management new rules on integrated permitting and on collection of emissions data were approved in February and March 2002 respectively.

It is quite clear that, at this stage of legal and economic development of the Baltic States, **a consistent enforcement of the newly established legal provisions is extremely important**.

As for the next steps towards EU integration in the domain of environmental pollution risk management, it is foreseeable that new legislative requirements will be

---

[1] It is worth noting that, in Latvia, the Polluter Pays Principle is now expressly recognized in the current version of article 3 of the Law on Environmental Protection: "*natural persons and legal persons shall cover all the costs, which are related to the assessment, reduction or rectification of the pollution caused as a result of their activities.*"

introduced upon approval of the proposal for a "Directive of the European Parliament and of the Council on environmental liability with regard to the prevention and remedying of environmental damage" presented by the Commission of the European Communities on January 23, 2002 [COM(2002) 17 final] and discussed earlier in this report (see *supra* Chapter 2).

As mentioned, the proposal is aimed at establishing an EU framework whereby environmental damage would be prevented or remedied in the Member States. In this context, the Commission of the European Communities recognized the role of environmental insurance as crucial for the successful achievement of the desired policy results. In light of the above, with respect to ecological insurance the Baltic States will soon be facing the same challenges of the current EU member countries.

II. Environment-related risks and insurance: market development issues

According to the information available through the local insurance supervisory authorities, at present specific insurance products like **environmental pollution insurance** or **natural disasters insurance** do not appear to be popular in the Estonian, Latvian and Lithuanian market. Sometimes, certain consequences of these environment-related risks are included in the general liability insurance coverage or in the general property coverage.

As illustrated earlier in this report, however, the general trend at the international level points towards the need to develop very specific and innovative products, aimed at addressing the peculiar problems posed by this new type of risks.

When dealing with the environmental pollution risk, for instance, one must cope with severe conditions of **factual and legal uncertainty**[1]. This is why gradual pollution risk is almost completely excluded from general liability policies in most if not all OECD countries. Coverage is provided under separate contracts on a **site-specific** basis because there is a special need for careful evaluation and classification of the risk to be transferred.

With the enactment of new environmental laws in compliance with the Polluter Pays Principle, the operators of hazardous activities in the Baltic States will face new risks, including the risk of being held liable for damages and for the remediation costs in case of a polluting event.

Choices made by law and policy makers in the course of implementation of EU requirements, therefore, will greatly affect the level of risk predictability. In other words, as the analysis conducted Chapter 2 of this report shows, several features of the underlying legal framework affect the insurability of environmental pollution risk and, consequently, the development of a pollution insurance market.

---

[1] See, *supra*, Chapter 2 of this report.

With respect to the current situation of the Baltic States, the issue is of great concern and the growth of a specialized **environmental insurance market** appears to be crucial in this field. Insurance, in fact, would give effect to the **compensation** function of the new environmental liability regimes, providing the State and the injured parties with a reliable source of funds when pollution occurs. Moreover, with a view to reducing the risk of a polluting event, the insurance companies may be called upon to act as a **private surrogate regulator**, enhancing the incentives for the operators to adopt better prevention measures. Furthermore, since the payment of premiums can be conceived as an *ex ante* **internalization of environmental costs**, supporting the development of new environmental insurance products appears to be an effective strategy for the full implementation of the Polluter Pays Principle.

In order to encourage and stimulate the development and growth of the pollution insurance market, law and policy makers in the Baltic States, as elsewhere, should put their best efforts in circumscribing, limiting and defining with a sufficient level of clarity and predictability the financial risks associated with environmental pollution liabilities. Moreover, the enactment of rules mandating the responsibility for provision of adequate financial security, in a form to be approved by the competent authority (not necessarily insurance), seems highly advisable, in order to prevent the risk of insolvency.

As far as **natural catastrophe risk** is concerned, it shall be noted that the policy recommendations made in Chapter 3 of this report also apply to the situation in the Baltic States. In fact, it seems that so far the problem has not been fully addressed.

Lawmakers should careful consider the importance of a public-private partnership in the management of natural disasters. The analysis conducted in Chapter 3 of this report illustrates that the financial burden of natural catastrophe risk cannot be carried exclusively by the private insurance sector. Some of the major obstacles to insurability, however, may be overcome through the proactive intervention of the public sector.

In light of the above, Estonia, Latvia and Lithuania might be willing to envisage some sort of close co-operation between governments and the private sector, drawing on the experience of several OECD countries (see *infra* Chapter 3 § 4. and Table 2).

As mentioned, while insurance proves to be a reliable financial tool for managing and funding risks, because it specializes in reserving and investing collected funds for the purpose of claims payment, certain conditions of the natural catastrophe risks require public intervention in this area.

The public sector, for instance, can contribute providing the requisite legal framework, subsidizing the cost of administering the disaster management scheme, subsidizing the cost of insurance to the beneficiaries, or being a reinsurer of last resort.

It is worth recalling, moreover, that governments have the power to enforce the adoption of appropriate risk mitigation measures and to make catastrophe insurance coverage mandatory, thereby spreading the risk throughout the entire population.

With reference to the natural catastrophe risk, the access of local primary carriers to the international reinsurance market is also fundamental for a more effective geographical risk spreading.

The development of markets for disaster risk coverages, furthermore, may be affected by regulatory policies[1] that sometimes distort the incentives and undermine the ability of market forces to make necessary adjustments and operate effectively in managing catastrophe risk. Regulatory constraints, antitrust policies, fiscal issues, market entry/exit rules and restrictions concerning the admissibility of cat bonds and other alternative risk transfer mechanisms may influence the availability of catastrophe insurance coverage.

III. Conclusions

The concise remarks comprised in this last chapter of the report are aimed at calling the attention of law and policy makers in Estonia, Latvia and Lithuania (the Baltic States) to the proper role that the private insurance sector might play in the future management of environment-related risks. Of course, when dealing with transitional economies, one must also take into account the relative immaturity of the local insurance market and the difficulties that might be encountered in establishing a sound and reputable insurance business environment.

---

[1] See: Kunreuther, H.C. and R.J. Roth (ed.) (1998), Paying the Price: The Status and Role of Insurance Against Natural Disasters in the United States. Washington DC, Joseph Henry Press, especially at Chapter Eight (authored by Robert Klein).

BIBLIOGRAPHY

Abraham, K.S. (1986), Distributing Risk: Insurance, Legal Theory and Public Policy, New Haven: Yale University Press.

Abraham, K.S. (1988), Environmental Liability and The Limits of Insurance, 88 Columbia L. Rev. 942.

Abraham, K.S. (1991), Environmental Liability Insurance Law - an analysis of toxic torts and hazardous waste insurance coverage issues, Prentice Hall Law & Business.

Andersen T., Masci P. (2001), Economic Exposures to Natural Disasters. Public Policy and Alternative Risk. Management Approaches, 'Infrastructure and Financial Markets Review', vol.7 n.4, Dec. 2001.

Arrow, K. J. (1992). "Insurance, Risk and Resource Allocation." Foundations of Insurance Economics: Readings in Economic and Finance. G. Dionne and S. E. Harrington. Boston, Kluwer Academic Publishers.

Berliner, B. (1982), Limits of Insurability of Risks. Englewood Cliffs, NJ, Prentice-Hall, Inc.

Berliner, B., Spühler, J. (1990), Insurability issues associated with managing existing hazardous waste sites, in 'Integrating Insurance & Risk Management for Hazardous Waste', edited by Howard Kunreuther and Rajeev Gowda, Kluwer Academic Publishers.

Boyd, J. (2000), A market-based analysis of financial assurance issues associated with U.S. natural resource damage liability, Follow up study commissioned by the European Commission.

Calabresi Guido (1970), The cost of the accidents, New Haven: Yale University Press

Camerer, C.F. and Kunreuther, H.C. (1989), "Decision Processes for Low Probability Events: Policy Implications." Journal of Policy Analysis and Management 8 (1989): 565-592

Croson, D. and Kunreuther, H.C. (2000), "Customizing Indemnity Contracts and Indexed Cat Bonds for Natural Hazard Risks," Journal of Risk and Finance, Volume 1, Spring 2000

Faure, M.G. (ed.), Deterrence, Insurability and Compensation in Environmental Liability. Future Developments in the European Union. SpringerWienNewYork, 2003.

Faure, M.G., Grimeaud, D. (2000), Financial Assurance Issues of Environmental Liability – Report, Follow up study commissioned by the European Commission.

Faure, M.G., Hartlief, T. (1996), Compensation Funds versus Liability and Insurance for Remedying Environmental Damage, Review of European Community and International Environmental Law, Volume 5, Issue 4, 321-327.

Faure, M.G., The Limits to Insurability from a Law and Economics Perspective, Geneva Papers on Risk and Insurance, 1995, 454-462.

Freeman, P.K. and Kunreuther, H.C. (1997), Managing environmental risk through insurance, Boston [etc.]: Kluwer, c1997 (Studies in risk and uncertainty: 9).

Froot, K. A. (ed.) (1999). The Financing of Catastrophe Risk. Chicago, University of Chicago Press.

Gastel, R. (ed.) (2002), Catastrophes: insurance issues, Insurance Information Institute, III Insurance Issues Update, April 2002 (available in LEXIS).

Gülkan, P. (2001), Rebuilding the Sea of Marmara Region: Recent Structural Revisions in Turkey to Mitigate Disasters, Issues Paper for EERI Annual Meeting Session on Changes in Dealing with Risk in the International Arena February 7-10, 2001 Monterey, CA.

Guy Carpenter & Co., Inc. (2002), The World Catastrophe Reinsurance Market: 2002.

Hansmann H. and Kraakman R. (1991), Towards Unlimited Shareholder Liability for Corporate Torts, 100 Yale L. J. 1879

Kleindorfer, P.R. and Kunreuther, H.C. (1999), Challenges Facing the Insurance Industry in Managing Catastrophic Risks. in Froot, K. A. (ed.) The Financing of Catastrophe Risk. Chicago, University of Chicago Press: 149-189.

Koeman, Niels S.J. (ed.) (1999), Environmental Law in Europe, Kluwer Law International.

Kunreuther, H.C. (1996), Mitigating disaster losses through insurance, Journal of Risk and Uncertainty, 12:171-187.

Kunreuther, H.C. (2000), Insurance as a Cornerstone for Public–Private Sector Partnerships, Nat. Hazards Rev., 1, 126–136.

Kunreuther, H.C. (2000), Linking Insurance and Mitigation to Manage Natural Hazard Disaster Risk, *Handbook of Insurance,* Georges Dionne (Ed.), Kluwer Academic Publishers, Boston.

Kunreuther, H.C. (2001), Mitigation and Financial Risk Management for Natural Hazards, *The Geneva Papers on Risk and Insurance*, Vol. 26, n.2 (April 2001) 276-295.

Kunreuther, H.C. and R.J. Roth (ed.) (1998), Paying the Price: The Status and Role of Insurance Against Natural Disasters in the United States. Washington DC, Joseph Henry Press.

Kunreuther, H.C., Linnerooth-Bayer, J. (1999), The Financial Management of Catastrophic Flood Risks in Emerging Economy Countries, paper presented at Global Change and Catastrophic Risk Management, Laxenberg, Austria: IIASA, June 6-9, 1999.

Lewis, C. M. and Murdock, K. C. (1999). "Alternative Means of Redistributing Catastrophic Risk in a National Risk-Management System." in Froot, K. A. (ed.) The Financing of Catastrophe Risk. Chicago, National Bureau of Economic Research: 51-85.

Mattei, U. (1997), Comparative Law and Economics, Ann Arbor: Michigan Univ. Press

Mattei, U. and Monti, A. (2001), Comparative Law and Economics. Borrowing and Resistance, Global Jurist Frontiers, Vol. 1: No. 2, Article 5, 2001, Berkeley Electronic Press: http://www.bepress.com/gj/frontiers/vol1/iss2/art5

Meyer, P. et al. (1997), Tropical Cyclones, Zurich, Swiss Reinsurance Company.

North, D. (1990), Institutions, Institutional Change and Economic Performance, Cambridge University Press.

Pollner, J. (2000), Catastrophe Risk Management Using Alternative Risk Financing & Insurance Pooling Mechanisms: The Insurance Market and the Case of the Caribbean Region. Washington DC: World Bank.

Pozzo B. (1996), The Liability Problem in Modern Environmental Statutes, 4. *ERPL* 1996, 111-144.

Priest, G.L. (1996), The Government, the Market, and the Problem of Catastrophic Loss, Journal of Risk and Uncertainty, 12 (Number 2/3): 219-237.

Sacco, R. (1991), Legal Formants: A Dynamic Approach to Comparative Law, 39 Am. J. Comp. Law 1991, 1 ff., 349 ff.

Sen, A. (1999), Development as Freedom, New York, Alfred A. Knopf.

Shavell, S. (1980), Strict Liability Versus Negligence, 9 Journal of Legal Studies 1980, 1

Shavell, S. (1984), Liability for Harm versus Regulation of Safety, 13 Journal of Legal Studies 1984, 357 ff.

Shavell, S. (1986), The Judgment Proof Problem, 6 Int. Rev. Law and Econ., 1986, 45-58

Shavell, S. (1987), Economic Analysis of Accident Law, Harvard University Press.

Skogh, G (1998), Development risks, strict liability and the insurability of industrial hazards, Geneva Papers on Risk and Insurance, 87, 247.

Skogh, G. (1989), The transactions cost theory of insurance: contracting impediments and costs, Journal of Risk and Insurance, 726-732.

Spühler, J. (1999), Environmental insurance for enterprises. An insurance concept, Swiss Reinsurance Company, Zurich: Swiss Re Publishing.

Swiss Reinsurance Company (2002), Natural Catastrophes and man-made disasters in 2001, Swiss Re SIGMA series 1/2002. Zurich, Swiss Reinsurance Company.

Swiss Reinsurance Company (2003), Natural Catastrophes and man-made disasters in 2002, Swiss Re SIGMA series 2/2003. Zurich, Swiss Reinsurance Company.

ISSUES IN FINANCIAL SERVICES INTEGRATION:

IMPLICATIONS FOR BALTIC STATES

Harold Skipper

Abstract

This paper summarizes and synthesizes the current knowledge and opinions on the controversial and complex issue of financial services integration for the purpose of assisting policy makers in the Baltic countries as they wrestle with these issues. The paper begins with a discussion of the meanings ascribed to the phrase financial services integration. It then overviews the existing economic literature on the subject and of the key issues facing managers of integrated firms. Next the author classifies and summarizes the numerous public policy concerns that have been raised with integration. The paper closes with some speculations about the future of financial services integration in general and possible relevance for the Baltic countries in particular.

TABLE OF CONTENTS

INTRODUCTION

Will financial services integration lead us straight away to a brave new financial world in which operational and marketing efficiencies and innovation ensure ever greater consumer value and choice and a safer financial system? Or will it result in a handful of financial giants exercising their market power to sell high priced, unsuitable products to all but their wealthiest customers, while abusing customers' privacy and exposing the entire financial system to greater risk?

This paper summarizes and synthesizes the current knowledge and opinions on these and related issues for the purpose of assisting policy makers in the Baltic countries as they wrestle with these issues.[1]

We begin with a discussion of the meanings ascribed to the phrase financial services integration. We then offer a brief summary of the existing economic literature on the subject and of the key issues facing managers of integrated firms. Next we classify and summarize the numerous public policy concerns that have been raised with integration. The paper closes with some speculations about the future of financial services integration in general and possible relevance for the Baltic countries in particular.

---

[1] This paper is based on Skipper (2000).

CHAPTER 1

THE MULTIPLE MEANINGS AND FORMS
OF FINANCIAL SERVICES INTEGRATION

Because the term "financial services integration" is subject to multiple meanings, we need to be clear about how it is used. Additionally, because firms offering integrated financial services can be structured in multiple ways, we also should understand these different structural possibilities. As background, we first provide an overview of the leading financial intermediaries.

I. Overview of Financial Intermediaries

Financial intermediaries exist to bring savers, investors, and borrowers together. Financial intermediation is essential to economic development, and the more efficiently this activity is performed, the stronger can be economic growth, other things being equal. Banks, insurers, and securities firms comprise the three major classes of financial intermediaries. More specialized, large intermediaries include mutual funds and pension funds. In many markets, there exists also a range of other, usually smaller specialized intermediaries such as finance companies, real estate investment trusts, mortgage companies, and the like. While intermediaries compete in asset management and risk management, all specialize.

Of the world's 500 largest companies in 2002, 120 were financial intermediaries, broken down as follows: 62 banks, 48 insurers, six diversified financial firms, and four securities firms.[1] Banks accounted for 44.8 percent of the total revenues of the 120 firms, with insurers following closely at 40.5 percent, and diversified financials and securities firms accounting for 10.7 and 4.0 percent respectively. These figures omit mutual funds and pension funds.

Banks. Banks specialize in relatively short-term asset management, credit extensions, and payment services. Of the world's 50 largest banks based on revenues in 2001, 29 were European, 11 North American, and eight Asian. From year-end 1991 through mid-2001, annual stock returns averaged 19 percent for U.S. banks, 14 percent for European banks, and minus 10 percent for Japanese banks. The share of revenues and assets under management by banks worldwide continues to decline relative to other financial intermediaries.

Insurers. Non-life insurers underwrite, price, and finance primarily hazard risks for individuals and businesses and manage relatively short-term assets. Life insurers underwrite, price, and finance mainly mortality-related risks and manage comparatively long-term assets. Life insurers' revenues are twice those of non-life insurers, and they manage more than twice the assets of non-life insurers. Of the world's 48 largest

---

[1] Data given in this section come from Fortune (2002), Swiss Re (2001), and Dow Jones (2002).

insurers based on 2001 revenues, North America and Europe each claim 17, Asia has 12, and other domiciles account for the remaining two insurers. From year-end 1991 through mid-2001, annual stock returns averaged 18 percent for U.S. insurers, 11 percent for European insurers, and minus 3 percent for Japanese insurers. Insurers' worldwide shares of revenues and assets under management have declined relative to other financial intermediaries.

Securities Firms. Securities firms underwrite and distribute debt and equity issues, provide advisory services to individuals and institutions, and provide brokerage services. Some securities firms specialize in only a few functions (e.g., retail brokerage) whereas others offer all services. Profitability of securities firms is, on average, higher than that for banks and insurers, but also much more volatile. Five firms dominate this concentrated market.

Mutual Funds. Mutual funds are pools of managed assets offering savers convenient access to the securities markets. In the U.S., funds are sold predominately through securities brokers or directly to the public at no commission charges. In Europe, funds are sold predominately through banks. The number of mutual funds worldwide continues to grow rapidly, as do assets under management. From 1995 to 2000, assets under management more than doubled to US$12.0 trillion, reaching 60 percent of total bank assets under management worldwide and easily surpassing insurers' assets under management. The world's largest mutual funds are stand-alone firms and generally are not managed by other financial intermediaries, except in Europe.

Pension Funds. Private pension funds specialize in managing diversified portfolios of assets dedicated to providing retirement income to plan participants. Pension plans may be established by employers to provide retirement income for their workers or by individuals, with the former dominating worldwide. Pension fund assets might be managed by the fund itself or any other financial intermediary or by the individual. Thus, most of their assets are subsumed within the total assets of their managing intermediary, be it a bank, mutual fund, or life insurer. Pension funds generally are considered parts of corporations or government agencies and not separate entities, so do not appear in listings of large financial intermediaries worldwide. Nonetheless, we know that the growth in private pension funds worldwide has been enormous, fueled by aging, more affluent populations, favorable tax treatment, and revenue-starved public pension plans.

II. The Meaning of Financial Services Integration

Perhaps the most familiar definition of *financial services integration* is that it occurs whenever production or distribution of a financial service traditionally associated with one of the three major financial sectors is by actors from another sector. Terms such as *bancassurance, allfinanz*, universal banking, and financial conglomerates are all used to convey some notion of integration. Terminology, however, is not yet standard, so these terms carry different meanings for different people.

The above definition embraces production and/or distribution of financial services. The degree of integration may range from shallow to deep. The definition is not completely satisfactory, however, unless production is understood to include two dimensions: management and product. To understand this importance, it will be useful, first, to consider a *financial conglomerate* – commonly defined as any group of companies under common control whose exclusive or predominant activities consist of providing significant services in at least two of the three major financial sectors. (To meet the definition of a financial conglomerate within the European Union's conglomerate directive, the conglomerate must include an insurer and at least one financial intermediary from a different sector.)

Consider two financial conglomerates that, from a legal point of view, are identical. Each is composed of a non-operating holding company that owns a bank and an insurer. In one conglomerate, the bank and insurance company are managed as separate profit centers, with no effort made to integrate overall management and operations. Activities are aligned precisely with legal form. The other conglomerate, by contrast, has global control functions allowing management and operations at the group level. Activities align with target markets, not legal form. Profit centers cut across sectoral lines.

Both conglomerates might sell the same portfolio of products, so this dimension of production is indistinguishable. They are, however, managed quite differently. The latter group is more integrated, expecting that economies can be secured through operational integration.

The French term *bancassurance* most commonly refers to banks selling insurance products (and usually vice versa[1]). The German term *allfinanz* usually is synonymous with *bancassurance*, although it sometimes suggests integration via distribution across all three major sectors, as does *bancassurance* at times.

Universal banks usually are thought of as representing a greater degree of integration. According to many scholars, a theoretical definition of a universal bank allows it to manufacture and distribute all financial services within a single corporate structure (Saunders and Walter, 1994). As a practical matter, perhaps the most common concept of a universal bank is that of a financial institution that combines the production and distribution of commercial and investment banking within a single firm. Some universal banks distribute insurance but through a separate subsidiary.[2]

Under the earlier definition, a conglomerate must involve firms under common control, suggesting the possibility of integration at the level of production (both product

---

[1] Van den Berghe and Verweire (1998) use assurfinance to signify banking products being marketed through traditional insurance distribution channels.

[2] Some scholars, following the German model, further distinguish universal banks from other financial institutions through their holding of important equity positions and voting power in non-financial companies.

and management). Note, however, that the definition does not specify the structure of the conglomerate, insisting only on common control.

The business of a conglomerate consists exclusively or predominantly of providing services in at least two financial sectors. Thus, a universal bank ordinarily meets the definition, as would a *bancassurance* arrangement involving affiliated firms. A conglomerate that contains one or more financial services firms, but which is predominantly commercially or industrially oriented, does not meet this definition. Such a conglomerate is commonly referred to as a *mixed conglomerate*.

Financial services integration also occurs when firms in one sector create and sell products containing significant elements traditionally associated with products of another sector. Thus, variable (unit linked) annuities and life insurance combine elements of insurance and securities. The securitization of banks' asset cash flows (e.g., mortgages, credit card balances, and other debt portfolios) combines important elements of securities firms and banking. Alternative risk transfer techniques, such as catastrophe options, bonds, and equity puts, standby letters of credit, and finite risk transfer mechanisms, offer other examples. Money market mutual funds, offered by securities firms, are effectively demand deposit accounts. This product convergence trend can be expected to be an important force toward operational integration among banks, securities firms, insurers, and mutual funds.

Finally, financial services integration can occur at the level of the advisor, without necessarily any supply-side integration or even cooperation. Thus, personal financial planners, accountants, attorneys, risk management consultants, agents, brokers, and other personal and corporate advisors often effectively integrate financial services for their clients. They may sell products themselves or direct the client's purchasing behavior based on an integrated financial or risk management plan. Integration also occurs when employers or affinity groups offer a range of financial products to employees or group members, as, for example, when an employer offers a "cafeteria" of employee benefits that may be self-funded or funded through an insurer or other financial intermediary.

This paper focuses on integration at the supplier level. Thus, product and advisory integration receive scant attention here, although we recognize the importance of this type of integration.

III. Structures for Delivering Integrated Financial Services

Integrated financial services may be delivered through several structural forms. In general, however, they fall into one of five classifications.[1]

Full Integration. The most fully integrated operational form is one wherein all financial services are produced (underwritten) within and distributed by a single corporation, with all activities supported by a single capital base. Figure 1 illustrates

---

[1] This classification scheme follows that of Saunders and Walter (1994), p. 85.

this form which probably exists presently only in theory. The form is nonetheless important because it might represent a future structure of such firms, and provides a schema for thinking about the issues associated with regulation and management of financial conglomerates that, while sectorally separate for legal and regulatory purposes, might be operationally integrated.

Figure 1: Full Financial Services Integration

Banking Activities	Securities Activities	Insurance Activities	Other Financial Services

Universal Bank – German Variant. German universal banks, a step removed from the fully integrated firm above, represent the next structural form of integration. As illustrated in Figure 2, such firms combine commercial and investment banking within a single corporation but conduct other financial activities through separately capitalized subsidiaries owned by the universal bank. The German *grossbanken* ("big banks"), including Deutsche Bank, Dresdner Bank, and Commerzbank, are organized in this way, as are many regional banks. The large Swiss banks also are structured in this fashion, as are many other continental European financial institutions.

Figure 2: Partial Financial Services Integration
(Universal Bank – German Variant)

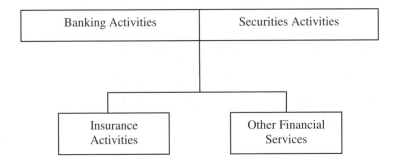

Bank or Insurer Parent. The third structural variation of financial conglomerates is one in which the parent company is a bank or an insurer. The parent owns one or more subsidiaries that produce other financial services and are separately capitalized. Figure 3 illustrates this approach, with the bank as the parent. This structure is common in the United Kingdom (U.K.), with Barclays and Lloyds TBS being examples.

Holding Company Arrangement. The fourth principal form of financial conglomerate is via a holding company arrangement. Typically, a non-operational holding company owns all or most of the shares in separately incorporated and capitalized sectoral subsidiaries, as illustrated in Figure 4. This arrangement is the evolving model for the United States (U.S.).

Figure 3: Financial Services Integration via Bank Ownership

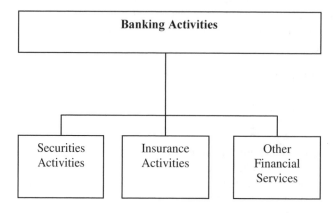

Figure 4: Integrated Financial Services via a Holding Company

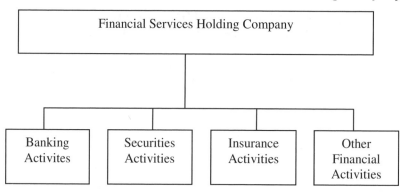

Joint Venture and Other Arrangements. Another form through which integrated financial services are provided involves joint venture and other arrangements between unaffiliated financial services firms. In such structures, two financial intermediaries – such as a bank and an insurer – form a joint venture firm, strategic alliance, joint marketing arrangement, or other formal arrangement through which one or both firms' products are sold.

The structure adopted in delivering integrated financial services is influenced by a myriad of factors. Besides the historical context of a country's financial services market, its regulation is critically important in this respect. But so too are issues such as market power, economies of scale and scope, operating efficiencies, and how best to address conflicts of interest. These and other issues are discussed later in this paper.

CHAPTER 2

THE ECONOMICS OF FINANCIAL SERVICES INTEGRATION

We now explore our existing understanding of the economics of integration. Integration is economically logical if it results in higher profits. One means of viewing this issue is to consider the stock market reaction to the announcement of cross-sectoral mergers and acquisitions. A positive reaction suggests an expectation of enhanced profitability. Two recent studies provide insight.

In their study of 54 merger and acquisition (M&A) deals covering 14 European banking markets, Cybo-Ottone and Murgia's (2000) results indicate positive gains in shareholder value are associated with the average domestic bank-to-bank merger and to bank/insurer deals but not bank expansion into investment banking. Carow (2001) conducted an event study around the announcement of the Citicorp/Travelers merger. He found that large banks and life insurers had significant share price increases, suggesting a market expectation of additional profitability accruing to these firms. Small banks, health insurers, and nonlife insurers experienced no increase.

Another means of examining the economics of financial services integration is to conduct studies on the firms themselves. Using this methodology, higher profits can flow from a reduction in operating costs, an increase in revenues, or any combination that yields increased profits (e.g., revenues increase more than costs increase). We now explore these issues in more depth.

I. Cost Effects

Financial services conglomerates could enjoy cost advantages through realizing economies of scale, economies of scope in production, or operational efficiencies.

A. *Economies of Scale*

Economies of scale exist if the average cost of production falls with increasing output, holding product mix constant. Economies of scale, in themselves, would not seem to justify the formation of multi-sectoral financial firms, although they may justify existing conglomerates growing larger.

The majority of studies on economies of scale of financial institutions have been conducted on U.S. firms, and, therefore, hold less relevance for scale economies with financial conglomerates, given the historical U.S. practice of having segregated financial institutions. Additionally, U.S. regulation historically had other highly restrictive elements, rendering such studies less relevant to the European financial scene.

Saunders and Walter (1994) studied the world's largest banks, including several universal banks, and found economies of scale only in the middle range of big banks.

The few other studies on economies of scale for universal banks find somewhat similar results. Growing from $1 billion to $10 billion in assets seems to gain scale, but growing from $10 billion to $100 billion seems to gain little.[1] Thus, we have some evidence for scale economies from the 1980s and early 1990s for financial conglomerates, but not for very large institutions. More recent work suggests that a historically more favorable European regulatory environment may contribute to the different results for European financial firms. For example, Vander Vennet (2002) found that a large sample of European universal banks and other financial conglomerates enjoyed neither scale benefits nor disadvantages, suggesting that the minimum efficient scale for such financial institutions, as least in Europe, has increased since the earlier studies and that diseconomies of scale pose few problems to further growth.

B. *Economies of Scope in Production.*

Economies of scope in production exist if multiple products can be produced at less cost than the sum of the costs of producing each separately. Economies of scope could be important in financial integration because of the ability to share overhead, technology, and other fixed costs across a range of products. Thus, the fixed costs of managing a client relationship would seem to lend themselves to sharing across a broad range of financial services (Herring and Santomero, 1990, p. 474).

Economies of scope could come about from investment operations (having a single investment unit for all sectors), information technology (having customer information consolidated and available for multiple uses), distribution (using distribution channels established for one sector to sell other products), and reputation (having the good reputation of one firm – e.g., a bank – enhance the sale of other conglomerate products). As with studies on economies of scale, most scope studies are on U.S. single-sector financial firms, finding that, where they exist, they are exhausted at fairly low levels of output. However, most studies were conducted over periods during which financial firms were undergoing great change, perhaps incurring substantial sunk costs that may have distorted results.

Diseconomies of scope are not unlikely. Financial conglomerates are large firms with substantial bureaucracies. They may suffer from inertia and an inability to respond quickly to changing markets and customer demand. They may lack creativity, experience "turf" battles, realize internal compensation conflicts that erode synergy, and suffer from serious internal cultural differences across sectors that inhibit cooperation and coordination necessary for synergy (Walter, 1997).

Also, not all customers will want to purchase financial products from a single conglomerate. They may be concerned about being treated impersonally, about a large firm not passing lower costs of operation to its smaller customers, about having their financial purchases concentrated within a single group (and foregoing diversification),

---

[1] See, generally, studies cited in Berger (1999).

or about use of personally identifiable information within the conglomerate family to the customer's detriment.

C. Operational Efficiencies.

Economies of scale and scope are static efficiency concepts, with studies focusing on size and product mix cost effects for a given time frame. *Dynamic efficiency*, involving product and process innovations and other operational efficiencies (also called X-efficiencies), might be even more important. Financial conglomerates might have an informational advantage over specialized firms in that they can more quickly develop products in response to changing technological or market conditions, especially products carrying attributes of multiple sectors. Indeed, several studies have found that technical inefficiencies (excess use of inputs) and allocative inefficiencies (suboptimal input mix) are large and dominate scale and scope economies.[1]

Considerable effort has gone into the measurement of X-efficiency of financial institutions. Berger and Humphery (1997) survey 130 studies on efficiency that covered 21 countries and used various efficiency and measurement methods. These studies included multiple time periods and all major financial intermediaries. It appears that the average unit costs in banking range from 20 to 25 percent above the costs of best practice firms.

Understandably, comparatively few efficiency studies have been conducted of financial conglomerates. Vander Vennet's (2002) study cited above is one of the few. His results suggest that universal banks enjoyed significantly higher average levels of operational efficiency than specialized banks and that this finding is most pronounced for other-than-German universal banks.

II. Revenue Effects

Two aspects of financial integration could give rise to important revenue effects: economies of scope in consumption and market power.

A. Economies of Scope in Consumption

Integration may enhance the earnings potential of a financial conglomerate through distribution of a greater product range. These *economies of scope in consumption* (demand-side economies of scope) could follow from the cross-marketing of investment, savings, credit, and insurance products. Many financial products are complements: mortgage loans and mortgage protection life insurance policies; auto loans and auto insurance; and wrap accounts and investment products. Customers could realize lower search, information, monitoring, and transactions costs by purchasing products from a conglomerate than by purchasing the same array of products from specialty firms. Private banking has always been designed to exploit such economies.

---

[1] See Group of Ten (2001) for an overview of the literature.

379

These economies may not entail lower priced products. In fact, if such consumption economies exist, customers presumably would be willing to pay more for products offered in this convenient way and costs may actually be higher, but presumably revenues would be higher still.

Evidence of such economies exists, although the literature is thin. Berger, Hancock, and Humphrey (1993) found that gains inherent in universal banking may lie more on the revenue than the cost side. Canals (1993) found that bank performance was improved by the increased revenues from new business units. Mutual fund activities increase bank profitability (Gallo, Apilado, and Kolari, 1996). Various risk-simulation studies conducted by Saunders and Walter (1994) suggest that combinations of banking, insurance, and securities activities may lead to a more stable profit stream, as each sector's cash flows are usually imperfectly correlated.

Boyd, Graham, and Hewitt (1993) found that simulated mergers of U.S. bank holding companies (BHCs) with life insurance and property/casualty insurance firms may reduce risk, but that mergers with securities firms would likely increase risk. Kwan (1997) found that U.S. BHCs gain potential diversification benefits from having securities subsidiaries because of low correlations between their returns and those of the other operating units of the BHC. Benston (1989) reports that returns for combined commercial and investment banking would be significantly higher, but without an increase in overall risk. Vander Vennet (2002) found that European financial conglomerates were more revenue efficient and enjoyed higher profits than specialized financial firms.

Further, Walter (1997) observes that network economies, a special type of economies of scope in consumption, are associated with some elements of universal banking. With network economies (positive externalities), relationships with end users represent a network structure wherein additional client linkages add value to existing clients by increasing the feasibility or reducing the cost of accessing them. These externalities tend to increase with the absolute size of the network itself and are characteristics of activities such as securities clearance and settlement, global custody, funds transfer and international cash management, foreign exchange and securities dealing, and the like.

B. Market Power

Large size can convey market power; i.e., the ability to affect price. To the extent that barriers to entry exist and a country's financial services market tends toward oligopoly, financial conglomerates may be able to charge higher prices, at least to some market segments, than they would charge in a less concentrated, more competitive market. In exercising their market power, such conglomerates would enhance their revenue (or at least profit) stream.

Until the mid-1990s, many countries strictly limited access to their financial services markets, especially by foreign firms, and sheltered highly concentrated markets. Government-sanctioned market power flows naturally in such markets. With the deregulation and liberalization trend worldwide, such markets seem likely to be the exception rather than the rule for the future. With fewer barriers to entry, more competitive markets with fewer opportunities to gain market power should evolve.

III. Profit Efficiency

Of course, a conglomerate could incur greater costs – resulting in cost inefficiency – yet realize greater revenues – from revenue efficiency – such that net profits increased or vice versa. Profit efficiency measures incorporate both cost and revenue effects and, therefore, are likely to be more relevant.

Estimates of profit efficiency tend to be sector specific. For banks, results are dispersed, averaging around 50 percent; that is, the average bank could be twice as profitable if it operated as efficiently as the most profitable bank (Group of Ten, 2001). For insurance, Berger et al. (2000) found mixed results when they examined profit scope economies. Large insurers that emphasized multiple personal lines of insurance and that had vertically integrated distribution systems dominated single-line firms in profit efficiency. Small insurers, by contract, that emphasized commercial lines and used non-integrated distribution systems dominated the large insurers.

For financial conglomerates, Vander Vennet (2002) found that European universal banks (except for those in Germany) were more profit efficient than non-universal banks. He suggests that the trend toward cross-financial services specialization could lead to a more efficient banking system.

IV. Relationship between Effects and Operational Structure

If integration yields positive microeconomic cost effects, one would expect to find conglomerates moving toward production and operational integration. Back-office operations such as investment, accounting, information technology, risk management, and the like would more likely be the basis for realizing economic gains. Synergies would likely relate to both the corporate and retail markets.

If integration yields positive microeconomic revenue effects, one would expect to find financial integration more toward distribution. It may be that little or nothing is gained by production and operational integration. In such instances, *bancassurance* arrangements, with or without affiliation, would be sufficient. Synergies would likely relate more to the retail than to the corporate market.

CHAPTER 3

MANAGEMENT ISSUES IN INTEGRATION

The preceding discussion highlighted several management challenges associated with financial services integration but did so in the terminology of the economist. This section translates some of those economic concepts into practical management concerns.

I. Group Structure

After establishing the group's mission and strategy, management must decide on the most desirable operational structure. We can distinguish between *de jure* and *de facto* structures. Whereas the formal structure must comply with legal requirements (e.g., conduct insurance operations in an insurance subsidiary), this should not necessarily dictate the operational structure. In fact, adopting the legal structure as the operational basis could fail to capture hoped-for economies, as alluded to earlier.

Group structure decisions also relate to whether the necessary manufacturing platforms for financial services will be acquired or created *de novo*. Of course, such decisions need not be the same from market to market or over time.

In general, organic ("greenfield") growth leads to fewer cultural difficulties and allows operations to be oriented more quickly and efficiently toward the group's mission. Many observers believe that organic growth has been more successful than growth through acquisition.

On the other hand, organic growth means that the group is unlikely to be a major player within a country's financial services market in the near term. If, as many financial conglomerates believe, being among the five or so largest financial institutions in the market is important for operational efficiency and profitability, organic growth may not be the best choice. This is especially true in mature markets, where consolidation is already well under way and opportunities for acquisitions abound. Organic growth tends to be more common in emerging markets than in mature markets.

II. Complexity

Integrated financial services firms are complex operations. This observation seems especially relevant when integration is accomplished via merger or acquisition. As noted in *The Economist*, "Managers are finding that, in practice, consolidation brings such nightmarish complexity that it often threatens to undo any costs savings or revenue synergies that the mergers might have achieved in the first place."[1]

---

[1] "Complex Equations," *The Economist* (June 5, 1999), p. 69.

Such complexity, however, is not associated solely with consolidation. For example, it has been observed that long-established European universal banks consistently subsidize unprofitable activities, seem reluctant to out-source nonessential operations, and rarely excel or become innovative in any one sector. Many are said to operate with a "silo" mentality. These observations may explain why they achieve a lower return on equity than U.S. commercial banks, with some observers contending that no European investment banks are capable of competing with U.S. institutions such as Morgan Stanley, Goldman Sachs, Bankers Trust, or J. P. Morgan (Kraus, 1998).

The problem of complexity seems largely to be ignored at present. As reported in *European Banker* (1999), it is as if consolidation and being big were not just necessary but sufficient conditions for success in financial services. Again, if the professional press is accurate, this seems particularly true for Europe's universal banks. In an examination of the annual reports of Europe's 50 largest banks, Lafferty Business Research found only one bank that questioned whether merger and consolidation were the appropriate answers to the advent of the European Monetary Union. Banco Popular, perhaps prophetically, noted: "It is, to say the least, surprising that there should be such widespread and critical [sic] acceptance of this need, with no precise distinction between types of business and without meticulous analysis of the many drawbacks that these processes may involve and of the problematic nature of their purported advantages" (*European Banker*, 1999).

III. Corporate Cultures

Corporate cultures vary across firms and across financial sectors and can lead to potentially crippling management problems. The investment bank corporate culture is one of entrepreneurship, risk taking, and incentive compensation. The commercial banking culture is one of relationship building, little risk, stability, and compensation schemes less related to performance. The insurance culture is bi-polar. Life insurance is associated with aggressiveness, marketing innovation, consultative selling, and incentive compensation. The non life insurance culture falls between that of life insurance and commercial banking. Non life products are largely demand pull, not demand push products like life insurance.

These cultural differences pose challenges for management of financial conglomerates, especially those resulting from merger and acquisition. Indeed, one-half of all mergers and acquisitions are unsuccessful, with the most frequently cited reason for failure being cultural differences (Tuohy, 1999). Cultural differences seem less of an obstacle when integration is organic.

Thus, a frequently reported difficulty with *bancassurance* is indifference by bank employees to insurance. They treat such products as sidelines or as too complex to sell within the traditional banking relationship (Higgins, 1999).

Another dimension of corporate culture seems to be related to national differences in management dedication to shareholder value. Economists classify this as an agency problem. In a study touching on this issue, Lafferty Business Research found that

European banks clustered around two distinct business approaches: focused banks and universal banks (*European Banker*, 1999).

IV. Inexperience/Lack of Expertise

Although perhaps not a problem for the long run, the lack of experience in managing an integrated financial services group can pose vexing short-term problems. This issue is particularly relevant in markets where financial integration has not existed formerly, either because of practice or regulatory prohibitions, such as in the U.S., Eastern Europe, and Asia. Financial conglomerates from other countries, particularly from Western Europe, may have a competitive advantage over domestic financial institutions in such markets.

Joint ventures and strategic alliances between domestic and experienced foreign firms may prove most appealing to both domestic and foreign entrants. Although foreign financial conglomerates have greater knowledge and insights into how to make integration work, local firms have a competitive advantage in understanding the local culture and in local relationships.

V. Marketing/Distribution Issues

Distribution issues can be among the most challenging for management of integrated financial institutions. Among the most troubling issues for financial conglomerates created via M&A has been how to deal with channel conflict. The concern, of course, is that marketing intermediaries, especially agents and brokers that have been the primary distribution outlet for one of the formerly independent institutions, face the possibility of disintermediation by new channels, such as a bank branches, direct response, or the internet.

The situation of ING – the first large-scale merger of a bank and an insurer – offers an example. ING was formed in 1991 by the merger of the insurance group Nationale-Nederlanden (NN) and the banking group NMB-Postbank which was itself a result of a 1989 merger between two important Dutch banks. At the time, NN was the largest insurance group and NMB-Postbank was the third largest banking group in the Netherlands.

In announcing the merger, NN indicated that it would design special insurance products to be sold through Postbank. Such products would compete with and be less expensive than those sold by NN's army of independent agents, which accounted for some 85 percent of NN's sales. Their agents promised a boycott. Only after NN agreed to limit Postbank distribution to very simple products, such as travel accident insurance and certain types of annuities, was the boycott canceled (Van den Berghe and Verweire, 1998). The channel conflict for ING has since eased, but remains a challenge for the group in the Dutch market.

Channel conflict seems to be less of a management challenge for (1) de novo *bancassurance* operations (e.g., the creation of Deutsche Lebensversicherungs AG by Deutsche Bank and the creation of Predica by Credit Agricole), (2) integration that does not involve agents or brokers (e.g., USAA Life and USAA and Maybank Life and Maybank in Malaysia), and (3) integration in countries with less mature financial markets (e.g., the Philippines and Poland).

Marketing issues are associated largely with demand-side economies of scope. As such, they usually are of greater concern with *bancassurance* integration than others, especially those related to investment, risk management, and other back office integration possibilities.

VI. Target Market Clarity

Management must be clear about the group's target market. History is littered with attempts at financial services integration that were unsuccessful largely because of ambiguity in this regard. For example, when Prudential (U.S.) acquired Bache many years ago, it was expected that Prudential – with its largely blue collar, lower middle-income target market – and Bache – with its largely white collar, upper-income target market – would cross-market each other's products. That the experiment failed is unsurprising, in retrospect.

To date, most success in financial services integration has been in the retail market. Within the retail sector, greatest success has been with middle and lower-income markets. The affluent market seems largely to be the province of financial planners and independent agents and brokers. Indeed, some years ago, it was predicted that *bancassureurs* would capture one-third of the U.K. life insurance market. Their share today is about one-eighth. Independent financial advisors, by contrast, now control more than one-half of the market, up from less than one-third a few years ago (O'Conner, 1999). These advisors have expanded their own product offerings; in effect, offering integration at the advisory level and blunting bank distribution.

In selecting the target market, management will simultaneously be determining the classes of products to be offered. The emphasis might be on the retail market, the corporate market, or both. Different demographic, economic, and geographic emphasis will be taken with each broad market segment.

Management will decide which asset accumulation, debt management, and asset protection products to manufacture and through which channels to distribute them. In this connection, an issue confronting all financial conglomerates is the extent to which it is better to manufacture the desired product or to market other institutions' products through their distribution channels.

Management of some financial conglomerates seemingly is concerned that some financial products carry the potential of creating diseconomies for scope. Property/casualty insurance is perhaps the most commonly discussed product line in this regard. An insightful story making the rounds is that of a superb banking customer taking her entire account elsewhere because the group's insurer denied automobile insurance to her 17-year old son who had two speeding tickets. What is the anticipated effect on a good securities customer of being dissatisfied with a property insurance claim settlement? The recent divestiture by Citigroup of its Travelers (non-life) insurance subsidiary speaks directly to this point. Many conglomerates have chosen to avoid the manufacture of property/casualty insurance for reasons of this type, with some not even making it available via marketing arrangements.

VII.   Financial Management Issues

For financial institutions and conglomerates interested in manufacturing their own products, financial management should be a core competency. Two areas of financial management seem to be particularly important: risk management and performance appraisal.

Only in the past few years have risk management issues been addressed in anything resembling an integrated way by financial institutions. Even then, this has occurred chiefly within individual financial institutions, not across institutions within a group, with some notable exceptions. Moreover, the focus of risk management differs considerably based on sector and product line. Credit risk, interest rate risk, liquidity risk, operating risk, and foreign exchange risk vary greatly from line to line and even product to product within the same line.[1] For example, interest rate risk for a securities firm ordinarily is far less important than it is for a life insurer.

A challenge for management of financial conglomerates is, first, understanding the risk profile of the group as a whole rather than its parts in isolation. Second, management must develop risk management policies and techniques appropriate for the entirety of the group. If synergies are to be realized through integration, one would fully expect them to arise, among other places, through a holistic approach to measuring and managing risk.

Related to holistic risk management is the issue of how best to appraise the financial performance of the entire group. Banks, insurers, and securities firms have used different techniques. Banks historically have focused on interest spread, with return on equity of more recent importance. Life insurers increasingly use embedded value analysis. Property/casualty insurers use combined ratios and return on equity. How are these diverse techniques to be reconciled (if at all) for the benefit of management and ultimately shareholders?

---

[1] For an overview of the risk profiles of different financial intermediaries, see Santomero and Babbel (1997), chap. 25.

VIII.   Conflicts of Interest

The potential for internal conflicts of interest (agency problems) is endemic to financial services integration.[1] Conflicts of interest exist when incentives within the group do not align with the customer's best interest. The major classes of conflicts of interest include the following:

- *Salesperson's stake.* It has been argued that when one financial institution within a conglomerate has the power to sell affiliates' products, salespeople and managers are less likely to offer objective product advice to customers. Rather they will have a stake in pushing the conglomerate's products, possibly to the disadvantage of the customer.

- *Stuffing fiduciary accounts.* In underwriting securities, the investment operation of a financial conglomerate may seek to minimize a potential loss by "stuffing" the unwanted securities into customers' accounts over which it has discretionary authority.

- *Bankruptcy-risk transfer.* Because of its relationship with its commercial loan or commercial insurance customers, the group may secure private information that a customer's bankruptcy risk has increased. The group may have an incentive to induce the firm to issue bonds or equities – underwritten by its securities operation – to an unsuspecting public. Proceeds could be used to reduce the bank loan, thus effectively transferring the bank's credit risk outside the group, and earning fees or underwriting spreads.

- *Third-party loans.* A conglomerate may have an incentive to make below-market loans to customers of its securities operation on the condition that the proceeds are used to purchase products sold by other units, such as securities or life insurance.

- *Tie-in sales.* A bank could use the threat of withholding or rationing credit to coerce a customer into purchasing other conglomerate products, such as insurance or securities.

- *Internal information transfer.* One unit of the conglomerate may secure material, private information about a customer that enables other units to charge higher prices than otherwise to that customer. (The result also could be lower prices.) For example, in underwriting a life insurance policy, the insurer might discover that the proposed insured had a substantial health problem. Information about this problem might influence a mortgage loan decision by the group's bank. Irrespective of whether the customer might suffer harm, the important issue of the extent to which he or she should be

---

[1] This section draws from Walter (1997).

able to control the flow of personally identifiable information within a financial conglomerate remains an important public policy (and, therefore, management) concern.

Incentive conflicts are managed by rearranging the incentives to be more compatible with the desired result (a market solution) or through regulation. Most universal banking systems are said to rely on market incentives (Walter, 1997). The U.S. historically has relied more heavily on regulation, including "firewalls" between activities potentially giving rise to incentive conflicts.

In general, conglomerates deal with potential conflicts of interest by seeking to instill a sense of professionalism and ethical conduct within salespeople and employees. Training, close supervision, and internal monitoring are essential. Further, the group's reputation and competition act as disciplinary mechanisms. The value of future business (goodwill) is greatly affected by the group's market reputation (franchise), as recent accounting, market conduct, and trading scandals have demonstrated.

Preventing or mitigating the adverse effects of internal conflicts of interest is expensive. Training and monitoring systems are costly. Building internal firewalls or creating other substantial limitations on information sharing within the group can defeat the very reason for integration.

CHAPTER 4

OVERVIEW OF REGULATION OF FINANCIAL CONGLOMERATES INTERNATIONALLY

Details of financial institution regulation vary greatly from country to country. This observation applies particularly to prudential regulation, although some harmonization has been achieved in banking through the Basle Accord. Some generalizations can be drawn, however, in the extent of financial activities that countries permit within a financial conglomerate and the overall mode of regulation.

I. Permissible Activities

In a survey of 54 of the world's major financial centers, the Institute of International Bankers (2002) found that the majority, especially the largest centers, permit financial conglomerates to undertake banking, insurance, and security activities. The survey does not speak to the important issue of consistency of prudential oversight across sectors.

Table 1 gives a summary of the survey. It shows that the overwhelming majority of countries allow joint banking and securities activities, with most permitting banks to undertake securities activities within the bank itself. Several others require some or all securities activities to be undertaken through subsidiaries or affiliates. Of the countries surveyed, only China prohibits any joint undertakings.

The situation with insurance is somewhat different. Although the information source is not completely clear, it appears that few, if any, countries permit insurance underwriting within a bank. The majority allows joint arrangements, but through subsidiaries or affiliates. Several countries prohibit any affiliation between insurance and banking, with a few others prohibiting banks from owning insurers but allowing them to act as agents or brokers for unaffiliated insurers.

II. Structure of Regulatory Authority

The majority of countries regulate financial conglomerates on a functional basis; that is, banking and insurance (and often securities also) oversight are separate, with each sector having its own regulator. Several countries with functional regulation, however, establish a lead regulator for conglomerates, based on its principal activity. Thus, if a conglomerate's main activity is commercial banking, the bank regulator is the lead regulator. He or she is responsible for overseeing the entire group's operation and ensuring coordination of responses among functional supervisors. This does not mean that the lead regulator usurps the power of other regulators, however.

An important trend during the past few years is the implementation of consolidated financial services regulation within several countries. For example, new regulatory agencies with responsibilities for consolidated oversight of banks and other financial institutions have been established in Australia, Korea, Japan, Singapore, and the U.K. Canada, Denmark, Norway, and Sweden have had consolidated regulation for several years. Table 2 summarizes the regulatory approaches of several major financial centers as of 1998 [Institute of International Bankers (1998)].

Table 1: Permissible Activities for Banking Organizations in Various Centers (2002)

Securities			Insurance	
Permitted Through the Same Legal Entity	Permitted Through Subsidiaries or Affiliates	Not Permitted	Permitted Through Subsidiaries or Affiliates only	Not Permitted
Argentina	Brazil	China	Argentina[4]	China
Australia	Canada		Australia[2]	Colombia
Austria	Colombia		Austria[2]	India
			Bahrain[3]	
Bahrain	Egypt		Belgium[2]	Israel
Belgium	Greece		Bermuda[2]	Pakistan
Bermuda	India		Bolivia[2]	Panama
Bolivia	Indonesia		Brazil[2]	Peru
Cayman Islands	Israel		Canada[2]	Russia
Chile	Japan		Cayman Islands	
Czech Republic	Korea		Chile[3]	
Denmark	Mexico		Czech Republic[2]	
Estonia	Panama		Denmark[2]	
Finland	Philippines		Egypt[2]	
France	Poland		Estonia[2]	
Germany	Romania		Finland[3]	
Hong Kong	Singapore		France[2]	
Ireland	United States		Germany[2]	
Italy				
Latvia			Greece[1]	
Luxembourg			Hong Kong[1]	
New Zealand			Japan[2]	
The Netherlands			Indonesia[2]	
Nigeria			Ireland[2]	
Norway			Italy[1]	
Pakistan			Korea[2]	
Peru				
Portugal			Latvia[2]	
Russia			Luxembourg[2]	
South Africa			Mexico[2]	
Spain			The Netherlands[2]	
Sweden			New Zealand[2]	
Switzerland			Nigeria[2]	
Turkey			Norway[2]	
United Kingdom			Philippines[2]	
Uruguay			Poland	
Venezuela			Portugal[2]	
			Romania[3]	
			Singapore[2]	
			South Africa[1]	
			Spain[2]	
			Sweden	
			Switzerland[2]	
			Turkey[3]	
			United Kingdom[2]	
			United States[2]	
			Uruguay[2]	
			Venezuela[2]	

[1] With limits.   [2] Through subsidiaries or affiliates only.
[3] Brokerage or agency only.   [4] Pensions only.

Table 2: Regulation of Financial Conglomerates (1998)

Single Regulator Oversees Activities of Financial Conglomerates as a Whole	Identity of the Lead Regulator for a Financial Conglomerate Determined on the Basis of the Financial Conglomerate's Principal Activity	Financial Conglomerates Operate without a Single or Lead Regulator
Australia Bolivia Canada[1] Cayman Islands Columbia Denmark Japan Norway Peru Singapore Sweden United Kingdom	Argentina[2] Austria Belgium Chile Estonia[3] Greece Ireland Israel Latvia[4] Philippines[5] Spain United States[6] Venezuela	Czech Republic Finland France Germany Hong Kong Italy Luxembourg Netherlands Panama[7] Poland Portugal Romania South Africa Switzerland Turkey Uruguay[8]

[1] The Office of the Superintendent of Financial Services oversees the operations of financial conglomerates at the federal level. Certain companies within a financial conglomerate (e.g., securities firms and insurance companies) may also be subject to supervision by provincial authorities.

[2] Only financial conglomerates headed by banks are subject to consolidated regulation.

[3] The Central Bank is the lead regulator of financial conglomerates that include banks. Financial conglomerates that do not include banks do not have a lead regulator.

[4] Effective January I, I999, but only with respect to conglomerates headed by credit institutions.

[5] The Central Bank has supervisory authority over banks and their subsidiaries and affiliates, as well as nonbank financial institutions with quasi-banking or trust authority. The Office of the Insurance Commissioner supervises insurance companies that are subsidiaries or affiliates of banks. Nonbank financial institutions that are subsidiaries and affiliates of banks and other financial institutions where their charter provides that they will be under the Central Bank's supervision are regulated jointly by the Central Bank and the Securities and Exchange Commission (SEC). The SEC regulates other nonbank financial institutions that do not fall under these classifications.

[6] Financial conglomerates that include banks are regulated at the holding company level by the Federal Reserve. Nonbank financial conglomerates (i.e., those comprised of only nonbank financial institutions such as securities firms, insurance companies, and commercial finance companies) are not regulated at the group level, although the Securities and Exchange Commission requires registered broker-dealers to file quarterly risk assessment reports regarding their material affiliates. Banks may affiliate with securities firms and insurance companies.

[7] Only financial conglomerates that include banks are regulated on a group-wide basis.

[8] The Central Bank regulates separate companies within a financial conglomerate (e.g. banks, insurance companies, investment fund managers, and pension fund managers) but not the group as a whole.

III. Governmental Actions Affecting Financial Services Integration

The Asian and other financial crises of the 1990s brought forceful attention to how inadequate financial regulation adversely affects national economies and to the need for better international regulatory coordination and cooperation. Since then, financial regulation has become less diverse, with the major intergovernmental organizations involved in financial regulation playing more active and constructive roles. While these actions have not, for the most part, been directed toward integration, they nonetheless have provided impetus for this result through efforts to address cross-sectoral financial issues.

Other governmental actions, not explicitly aimed at financial services integration, are having or promise to have potentially important positive effects on integration. For example, the trend towards allowing mutual insurers and banks to convert to shareholder-owned firms opens up new opportunities for financial conglomeration. Demutualization has been particularly important in Australia, Canada, South Africa, the U.K., and the U.S.

Privatization of banks and insurers in several countries similarly created opportunities. Privatizations have occurred in Belgium, the Czech Republic, Finland, France, Israel, Norway, Peru, Poland, Turkey, the Baltic counties, and Venezuela.

Significant combinations of banks and insurance companies occurred within the past few years in Denmark, Norway, Switzerland, and the U.S., while consolidation of domestic banks, insurers, and securities firms continues in many countries. Foreign financial institutions developed, expanded, or have been given new authority to develop or expand their presence in many markets during the past few years.

CHAPTER 5

PUBLIC POLICY CONCERNS IN INTEGRATION

Many observers and government policy makers express concern about certain aspects of financial services integration.[1] The question is whether new or additional regulation is needed to protect consumers or the financial system.

I.   Categories of Market Imperfections

In considering this question, we should first be clear about the generic types of market imperfections of concern to financial services regulators. These market imperfections fall into three broad categories: information problems, market power, and negative externalities. *Information problems* exist when the information that buyers or sellers have is deficient in some way, such as being incomplete or inaccurate. Thus, insurance buyers typically have incomplete information about the policies that they purchase and the insurer's financial solidity. This information asymmetry – the "lemons" problem – means that customers are at an information disadvantage vis-à-vis the insurer and its agents, which could lead customers unknowingly to purchase poor-value insurance or purchase it from financially unsound insurers. Hence, government intervention is justified to minimize the chances of consumers being harmed because of insurer insolvency or misleading or incomplete marketing information.

As noted earlier, *market power* exists when the seller (or buyer) can exercise meaningful control over prices. If a market were reasonably competitive, all sellers would be forced by competition to charge more or less the same prices. Firms seek to create market power and thus enhance profitability.

Market power can result from increasing returns to scale and from concerted practices among competitors that restrain competition, such as market sharing arrangements, pricing collusion, or exclusive dealings. In many instances, regulation is the source of market power for companies, as when government creates unreasonable barriers to entry for new competitors or mandates price controls (as in mandating interest rates on demand deposits or premiums for insurance policies).

Negative externalities exist when a firm's activities impose uncompensated costs on others. The most important negative externality in financial services stems from the possibility of systemic risks. *Systemic risks* exist because the difficulties of financial intermediaries can cause harm elsewhere within an economy. We can identify two types of systemic risks. The first – *cascading failures* – exists when the failure of one financial institution is the proximate cause of the failure of others. This can occur, for example, if a bank's default on its short-term credit obligations to other banks precipitates other bank failures – ultimately causing harm to the real economy.

---

[1] For an interesting analysis of unfavorable outcomes, see Wilmarth (2002).

The second type of systemic risk is a *run* in which many depositors (or other creditors) demand their money at once. Runs are caused by a loss of confidence in the financial institution, often precipitated by a real or imagined fear of insolvency. The failure of one or more banks can then precipitate runs on otherwise solvent banks, causing their failure. Similar runs in securities markets can lead to crashes.

II. Categories of Regulation

Government regulation of financial intermediaries is justified when market imperfections could cause substantial economic harm to consumers or the economy and, importantly, government intervention can ameliorate the harm.   Governments are not always capable of ameliorating harm. (Just as there are *market* imperfections, so too are there *government* imperfections.)   Generally, regulatory intervention falls into three categories: prudential, market conduct, and competition policy.

Prudential regulation is concerned with the financial condition of the financial intermediary.   Market conduct regulation addresses the marketing behavior of the intermediary and its agents. Competition policy (antitrust) regulation is concerned with actions of intermediaries that have the effect of substantially lessening competition. Prudential regulation evolved primarily because of information problems and negative externalities (especially for banking).   Market conduct regulation evolved primarily because of information problems. Competition policy regulation evolved because of market power concerns. Prudential regulation has been and remains the most critical element in government oversight of financial intermediaries.

III. Multinational Public Policy Initiatives

Financial services integration raises questions whether it introduces additional or more complex market imperfections and, therefore, whether different or additional regulation is needed. These questions are limited neither by national boundaries nor to a single sector. With the continued internationalization of financial services, it was recognized that an international approach was desirable.

Thus, at the initiative of the Basle Committee on Banking Supervision (BCBS), an informal group of banking, securities, and insurance regulators was formed in 1993 to examine issues relating to supervision of financial conglomerates. The report (The Tripartite Group, 1995) was the first to address cross-sectoral issues associated with integration on an international level.

A more formal approach emerged in 1996 with the creation of the Joint Forum on Financial Conglomerates (Joint Forum), which was charged with taking forward the work of the Tripartite Group.[1] The Joint Forum is comprised of an equal number of senior bank, securities, and insurance supervisors representing the BCBS, the International Organization of Securities Commissions (IOSCO), and the International

---

[1] See http://www.bis.org/bcbs/jointforum.htm

Association of Insurance Supervisors (IAIS). Thirteen countries are represented in the Joint Forum, with the EU attending in an observer capacity.

The Joint Forum has issued papers addressing the following topics:

- capital adequacy – these papers outline measurement techniques and principles to facilitate the assessment of capital adequacy on a group-wide basis

- fit and proper requirements – this paper provides guidance to ensure that supervisors of entities within financial conglomerates are able to exercise their responsibilities to assess whether those entities are soundly and prudently managed

- sharing of information by supervisors – these papers set out general principles and a framework for facilitating information sharing between sector supervisors

- coordination of activities by supervisors – this paper provides supervisors guidance on cooperation and selection of a coordinator (lead) regulator in emergency and non-emergency situations

- intra-group transactions and exposure principles and risk concentration principles – these papers provide supervisors with principles for ensuring the prudent management and control of such transactions and exposures and of risk concentrations.

Additional, but limited, work on issues related to financial integration is being carried out by other international bodies. The Financial Stability Forum encourages the adoption of 12 core economic and financial standards that are internationally accepted as important for sound, stable, and well functioning financial systems.[1]

The Financial Sector Assessment Program, a joint venture of the World Bank and the International Monetary Fund, seeks to promote the soundness of financial systems in member countries. Supported by experts from a range of national agencies and standard-setting bodies, work under the program seeks to identify the strengths and vulnerabilities of a country's financial system, to determine how key sources of risk are being managed, to ascertain the sector's developmental and technical assistance needs, and to help prioritize policy responses.[2]

The International Network of Pensions Regulators and Supervisors, created in 2000, provides a forum for policy dialogue and cooperation on regulatory, supervisory,

---

[1] See http://www.fsforum.org/home/home.html

[2] See http://www.imf.org/external/NP/fsap/fsap.asp

and financial issues related to pensions.[1] Finally, a useful report was issued in 2001 by the Multidisciplinary Working Group on Financial Disclosure – sponsored jointly by the BCBS, IOSCO, and the IAIS – that addressed key issues related to enhanced disclosure by financial institutions and how to promote market discipline in financial risk management.[2]

IV. Public Policy Issues in Integration

The discussion below draws from the above and other sources. Our focus is on only those public policy issues that arise from integration, not on issues of the type ordinarily dealt with by sectoral regulation alone.[3] The discussion is framed around the three classes of market imperfections and associated typical regulatory responses.

A. Information Problems

This area addresses potential information problems that could accompany integration. The problems are clustered around prudential and market conduct regulation. As will be seen, prudential issues dominate.

1. Prudential Issues

At least six prudential issues have been mentioned as flowing from financial integration. These issues are presented and discussed below as if they were distinct from each other, for ease of exposition. Of course, they relate to each other, often intimately so. They include the following:

- Transparency

- Contagion

- Double and multiple gearing

- Unregulated group entities

- Fit and proper requirements

- Regulatory arbitrage

---

[1] See http://www.inprs.org/objectives.asp

[2] See http://www.bis.org/publ/joint01.htm

[3] Thus, we ignore the important issue of whether financial institutions should be permitted extensive equity investments in or other control of commercial businesses and vice versa, as this issue applies equally to isolated financial institutions.

Transparency.

Overarching all public policy concerns about financial services integration is the issue of group transparency. As it relates mainly, but not exclusively, to prudential concerns, we cover it here. Transparency concerns the extent to which accurate, complete, timely, and relevant information about the financial group is readily available to regulators. Transparency also is sometimes considered as encompassing the availability of such information to other interested parties, such as customers (especially corporate customers), citizens, rating agencies, and marketing intermediaries. This form of transparency often is classified as disclosure.

Using the narrower definition, regulators are concerned about the possibility of opaque management, ownership, and legal structures. If supervisors do not fully understand these structures, they may be unable to assess properly either the totality of the risks faced by the group or the risk that non-regulated members of the group may pose to the regulated members.

The structures of financial groups vary greatly because of tax, legal, cultural, regulatory, and historical considerations. Complexity is multiplied with such groups. Regulators are concerned that they be able to understand fully the lines of accountability relevant to their tasks. Large international financial conglomerates can be particularly complex, making effective regulation more difficult, especially with multiple national and international sectoral regulators. There is concern that some groups may choose complex structures to make their operations opaque in order to avoid or impede effective regulation (The Tripartite Group, 1995, p. 29). To avoid these problems, regulators must have the power to secure needed information from the group itself or from other regulators.

Contagion.

Contagion entails the risk that financial difficulties encountered by one unit in a financial conglomerate could have adverse effects on the financial stability of the group as a whole or possibly on the entire market in which the constituent parts operate (i.e., negative externalities). Close monitoring of the relationships among entities in the group is of paramount importance. Adequate transparency minimizes the risk of contagion.

The Tripartite Group (1995, p. 19) identified two types of contagion. The first is psychological in that the market effectively transfers problems associated with one part of a conglomerate to other parts. The financial difficulties of an insurer within the group may be perceived as threatening to the financial performance of the bank, for example, irrespective of whether the perception comports with reality.

The second type relates to intra-group exposures. Intra-group exposures are direct or indirect claims of units within a conglomerate that are held by other conglomerate units. Some such exposures include the following:

- Credit extensions or lines of credit between affiliates

- Cross-shareholdings

- Intra-group trading in securities

- Insurance or other risk management services provided by one unit for another

- Intra-group guarantees and commitments

Intra-group exposures can have implications for both liquidity and group solvency. An example is a life insurer placing its premiums on deposit with its parent bank, a practice that might not be obvious to regulators. The Tripartite Group (1995, pp. 20 and 23) said that it was important for regulators to be made aware of all intra-group exposures and their specific purposes. Each sectoral regulator should then ensure that the pattern of activity and aggregate exposure between the regulated entity for which it is responsible and other group companies are not such that the failure of another company will undermine the regulated entity. Close coordination among regulators is essential, especially when uncertainties arise. The Tripartite Group admonished regulators that they must ensure that capital is increased or activities limited if the risk that other companies pose to the regulated entity appear to be unacceptable.

Double and Multiple Gearing.[1]

Double gearing, also called double leverage, occurs whenever one entity holds regulatory capital issued by another entity within the same group and the issuer is allowed to count the capital in its own balance sheet. Multiple gearing (leverage) occurs when the subsidiary firm in the previous instance itself sends regulatory capital downstream to a third-tier affiliate. Double and multiple gearing are special classes of intra-group exposures and ordinarily are associated with parents downstreaming capital to subsidiaries. The flow can be reversed or can be by a sister affiliate.

The principal issue raised with double and multiple gearing is less the ownership structure flowing from it and more the proper assessment of a financial conglomerate's consolidated capital. With double and multiple gearing, group capital derived directly from each entity's solo capital is likely overstated. For the most part, capital derived only from external sources provides support for the group. Consequently, assessments of group capital should exclude intra-group holdings of regulatory capital.

The Joint Forum (1999, Annexes 1 and 2) noted three methodologies used for adjusting financial data for double and multiple gearing. These methodologies also accommodate the important issue of capital adequacy assessment for groups containing subsidiaries that are not 100 percent owned by the group.

---

[1] This discussion draws from The Joint Forum (1999), pp. 8-9.

Unregulated Group Entities.

Additional information problems stemming from financial services integration can occur when the group contains an unregulated entity; that is, one not subject to oversight by any sectoral regulator. One such issue is excessive leveraging.[1] Excessive leveraging, another class of intra-group exposure, can occur when an unregulated parent issues debt or other instruments not acceptable as regulatory capital in a downstream entity and downstreams the proceeds to a subsidiary firm in the form of equity or other regulatory capital. The subsidiary's effective leverage may be greater than appears on a solo basis. Such leverage is not inherently unsafe but can become so if undue stress is placed on the regulated subsidiary because of the parent's obligation to service the debt.

With an unregulated holding company, an assessment of group-wide capital adequacy should encompass the effect of the holding company's structure. Regulators will, therefore, need to be able to obtain information about the holding company's ability to service all external debt.

Excessive leveraging as well as double and multiple gearing can also occur when the unregulated entity is an intermediate holding company. The group-wide capital assessment should eliminate the effect of such holding companies. Such intermediate holding companies typically are non-trading entities whose only assets are their investments in subsidiaries or that provide services to other companies.

Finally, some unregulated group entities conduct activities similar to those of regulated companies; for example, leasing, factoring, and reinsurance. In such instances, a comparable or notional capital proxy may be estimated by applying to the unregulated entity the capital requirements of the most analogous regulated industry. Unregulated non-financial entities normally would be excluded from the assessment of the group.

Fit and Proper Requirements.[2]

The probity and competence of the top management of banks, securities firms, and insurers are critical to the achievement of regulatory objectives, particularly as relates to prudential aspects. An effective and comprehensive supervisory regime should include controls designed to encourage the continued satisfaction of the fitness, propriety, or other qualification tests of supervisors and to allow supervisory intervention where necessary. The application of such tests for managers, directors, and key shareholders is a common regulatory mechanism for supervisors to ensure that the institutions for which they have supervisory responsibility are operated in a sound and prudent manner.

The organizational and managerial structure of financial conglomerates adds complexity for supervisors seeking to ensure the fitness, propriety, and other qualifications of the top management of regulated entities. The management of such

---

[1] This discussion draws from The Joint Forum (1999), pp. 9-10.

[2] This discussion draws from The Joint Forum (1999), pp. 41-44.

entities can be influenced by individuals who may not be managers or directors of the regulated entities themselves. Thus, managers and directors of unregulated entities, such as those within an unregulated upstream holding company, can exercise a material influence over many aspects of the regulated entities' business and can also play a key role in controlling risks in the various entities of the group.

Additionally, for multinational financial conglomerates, issues of supervisory jurisdiction arise. A supervisor's reach may not extend beyond national boundaries. This raises the issue of the sharing of information among supervisors with respect to individuals (and companies, see below).

To address these concerns, the Joint Forum (1999, p. 43) recommended that fitness, propriety, or other qualification tests should be applied to managers and directors of other entities in a conglomerate if they exercise a material or controlling influence on the operation of regulated entities. Tests should apply as well to individuals holding substantial ownership or who can exercise material influence on regulated entities within the conglomerate.

Regulatory Arbitrage.

Financial conglomerates should be expected to undertake their activities in ways that minimize their regulatory burdens and taxes. Of course, tax treatment, accounting standards, investment restrictions, capital adequacy requirements, and other elements of regulation differ between types of financial intermediaries and across countries. To the extent that sectoral regulations and taxation differ, arbitrage possibilities are created.

For example, regulations typically limit the maximum exposure that credit institutions may undertake with respect to a single client or group of related clients. Thus, in the EU, loans or other exposures to a single client may not exceed 25 percent of a bank's free capital. In contrast, limitations on insurers' counterparty exposures generally are unrelated to their capital. It is possible for an insurer's exposure to a single client to exceed 100 percent of its capital. Even in countries that subject all major types of financial intermediaries to capital-related limitations (e.g., the U.S.), they are rarely the same across different types of intermediaries. Similar examples are found with capital requirements in connection with other investments and products.

Arbitrage possibilities influence decisions about the structure of the group. If the parent firm is a regulated financial institution, as is common with banks in the U.K., the group itself could be subject to regulations applicable to that institution. The parent is fully subject to regulatory oversight. If the parent firm is an unregulated entity, many of its activities may pass outside regulatory scrutiny.

With continued internationalization and convergence of financial services, the material differences in sectoral and cross-national regulation will gradually disappear, as governments individually and collectively converge toward more common approaches.[1] In

---

[1] For a discussion of these issues, see Barfield (1996).

the interim, however, arbitrage is possible. In some instances, it may result in no meaningful weakening of regulation; in others, the opposite. The Tripartite Group (1995, p. 35) believed that regulatory arbitrage in relation to core activities in most jurisdictions was rare. That there is scope for arbitrage, however, suggests that it must be considered carefully. The suggested solutions to this issue are to move toward consolidated financial regulation where such differences are eliminated or to ensure that sectoral regulators cooperate fully with each other to identify and, if necessary, address such instances collectively.

2. Market Conduct Issues

Market conduct regulation is the other major regulatory category intended primarily to address information problems. The information asymmetry problems here are conflicts of interest (agency problems). Concern has been expressed that conflicts of interest within integrated financial services groups might lead to deficiencies in market conduct. These conflicts of interest were discussed above in connection with management issues in financial conglomeration. Additionally, there may be greater scope for churning of a customer's investments within a conglomerate structure.

As between commercial and investment banking activities, most authorities seem to doubt the importance of such conflicts of interest, with many noting that financial firms have strong reputational incentives to address these potential problems internally. As between insurance and banking activities, the same reputational incentives should apply, plus there have been comparatively few instances of bank/insurance tie-in sales (Kelley, 1985; Diamond, 1989; *Bank Powers*, 1990; Benston, 1990 and 1994).

To the extent that proper private incentives and appropriate management control are insufficient to address conflicts of interest, a regulatory response may be called for. Already, most potential conflicts are illegal.

B. Market Power

The second major classification of market imperfections addressed by regulation is market power. Market power could, in theory, arise from size alone if barriers to entry are great. It also could evolve through predatory pricing.

An established, large conglomerate could sell at less than the cost of production if it wished to drive out smaller competitors or to discourage new entrants. As a practical matter, this option seems remote, provided there are not substantial barriers to entry (Skipper, 1997). For every large national or multinational financial conglomerate that might attempt such practices, there are several others with the financial capacity to weather the storm. Existing competition law would seem to be sufficient, if enforced reasonably, to prohibit or punish concerted anti-competitive behavior by conglomerates. An exception could occur if the collusion occurred outside of a national market but with respect to that national market, such as by large international financial conglomerates.

C. Negative Externalities

The third major classification of market imperfection addressed by financial services regulation is negative externalities. The principal negative externality is systemic risk, most commonly associated with commercial banking. The public policy question is whether financial service conglomerates pose a greater risk to system-wide financial stability than do solo institutions. If they do, their failure could both create greater harm to the real economy and impose greater costs on taxpayers.

1. Are Financial Conglomerates Riskier?

In an examination of the studies on the effects on risk and return of combining banking and non-bank financial activities, Kwan and Laderman (1999) conclude that the studies generally show that both securities activities and insurance (agency and underwriting) are riskier and more profitable than banking. The literature also suggests, however, that such activities provide diversification benefits, with the result that they offer the potential to reduce bankruptcy risk.[1]

Barth, Caprio, and Levine (2001) investigated the much discussed issue of whether restrictions on commercial banks engaging in securities, insurance, and real estate rendered national financial systems less efficient but more stable, as many policy makers have contended. The authors found no reliable statistical relationship between integration restrictiveness and level of economic development. Interestingly, they found restrictions on banks' engaging in securities activities were associated with higher interest rate margins and greater likelihood of suffering a financial crisis, thus suggesting integration at this level promotes efficiency and financial stability.

Hence, it appears that financial services integration could lead to a reduction in systemic risk. This hoped-for benefit, however, might not materialize if the smaller likelihood of failure (because of diversification) is accompanied by a much higher severity associated with those failures that do occur. That is, if financial firms are larger because of integration (a likely result), their now-less-frequent failure might cause greater harm to the financial system. In turn, government authorities presumably would be more likely to take a "too-big-to-fail" (TBTF) position.

The moral hazard problems of a TBTF policy are well known. If customers (depositors, insureds, creditors, etc.) believe that they will be made whole financially were the financial institution to fail, they have much less incentive to monitor the institution and to cease doing business with it if it takes on more risk. In turn, managers (with shareholder approval) might take on greater risk than they would otherwise (Boyd and Gertler, 1993). Thus, it is possible that large financial conglomerates, contrary to

---

[1] Exceptions occur in certain securities activities. According to Kwan and Laderman (1999), the literature suggests that, while securities trading tends to be more profitable and riskier than banking, it may not provide diversification benefits because of its high stand-alone risk.

the findings of the literature, could be riskier even in the face of diversification benefits. This increased riskiness would have stemmed, however, from an increase in the risk appetite of managers and shareholders, brought about because of a TBTF policy or other reasons.

2. Safety Net Issues

Governments build so-called safety nets into financial systems to minimize systemic risks. The safety net includes deposit insurance or other guarantee arrangements, the discount window, and payment system guarantees. Does financial service integration pose additional burdens on the safety net, with resultant taxpayer exposure?

As with a TBTF policy, safety nets create moral hazard problems. Customer incentives to monitor the condition of financial institutions with which they do business is diminished, so managers are prone to take on more risk than they otherwise would. An expansion of banking activities through integration, thus, could lead to excessive risk taking that could weaken the fabric of the financial system (Mishkin, 1999).

Neither the TBTF nor the safety net issue is new. Suggested reform proposals include the following:

- eliminate deposit insurance (Edwards, 1996)

- price deposit insurance premiums to reflect institutional risk[1]

- limit deposit insurance protection to narrow banking[2]

- increase capital requirements and enact stricter closure rules (Benston and Kaufman, 1988)

- practice more vigilant supervision

- impose a program of "constructive ambiguity" onto the safety net (Mishkin, 1999)

These and other proposals to address the moral hazard issue seem as applicable in an integrated financial services world as in a segregated one. Supervision admittedly will be more complex as will problems of regulatory arbitrage such as moving the underwriting of products from units not within the safety net to units enjoying safety net protection. To the extent that these problems prove valid, however, they are not caused by integration but by government failure. As such, the first-best solution is governmental reform, not limitations on integration.

---

[1] For a discussion of this proposal, see Saunders (1997), chap. 18.

[2] For a discussion of this proposal, see Mishkin (1999).

V. The Relationship between Integration and Regulatory Structure

A final public policy concern is whether existing regulatory structures are appropriate in an integrated financial world. If financial sectors are integrating, should supervisors do the same? The underlying issue is what regulatory structure minimizes the chances of government failure in ameliorating market imperfections and does so most efficiently.

The case for consolidated regulation is both compelling and obvious. To have true consolidated regulation, it would seem that the single regulator should:

- have oversight responsibilities for all or most types of financial intermediaries, especially banks and insurers

- work under laws that are not inconsistent across types of intermediaries

- apply comparable (although not necessarily identical) regulation to all intermediaries and cross-sectoral competing products, ensuring equality of competitive opportunity between types of intermediaries

Having a single supervisory body could minimize the problems of information sharing and coordination associated with sectoral supervisors, at least at the national level. In concept, it would permit a less complex approach for addressing issues such as transparency, multiple and excessive gearing, fit and proper requirements, and contagion. Needed harmonization of accounting and capital adequacy requirements across financial intermediaries would, in theory, be facilitated. Opportunities for regulatory arbitrage should be lessened.

On the other hand, it is argued that existing solo regulatory approaches, augmented by information sharing and agreement on coordination issues, are adequate and involve less disruption. There is something to be said for building on existing structures.

Moreover, the objectives of regulation vary by sector. Banking supervision is oriented more toward stability of the financial system as a whole, rather than the solidity of individual banks or efficiency, and relies on consolidated regulation. Systemic risks are not as important in insurance as they are in banking or even securities (Skipper, 1996). Securities regulation is oriented more toward consumer protection through disclosure and market efficiency than toward system stability. Insurance regulation is oriented more toward financial soundness of individual insurers and fairness, with less focus on systemic risks and efficiency.

Additionally, arguments have been made that product differences justify solo regulatory approaches. Insurance products tend to be more complex and often involve much longer guarantees than banking and securities products. As a consequence, risk and risk management practices differ by sector and regulatory specialization offers greater efficiency.

This debate might be moot to some extent. Already many banking regulators have captured the "high ground" of consolidated regulation because of their charge to protect the financial system against systemic risks and because they already focus their regulatory efforts at the group level. Thus, so the argument goes, if a financial conglomerate contains a commercial bank, the banking supervisor should have an important voice in the supervision of the group.

No international consensus has yet emerged on this issue, although the trend is toward consolidated approaches. Some countries already have consolidated supervision, including the U.K., Australia, Canada, Denmark, Sweden, Singapore, Japan, and Korea, and others have recently moved in this direction, including Austria, Bahrain, Germany, and Ireland. Most countries retain sectoral regulation for banking, securities, and insurance, although some include investment banking within the overall banking function.[1]

According to Thompson (1999), Deputy Superintendent of Canada's consolidated regulator, the case for consolidated regulation is strongest in a market that exhibits the following characteristics:

- similar products and services are offered by different types of intermediaries in the same market segments

- institutions in competing sectors have similar strategies for growth and development in home and/or international markets

- institutions in one sector create systemic risk exposure for another sector

- competing sectors are at a similar and advanced stage of development

- institutions are combining in ways that make it difficult to distinguish a bank from an insurance company

- the financial services industry is pushing for reform to meet competitive pressures

Clearly, the larger the financial services market of a country, the greater the complexity and difficulty in moving to consolidated regulation. Thus, for example, substantial regulatory change in the U.S. financial regulatory system would seem problematical, even though, according to *The Economist* (October 30, 1999, p. 19), "[U.S. regulation] is hopelessly fragmented and costly." In contrast, the more modest in size is a country's financial sector, the easier it should be to move to consolidated approaches.

---

[1] For recent information on practices in 43 major countries, see http://www.iib.org/gs2002.pdf.

CHAPTER 6

ISSUES IN FINANCIAL SERVICES INTEGRATION
FOR THE BALTIC COUNTRIES

The three Baltic countries have several commonalities. They began the arduous process of building the infrastructure essential to fully functional financial markets and institutions only somewhat more than ten years ago. All have accomplished much in a relatively short span of years. Each has also overcome difficulties, including banking crises.

I.   The Current Situations

During the latter part of the 1990s, the Baltic countries began substantial reform of their financial sectors. Faster privatizations and new legislation and supervisory institutions followed. Consequently, the financial sectors of the Baltic countries have evolved rapidly in recent years, with no immediate threats to their stability according to the 2001 IMF/World Bank financial sector assessments.

Each country's financial market is dominated by the banking sector, although each remains small in comparison to those of the EU countries. Of course, one reason for small financial markets is the comparatively small economies.

After privatization and increased capital requirements that caused many mergers, the banking sector in each country became largely foreign-owned and highly concentrated, as the table below shows. The Lithuanian banking sector is smaller than its counterparts in Estonia and Latvia. However, with the end of privatization of the sector in 2002, it seems to be getting more efficient. The comparatively high number of Latvian's banks is partially explained because ten banks primarily handle investment of Russian money in Western Europe.

Table 3:Selected Data on the Banking Sectors of the Baltic Countries

	Estonia	Latvia	Lithuania
Number of banks	7	22	14
Share capital owned by foreigners, %	85	70	90
Share of total bank assets controlled by two largest banks	80	50 (top 3 banks)	70
Assets as % of GDP	80	80	30
Share of non-performing loans, %	0.8	1.9	4.8

Sources: Baltic Economies – Bimonthly Review, 3/03, Bank of Finland Institute for Economies in Transition, BOFIT and Koivu (2002).

High bank concentration has occurred also at the Baltic level, with foreign owners controlling almost all large banks and most operating in all three countries. The presence of foreign banks has, however, brought stability. Moreover, as many of these banks have extensive experience already in integrated financial services, such expertise should be easily transferable to the Baltic countries, thus permitting less costly, more rapid market adjustments than otherwise might occur.

The bond and security markets in each of the countries are particularly under developed. Also, while their insurance sectors are generally growing rapidly, they remain quite small in comparison to their banking sectors.

II. Issues

Although the Baltic countries' financial markets share commonalties, it would be wrong to assume that the issues in financial services integration are necessarily the same for each country. Important differences have already led to distinctive characteristics.

A. Consolidated Regulation

Thus, on the issue of whether to move to consolidated supervision of the banking, insurance, and securities sectors, Estonia and Latvia have already answered. Latvia moved to a unified regulatory agency – the Financial and Capital Markets Commission (FCMC) – in July 2001. Effective January 1, 2002, the unified Estonian Financial Supervision Authority (FSA) became responsible for banking, insurance, and securities market supervision. Each is an autonomous agency.

The IMF/World Bank 2001 financial sector assessment for Lithuania identified some areas of desirable regulatory improvement, particularly in insurance supervision. Also, the assessment recommended greater information sharing and coordination among the various financial supervisory agencies and, in the long term, consideration of a more formally integrated system of regulation. The unwritten implication would seem to be that Lithuania, with somewhat less developed financial markets and supervision than the other two Baltic countries, might first ensure that the sectoral regulators meet international core principles and enhanced cooperation and then consider a consolidated approach.

B. Market Oversight

Financial services integration can render markets even more concentrated. Highly concentrated markets lend themselves to anti-competitive behavior and market conduct violations. While strong legislation and enforcement can obviate these concerns, it goes almost without stating that they first must be acknowledged and safeguards instituted. That each country continues to bring its laws and supervision into alignment with EU standards suggests that these matters will be addressed.

Even so, it seems important for authorities to continue to seek means of enhancing competition within their markets, particularly given the dominance of banks. More vigorous stock and bond markets would seem to be especially important in this respect, and recent pension reforms heighten prospects for achievement of this goal. Additionally, even stronger foreign involvement – or at least the perception of the easy possibility of more such involvement – could be positive. Certainly, the provision of cross-border services that will accompany EU membership will also strengthen competition. At the same time, it must be recognized that effective and efficient supervision will be an even greater challenge. This statement is especially relevant to the Baltic countries whose citizens have perhaps less sophistication in individual financial security decision-making than found in the EU.

C. Too Big to Fail

A final issue that seems relevant to the Baltic countries in their examination of financial services integration stems directly from the concentrated nature of their markets. As noted above, financial services integration has the potential for greater concentration and, therefore, even larger financial institutions. With ever larger financial conglomerates and financial institutions, the question naturally arises as to whether some might be considered by policy makers as too big to be permitted to fail. As discussed earlier in this paper, this can lead to undesirable moral hazard problems. Several responses are possible to this concern, one of which is greater competition.

III. EU Accession

The approaching EU memberships have caused and will continue to cause the governments of the Baltic countries to examine the above and dozens of related issues. In each such instance, it is reasonable to expect resolution in favor of greater integration within the EU and closer international cooperation. In turn, competition should grow in each country, with positive results for economic development and citizen welfare. Policy makers must be especially vigilant, however, to ensure that consumer trust is not abused by some financial service purveyors and their representatives which might seek to take unfair advantage of what they perceive as less informed buyers.

CHAPTER 7

THE FUTURE OF FINANCIAL SERVICES INTEGRATION

Services in general and financial services in particular lie at the center of all developed economies. Financial services innovation and production efficiency are essential to economic development. The question is how integrated financial services fit into this evolution and whether it poses unacceptable risks to consumers and the financial system.

Whether integration leads to economies of scale or scope or greater efficiencies cannot be answered with confidence at this time. In one sense, however, the answers are irrelevant. The present pressures for integration seem strong. Financial firms are battling for customers and understand that they must allow potential and present customers to conduct their financial affairs in ways most convenient to them. This translates into figuring out how to make available a range of financial products and services through multiple distribution channels and how to offer multiple service points. Our poor understanding of the possibilities for technology to assist in making integration work hinders the making of sound forecasts.

With time being the currency of the future, the opportunities for economies of scope in consumption seem to loom large. Securing these economies does not require financial conglomeration, however. It requires integration only at the interface of the customer and the distributor (advisor), and that distributor can as easily be Microsoft as Citigroup representatives.

The market will determine whether financial conglomeration makes good business sense and, if so, the optimum operational structure. One can imagine different outcomes in different markets, depending on cultural, historical, and economic factors, such as stage of development. Additionally, even for markets in which some financial firms move aggressively to integrate, we will find many that decide that specialization offers greater opportunities. These trends seem contradictory, but they need not be. Important market segments will prefer specialized service providers, in part because their needs will themselves be highly specialized (e.g., large businesses and wealthy individuals). Additionally, we should not be surprised to find that specialized financial institutions are able to develop a better understanding of their narrower target markets and corresponding core competencies, allowing them to compete effectively with conglomerates.

The globalization of business in particular and financial services specifically fosters integration. One has but to consider whether the recent U.S. reforms would have been enacted or as sweeping without the compelling arguments from U.S. financial institutions that they were at a competitive disadvantage internationally under former U.S. law.

A byproduct of globalization and liberalization, especially for mature markets, is consolidation aided by demutualization, both of which seem destined to continue. Look particularly for greater consolidation activity in Japan, Germany, the U.S. in the commercial banking and insurance sectors, and in France. In all instances, important transparency and fairness issues must be addressed.

Integration seems to be further advanced in Australia and the Netherlands than other countries, with France and the U.K. not far removed. Each of these and other countries with reasonably advanced integration offer a wealth of experiences for countries that are not as far along. At the same time, however, care must be taken to recognize those situations or elements that do not travel well. For example, unique circumstances aiding integration in Australia, France, the Netherlands, Spain, and the U.K. may not exist in other markets.

The public policy concerns accompanying financial services integration are rational but seem manageable with reasonable and timely governmental responses. The question is whether governments will adjust fast enough to minimize possibilities of systemic and substantial consumer harm and whether their adjustments will be no more burdensome on business than necessary. Both the management and regulation of conflicts of interest might pose the greatest challenges.

Within the U.S. and between the U.S. and the EU, the privacy issue stands out. Lowering the costs of gathering, storing, and using (including sharing) information lies at the heart of integration. Network externalities might also accompany integration. An unresolved issue is how to achieve the appropriate balance between an individual's right to control the flow of personally identifiable information about him- or herself and a business's (and ultimately, customers') desire for information efficiencies. A reasonable approach would seem to be to allow explicit consumer consent to share sensitive personal information between affiliated companies.

The integration trend will push regulatory convergence in two dimensions. First, with integration and product convergence, those aspects of national regulation and taxation that are specific to one financial sector or its products can be expected to cause increasing distortion. Firms will offer products and structure themselves in ways that minimize their regulatory burdens and taxes; i.e., regulatory and tax arbitrage will ensue. This will continue to drive governments to seek greater horizontal equity in financial institution and product regulation and in taxation. In turn, this will lead to national regulatory and tax convergence. This could facilitate the move by more nations toward consolidated regulation.

Second, international differences in regulation and taxation of financial institutions and products increasingly will afford opportunities for international regulatory and tax arbitrage. This is especially true as markets continue to liberalize and as the cross-border provision of financial services grows, facilitated by the internet. Again, it is logical that firms will take advantage of these differences. Pressure will mount for governments to harmonize key elements of tax and regulation. A danger is that governments will succumb to the sirens' song of *de jure* harmonization and harmonize the wrong things or harmonize at the wrong level, thereby stifling innovation and efficiency. The superior approach is gradual convergence through mutual recognition and establishment of regulatory principles (Skipper, 1998). In this process, the importance of some meaningful degree of accounting harmonization internationally cannot be overemphasized.

Many knowledgeable observers believe that the financial world of the future will be dominated by a dozen or so financial conglomerates. Even if accurate, oligopolistic markets can remain competitive and innovative if barriers to entry remain low, especially to foreign financial service suppliers. And certainly, specialist suppliers, even if small, will provoke continuous improvement by the giants. Irrespective of which view proves correct, changing demographics and economic prosperity ensure a growing role for financial service providers and distributors.

BIBLIOGRAPHY

Bank Powers: Issues Relating to Banks Selling Insurance. 1990. Washington, D.C. General Accounting Office.

Barfield, C.E., ed. 1996. *International Financial Markets: Harmonization versus Competition.* Washington, D.C. AEI Press.

Barth, J.R., Caprio, Jr., G., and Levine, R. 2001. "Banking Systems around the Globe: Do Regulation and Ownership Affect Performance and Stability?" in F. S. Mishkin, ed., *Prudential Supervision: What Works and What Doesn't.* Chicago. U. of Chicago Press, 31-95.

Benston, G.J. 1989. "The Federal Safety Net and the Repeal of the Glass-Steagall Act's Separation of Commercial and Investment Banking," *Journal of Financial Services Research.* October, 2, 287-306.

Benston, G.J. 1990. *The Evidence on the Passage and Continuation of the Glass-Steagall Act's Separation of Commercial and Investment Banking: Analysis of a Hoax.* New York. Oxford University Press.

Benston, G.J. 1994. "Universal Banking," *Journal of Economic Perspectives.* Summer, 3, 121-143.

Benston, G.J. and Kaufman, G.G. 1988. in W. S. Haraf and R. M. Kushmeider, eds., *Restructuring Banking and Financial Services in America.* Washington, D.C. American Enterprise Institute.

Berger, A.N. 1999. "The Integration of the Financial Services Industry: Where are the Efficiencies?" *North American Actuarial Journal,* 4, 25-52.

Berger, A.N., Cummins, J.D., Weiss, M.A., and Zi, Hongmin. 2000. "Conglomeration versus Strategic Focus: Evidence from the Insurance Industry," *Journal of Financial Intermediation,* 9, 232-262.

Berger, A.N. and Humphrey, D.B. 1997. "Efficiency of Financial Institutions: International Survey and Directions for Future Research," *European Journal of Operational Research,* 98, 178-212.

Berger, A.N., Hancock, D. and Humphrey, D.B. 1993. "Bank Efficiency Derived from the Profit Function," *Journal of Banking and Finance,* 17, 317-347.

Boyd, J.H. and Gertler, M. 1993. "US Commercial Banking: Trends, Cycles, and Policy," *NBER Macroeconomics Annual.*

Boyd, J.H., Graham, S.L., and Hewitt, R.S. 1993. "Banking Holding Company Mergers with Nonbank Financial Firms: Effects on the Risk of Failure," *Journal of Banking and Finance,* Feb., 43-63.

Canals, J. 1993. *Competitive Strategies in European Banking.* Oxford. Oxford University Press.

Carow, K.A. (2001). "Citicorp-Travelers Group Merger: Challenging Barriers Between Banking and Insurance," *Journal of Banking and Finance,* 25, 1553-1571.

Cybo-Ottone, A. and Murgia, M. (2000). "Mergers and Shareholder Wealth in European Banking," *Journal of Banking and Finance*, 24, 834-859.

Diamond, D. 1984. "Financial Intermediation and Delegated Monitoring," *Review of Economic Studies,* 51, July.

Dow Jones. 2002. *Global Indexes* at http://averages.dowjones.com/jsp/index.jsp.

Edwards, F.R. 1996. *The New Finance: Regulation and Financial Stability.* Washington, D.C. American Enterprise Institute.

European Banker. 1999. "Bigger Size Fits All," January 1.

Gallo, J.G., Apilado, V.P., and Kolari, J.W. 1996. "Commercial Bank Mutual Fund Activities: Implications for Bank Risk and Profitability," *Journal of Banking and Finance*, Dec., 1775-1791.

Fortune. 2002. *Global 500* at http://www.fortune.com/fortune/global500

Herring, R.J. and Santomero, A.M. 1990. "The Corporate Structure of Financial Conglomerates," *Journal of Financial Services Research*, Dec., 471-497.

Higgins, M. 1999. "Breaking Tradition: Creating Tomorrow's Leading Retail Bank," *Bank News.* September 1.

Group of Ten. 2001. "Chapter V: The Effects of Consolidation on Efficiency, Competition and Credit Flows," in *Report on Consolidation in the Financial Sector.*

Institute of International Bankers. 1998. *Global Survey 1998.*

Institute of International Bankers. 2002. *Global Survey 2002.*

Joint Forum on Financial Conglomerates. 1999. *Supervision of Financial Conglomerates.*

Kelley, E.J., III. 1985. "Conflicts of Interest: A Legal View," in *Deregulating Wall Street; Commercial Bank Penetration of the Securities Market,* New York. John Wiley and Sons.

Koivu, Tuuli (2002). "Banking and Finance in the Baltic Countries" at Bank of Finland Institute for Economies in Transition, November, at www.bof.fi/bofit.

Kraus, J.R. 1998. "Europe's Universal Banks: Flawed Models," *American Banker,* June 8.

Kwan, S.H. 1997. "Securities Activities by Commercial Banking Firms' Section 20 Subsidiaries: Risk, Return, and Diversification Benefits," *Federal Reserve Bank of San Francisco Economic Review*, October.

Kwan, S.H. and Laderman, E.S. 1999. "On the Portfolio Effects of Financial Convergence – A Review of the Literature," *Federal Reserve Bank of San Francisco Economic Review*, January 1.

Mishkin, F.S. 1999. "Financial Consolidation: Dangers and Opportunities," *Journal of Banking and Finance*, 23, 675-691.

O'Connor, R. 1999. "UK Bancassurance: Will it Play in Peoria?" *Banking Strategies*, Sept./Oct.

Santomero, A.M. and Babbel D.F. 1997. *Financial Markets, Instruments, and Institutions.* Chicago. Irwin.

Saunder, A. 1997. *Financial Institutions Management.* Chicago. Irwin.

Saunders, A. and Walter, I. 1994. *Universal Banking in The United States.* New York. Oxford University Press.

Skipper, Jr., H.D. 1997. *Foreign Insurers in Emerging Markets: Issues and Concerns.* Washington, D.C. International Insurance Foundation.

Skipper, Jr., H.D. 2000. "Financial Services Integration Worldwide: Promises and Pitfalls," *North American Actuarial Journal,* 4, 71-108.

Skipper, Jr., H.D. 1996. "International Trade in Insurance," in Claude E. Barfield, ed., *International Financial Markets: Harmonization versus Competition.* Washington, D.C. AEI Press. 151-223.

Skipper, H.D., Jr. 1998. "Regulatory Harmonization and Mutual Recognition in Insurance," in H.D. Skipper, Jr., ed., *International Risk and Insurance: An Environmental/Managerial Approach.* Boston. Irwin McGraw Hill.

Survey of International Banking. 1999. *The Economist.* April 17.

Swiss Re. 2001. *World Financial Centres: New Horizons in Insurance and Banking,* 7.

Thompson, J. 1999. "Financial Services Reform: Basic Components, Position and Prognosis," presented at the Conference on Insurance and Financial Services Regulation. Hartford.

The Tripartite Group of Bank, Securities, and Insurance Regulators. *1995. The Supervision of Financial Conglomerates.*

Tuohy, M.R. 1999. "Financial Services: What Lies Ahead?" *Emphasis,* 3, 32.

Van den Berghe, L.A.A. and Verweire, K. 1998. *Creating the Future with All Finance and Financial Conglomerates.* Boston. Kluwer Academic Publishers.

Vander Vennet, R. 2002. "Cost and Profit Efficiency in Financial Conglomerates and Universal Banks in Europe," *Journal of Money, Credit, and Banking,* 34, 254-282.

Walter, I. 1997. "Universal Banking: A Shareholder Value Perspective," *European Management Journal,* 15, August.

Wilmarth, Jr., A.E. 2002. "The Transformation of the U. S. Financial Services Industry, 1975-2000: Competition, Consolidation, and Increased Risks," *University of Illinois Law Review,* 2.

www.bis.org/bcbs/jointforum.htm

www.fsforum.org/home/home.html

www.iib.org/

www.imf.org/external/NP/fsap/fsap.asp

www.inprs.org/objectives.asp

ANNEXES

TWENTY INSURANCE GUIDELINES FOR ECONOMIES IN TRANSITION[1]

DETAILED PRINCIPLES FOR THE REGULATION AND SUPERVISION OF INSURANCE MARKETS IN ECONOMIES IN TRANSITION

TWENTY INSURANCE GUIDELINES FOR INSURANCE REGULATION AND SUPERVISION IN ECONOMIES IN TRANSITION

RULE N°1 Adequate prudential and regulatory provisions should be enforced in order to ensure the soundness of the insurance markets, the protection of the consumers and the stability of the economy as a whole. Over-regulation should be avoided. The insurance regulatory framework must be adapted to the characteristics of individual countries and encourage the stability, whilst maintaining the necessary flexibility to meet developments in the market.

RULE N°2 Sufficiently strict licensing criteria should govern the establishment of insurance companies. Among these criteria, the testing of the nature and adequacy of the financial resources of insurance companies, in particular through analysis of

---

[1]   Both the guidelines and the detailed principles were endorsed by the three Baltic states among 38 other countries (including OECD countries and other Central and Eastern European countries) during the Second East/West Conference on insurance systems in economies in transition held in Warsaw on 3-4 April 1997.

business plan and the requirement for a relevant minimum level of capital (taking account of inflation) deserves particular consideration. Other key requirements are related to the assessment of the ability of the company to meet legal, accounting and technical requirements and last but not least requirements for a competent management (fit and proper provisions).

RULE N°3 The underwriting of insurance risks should be restricted to insurance companies, which may transact insurance (and connected) operations only. Life and non-life activities should be separated (in distinct companies), so that one activity cannot be required to support the other. The distribution of insurance products by entities from other sectors may be authorised. Risks associated with the activities and structure of financial conglomerates should be adequately monitored.

RULE N°4 Establishment of foreign insurance companies should be based on prudential but non discriminatory rules. Liberalisation of cross-border operations, at least concerning reinsurance and international risks, should be encouraged.

RULE N°5 Adequate insurance contract laws should be established. Rules governing contractual rights and obligations as well as related sanctions, are essential for the protection of both contractual and third parties and indispensable for the development of legal stability. In the absence of contract laws, the approval of policy conditions by the supervisory authority may prove all the more necessary.

RULE N°6 Due to the crucial economic and social role of insurance in the development of an economy, consideration should be given to tax facilities in the life-insurance and pensions field in the economies in transition.

RULE N°7 The establishment of a supervisory body is essential. The supervisors should be professionally independent and properly trained and impartial. The supervisory body should have sufficient personnel and financial resources as well as adequate powers (including sanctions) to carry out its tasks.

RULE N°8 The examination of records and on site inspections of insurance companies are at the core of the work of the supervisor. An adequate reporting system is essential to achieve this task properly. The secrecy of information communication to and between supervisors should be safeguarded.

RULE N°9 Monitoring solvency margins and capital ratios constitutes a key element of dynamic supervision. But adequate tarification and prudent technical provisions backed by reliable and equivalent assets remain the fundamental requirements for maintaining solvency. Adequate business management and reinsurance activities are also indispensable to safeguard the soundness of the companies.

RULE N°10 Initially at least, it may be advisable for economies in transition to request the submission of premium rates and insurance products for prior approval.

Supervision of tariffs and products should however be adapted to the particular situation of each country and reassessed at a later stage according to the development and progress of the market.

RULE N°11 Supervisory authorities should take adequate, effective and prompt measures to prevent insurance companies from defaulting, and to arrange an orderly run-off or the transfer of portfolio to a sound company. Appropriate winding-up procedures should be enforced. Under certain conditions, and particularly if the national market comprises a sufficient number of potential contributors with a broad spread of risks, the creation of a compensation fund could be considered.

RULE N°12 Standardised accounting rules are essential to ensure the transparency and comparability of the financial situation of insurance companies. Adequate insurance accounting rules and requirements for reporting and disclosure have to be set as a priority action. The compilation of statistical data regarding the frequency and severity of losses is an essential condition for computing tariffs and technical provisions accurately. Tariffs should be based on statistical data. Actuarial techniques are a key component of insurance management; the role of the actuarial profession could be encouraged.

RULE N°13 Investment regulation should ensure that both security and profitability requirements are respected. It should promote the diversification, spread and liquidity of investment portfolios as well as the maturity and currency matching of assets and liabilities, although some temporary dispensations to the last principle may be necessary. In any case, account should be taken of the country's current economic environment. Regulations might include a list of admitted assets on which ceilings may be set and requirements on the way in which investments should be valued.

RULE N°14 Regulation should not restrict free access to international reinsurance markets. Compulsory cessions of risks to domestic/national reinsurers should therefore be avoided. The collection and monitoring of information relating to reinsurance companies should be established. International co-operation is particularly important to obtain accurate information and should be strengthened.

RULE N°15 Insurance intermediaries should be registered in order to ensure their compliance with selected criteria. Insurance intermediaries should possess appropriate qualifications and provide adequate information to policyholders including disclosure of limits to their independence such as significant ties with insurance companies. Insurance brokers should possess either financial guarantees or professional liability insurance.

RULE N°16 Compulsory insurance may be justified in respect of certain forms of social protection and might be considered in other areas where the risks covered are particularly serious, or where premium payments should be divided on an equitable basis among the policyholders group under consideration. Compulsory insurance is particularly recommended for automobile third party liability. Guarantee funds could be created to compensate victims when there is no insurance cover. Tariffs for compulsory insurance should also be based on statistical data. Adequate monitoring systems should be established. Compulsory insurance should not be restricted to former monopolies or State owned companies.

RULE N°17   Regulations should allow for fair competition within the insurance and reinsurance market. The process of dismantling monopolies and the privatisation of government owned insurance companies should be strongly encouraged.

RULE N°18   The activities of insurance companies in the pensions and health insurance field should be encouraged within an appropriate regulatory and supervisory framework. Regulations should endeavour to ensure fair treatment between all private companies operating in these areas.

RULE N°19   Governments should strengthen co-operation in order to exchange information on insurance regulation and supervision, facilitate the monitoring of the activities of foreign insurance and reinsurance companies and promote the development of sound, modern and open insurance markets.

RULE N°20   The insurance industry should be encouraged to set up its own business guidelines and to develop adequate training structures. Self-regulatory principles and organisations, including professional bodies, can complement usefully the public supervisory structure.

DETAILED PRINCIPLES FOR THE REGULATION AND SUPERVISION OF INSURANCE MARKETS IN ECONOMIES IN TRANSITION

Although general guiding principles can be set forth for the benefit of the regulatory and supervisory authorities of countries in transition, those principles are applicable only if they are adapted to the economic environment as well as to the historical and cultural context of each country. Specifically, a number of regulations enforced in countries where the insurance sector has attained an advanced degree of maturity can only be progressively incorporated into economies in transition. Also, certain regulatory provisions that have long existed in OECD countries, but are nowadays no longer justified due to changes in the economic and regulatory environment of those countries, may be appropriate in light of the current stage of development of certain countries in transition.

In addition, insurance regulations should be flexible so as to evolve in accordance with changes in the economic environment and the insurance market. For that reason, it could be appropriate to incorporate certain provisions not in the law itself but rather in implementing regulations that are easier to amend. Maintaining this margin of flexibility is also perfectly compatible with preserving legal predictability, which economic agents require.

In order for the regulations to have the desired effect, they should stipulate obligations as well as provide for realistic penalties in the event of non-compliance with the applicable statutory and regulatory provisions.

Finally, special mention should be made of the importance of having different regulations applying to life and non-life insurance. Each of those branches operates under its own constraints and requires specific management and regulatory structures.

The paragraphs which follow contain observations concerning some of the fundamental aspects of insurance regulation and supervision to be addressed by economies in transition. The order and length of these paragraphs should not be taken as an indication of their relative importance as regards the policies governing insurance.

Licensing

Sufficiently strict conditions governing the formal approval of insurance companies serve to guarantee the protection of insurance users and ensure that fair, competitive conditions exist among companies in the domestic market. In most OECD countries, separate licenses are issued for each class of insurance (or for several classes grouped under a common denomination) usually in the six months following the filing of applications, and they are generally permanent.

Experts agree on the importance of a certain number of criteria that must be met by an insurer seeking to be licensed. Among those, the first may be the strict testing of the nature and adequacy of the financial resources of insurance companies at the time they go into business, an essential condition for ensuring that they have the financial strength needed to operate. The minimum required capital is that which would enable a company to meet certain contingencies inherent in its business. The amount of such capital (expressed in a manner that takes inflation into account) varies according to the insurance class in question and to the specific conditions prevailing in different markets. Lastly, a deposit, either of a fixed or variable amount, may be required in addition to the minimum capital requirement.

In addition to these financial standards, economies in transition should not fail to impose other licensing criteria, which have been used in all OECD countries. They concern in particular:

- legal requirements, *i.e.*, in particular, conformity of the form of business organisation adopted by the company, filing of bylaws and general terms and conditions of policies, insurance specialisation;

- accounting requirements, *i.e.* filing of opening balance sheet, budget and income statement, proof that the company has the required minimum capital, etc.;

- technical requirements, *i.e.* filing of premium rates for information or, if applicable, for approval, as well as of the technical bases used in tarification and planned technical provisions, and of reinsurance contracts;

- managerial requirements, *i.e.* demonstration that officers are fit and proper, and that the shareholders are reputable.

Supervision of insurance companies

In many economies in transition policyholders are highly vulnerable because they lack access to reliable information on products, intermediaries and insurance companies, while insurers are still short on training and experience and there can be significant gaps in regulatory coverage. The implementation of adequate supervision for the insurance sector would be a first step towards removing those deficiencies.

Regardless of which structure is chosen for supervisory bodies (independent authority, ministry of finance division, etc.), experts in charge of supervising insurance companies must be properly trained and impartial.

The examination of records is at the core of the work of supervisors. They analyse records supplied by insurance firms and may request any additional accounting or business document they deem necessary for their audit. Thorough on-site investigations are an indispensable complement of audits of records. *A priori* supervision is also particularly recommended in countries where economic structures and comprehensive regulations have not yet been developed. The prevention and detection of insurers' financial problems would enable the supervisory authorities of countries in transition not only to safeguard the solvency of companies, but also, in a more general way, to promote public confidence in recently privatised institutions within a business sector about which the public may still be unfamiliar.

The duties of supervisory authorities should focus on the following general areas:

- supervision with respect to legal obligations: compliance with existing legal provisions, by-laws of the company, general terms and conditions of insurance policies;

- financial supervisions: own funds, technical provisions, assets, monitoring of business activities;

- audit of interim and annual financial statements;

- actuarial supervision: tariffs, technical or mathematical provisions;

- management supervision: fit and proper requirements of company officers, reputation of strategic shareholders;

- economic supervision: conditions prevailing in the marketplace, statistics.

Initially at least, it may be advisable in economies in transition to submit premium rates for prior approval. This practice would efficiently safeguard the financial soundness of insurance companies, which might otherwise be tempted to engage in rate wars, thereby running the risk of putting their solvency in jeopardy. On the other hand, excessively high tariffs would penalise policyholders. Above all, in economies in transition, the lack of experience of insurance management, combined with the shortage of basic statistical data such as the frequency and severity of losses, can make it difficult or, indeed, impossible to set premiums rates based on actual risk exposure.

Regulatory and supervisory authorities may therefore have to draft regulations on premium rates on the basis of probability assumptions. In addition, they will have to compensate for the difficulty of individual data collection by seeing to it that a national body of statistics is being established.

Similarly, it seems advisable that the insurance products offered for sale be examined by the supervisory authority, so that consumers will not be harmed by inappropriate policy conditions. The risk of asymmetry in the information available to the insurer and to the insured is even greater in economies in transition, due to insufficient disclosure of information on insurance products and companies.

Supervision of premium rates and policy conditions must however be adapted to the particular situation of each country, and reassessed at a later stage according to the development and progress of the market.

Prudential rules in OECD countries also include requirements for solvency thresholds or margins which correspond to the minimum amount of capitalisation required for the type of business written by the company, in order to cope with the contingencies associated with that business or to offset any shortfalls in the technical provisions set aside. That margin, which is computed for individual companies on the basis of their commitments, constitutes the first step towards dynamic supervision. It may be appropriate for it to reflect as much as possible the nature and diversity of the risks to which the company is exposed, using as models those recently developed by certain OECD Member countries. Nevertheless, a solvency margin that matches regulatory standards should not be deemed by the management or supervisory authority to be the end-result of the assets-liabilities management and a fail-safe guarantee of the financial soundness of the company under consideration. Furthermore, the mechanism for setting margins may be affected in a situation of high inflation. Above all, the margin is only an instrument for measuring and monitoring solvency; adequate tarification, investments that correspond to technical commitments and sufficient technical provisions remain the main pillars of solvency.

The setting aside of technical (or mathematical) provisions in an amount sufficient to meet at all times the company's commitments vis-à-vis the insured remains at the very core of insurance business. Most countries have agreed on the definition of technical provisions to be set aside. Among those, the following non-life provisions can be quoted: provisions for unearned premiums, provisions for unexpired risks, provisions for claims outstanding or equalisation reserves.

The method used for setting the amount of these provisions, whether imposed or regulated, should be based on national statistical data. At first, it is likely that computing for the purpose of setting technical provisions will have to be based on probability assumptions, owing to the absence of reliable nation-wide statistics (such as mortality tables for life insurance) in most countries in transition.

It seems essential that the supervisory authorities be given adequate sanction powers in the event insurers fail to comply with legal provisions governing the setting aside of technical provisions. Under these circumstances, it would in particular be advisable that a company no longer has the unrestricted use of its assets.

More generally, in order to perform adequately its duties, the supervisory authority will have to develop an on-going dialogue with insurers so as to appear as a partner of companies' success, instead of being confined to a coercive role.

Investments

In OECD countries, regulations governing the management of assets are based on a list of "admissible" investments. In order to ensure that requirements of both safety and profitability are respected, countries in transition may also adopt a series of principles (listed below), which have proved useful in this respect in more advanced markets.

Diversification, spread and liquidity

Ceilings may be set on admitted investments, by type of investment and in percentage terms rather than in absolute value, so as to reduce the risk of default or of liquidity shortages associated with certain types of investments, as well as to ensure that portfolios are sufficiently diversified. A ceiling may also be set for given investments (according to the principle of spreading investments within each category). Although OECD countries now very seldom set floor limits, such practices were sometimes used in the past, especially to encourage investments with a low risk of loss or lack of liquidity.

When setting ceilings, the impact of the method used for establishing the value of investments must be taken into consideration (for example through a prudent assessment of investments). Lastly, insurance companies are generally advised against having recourse to debt to finance long-term investments.

At this stage, regulatory and supervisory authorities should make sure that a distinction applies between the treatment of investments representing technical reserves and that of investments of the capital base. The latter has a role to play in the long run, particularly with respect to the funding of the company's future growth, and it would be sound policy to let companies earn a high return on the investment of their capital base, so that they may reinforce their financial resources. However, the buffer effect of the capital base in its role as a complement to technical provisions and possible equalisation reserves may serve as grounds for justifying restrictions placed on investments of these funds. Thus, one will also have to distinguish, within owners' equity itself, between the minimum required capital and the free capital. While there is a need for regulations on the investment of the minimum capital - which ought to be readily available to pay exceptionally high claims - those concerning the investment of the free capital seem less justified.

Localisation

The domestic location and/or custody of certificates of investments corresponding to technical reserves can be of particular importance in countries in transition. This makes it possible for them to ward off two problems to which they may be exposed more frequently than OECD countries, namely difficulties in establishing proof of ownership and the possibility of fraud by companies. Those provisions should not constitute an obstacle to the balance of investments.

Currency matching

The currency matching rule refers to the fact that investments ought to be in the same currency as commitments. In the case of economies in transition, the current fragility of their national currency as compared to those of foreign countries in which foreign investments can be made, may lead to tolerate a certain degree of flexibility. Regulations should simply state in what foreign currencies investments may be made. Also, arguments in favour of the matching of currencies in which the shareholders' equity of companies is invested are less convincing. Lastly, the fact that a national currency is fragile justifies even more that insurers and reinsurers should at least be authorised to hold foreign-currency reserves in the amount of their commitments payable in those currencies; this is the case, for instance, for reinsurance policies between domestic insurers and foreign reinsurance companies.

Maturity matching

One of the primary objectives of insurance companies in managing their assets, in particular in the life-insurance sector, is to ensure that the maturity of those assets matches that of their commitments, so as to reduce the risk of changes in interest rates. Partial and temporary exemptions from that rule may be considered in certain countries, given their economic situation (tightness of capital markets, rampant inflation, concerns about investments in domestic securities, etc.).

Insolvency and management of troubled companies

Clear instructions should exist regarding what is to be done about insolvent insurers through legislation covering all matters connected with the management of troubled companies, including standards used to establish insolvency, the basis for choosing between rehabilitation and liquidation, recovery measures available (premium rate increase, freezing of assets, request for reinsurance plans, injection of capital, etc.), the revocation of licenses, conditions under which policies may be transferred to a sound company (often resulting in the rights of policyholders being safeguarded), the role of the liquidator and the ranking of creditors' claims.

In most OECD countries, it is generally accepted that supervisory authorities should do everything in their power to prevent an insurance company from defaulting, as this would be damaging to the entire insurance sector.

Some countries have also opted in favour of guarantee funds which pay the claims of insolvent companies. However, in countries in transition, the advisability of creating such a fund should be assessed by looking at its costs, which could weaken participating companies, and at the possible aggravation of moral hazard that the establishment of such a fund may cause - as compared with the possible benefits derived from it.

Liberalisation and competition in the insurance sector

While implementing a programme of removing monopolies and privatising state-owned companies, economies in transition are preparing for the advent of a globally competitive insurance market. In this connection, the regulatory and supervisory authorities of countries in transition would be well advised to ensure that state-owned companies and private firms are treated equally, although it may be justifiable to hold on to certain exclusive rights, such as in the field of export credits and political risks, which are generally areas covered by companies run by the state.

The danger inherent in a policy of closed markets should also be underscored, and competition encouraged, free of discrimination based on companies' nationality. The presence of subsidiaries or branches of foreign insurers, as well as the acquisition by foreign companies of minority or majority interests (the restriction of ownership to a minority of the shares may dissuade foreign companies from entering the market), contribute to the development of the domestic insurance sector. Foreign presence brings with it innovation and transfers of know-how, while at the same time giving access to additional financial resources, improving insurance rules, fostering greater diversification of business, expanding capacity so that a steep growth in demand will not be held back by the small size of the domestic insurance sector, broadening the scope of products offered and increasing financial security, to mention only the main advantages. While prudential regulation of investment is necessary, discriminatory provisions or practices which would constitute obstacles to investments by foreign insurance companies should be avoided and the adoption is recommended of a relatively liberal attitude towards exchange controls.

Distribution of insurance products

The emergence of new insurance companies and new insurance products requires the development of modern distribution networks, with the possibility of an adequate combination of several types of intermediaries (insurance company staff, agents, brokers, direct sales, etc.). Considering that in many cases only intermediaries have contact with consumers, it might be recommended that regulations covering intermediaries be adopted, at least insofar as brokers are concerned (insurance companies being often in a position to exercise at least indirect control over agents). These regulations would cover issues such as registration, required business qualifications and ethical standards, along with financial security (including the need for professional liability coverage).

Supervisory authorities should see to it that intermediaries conduct their business as transparently as possible; specifically, they should disclose to their clients their status on any ties that they may have to insurance companies, along with providing extensive information on, and explanations of, policies to policyholders.

Insurance accounting

Accurate accounting provides authorities with the practical means to perform proper supervision, while at the same time being a resourceful instrument for the management of companies.

Widely available financial statements and proper financial information are important assets both for the supervisory authorities and the insurance market. That is why, in OECD countries, insurers are required by law to issue financial statements certified by an independent auditor as fair and accurate.

There is no doubt as to the advantage of standardising accounting rules at the national level in terms of disclosure and comparability of the financial positions of companies (this concerns mainly the presentation of annual financial statements, evaluation rules, the contents of notes to the financial statements and of the annual report, the presentation of consolidated financial statements, auditing and publication, as well as sanction measures).

Among the accounting problems encountered in economies in transition, those having to do with valuation and assessments are particularly thorny. The evaluation of technical commitments should for instance be made through several approaches involving looking at past and future performance. In several countries in transition, owing to the absence of a genuine market, prudential rules may play a particularly important role in the valuation of assets, regardless of the assessment method used (none has been universally endorsed, even within the OECD, where certain countries use book/acquisition value and others emphasise market value). In addition, a periodic reassessment of certain assets, such as buildings, seems necessary. Lastly, it is important to make allowance for inflation, which is high in many of those economies and makes it even more difficult to keep a prudent and fair accounting that accurately reflects the financial position of companies.

Statistics

The compiling of nation-wide statistical data, particularly regarding the frequency and severity of losses (mortality tables in life insurance) is a *sine qua non* condition for computing tariffs and technical reserves accurately. Compiling could be done by the supervisory authority or by a specialised body. It would make sense that it focuses initially on key insurance classes, such as automobile liability insurance and fire insurance.

Furthermore, the creation of a reliable statistical instrument is the only way for insurance companies to demonstrate to the tax authorities that they are justified in setting aside certain amounts to cover their commitments.

Contract law

In an environment where markets are opening up, the insurance sector is rapidly expanding, and the number of participants and complexity of products are on the rise, the protection of insurance policyholders in economies in transition also requires the enactment of a contract law or the improvement of the existing one. It is a way for lawmakers to bring the rights and obligations of the parties into balance and to devise sanction measures proportionate to the violations committed.

A certain number of general principles, which served as guidelines for the enactment of contract laws in OECD countries, may be listed for the benefit of countries in transition. For instance, the distinction between policies providing for indemnities and those paying flat sums should be clear, including the various legal consequences thereof (differences in the amount of compensation in the event of a loss in particular). The importance of establishing the exact time at which contracts are executed and go into effect, their life, as well as the issue of proof of contract, should also be underscored. A contract implies obligations on the part of the company but also on that of the insured, including that of declaring loss exposure (and the possible aggravation thereof), paying premiums and reporting damages or losses. The possibility that a policyholder may be underinsured should not be overlooked, anymore than that of intentional losses or wrongful conduct, which constitute grounds for exclusion from coverage. In order to be complete, insurance contract law also needs to refer to the rights of third parties to compensation or with respect to the insurer, as well as providing for the modalities of disputes settlement.

Besides the technical aspects of contract law, some leeway is left for each government to determine the degree of protection it wishes to provide for policyholders, with due regard to the cost of restrictions under consideration and to the supervisory capabilities they require.

Compulsory insurance

Insurance is made compulsory out of a desire to protect the whole or part of the public. In addition, compulsory insurance enables the state to cease being financially responsible for certain losses which they otherwise would have to compensate.

With the exception of automobile liability, it is hard to suggest for which kind of risks insurance cover should be compulsory. The need for certain types of compulsory insurance will be appraised differently from one country to another. At most, it can be stated that compulsory insurance seems advisable in the case of the following types of cover:

- in branches which are more closely related to the social sector than to private insurance;

- in specific areas where compulsory insurance is justified by the seriousness of risk exposure and/or by its generalised nature (automobile liability or occupational accidents for instance);

- in areas where premium payments should be divided on an equitable basis among the policyholders group under consideration.

Lastly, insurance can reasonably be made compulsory only in those sectors for which effective oversight is available at a reasonable cost.

Concern for losses incurred by third parties may also justify the implementation of mechanisms that serve to compensate for non-compliance with insurance requirements, or for the default of an insurer (*e.g.* guarantee fund for automobile liability insurance).

In most instances, the setting of uniform rates is not required, since competition will normally have an impact in the field of compulsory insurance as for other insurance categories. Should it be deemed preferable to set rates, it is important that tariffs take into account available statistical data and the economic situation of the sector under consideration.

Specialisation

Specialisation by companies along the lines of life and non-life insurance ensures that assets are managed separately and that losses incurred, for instance, in the non life-insurance sector will not affect life policyholders.

At the inter-sectoral level, the experience of OECD countries calls for prudence with respect to structures of the bank/insurance type, at least at this stage of development of the markets of economies in transition. The technical specificities of these businesses (such as that of non-life insurance for instance, whose management is highly complex, both in the setting of insurance premium levels and in assessing claims and how to compensate for them), along with the specificity of prudential rules applicable to the insurance sector, the risk of transfers of credit or dividends, exposure to conflicts of interest, contagion involving various constituent parts of a conglomerate or double gearing are just some of the reasons why these structures should be carefully monitored.

Taxation of life insurance

In light of the potential economic and social role of life insurance in countries in transition as well as of the obstacles to the purchase of life insurance (high rate of inflation, absence of insurance culture, very high nominal interest paid on cash savings, lack of knowledge about products, impossibility to guarantee an attractive rate of return on long-term policies, etc.) the establishment of tax incentives may be considered in order to promote this market. Incentives could for instance come in the form of tax deductions or credits for premiums paid by individuals on certain policies. Premiums paid by employers on policies providing reasonable life-insurance benefits on behalf of employees could also be tax deductible by employers and employees would not have to pay taxes on them.

Lastly, regardless of the tax model selected, it seems particularly advisable to keep its administration very simple in countries which often lack the means to enforce tax compliance.

Actuaries

The complexity and specific nature of actuarial work warrants encouraging the promotion of the actuarial profession. Actuaries can contribute in a useful way to the performance of very important tasks by insurance companies, such as calculating premium rates, calculating the amount of technical provisions, assessing contractual obligations, as well as preparing financial reports, monitoring solvency margins, developing insurance products, consulting on investment strategies, participating in the development of computer systems or making arrangements for reinsurance. In almost all OECD countries, insurance companies are required by law to appoint actuaries. This precaution seems all the more relevant at an initial stage, in order for this profession to be recognised.

Reinsurance

Adequate and effective reinsurance enables insurance companies to share risks with others, limit losses from large risks and, in a more general way, to streamline their risk portfolio and to allocate technical income and expenses over time. In many ways, such objectives are incompatible with regulations still in effect in certain economies in transition, in particular those concerning the compulsory cession of reinsurance. Only through free access to the wider international reinsurance market can the ceding company be ensured of getting the best product at a competitive price.

In addition, supervisory authorities should endeavour to protect insurers against the collapse of reinsurers. Supervisory authorities could start out by monitoring reinsurance transactions through an audit of the financial statements and notes thereto (in particular reinsurance agreements) of ceding companies. It is also very useful to compile as much information as possible on reinsurers, their solvency and liquidity (including through rating agencies), as well as, more generally, on the overall impact of ceding risks, taking into consideration all significant transactions with respect to claims, commissions and brokers' fees. Supervisory authorities from different countries may wish to consider working closely together in this area.

Private pension systems

The governments of OECD countries as well as of many economies in transition are experiencing growing difficulties in supporting pay-as-you-go pension systems. Current pension systems are therefore bound to be revised, while funded systems should grow in importance. In this context, the private sector will become responsible for a progressively larger share of pensions. At a macro-economic level, this trend is expected to provide a powerful boost to long-term savings. Hence, consideration could be given, among others, to tax incentives and regulations aimed at promoting the establishment of employee pension plans by employers. The role played by insurance companies in the financing of private pension systems will also have to be examined.